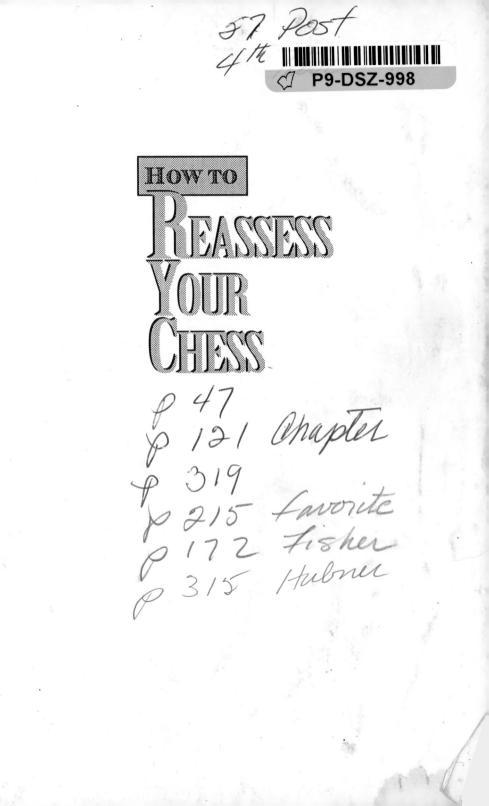

HOW TO
REASSESS
YOUR
CHESS

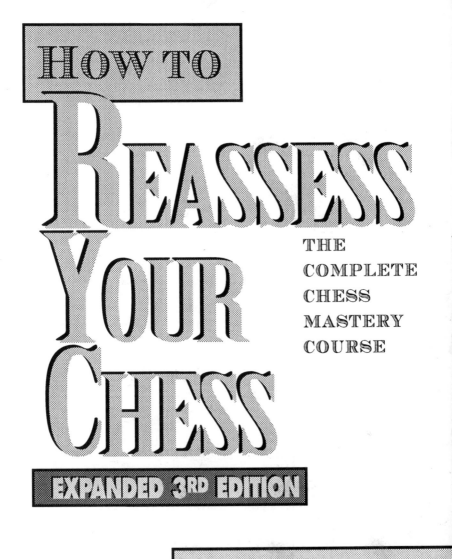

HOW TO
REASSESS YOUR CHESS

THE
COMPLETE
CHESS
MASTERY
COURSE

EXPANDED 3RD EDITION

JEREMY SILMAN
INTERNATIONAL MASTER

SILES PRESS ◆ LOS ANGELES

First Siles Press Edition

10 9 8 7 6 5 4 3

Library of Congress Cataloging-in-Publication Data

Silman, Jeremy.
How to reassess your chess : the complete chess mastery course /
Jeremy Silman. — 1st Siles Press ed.
p. cm.
Originally published : Expanded 3rd ed. Los Angeles : Summit Pub., c 1993
Includes bibliographical references (p.   ).
1. Chess.   I. Title
GV1449.5.S553 1997   794.1'2—dc21   97-5576

ISBN:1-890085-00-6

Cover design by Heidi Frieder
Cover photograph and illustration by Daniela Schmid

Printed and bound in the United States of America

Siles Press
3624 Shannon Road
Los Angeles CA 90027

Dedicated to Steven Christopher—the kindest gentleman I've ever met in my chess travels. This book would not exist without his help and encouragement.

CONTENTS

KEY TO NOTATION AND SYMBOLS

=/Equality or equal chances
+=/White has a slight advantage
+-/White has a clear advantage
++-/White has a winning advantage
=+/Black has a slight advantage
-+/Black has a clear advantage
-++/Black has a winning advantage
!/Excellent move
!!/Brilliant move
?/Poor move
??/Blunder
!?/Interesting move
?!/Dubious move

At times you will see a backslash standing between two symbols (like: +-/=). The first symbol stands for the result if it is White to move. The second symbol is for Black to move. ++-/= means that White to move wins and Black to move draws. -++/++- means that Black wins if it is White to move while White wins if it Black to move.

PREFACE TO THE THIRD EDITION

I originally wrote this book when I noticed that most of the 'instructional' chess books really offered no instruction at all. Most chess literature offers a bunch of positions that cater to a theme but never explain how to implement the examples into your own game. I wanted to give the serious chess student (from class D to Expert) a way to really improve his or her play—a serious study of this book should enable the reader to achieve this goal.

I have been more than gratified by the many kind words given to *How To Reassess Your Chess* by players all over the world. These positive comments show me that the book is doing its job—it's helping people to better understand chess.

For this third edition I have created new chapters, added lots of important examples to already existing chapters, and clarified any obscure language that might have detracted from the instructional value of the text.

I hope *How To Reassess Your Chess* brings you many hours of pleasure and opens up new levels of understanding to the game that we all love.

Jeremy Silman
Beverly Hills, 1993

INTRODUCTION

Often when I talk to players of D-A strength I am surprised to find how little they know about the game. Moreover, when I recommend a book for them to study they often tell me it was over their head—that they had difficulty understanding its content.

In particular, I have found that most players have problems with the following subjects:

1) A lack of understanding concerning the true purpose of the opening.
2) No knowledge of planning and the thinking processes that make it happen.
3) No understanding of the most elementary endings.
4) How all three of these subjects are closely connected.

This lack of understanding of the fundamentals often continues for a lifetime. Typical is the following story:

John Everyman was taught how to play chess by his father at the age of twelve. At first he learned the basic rules and then, after he gained some experience, he memorized various mating patterns. Everyman was told that he should learn some endgame positions also and so, with a heavy heart, he took the time to figure out how to mate in such one-sided situations as King and Rook vs. King. However, he generally found endings boring and not worthy of attention. Everyman was an attacker; he loved chasing an opponent's King across the board. To this end he studied chess problems and a few basic texts on combination. Everyman reigned supreme on his block; few could put up even the tiniest resistance. His ego bursting with power, Everyman decided to extend his area of dominance—he joined a chess club.

Against these new, more seasoned adversaries, Everyman could do little. He would try to attack, but his cowardly opponents would take a pawn, trade all the pieces off, and eventually win the resultant endgame. Obviously he had gotten involved in a club of wimps—real men would never play such chicken chess! Nevertheless, his style slowly went through certain transformations. Everyman learned to avoid weak pawns, develop all his pieces before attacking, try to avoid loss of material, etc. Everyman didn't particularly like these changes, but he liked losing to a bunch of wimps even less!

The years rolled by with Everyman memorizing a few opening variations and refining the various positional lessons he had been given by the other members. Soon Everyman was top dog in the club. His ego soared to new heights; it was time for further expansion. Everyman started to compete in tournaments. At first his results were shaky; the chess clock unnerved him and, in general, he was looked down on by the top players.

This proved to be temporary though—in a way it was a rite of initiation. As he became more familiar with the atmosphere of tournaments and as he picked up a few new strategies, Everyman started winning games with regularity. When he got his rating published he felt great pride—1802, a class 'A' player!

More time swam by and Everyman continued to hone his skills. When not working or spending time with his family, Everyman would sit back and memorize a few more opening lines and, at times, leaf through a tedious middlegame manual. Eventually Everyman achieved an Expert ranking and try as he might he could never get beyond it.

This did not have to be the case. Everyman was stuck because his foundation was rotten. His knowledge was slipshod and imcomplete. Most importantly, he never viewed the game as a homogeneous whole. Instead, everything was made of dis-jointed fragments.

Despite mediocre learning techniques, Everyman had reached the expert level. Unfortunately, this same mediocrity was now acting as an anchor and was effectively preventing him from getting any better. The truth wasn't pretty, but unless he destroyed that rotten foundation and learned everything again from scratch he would never get over the expert hump.

Everyman's story is common. Most players reach a peak and find themselves trapped there—A prisoner of their mind's erroneous dogmas.

Are you in a similar situation? Are you willing to rebuild your foundation, make a change, and reach new heights? If you are, then empty your brain of preconceived ideas, open you eyes, and prepare to be the player you always knew you *could* be.

The purpose of this book is to offer a complete course of study to the serious student. You will be taught the basic endgames, middlegame concepts, and the true purpose of the chess openings. You will be shown how to structure your thinking processes and how to come up with plans based on the needs of any given position. Tests, basic rules, and other recommendations will also be included. You will learn how to train yourself and be given all the tools necessary to do this.

This book is writen on many levels. Much very basic material is included. Study it! Even if you feel you know it, still go over it again. Some of the material will be a bit advanced for many players. Do the best you can with it. Reread this book every six months. You will often find that the material that was once an enigma becomes crystal clear with the passage of a little time.

This is not simply another tome on the middlegame! Instead I offer a method of controlled thought—we will examine many different aspects of chess, but always through the confines of that method. Enough material is given in each chapter to get a point across. A complete explanation of each subject would take many thousands of pages. A list of recommended literature is given at the end of this book for those who wish to delve deeper into various topics.

It is my contention that any student who seriously studies this book and continues the work schedules therein can eventually achieve a master ranking.

One pitfall must be mentioned before we finish this introduction and get into the actual lessons. Most players have developed a certain proficiency with their styles. They are skilled in their mediocrity. When you start changing the way you think about the game, you may find your results will actually get worse! Don't panic. As you master the materials in this book your downward plunge will reverse itself and you will soon find yourself at a point of understanding and achievement far beyond anything you have previously obtained. Of couse, a fall in strength is not necessary. Everyone will react differenty to the information inside. One gentleman had an 'A' rating for years but had never won an 'A' section. After one lesson something 'clicked' and he won two tournaments straight, both with 5-0 scores!

May things go so well for you!

PART ONE

BASIC ENDGAMES

This part of the book is an anomally—it really should not be here! I've struggled long and hard with the simple fact that basic endgames have nothing to do with my general theme. Why then, have I decided to include this section? In a way the answer is less a matter of reason and more a question of conscience. Quite simply: *EVERYONE* needs to know the basics of endgame play. Unfortunately I have found that players of every class have very little (if any) knowledge of this subject. Since the material in this section represents the building blocks of all endgames, I feel compelled to offer it here and BEG you to take the time to master it. Your reward will be many saves from poor positions and numerous wins from endings that you never would have gone into in the past.

Remember that I am only giving basic endgame material that I think you simply *must* know. For a deeper study of the subject, there are numerous books on the market that just explore this area of the game (see the recommended reading list at the end of this book).

I will take it for granted that the student is already familiar with the basic mates such as King and Queen vs. King, King and Rook vs. King, etc. More complex (and appropriate) endgame considerations will be studied later (see Part Thirteen: Imbalances In The Endgame).

UNDERSTANDING THE KING

Throughout a chess game a player hides his King away on the sidelines where it quivers in a perpetual state of fear. Of course, this is easy to understand—a state of martial law exists on the chessboard and a wandering King will be quickly executed by a vindictive Queen and her cohorts. This matriarchy exists as long as the all-powerful Queens roam. Eventually though, all goes quiet; the warring factions have bludgeoned each other into oblivion and only the Kings and a few faithful pawns are left (a remaining Knight, Bishop, or Rook may also exist, acting as small dogs that bark and snap at the King's heals).

When the board is finally cleared of hostile pieces the Kings finally become supreme. Now, safe from attack from the extinct larger pieces, the Kings are free to leave their respective bunkers and go for a stroll. At times what's left of the two male run armies give up hostilities and make peace—a draw is declared. More often than not though, the King, so recently freed from the bullying presence of the dominating Queen, finds himself lonely. He misses his lady and goes in search of a new one. Thus the queening of a pawn becomes his sole ambition and he roams the face of the board in an effort to turn this dream into reality.

In this chapter we will strive to understand the basic movements of the King and the relation that the opposing Kings have to each other.

Opposition

The fight between Kings to determine which one is stronger is called the *opposition* (diagram #1).

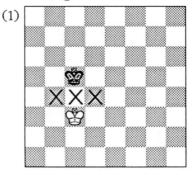

Both Kings would like to advance but they are placed in a way that prevents their counterpart from doing so. In this type of situation it is disadvantageous to have the move since you must then give up control of one of the critical 'X' squares and allow the enemy King to advance. With this in mind, we can see that White to move gives Black the opposition since 1.Kd3 allows 1...Kb4, while 1.Kb3 allows 1...Kd4. In both cases, Black's King is making headway into White's position.

Diagram #2 demonstrates the same concept, only in extended form.

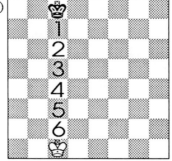

This is called the distant opposition. The rule is: *Whoever is to move when there is an odd number of squares between the Kings does not have the opposition.* The reverse is: *Whoever is to move*

when there is an even number of squares between the Kings does have the opposition. If they continue to walk towards each other we will arrive at diagram #1 again.

These same rules also apply to diagonals (diagram #3).

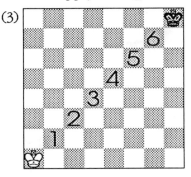

If it is White to move then who has the opposition? The answer is that White does since there is an even number of squares between the Kings. Thus White would play 1.Kb2 which would leave Black on the move with an odd number of squares between the Kings.

It now should not be difficult to determine who has the opposition when the Kings connect on a rank, file, or diagonal. But what if they fail to connect altogether? Does one then need to work out difficult mathematical formulas? Hardly! Let's look at diagram #4.

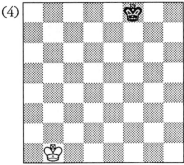

In non-connecting situations the rule is: *Move the King to a square or rectangle in which each corner is the same color.* Diagram #5 (next page) will illustrate this.

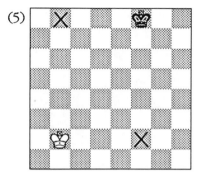

(5)

White has just played **1.Kb2**. The connecting points b2, b8, f8, and f2 are all dark squares and form a rectangle. After **1.Kb2** White has the opposition. Let's see if I'm telling the truth: **1...Ke8** (1...Kf7 2.Kb3 gives us direct diagonal opposition) **2.Kc2 Kf8** (2...Kd7 3.Kd3 or 2...Kd8 3.Kd2 both give us direct connections) **3.Kd2 Kg8 4.Ke2 Kh8 5.Kf2 Kh7 6.Kf3 Kh8 7.Kf4** and Black can no longer avoid a direct connection (7...Kh7 8.Kf5; 7...Kg7 8.Kg5; 7...Kg8 8.Kg4). Note that each time someone moves, a new series of connection points are formed.

OUTFLANKING

Outflanking is a simple but useful tool to know. With it a player can make inroads into a position that were not otherwise possible. Admittedly, this often costs the opposition but it must be remembered that *the opposition is only a means to an end, not the end itself!*

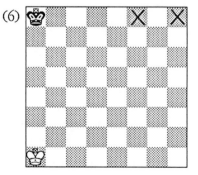

(6)

A close study of diagram #6 and its correct handling will teach the student the finer points of opposition and outflanking. White to play has the opposition. His goal is to reach f8, g8 or h8 in at most seventeen moves. Black will constantly try to stop this. **1.Ka2!** The only way to take the opposition. The more direct path fails because it allows Black to take the opposition: 1.Kb2? Kb8! 2.Kc3 Kc7 3.Kd4 Kd6 4.Ke4 Ke6 and White will not get close to his targets. **1...Kb8!** A fine defensive move! Now 2.Ka3? loses the opposition since Black has his choice of two squares on the a-file and thus can make it either odd or even (2...Ka7!). White will also fail to reach his goals after 2.Kb3? Kb7. **2.Kb2** Heading over to the target side of the board. **2...Kc8** Still keeping White's options to a minimum. The seemingly more active 2...Kc7 3.Kc3 only aids White. **3.Kc2** Still heading for the kingside. Instead White could try to outflank Black, but at the moment this would fail to achieve the set goal. Let's look at an example of outflanking: **3.Ka3**

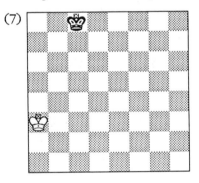

(7)

By putting a file between the Kings, White prevents Black from taking direct opposition while simultaneously making forward progress. This process is called outflanking. After 3.Ka3 Black can take the opposition with 3...Kc7 (forming connecting points on c7, c3, a3, and a7) but White will be able to move forward. 4.Ka4 Kc6 5.Ka5 Kc5 6.Ka6 Kc6. White has managed to make inroads into Black's position but he will never be able to get over to the kingside.

To solve diagram #6 White must first go to the target side of the board (kingside) and only *then* outflank his opponent. The logic for this is easy to understand: when you are on the kingside, any forward motion will allow White to land on his goal squares. **3...Kd8** (after 3.Kc2) **4.Kd2 Ke8 5.Ke2 Kf8 6.Kf2 Kg8 7.Kg2** White is now on the optimum file since his King stands in between the target squares. **7...Kh8 8.Kf3** The outflanking process finally takes place. **8...Kg7** Black could take the opposition by 8...Kh7 but after 9.Kf4 Kh6 10.Kf5 Kh5 11.Kf6 White would be able to conquer the target square on f8. This idea of giving up the opposition for a higher prize is a major part of outflanking. **9.Kg3!** Satisfied that he has advanced one rank, White retakes the opposition. Blunders would be 9.Kf4? Kf6 and 9.Kg4? Kg6. In both cases White will never reach his goal. **9...Kf7** 9...Kh7 10.Kf4 leads to the same type of play. **10.Kh4!** Another outflanking maneuver. White once again offers Black the opposition. **10...Kg6** And Black once again refuses to take it! After 10...Kf6 11.Kh5 Kf5 Black would clearly have the opposition but White would dance forward with 12.Kh6 and claim h8 for himself. **11.Kg4** Grabbing the opposition again. **11...Kh6** Or 11...Kf7 12.Kf5 Kg7 13.Kg5 Kh7 14.Kf6, etc. **12.Kf5 Kg7 13.Kg5 Kf7 14.Kh6 Kg8 15.Kg6 Kf8 16.Kh7** and White cannot be prevented from achieving his goal by 17.Kh8.

Please study the information on the opposition and outflanking carefully. Don't let the scientific names or the strange numbers and lines in the diagrams scare you away from learning something that is both easy to understand and highly useful! I should add that the position in diagram #6 is a fun one to show friends. They will not be able to solve it and will be amazed when you demonstrate how one King can actually be stronger than another just by understanding the basics of the opposition and outflanking.

KING AND PAWN ENDGAMES

In endgames with only Kings and pawns present, the opposition takes on a huge importance. This means that if the reader has not fully grasped the material in the previous chapter, I recommend that he go back and carefully reread it.

With King and pawn vs. King the battle revolves around the queening square of the pawn. If White can gain control of this square he will queen his pawn and win the game. If not, then a draw will result. The opposition will be the means by which White succeeds or fails in his quest (rook pawns form the exceptions and such situations will be studied at the end of this chapter).

(8) 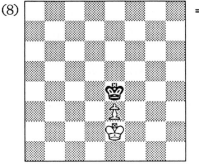 =

Diagram #8 is an extremely common position. White is a pawn ahead and wishes to advance it to e8. Black means to prevent this and at the moment is firmly blocking its path. Nevertheless, White can force the advance of his pawn. Black's ability to draw depends on his knowledge of the opposition and his keeping control of the queening square (e8). **1.Kf2 Ke5** I have often seen beginners play the atrocious 1...Kd3??. After 2.Kf3 Black's King is no longer blocking the pawn and must sit on the sidelines and watch it promote. **2.Kf3 Kf5 3.e4+ Ke5 4.Ke3** White has the opposition and Black has to give ground. **4...Ke6!** After this fine move White can only keep the opposition by playing 5.Ke2 (which does nothing to help advance the pawn) or 5.Ke4 (which is illegal). Black's plan is simple: *He intends to always jump in front of the pawn when possible. When this is impossible, Black will always move straight backwards so that when White's King comes up Black can step in front of it and take the opposition.* For example, if Black had played 4...Kf6 White would play 5.Kf4 and take the opposition. **5.Kf4** Else Black would go back to e5. **5...Kf6** Once again, if Black had played 4...Kf6 then 5.Kf4 leaves Black to move and White with the opposition. After the correct 4...Ke6! 5.Kf4 Kf6 we have the same position but with *White* to move—thus Black is the one who has gained the opposition. **6.e5+ Ke6 7.Ke4** Temporarily taking the opposition. **7...Ke7** Continuing to step straight back. Now White would have to play 8.Ke5 in order to retain the opposition. Since this is illegal, it will once again switch over to Black. **8.Kd5 Kd7** Obviously not 8...Kf7?? 9.Kd6 when White is allowed to come forward. **9.e6+ Ke7 10.Ke5 Ke8!** When it counts the most. Any other move would lose. For example, 10...Kd8?? 11.Kd6 Ke8 12.e7 Kf7 13.Kd7 when White has gained control of e8 and will easily queen his pawn. **11.Kf5** Hoping for 11...Kd8?? or 11...Kf8?? when 12.Kf6 would take the opposition and win after 12...Ke8 13.e7 followed by 14.Kf7. **11...Ke7** Always jump in front of the pawn when possible. **12.Ke5 Ke8! 13.Kf6 Kf8 14.e7+ Ke8 15.Ke6** Stalemate and thus drawn.

Drawing this position should become second nature to you. Get a friend to take the King and pawn while you try to save the game with the lone King. Use a chess clock and give yourself twenty seconds (the player with the King and pawn can take as much time as he wants) for an infinite number of moves. After a few practice sessions thought will not be necessary—your hand will know how to draw this in your sleep.

With King and pawn vs. King, *White's main hope to win occurs when his King is in front of the pawn.* Diagram #9 illustrates this point.

(9) 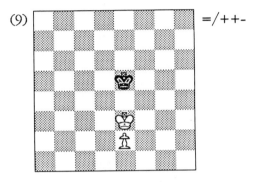 =/++-

White to move is a draw because Black has the opposition: **1.Kd3 Kd5 2.e4+** 2.Kc3 Ke4 or 2.Ke3 Ke5 are no better. **2...Ke5 3.Ke3 Ke6** with an easy draw as in diagram #8.

Black to move (from Diagram #9) is a different story. White now has the opposition and wherever the Black King moves it will allow White's monarch to advance: **1...Kd5** The same type of play follows 1...Kf5 2.Kd4 while 1...Kd6 2.Kd4 Ke6 3.Ke4 Kd6 4.Kf5 is also not difficult. **2.Kf4!** White wants to control the pawn's queening square. The rule to follow is: *Advance your King as far as possible without endangering the pawn,* making sure to take the opposition at the critical moments. With the King far advanced White can take the opposition at any time because he will always have tempo moves with his pawn. **2...Kd6** Other tries:

1) 2...Kd4 3.e4 (3.e3+ Kd5 4.Kf5 is also good) 3...Kc5 4.Ke5! (stopping Black from getting in front of the pawn) 4...Kc6 5.Ke6 Kc7 6.Ke7 followed by e5, e6, Kf7, e7, and e8=Q.

2) 2...Ke6 3.Ke4! (and not 3.e4?? Kf6 with a basic draw) 3...Kf6 4.Kd5 Kf5 5.e4+ (avoiding 5.Kd6?? Ke4 when the pawn will be eaten) 5...Kf6 6.Kd6! (6.e5+?? Ke7) 6...Kf7 7.e5 (threatening 8.Kd7) 7...Ke8 8.Ke6! (Retaking the

opposition. A blunder would be 8.e6?? Kd8 9.e7+ Ke8 10.Ke6 stalemate) 8...Kd8 9.Kf7 winning.

3.Kf5 Ke7 Or 3...Kd5 4.e4+ Kd6 5.Kf6 **4.Ke5 Kf7 5.Kd6 Kf6 6.e4 Kf7 7.e5** 7.Kd7 Kf6 8.Kd6 wastes time. **7...Ke8** Else White would play 8.Kd7 with control over e8. **8.Ke6!** Grabbing the opposition. Naturally 8.e6?? would allow Black to gain the opposition by 8...Kd8 with a draw. **8...Kd8 9.Kf7** White has gained control of the critical e8 square and will shortly queen his pawn.

(10)  ++-

Diagram #10 is similar to diagram #9 but here White wins irrespective of whose move it is because he has the opposition (thanks to the pawn move available to him). White to move would play **1.e3!**, taking the opposition and winning as in diagram #9.

As a player gains more experience he will discover that a Rook pawn will often provide exceptions to rules that we normally take for granted (see diagram #11).

(11) 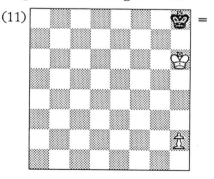 =

Usually such a fine King position for White would guarantee him the win. In this case however, Black will experience no difficulties in drawing because he cannot be flushed out of the corner. **1.h4 Kg8 2.h5 Kh8 3.Kg6 Kg8 4.h6 Kh8 5.h7** stalemate.

(12)

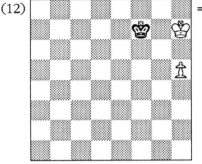

=

Diagram #12 shows another strange Rook pawn result. Black, who has no material at all, stalemates the stronger side. **1.h6** 1.Kh6 Kg8 is also a basic draw, as was seen in diagram #11. **1...Kf8 2.Kh8** Or 2.Kg6 Kg8, etc. **2...Kf7 3.h7 Kf8** stalemate.

It's clear that the opposition doesn't mean much when the only remaining pawn is a Rook pawn. White must control the queening square *and* avoid having his King trapped in the corner if he hopes to win.

To complete our discussion of King and pawn endgames, let's touch upon an old fashioned pawn vs. King foot race. If a King is far away from an enemy pawn, how can you tell if it will arrive in time to stop it from queening? Is it a matter of calculation? No, it's actually quite a simple process.

(13)

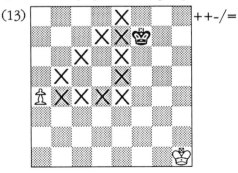

++-/=

Diagram #13 shows a quick and easy method. Create a diagonal extension (from a4 to e8) and side extension (a4 to e4) from the pawn. Connect up its points and make a border. If the King is not within or on this border the pawn will promote.

In the diagram (#13), Black to move draws by 1...Ke8 or 1...Ke7 or 1...Ke6, all of which are on the border. White to move wins by 1.a5, creating a new triangle (from a5 to d8 to d5) that Black cannot enter.

ROOK AND PAWN ENDGAMES

Endings with just Rooks and pawns are the most common form of endgame. The two basic positions that must be thoroughly known in Rook endings are the Lucena and Philidor positions.

The *Lucena Position* is the key to understanding any Rook endgame. It is the position that the stronger side strives to achieve. Diagram #14 shows the beginnings of Lucena's position.

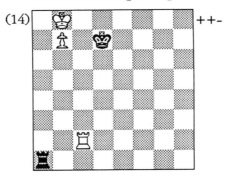

(14) ++-

Here many beginners try things like 1.Rc7+ Kd8 2.Rc8+ Kd7 3.Rh8 Ra2 4.Rh7+ but after 4...Kd8 White is not getting anywhere. Correct is **1.Rd2+** forcing Black's King to the e-file since 1...Kc6?? 2.Kc8 wins instantly for White. This leads us to our first major rule of Rook endgames: *It is always a good idea to trap the enemy King as far away as possible from the scene of action.* This rule applies to *all* Rook endgames. **1...Ke7 2.Rd4!** The key to this endgame (this Rook maneuver, for some reason or other, is called "building a bridge"). The logical 2.Kc7 fails to 2...Rc1+

15

3.Kb6 Rb1+ 4.Kc6 Rc1+ 5.Kd5 Rb1 and White must return with his King and run back to his hole on b8. The point of 2.Rd4! is that White's King can now come out since it will have the Rook to block the checks. **2...Ke6 3.Kc7 Rc1+ 4.Kb6 Rb1+ 5.Kc6 Rb2** The point of White's play is best seen after 5...Rc1+ 6.Kb5 Rb1+ 7.Rb4 with an immediate win. **6.Re4+** Pushing Black even further away. Also good is 6.Rd6+ Ke7 7.Rd5 followed by 8.Rb5. I should mention that Black had a trap in mind, namely 6.Rd5?? (hoping to play 7.Rb5) 6...Rxb7! with a draw. **6...Kf5 7.Rc4** followed by 8.Kc7 and 9.b8=Q.

It is clear that the defender must not allow the opponent to gain the Lucena Position. In general, *don't allow the side with the extra pawn to get his King in front of his pawn.*

Another thing that the defending side must avoid is the dreaded passive Rook. Diagram #15 shows a typical example.

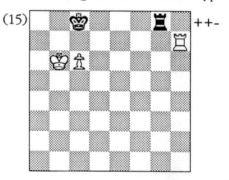

(15) ++-

Black loses because his Rook is passively placed on the back rank. If he ever tries to move to a more active post via something like 1...Rg1 (if it was Black to move) then 2.Rh8 would mate him. **1.Ra7** This idea of switching over to the other side is very important because it shows that Black's Rook was not really controlling the whole back rank after all. **1...Kb8 2.c7+ Kc8 3.Ra8+**, etc.

White wins in a similar fashion with a center pawn (diagram #16).

(16)

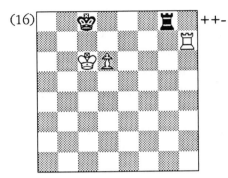

++-

1.Ra7 And not 1.d7+?? Kd8 with a draw since White's Rook can no longer swing over to a7. Never push this pawn unless it is immediately decisive. *The pawn acts as cover for your King—pushing it destroys that cover.* **1...Kb8 2.Rb7+ Ka8** 2...Kc8? 3.d7+. **3.Rb1** Not completely necessary but it is always a good idea to put one's Rook on a safe square far away from the enemy King. Now Black's King is trapped out of play. This leaves us in a King and pawn vs. Rook situation which will inevitably lead to the loss of Black's Rook. **3...Rc8+** Else White would play 4.Kc7, 5.d7, and 6.d8=Q. **4.Kd7 Rc2 5.Ke7 Re2+ 6.Kd8 Rd2 7.d7 Re2 8.Rb4** with a *Lucena Position.*

Lest White get the idea that he can win any passive Rook situation, let me point out that a Knight pawn or Rook pawn form an exception to the usual rules (see diagram #17).

(17)

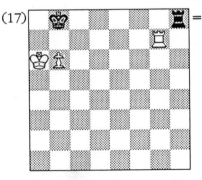

=

The game is drawn because White's Rook cannot successfully switch over to the other side of the board simply because there is no other side to go to! For example: **1.Ra7** (1.Rb7+ Ka8

2.Ra7+ Kb8 amounts to the same thing) **1...Rg8** 1...Rh1 intending 2...Ra1+ is also a clean draw. After 1...Rg8 White cannot make progress since **2.b7??** takes away White's cover and actually loses to **2...Rg6+.**

If Black (For illustrative purposes Black is often considered the inferior side) is in a Rook and pawn vs. Rook situation he can usually draw by avoiding a passive Rook, avoiding the Lucena Position, and making use of Philidor's defensive plan.

(18)

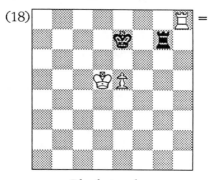

Black to play

Diagram #18 is a seemingly strong position for White, who is a pawn up with more active pieces. Nevertheless, Black draws easily by **1...Rg6!** Inferior is 1...Rg1 2.Rh7+ Ke8 3.Kd6 when 3...Rg6+?? 4.e6 Rg8 5.Ra7 leads to a hopeless passive Rook position (as in diagram #18), while 3...Rd1+? 4.Ke6 forces Black's King out of its hole. However, even after the inferior 1...Rg1 2.Rh7+ Ke8 3.Kd6 Black *can* draw by playing like a genius: 3...Re1! (the only good move) 4.Rh8+ Kf7 5.Rh7+ (If Black's Rook were not on the e-file White could play 5.e6+) 5...Ke8 6.Ke6 Kf8! (Here we come to an important rule. If your King is forced to leave the queening square of the pawn and run to one side or the other, *always run to the short side of the board.* The reason for this is that later you may wish to check his King from the side. In that case Black would move his Rook to the a-file so that there is as much room as possible between the enemy King and his Rook. If the Black King went to d8 and subsequently to c7 it might get in the way of the Rook's checking powers on the queenside) 7.Rh8+ Kg7 8.Ra8 Re2 (pass) 9.Kd6 Kf7! (And not 9...Rd2+? 10.Ke7) 10.Ra7+ Ke8 11.Ke6 Kf8! 12.Ra8+ Kg7 13.Re8 (Intending 14.Kd7 when 14...Kf7 fails to 15.e6+, while 14...Rd2+ also is nothing due to 15.Ke7) 13...Ra2! (threatening 14...Ra6+) 14.Rd8 (To block the checks) 14...Re2! and White is unable to make any progress. So it's clear that Black can draw even without 1...Rg6!, but he would have to know what he is doing if he expects to hold the game. Why make things difficult? It's very easy after 1...Rg6!. **2.Rh7+ Ke8** Now we can see the point of 1...Rg6!—White's King is unable to advance. Since Black simply intends to pass with moves like ...Ra6, ...Rb6, etc., White eventually has to advance his pawn. **3.e6** Threatening to win by 4.Kd6. **3...Rg1!** Activating the Rook only *after* the pawn is pushed. White now has no pawn shelter and a draw results since 4...Rd1+ with a perpetual check will follow (If White avoids this by 4.Rh4 Black can get an easy draw by 4...Ke7 or he can trade Rooks and go into a dead drawn King and pawn endgame).

The *Philidor technique* may seem somewhat complicated to some of you. However, just a little work will make it easy to understand. Please take the time to master this extremely important position!

Solve These Problems

(19)

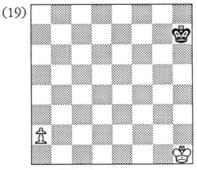

Black to move.

Can he stop the pawn?

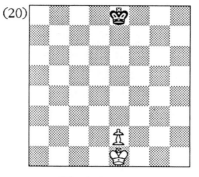

Black to move.

Can he draw the game?

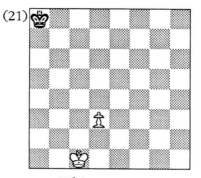

White to move.

Can he win?

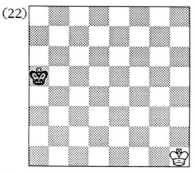

White to move and take the opposition.

How?

(23)

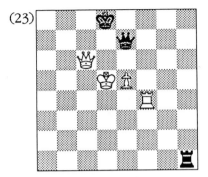

Black to play.
Is it safe for Black to trade Queens in this position?

PART TWO

THINKING TECHNIQUES AND THE LIST OF IMBALANCES

"A sound plan makes us all heroes, the absence of a plan, idiots."
—G.M. Kotov quoting a mysterious 'chess sage.'

At some time or other every tournament player learns a few opening lines, some tactical ideas, and the most basic mating patterns. As he gets better and more experienced he adds to this knowledge. However, the one thing that just about everybody has problems with is planning. From class 'E' to Master, I get blank stares when asking what plan they had in mind in a particular position. Usually their choice of plan (if they have any plan at all) is based on emotional rather than scientific considerations. By emotional I mean that the typical player does what he *feels* like doing rather than what the board *wants* him to do. *If you want to be successful, you have to base your plans on specific criteria on the board, not on your mood at any given time!*

An example of this can almost certainly be found in a large number of your tournament games. In the thick of battle with your clock ticking, how many times have you decided that you want to mate the enemy King? The position may call for something quite different but *you* decide to go for a kingside attack because you like playing for a quick checkmate. When victory comes (usually against weaker opposition) you congratulate yourself on a brilliant concept. When defeat appears (a common occurance) you bemoan your fate and blame it on a particular move, your recent divorce, the noise level, the blonde across the hall, or a host of other excuses.

What is this mysterious allusion to the chess board's desires? What are the criteria that we are going to have to become aware of and how do we master their use? What, exactly, is a plan?

WHAT IS A PLAN?

Though every chess instructor sings the praises of planning, few authors bother to tell us what a plan is and, more importantly, how to create one. In his excellent glossary of chess terms (found in *How to Open a Chess Game*[1]), Grandmaster Larry Evans avoids the problem by leaving out the word 'plan' altogether. Kotov, in his classic work, *Think Like a Grandmaster*[2], teaches us how to calculate but neglects to explain planning (to be fair I must mention that Mr. Kotov does address this question in his book *Play Like a Grandmaster*[3]. However, his explanations tend to be over the head of the average player). Even encyclopedic texts like the *Oxford Companion to Chess*[4] tries to make 'planning' a non-existent word.

Only Harry Golombek in his *Encyclopedia Of Chess* bothers to give us a basic definition: "Planning is the process by which a player utilizes the advantages and minimizes the drawbacks of his position. In order to promise success, planning is thus always based on a diagnosis of the existing characteristics of a position; it is therefore most difficult when the position is evenly balanced, and easiest when there is only one plan to satisfy the demands of the position."[5]

[1] *How to Open a Chess Game,* by Larry Evans, Svetozar Gligoric, Vlastimil Hort, Paul Keres, Bent Larsen, Tigran Petrosian, Lajos Portisch, R.H.M. Press, New York, 1974.
[2] *Think Like a Grandmaster,* by Alexander Kotov, B.T. Batsford Ltd., London, 1978
[3] *Play Like a Grandmaster,* by Alexander Kotov, B.T. Batsford Ltd., London, 1971
[4] *The Oxford Companion to Chess, Second Edition,* by David Hooper and Kenneth Whyld, Oxford University Press, Oxford, 1992
[5] *The Encyclopedia of Chess,* Edited by Harry Golombek, B.T. Batsford Ltd., London, 1977, p. 242

IMBALANCES AND THE 'SILMAN THINKING TECHNIQUE'

To define the word 'plan' does not necessarily mean that we know how to create one in an actual game. As Golombek said, this calls for the ability to recognize the existing characteristics of a position. To successfully penetrate into the mysteries of the chess board you have to be aware of the magic word of chess: **IMBALANCE.** An imbalance in chess denotes any difference in the two respective positions. To think that the purpose of chess is solely to checkmate the opposing King is much too simplistic. The real goal of a chess game is to create an imbalance and try to build a situation in which it is favorable for you. An understanding of this statement shows that an imbalance is not necessarily an advantage. It is simply a difference. It is the player's responsibility to turn that difference into an advantage.

Here is a breakdown of the different imbalances:

1) *Superior Minor Piece* (the interplay between Bishops and Knights).

2) *Pawn Structure* (a broad subject that encompasses doubled pawns, isolated pawns, etc).

3) *Space* (the annexation of territory on a chess board).

4) *Material* (owning pieces of greater value than the opponent's).

5) *Control of a key file or square* (files and diagonals act as pathways for your pieces, while squares act as homes).

6) *Lead in development* (more force in a specific area of the board).

7) *Initiative* (dictating the tempo of a game).

Recognizing these imbalances (you will find definitions to all these terms in the Glossary at the end of this book) and understanding their relationship to planning will be the main focus of this book. If we are to use these things properly we must be able to break down our thinking in a way that allows us to dissect any particular position. Here are the stages of my thinking technique that enables us to accomplish this:

1) Figure out the positive and negative imbalances for *both sides.*

2) Figure out the side of the board you wish to play on. *You can only play where a favorable imbalance or the possibility of creating a favorable imbalance exists.*

3) Don't calculate! Instead, dream up various fantasy positions, i.e., the positions you would most like to achieve.

4) Once you find a fantasy position that makes you happy, you must figure out if you can reach it. If you find that your choice was not possible to implement, you must create another dream position that is easier to achieve.

5) Only now do you look at the moves you wish to calculate (called *candidate moves*). The candidate moves are all the moves that lead to our dream position. This will be discussed fully in Part Three of this book.

Let's now take a look at this thinking technique in action. If it seems difficult don't panic! It just takes practice. Nobody ever said that getting your thoughts to work in a structured way would be easy!

After the opening moves **1.c4 e5 2.Nc3 Nf6 3.g3 Bb4 4.Bg2 0-0 5.e4 Bxc3 6.bxc3 c6 7.Ba3 Re8 8.Qb3 d6 9.Ne2 Na6 10.d3 Nc5 11.Qc2** we get the position in diagram #24.

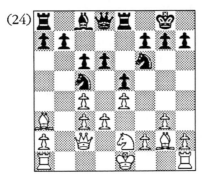

(24)

Saidy-Silman, Los Angeles 1989.
Black to move.

What should Black do? He wants to avoid simple developing moves like 11...Bd7 or 11...Be6 since they are not part of a particular plan. To say that your plan is just to develop your pieces is a cop-out! Remember: *First* find a plan and then develop your forces around it! *Never* mindlessly develop and expect to find a plan at some later point in the game.

The first thing we have to do is figure out the imbalances. White has the two Bishop's, but at the moment the Bishop on g2 is inactive and the Black Knight on c5 is very well placed—this Knight is just as good as any Bishop. White has doubled pawns but are not weak in this position. The c4 pawn gives White added control of the d5 square while its siamese twin on c3 controls the d4 square, thus preventing Black from rushing a Knight there by ...Ne6-d4. The final imbalance of note is the lack of open files for the Rooks. The only one available is the b-file, something that White can use if he so wishes.

Since material is even and nobody has an edge in space or development, that ends our breakdown of the imbalances in this position. Keep in mind that we are just listing them, not judging their respective values.

Next we have to figure out which side of the board to play on. Remember that *you should only play where a favorable imbalance or the possibility of creating one exists.* This is extremely important! Let's say Black loved to attack. Nothing pleased him more than mating the opponent's King. Such a player would naturally look to the kingside first in just about any situation. In this case what factors exist on the kingside that favor Black? The answer is none! With no White weakness there and few Black pieces aiming in that direction (you won't mate with just the c8 Bishop and the f6 Knight) Black has little to hope for on that wing. Perhaps he is emotionally ready to start some sort of 'do or die' charge, but his position is not backing him up. Black must calm down and look elsewhere.

Since the kingside doesn't seem to be the promised land, we will turn our attentions to the center. Here we have some hope for play because both our Knight's influence this sector of the board. However, since there are no ready-made squares or weaknesses to go for, we would be forced to crack it open with a central advance. Thus a centrally based plan would revolve around the break with ...d6-d5. Since this type of advance would give us more central territory and potential open files for our Rooks it is worth pursuing. Once we find an interesting path we go to our next step: the creation of fantasy positions. Note that we are still not calculating any variations!

A fantasy position is just that—a fantasy. We place the pieces wherever we want them in order to carry out the plan, in this case ...d6-d5. Here we note that our Knight on c5 would hang if we moved the d-pawn too quickly. So we must give this piece support. We also must be careful that the resultant opening up of the center does not activate White's Bishops. To this end we would like to trade off or at least challenge White's Bishop on g2 (this goes along with a rule that we will study in a later lesson: *If the opponent has the two Bishops, trade one Bishop off. This will lead to a more manageable Bishop vs. Knight situation*). To fulfill these ideas we come up with the following setup:

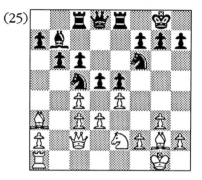

Notice what was done. Black just placed his pieces and pawns in the desired positions...*he didn't move them there!* He then decides if achieving this leads anywhere. A glance at the diagram shows that Black would have good play. However it must be admitted that the construction of this setup would take several moves. What would White be doing in the meantime? To answer this you would go through these same stages for your opponent. As it turns out, White's correct plan is to play for kingside expansion by an f2-f4 advance. Notice that this can be done very quickly via 12.0-0 and 13.f4. So what we end up with is an interesting plan of central expansion for Black that would hopefully counteract White's theme of a kingside pawn storm. The one problem is timing; White's plan is faster than ours. If we decided that we wanted to play this way we would then look for the candidate moves, e.g. all the moves that aid us in setting up the desired position. In this case only one move comes into consideration, namely 11...b6. We would then analyze it and, if everything checked out we would store it away as a playable idea. We still don't want to play it because we have yet to explore the possibility of a queenside plan.

We now turn our attention to the queenside. Are there any weaknesses there to attack? No. However our strong c5 Knight is placed there and White's doubled pawns (which at the moment are by no means weak) are also on that side. Since we have no clear targets to attack, can we create one? Can we open lines there? Yes, with ....b7-b5 we can force an immediate crisis.

After 11...b5 12.cxb5 cxb5 Black would have made a gain in queenside territory and also created a weakness in White's camp—a backward pawn on c3. To make matters even better, this pawn lies on a newly opened file. Our plan would then be obvious: Move our Bishop, place a Rook on c8, and put pressure on White's weak and accessible pawn on c3.

So it turns out that we have a choice. Play in the center or on the queenside. In the game Black chose the queenside simply because it is the faster plan.

Note that Black is not worried about White playing Bxc5 since after ...dxc5 Black could make use of the newly opened d-file to attack the backward pawn on d3. **11...b5! 12.cxb5 cxb5 13.0-0 Bb7!?** A tough choice. Black wants to put his Rook on c8 as quickly as possible but he is not sure where to place his Bishop. A good alternative is 13...a5 followed by 14...Ba6 when White must always worry about a discovered attack on his d3 pawn by ...b5-b4. Black finally decided on 13...Bb7 because he felt that after ...Rc8 he would be in a position to play for an eventual break in the center with ...d6-d5. **14.Rab1 Rc8?!** The intended move. However he first should have defended his b5 pawn and his b7 Bishop by 14...Qd7. Now White is able to get rid of his weakness on c3—a great shame since the creation of that weakness was the whole point of Black's earlier play. **15.c4!** Avoiding 15.Rxb5? Ba6 when the pawn on d3 would die. Now Black must avoid falling for a trap: 15...bxc4?? 16.Bxc5 dxc5 17.Rxb7 cxd3 18.Qc4 and Black cannot recapture his piece since White threatens 19.Qxf7+.

At this point the student should be able to deduce the importance of creating weak, attackable points in the enemy camp. If you happen to possess one of these weaknesses you should do everything you can to get rid of it. In our present game, by pouncing on Black's error and getting rid of his weakness, White throws Black on the defensive. **15...a6 16.cxb5 axb5 17.Qd2** 17.Rxb5? was still bad due to 17...Ba6. Now, due to his inaccuracy on the 14th move, Black must come up with a new plan. Since White's pawn weakness is now on a2, Black redirects his guns on that point. **17...Ra8 18.Bb4** White wants to hold onto his two Bishops. He gains nothing after 18.Bxc5 dxc5 19.Rxb5 Ba6 20.Rb3 c4.

After 18.Bb4 Black has to find a way to activate his Bishop and create new attackable points in White's position. If Black plays passively White will continue with Nc3 and Rfc1 with pressure on c5 and b5. **18...Na4!** Now if White's Knight comes to c3, Black can trade it off. Another benefit of ...Na4 is that Black is finally in a position to play ...d5 since the Knight would no longer be hanging on c5. Why play ...d5? The reasoning is this: After ...d5, if White captures by exd5 he would be left with a weak isolated pawn on d3. If he leaves his pawn on e4, then after Black trades pawns by ...dxe4 White's e4 pawn would be vulnerable to several of the Black pieces. Just another example of Black striving to create pawn weaknesses in the enemy camp. **19.Nc3 Nxc3 20.Bxc3 d5!** Using tactical means to create the desired target on e4. White cannot play 21.Rxb5 due to 21...Ba6 and 22...dxe4. **21.Qe2 Ra4!** Still whacking away at the e4 pawn and preparing to double on the a-file and intensify the pressure on the weak a-pawn. **22.Qb2 Qa8!**

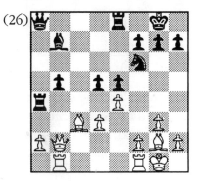

(26)

Black relentlessly steps up the pressure on both e4 and a2. **23.Bxe5 Rxa2**, 1/2-1/2. The White Queen wants to guard the e5 Bishop so Black would have a perpetual on the Queen after 24.Qd4 Ra4 25.Qc3 Ra3 etc.

This thinking technique is quite effective but requires a good deal of practice to master. However, if you are lazy (or simply don't have much time to put into the study of chess) it might interest you to know that a firm understanding of the imbalances alone can provide a sort of fast-food method of planning. Just find the imbalances and try to make use of them. The majority of this book is devoted to a detailed study of each imbalance. When you have mastered the subject, you can use just the imbalances to determine what you wish to do or use imbalances in relation to the thinking technique that has just been examined.

Solve This Problem

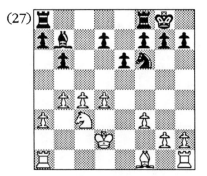

(27)

Black to play.

After **1.d4 e6 2.c4 Nf6 3.Nc3 Bb4 4.Qc2 c5 5.dxc5 0-0 6.a3 Bxc5 7.Nf3 Nc6 8.Bg5 Nd4 9.Nxd4 Bxd4 10.e3 Qa5 11.exd4 Qxg5 12.Qd2 Qxd2+ 13.Kxd2 b6 14.b4 Bb7 15.f3** we reach the position in diagram #27. What are the imbalances and what is White's plan?

PART THREE

CALCULATION AND COMBINATIONS

When most people sit down at a chessboard they look desperately at their pieces for a hint, a clue, a sign—anything that would help them know what to do. Calculating variations madly without any goal in mind, they think that chess is nothing more than a quick mating attack or a search for a pretty combination that can knock an opponent out of the game. Though Part Two of this book hopefully destroyed this view, it *is* important to know how to do these things (calculation and spotting combinations) when the proper situation arises. This section discusses Kotov's method of calculation and also deals with a system that allows you to understand when combinations may or may not exist.

CALCULATION

It is very common for the chess amateur to wonder how many moves ahead a Grandmaster usually calculates. When the great Richard Reti was asked this question he said, "One move." Alekhine, on the other hand, loved to present a combination from one of his games and say "the point" when he was over a dozen moves into it, thereby claiming that he had seen everything till the very end.

Was one of these legendary Grandmasters pulling our collective legs or are there some top players who simply can't calculate? The answer lies somewhere in between. Of course, some Grandmasters *can* calculate better than others (Alekhine was one of the finest calculaters in history). However, virtually every GM has the ability to see many moves ahead. The point is that many positions don't call for calculation at all; hence Reti's 'one move' claim. Diagram #28 illustrates this concept in a simple way.

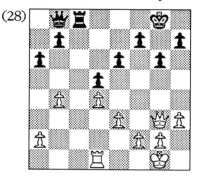

(28)

White to move

In this position no good international player would hesitate to play **1.Qxb8 Rxb8 2.Rc1** followed by 3.Rc7 with a clear advantage due to the dominant placement of his Rook on the only open file. To calculate any variations at all would be a complete waste of time.

The same reasoning can be applied to diagram #29.

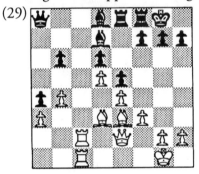

(29)

White to move.

White enjoys a clear advantage in space on the queenside and control of the open c-file. He would like to put more pressure on the weakened pawns on b6 and a4 but Black's light-squared Bishop defends a4 and keeps the White Rooks out of c6. It would not take a master more than a nano-second to see and play the obvious **1.Bb5!**, trading off his bad Bishop for Black's useful defensive piece. After this inevitable exchange White would gain enormous pressure on the Black position by continuing with Rc6 and Qb5. Once again, no calculation would be necessary.

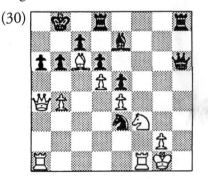

(30)

White to play.

In general, calculation is necessary to verify the tactical worth of a move that seems to take care of the needs of a given position. In diagram #30 we have a situation that is anything but subtle. It's clear that both sides are trying to mate the other and, if he can get away with it, White would love to play 1.Qxa6 when mate on a8 or b7 is unstoppable if Black doesn't execute White first.

Since the position screams for 1.Qxa6 to be played, White has only to calculate the consequences of a Black checking onslaught to see if it is a correct decision *tactically*. As it turns out, Black gets some macho checks and then has to resign: **1.Qxa6 Qh1+ 2.Kf2 Qxg2+ 3.Kxe3 Bg5+ 4.Kd3**, 1-0.

We can see then, that in both positional and tactical situations you must use my thinking technique (or at least carefully weigh the imbalances) to find the proper plan or move. You only bother calculating once the correct plan is clear and once you settle upon a move that helps your plan come to fruition.

(31)

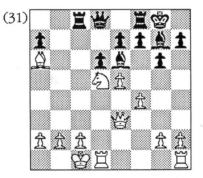

Kelson-Silman, Reno 1993.
Black to play.

In diagram #31 we see that Black is a pawn down and his Rook on c8 is attacked. On the basis of these two factors we might conclude that White is in control. However, when we factor in Black's two Bishops, safe King, and the open lines and files that lead right to the White monarch, we get quite a different picture.

Since we want to save the Black Rook, and since if the White Knight didn't stand on d5 (where it keeps the Queen at bay defending the e7-pawn) Black would be able to continue his attack by ...Qa5, Black decides that he would like to play **1...Rc5!**, bringing his Rook to safety and attacking the impudent horse. The only question left to be answered is, "Does the move have a tactical refutation?" At this point all you can do is calculate the consequenses. To do this we will borrow Kotov's suggestion that candidate moves be used. A candidate move is all the possible (meaning reasonable) replies your opponent might make (or if it was your move—all the moves that lead to the fullfillment of your plan). Kotov recommends that you mentally list these possibilities, so on paper the choices would be like this: A) 2.c4; B) 2.Qe4; C) 2.Nc3; D) 2.Nb4; E) 2.Bb7; F) 2.Qxc5; G) 2.Nxe7+. Note that all these moves either defend the hanging Knight or try to take advantage of the fact that Black's Queen is sitting on the same line as the White Rook on d1.

So far then, we have used the Silman Thinking Technique to find our correct plan (no calculation), discovered the move that strives to make our plan a reality (still no calculation), and listed our opponent's intelligent replies (sorry—we haven't started to calculate yet). Only when all this is done do we actually calculate each White move in our mental list to see if 1...Rc5 is actually correct:

A) 2.c4 Bxd5 3.Rxd5 Rxd5 4.cxd5 Qa5 gives Black a strong attack (this occured in the actual game).

B) 2.Qe4?? allows the Knight to remain on d5 but runs into 2...Bf5!.

C) 2.Nc3 Qa5 gives Black the kind of attacking position he has been dreaming of. No further calculation would be necessary; you have a beautiful position—there is no necessity to figure everything out to the end.

D) 2.Nb4 also gives Black a tasty position. Black would only have to figure out (calculate) if 2...Qb6 is better than 2...Qa5.

E) 2.Bb7!? is ugly but keeps the Knight rooted to d5. At the very least Black could win back his pawn by 2...Bxd5 3.Bxd5 Qa5 when White's bit on e5 falls.

F) 2.Qxc5?? dxc5 3.Nf6+ exf6 4.Rxd8 Rxd8 and Black ends up with an extra piece.

G) 2.Nxe7+ almost refutes 1...Rc5. However, 'almost' isn't good enough: 2...Qxe7 3.exd6 and now instead of 3...Qf6 4.Qxc5 Qxb2+ which allows White to keep fighting with 5.Kd2, Black can win immediately with the pretty 3...Rxc2+! 4.Kxc2 Bf5+ 5.Kd2 Qxd6+ 6.Bd3 Qb4+ 7.Ke2 Bg4+ 8.Kf2 Bd4.

Interestingly enough, old experienced dogs like myself will often avoid calculation even in this type of complicated situation and just play 1...Rc5 cold turkey (of course, we would still use the thinking technique to find the correct plan)! Why? Are we tempting fate or are we getting some sort of rush from the knowledge that we might be hammered at any moment? The simple truth is that ...Rc5 is the move that the position calls for. Since the *board* wants it to be played, I may trust in my instincts and give it a go, secure in the knowledge that the ultimate spiritual truth of the chessboard will not prove me wrong (on occasion I *have* been punished for such unabashed idealism; so beware—the Goddess Caissa does not always heap rewards on her devotees).

Normally you may want to look a couple of moves ahead to make sure that everything is in order. Of course, once in a while very deep calculation is a must—you simply *have* to look deeply into the position.

(32)
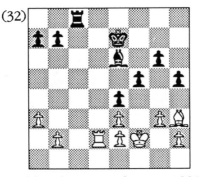

Eddy-Silman, Anchorage 1993.
Black to play.

In diagram #32 Black has a winning advantage because White's Bishop is entombed on the kingside. However, Black made a point of calculating over 20 moves ahead to insure that the zugzwang he had in mind was really going to happen. The first part of Black's calculations concerned keeping White's King out of c3 (after a trade of Rooks) by placing a pawn on b4. **1...a5 2.Ke1 Bb3 3.Kf2 Rc1 4.Bg2 g5 5.h3 g4 6.h4 b5 7.Bf1 Ke6?** An inaccuracy. Black could have kept White's counterplay to a minimum by 7...Rc8 8.Ke1 Ke6 9.Bg2 Rc1+ 10.Kf2 Rc2, when things would have turned out as they did in the actual game. **8.Bg2?** His last chance was 8.Rd8 Rc2 9.Rh8 with fighting chances. **8...Rc2 9.Ke1 Rxd2 10.Kxd2 b4 11.axb4 axb4 12.Bh1 Kd5 13.Bg2 Kc4 14.Bf1 Ba4 15.Kc1 Kb3 16.Kb1 Bb5 17.Kc1 Ka2 18.Kc2 Ba4+** Black also wins with 18...Bc4 19.Kc1 b3. **19.Kc1 Bd1! 20.Bg2** The sad state of White's Bishop would be highlighted after 20.Kxd1 Kxb2 when nothing can be done to stop Black from promoting his b-pawn. **20...Bxe2 21.Kc2 Bd3+ 22.Kc1 b3 23.Bh1 Bf1**, 0-1. Believe it or not, Black saw this position (and variations of it) when he played 1...a5. The depth of this calculation was made possible by the fact that White was helpless and could only go back and forth. The lack of side variations can make a calculation of any size rather easy for the international player.

There are games though, where calculations were made of

such amazing length and complexity that it almost boggles the mind. The following example is one of the most famous of these cases.

Reti-Alekhine, Baden Baden 1925. **1.g3 e5 2.Nf3 e4 3.Nd4 d5 4.d3 exd3 5.Qxd3 Nf6 6.Bg2 Bb4+ 7.Bd2 Bxd2+ 8.Nxd2 0-0 9.c4** Starting play in the center and trying to increase the scope of his Bishop on g2. **9...Na6 10.cxd5 Nb4 11.Qc4 Nbxd5 12.N2b3 c6 13.0-0 Re8 14.Rfd1 Bg4 15.Rd2 Qc8 16.Nc5** White has prevented any active play in the center and intends to roll Black up on the queenside by b2-b4-b5. Since Black has more pieces on the kingside, his only chance is to generate some threats in that sector. **16...Bh3** A natural move that entails a good deal of calculation. While it's clear that Black would like to get rid of White's powerful Bishop, he must make sure that 17.Bxh3 Qxh3 18.Nxb7 doesn't just drop all his queenside pawns: 18...Ng4 19.Nf3 Nde3! 20.fxe3 Nxe3 21.Qxf7+ Kh8! (21...Kxf7?? 22.Ng5+ picks up the Black Queen) 22.Nh4 Rf8 and any Queen move gets mated by 23...Rf1+. Black was only able to play 16...Bh3 after he saw that the b-pawn is taboo. **17.Bf3 Bg4 18.Bg2 Bh3 19.Bf3 Bg4 20.Bh1** White refuses the draw by repetition and instead tries for the win. He knows that his queenside attack will eventually pay dividends and he does not believe that Black's kingside counterplay will really lead to anything. In a way, this is typical of the mentality of kingside attacks vs. queenside attacks. The queenside attack is effective in a middlegame *and* in an endgame because the target is usually a weak pawn or square. A kingside attack usually aims at the enemy King. This means that a Queen trade will favor the queenside attack since the guy going after the King needs the Queen to head the mating attack. In other words, the side with the queenside attack is willing to put up with a few insults to his King—he is getting endgame odds (the long range chances) in return! **20...h5!** Preparing to weaken White's kingside pawn shelter. **21.b4 a6 22.Rc1 h4** Neither side wastes any time in trying to make his plan bear fruit. Mutual attacking situations always call for speed. If you hesitate and lose confidence in your ideas, you will be utterly consumed. **23.a4 hxg3 24.hxg3 Qc7** Eyeing the newly weakened g3 point. **25.b5** Forging ahead but underestimating Black's possibilities. **25...axb5 26.axb5 Re3!**

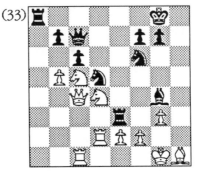

(33)

The storm breaks! A neverending stream of tactical ideas now beat White to a pulp. **27.Nf3** It's obvious that 27.fxe3 Qxg3+ 28.Bg2 Nxe3 is hopeless for White. Another way of stopping Black's threatened 27...Rxg3+ is 27.Kh2, but then Alekhine intended 27...Raa3! 28.Ncb3 (28.fxe3 Nxe3 is winning for Black due to his dual threats of 29...Nxc4 and 29...Nf1+) 28...Qe5! (everything rushes over to the kingside) 29.bxc6 bxc6 and now 30.fxe3 is still bad because of 30...Qh5+ followed by 31...Qh3 (Analysis by Alekhine). Alekhine claims that 27.Bf3! was White's best chance, though Black would retain an advantage after 27...Bxf3 28.exf3 cxb5 29.Nxb5 Qa5. **27...cxb5 28.Qxb5 Nc3! 29.Qxb7 Qxb7 30.Nxb7 Nxe2+ 31.Kh2** Black would still be on top after 31.Kf1 Nxg3+ 32.fxg3 Bxf3. **31...Ne4!** Still hammering away at White. Now 32.fxe3? Nxd2 leaves Black with an extra Exchange. **32.Rc4 Nxf2** Black rightly avoids 32...Nxd2? 33.Nxd2 with threats against the Rook on e3 and the Bishop on g4. **33.Bg2 Be6!** This shows that when Alekhine played his thirty-first move he saw clear through to move forty-two! **34.R4c2 Ng4+ 35.Kh3 Ne5+ 36.Kh2 Rxf3! 37.Rxe2 Ng4+ 38.Kh3 Ne3+ 39.Kh2 Nxc2 40.Bxf3 Nd4**, 0-1. Reti (the guy who said he only looks one move ahead!) finally saw that

41.Re3 Nxf3+ 42.Rxf3 Bd5 wins the Knight on b7.

Impressive, but how do *we* do that? How can we learn to calculate such long, detailed variations? Truth is, very few players in history have been able to calculate as well as Alekhine. However, to reach the Master level you *do* have to have some tactical skills. Does this mean that you are doomed if you don't have a natural gift in this area? Of course not! Don't despair; every player, no matter how low his ranking, *can* hone his calculation skills. The only rub (naturally) is that it will take lots of hard work.

For those aspirants who desperately want to improve their tactical vision and are willing to do anything to achieve this goal, I offer the following advice:

1) Finish reading this book! When that is done you should create a special notebook. Purchase a collection of annotated games by Tal, Alekhine, or Kasparov. Take the side of our hero (Tal, Alekhine, or Kasparov) and play through the first ten moves or so until the opening is coming to an end and the middlegame seems to be starting. Then cover up the moves and figure out what is going on. Go through all the imbalances and the whole thinking technique. Figure out the proper plan and all the candidates that lead to its fulfillment. *Write all this down!* It doesn't matter how long it takes to work all this out, just get it all on paper. When your list of candidate moves is clear, analyze each one in detail in your head—don't move the pieces on the actual board. Once again you must write down all the analysis that you have come up with.

Once this task is completed you will look at the move that was actually played, check out the opponent's reply, and then do the whole thing over again. **A word of warning!** If the first move took you thirty minutes or even an hour or more to work everything out and get it on paper, feel free to take a break and continue the game at a future date. We are not after speed here, we are trying to develop your ability to make use of my thinking technique and to increase your powers of visualization.

When you have gone through this process for the whole game, go over the annotations in the book and compare them with the notes you made. See how close you came to following the logic of the game and compare any tactical operations to your own analysis. If you were way off, play over the correct analysis, see where you went wrong, and *don't get depressed.* You're not in a contest here; you are simply trying to better yourself.

As your notebook fills up, you will notice that your work is becoming more concise and accurate. You will take less time to understand more about the position. You *will* get better if you work at it.

2) Get a copy of Kotov's excellent book, *Think Like a Grandmaster.* Aside from being fun to read, it will help improve your powers of calculation. Keep in mind though, that *Think Like a Grandmaster* is an advanced book and requires a serious effort if you want to mine its treasures. Only read it *after* you have spent several months filling up your notebook with the exercise listed above.

Of course, all this is hard work and somewhat time-consuming. Not everyone will want to make such a commitment. For this majority of individuals, the completion of *How to Reassess Your Chess* and lots of over-the-board experience is quite enough to see a marked improvement in your play.

RULES OF COMBINATION

For most chessplayers a combination is a beautiful but mysterious thing. The feeling that it is fun to see but you could never do it yourself is rather common. However, it does not have to be this way! All combinations can be broken down into their scientific components and made readily understandable to the chess playing public. How to do this?

The first thing the student must realize is that there are certain rules of combination that make a combination possible. If these factors do not exist then a combination cannot exist either. Here is list of these rules. Remember that at least one of these factors must be present if a combination is to work:

1) *Open or weakened King. Also includes Stalemated King.*

2) *Undefended pieces (this does not include pawns!).*

3) *Inadequately defended pieces.*

We all can find a small combination that leads to mate in two when it appears in a book with the caption: 'White to mate in two.' However, during actual play there is nobody there who can nudge us and whisper in our ear, "You have a forced win. It's here; look for it now!!"

How to cure this problem? Do we look for a possible combination on every move? Of course not. All we have to do is keep our eyes open for one or more of the given rules of combination. *If you see these items in a given position, then and only then will you look for a possible combination!*

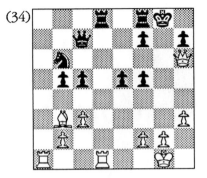

Alekhine-Junge, Warsaw 1942
White to play.

Instead of asking, "Does White have a combination?," let's ask, "Are any of the rules of combination present?" The first thing we notice is that Black's King is very open and unsafe. This gives us the 'go ahead' signal as far as the first rule is concerned. Next we should ask if any of Black's pieces are completely undefended. Yes, the Black Queen has no support at all (so rule #2 is also present). Finally we should note that Black has two pieces that are not well defended—his b6 Knight and the d8 Rook. The b6 Knight is loose because it is attacked once by our Queen on h6 and defended once by the c7 Queen. That means that if we can make the Queen move away we will snag the horse. The Rook on d8 is also loose because we can play Qg5+ and attack it twice with our Queen and d1 Rook. This means that all we have to do is make the f8 Rook or the Queen leave the defense of the d8 Rook and we will win it. Since all three rules are in existance we must look hard for a possible combination. However, don't just look for moves! Instead concentrate on the logic of what we are trying to accomplish, i.e. make the Black Queen or f8 Rook move away from the defense of the d8 Rook.

Before we go on from here I would like to caution the reader about a thing that I call the 'idiot combination.' We have all played an idiot combination at one time or another (I've done it countless times)—it's more of a psychological than an analytical error. An idiot combination is when you play a flashy series of moves not because of their great strength but because it's pretty and you would look good doing it. An example of this from diagram #34 is: 1.Rxd8 Rxd8 and now you call your friends over and triumphantly play 2.Ra7!!. Your chest swells and you swagger off to bask in the glory of your accomplishment. Of course, after 2...Qxa7 3.Qg5+ Kf8 4.Qxd8+ Kg7 you have done nothing but force a trade. In other words, you did something stupid, but you did it in style! Watch out for this psychological trap.

Another example of an idiot combination goes as follows: You have a clear advantage. You then spy a magnificent Queen sacrifice. There are four defenses, but the first three all lose brilliantly. So far so good. The fourth defense, however, allows the opponent to equalize the position. Sorry, but you have to ignore the Queen sacrifice and play something else! Remember this bit of advice: *Always expect your opponent to play the best move!*

Anyway, back to diagram #34. The solution to White's search is:

1.Bxf7+!! This seems shocking as everything in the world can capture our Bishop. However, all of Black's moves fail miserably:

1) 1...Kh8 allows a stalemated King. This means that any check is mate, thus 2.Qf6 mate.

2) 1...Kxf7 (this would win if not for the undefended Black Queen on c7) 2.Qxh7+ followed by 3.Qxc7.

3) 1...Rxf7 (now the Rook has been drawn away from the defense of d8) 2.Qg5+ and the d8 Rook falls.

1...Qxf7 2.Rxd8! Black could now resign since 2...Rxd8 loses to something that looks remarkably like a triple jump in checkers: 3.Qg5+ followed by 4.Qxd8+ and 5.Qxb6. **2...Na4** Any other Knight move allowed 3.Raa8. Now 3.Rad1 followed by 4.R1d7 is quite crushing but Alekhine, known as the sadist of the chess board, instead tortured his opponent with a 'quiet' move. **3.b3!** and Black resigned. 3...Nb6 hangs the Knight to 4.Qxb6. 3...Nxc3 4.Raa8 leads to mate. 3....Rxd8 4.Qg5+ wins back the Rook with check and then allows White to chop off the Knight with axb3. 3...Qxb3 4.Rxf8 is mate.

Go over this combination again and get a feel for the logic of it. It was all based on that loose Rook on d8 and White's desire to pull its defenders away.

To add one more thought to the subject of combinations, GM Y.Averbach has stated that the vast majority of combinations are based in one way or another on the theme of double attack. After I pondered this for awhile I was forced to agree with him. For example, the solution to diagram #34 was based on the double attack on the King and d8 Rook by Qg5+. Of course, a double attack is only made possible if some of the rules of combination exist. Our next game also illustrates this theme.

Aronin-Kantorovich, Moscow 1960. **1.e4 c5 2.Nf3 g6 3.c3 b6** A little experiment that doesn't turn out very well. **4.d4 Bb7 5.Bc4!** White immediately eyes the vunerable f7 square. Now 5...Bxe4 is met by either 6.Bxf7+ Kxf7 7.Ng5+ picking up the undefended piece on e4, or 6.Ng5! threatening the Bishop on e4 and a mate on f7 (note how the Ng5 move is a double attack *a la* Averbach). After 6.Ng5! Black would be forced to play 6...d5 when 7.Bb5+ Nd7 8.Nxe4 dxe4 9.dxc5 bxc5 10.Qa4 threatening 11.0-0 and 12.Rd1 (amongst other things) gives White a powerful initiative. **5...d5?** This breaks an important rule that states: *When behind in development don't open up the position.* The reason is simple—the more lines you open up the easier his pieces can get to you. **6.exd5 Bxd5 7.Qa4+ Bc6**

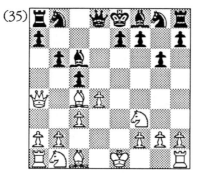

8.Ne5! Crushing! Black now resigned since 8...Bxa4 is mated by 9.Bxf7, while 8...Qc7 loses a piece to 9.Nxc6 Nxc6 10.d5. Once again, the game has been decided on a double attack, i.e. 8.Ne5 threatened both the f7 mate and the Bishop on c6.

That ends our very small discussion on combinations. For those of you who wish to make a detailed study of combinations (a rewarding experience) and their classifications (pins, forks, underpromotion, etc.), read *Winning Chess Tactics* by Seirawan and Silman (Microsoft Press).

Solve These Problems

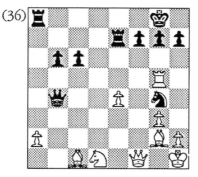

Black to play.

Who stands better and why? Also figure out how Black should best handle the attack on his Knight.

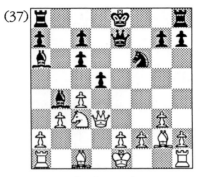

Black to play.

Black's Bishops look nice, but his center is under a lot of pressure. Who stands better here?

MINOR PIECES
IN THE MIDDLEGAME

We now come to the meat of the book—we will break down and explore all the imbalances. Part four is devoted to the study of minor pieces and their relations with each other. I give this subject first since I feel it is often ignored, underestimated, or simply misunderstood. This means that a deep knowledge of the minor pieces will give you a subtle weapon that sets you far above most of your opposition.

When I point out to a student that he has the two Bishops or a Knight versus a Bishop the usual reaction is lack of interest. Why should such a simple little thing be of any great importance? The fact is that games are constantly won or lost due to one side having a superior minor piece. However, this doesn't just 'happen.' Such a difference has to be carefully nurtured if you want it to obtain decisive significance. Personally I have won countless games by following the simplest of planning shortcuts: First I create some difference to work with (in this case let's say a Bishop versus the opponent's Knight). Next I create an atmosphere in which my Bishop will thrive—a non-locked pawn structure so that my Bishop will have open lines; getting his pawns on the color of my Bishop so that they will be vulnerable in an endgame; taking away advanced squares from his Knight so that his minor piece remains inactive. When all this is done I will steer the game into an ending in which my speedy Bishop eats his gimpy Knight alive.

In other words, I create an imbalance and devote all my energy into making it a positive force.

THE BISHOP

Many players are taught that Bishops tend to be somewhat stronger than Knights. This creates bigotry in the mind of the aspiring player that can lead to grave consequences if he buys into the lie. The truth is that Bishops and Knights are of equal value until you look at the position on the board. In other words, either piece can dominate the other under the right conditions.

Bishops can be divided into three groups:

1) *Good*
2) *Bad*
3) *Active*

A Bishop is considered *good* when its central pawns are not on its color and thus are not obstructing its activity.

A Bishop is considered *bad* when its central pawns are on its color and thus block it.

An *active* Bishop can be either bad or good; it's called active simply because it serves an active function.

In this chapter I will place the western 'white hat' on the head of the Bishops. Since we all would like to make Bishops heros when we possess them, let's see what kind of situations make them comfortable.

First Rule Concerning Bishops

If you have a bad Bishop you must correct it in one of the following ways:

1) *Trade it for an enemy piece of equal or greater value.*

For example, after the opening moves **1.e4 d6 2.d4 Nf6 3.Nc3 g6 4.Nf3 Bg7 5.Be2 0-0 6.0-0 Bg4 7.Be3 Nc6 8.Qd2 e5 9.dxe5 dxe5 10.Rad1 Qc8 11.Qc1 Rd8 12.Rxd8+ Qxd8 13.Rd1 Qf8 14.h3 Bxf3 15.Bxf3** we get diagram #38.

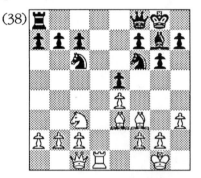

(38)

White has the two Bishops. His Bishop on e3 is particularly nice while its counterpart on g7 is bad. To correct this problem Black decides that he must trade his 'bad' Bishop for White's good one. Thus Black plays **15...h5** Intending ...Kh7 and ...Bh6. **16.Nb5 Rc8 17.c3** Taking away the d4 square from Black's Knight. **17...Kh7 18.Na3 Bh6 19.Bxh6 Qxh6 20.Qxh6+ Kxh6** with equality, Cramling-Yrjola, Gausdal 1984.

2) *Make it good by getting your central pawns off its color* (usually very difficult).

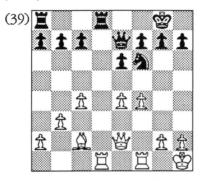

(39)

White has a bad Bishop. The fate of the game hangs in the balance because if it were Black's move he would jump at the chance to permanently entomb White's Bishop by 1...e5 when 2.fxe5 Nd7! would turn the pawn on e4 into a target (aside from giving the Knight a superb home on e5), while 2.f5 makes the thing on c2 as ugly as can be. White to move would avoid all this by 1.e5!. This gets the e4 pawn off the Bishop's color and grants his piece some measure of activity. Aside from the useful b1-h7 diagonal, the Bishop can also plant itself on e4 with possibilities on the h1-a8 line.

3) *Make it active by getting it outside the pawn chain* (an important rule to keep in mind).

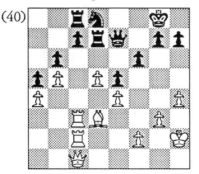

(40)

In diagram #40 Black is obviously in terrible trouble. His

weak pawn on c7 is barely hanging on. There is some hope though. White's Bishop is quite bad and Black threatens to play ...Nb7-c5 when his Knight would find an excellent post and the pressure on c7 would be alleviated. What can White do? If his Bishop could somehow join in the attack Black's game would certainly crack. Can this be achieved? The try 1.Bc4 threatening to win the Queen by 2.d6+ is bad because it is what I call a 'cross your fingers and hope' move. Black can easily defend by 1...Kh8 or 1...Kf8 when the Bishop has no purpose on c4. *Never play a move with the hope that the opponent won't see your threat!* This is a mistake that lower ranked players often make. Only play moves that help your position even if your opponent finds the best reply.

White's correct strategy is to get the Bishop outside the pawn chain by 1.Bf1! when the threat of 2.Bh3 is very embarrassing for Black. After the simple retreating move **1.Bf1** Black's game would fall apart.

Second Rule Concerning Bishops

Bishops are usually strongest in open positions. This is well known and obvious. The fewer pawns in the way of a Bishop the greater its scope. In general, Bishops tend to have an edge over Knights in open positions. I say 'in general' because there is no such thing as an all-encompassing rule in chess. *There are always exceptions!* Don't blindly follow these rules—use them as guidelines only.

Though it's impossible to break chess strategy down into a series of rules and regulations, a discriminating adherence to the ones given here will prove helpful in all phases of the game. Follow them in the opening, middlegame and the endgame. Due to this I feel it's fitting to give an endgame rule here.

Third Rule Concerning Bishops

In an endgame, with passed pawns on both sides of the board, Bishops tend to beat out Knights. This rule highlights the Bishop's greatest strength: its long-range abilities.

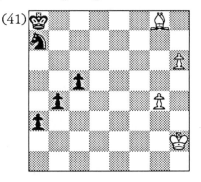

In diagram #41 both sides have passed pawns on the sixth rank. Black is even a pawn ahead, yet he is dead lost because his Knight is too slow to stop the White runner. Notice how White's Bishop can sit on the opposite side of the board and still stop Black's infantry. As stated earlier, the Bishop's long range powers are just too much for a Knight in these situations.

Using the Bishop

Now that you know what to look for, it's time to study various games and see what effect the Bishop has on the play.

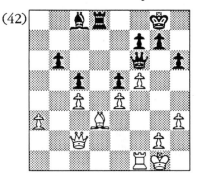

Diagram #42 shows a very favorable situation for Black. This is due to White's horrible Bishop. Black will play ...Rd4 followed by ...Qd6 and obtain great pressure on the open file (Black plays ...Rd4 before ...Qd6 because it's usually a good idea to lead with a Rook on open files).

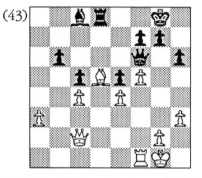

Botvinnik-Kan, Leningrad 1939.
White to play.

Now let's take a look at diagram #43. Here too White has a bad Bishop. In this case, however, it is extremely active. Thus White's Bishop is the superior piece even though Black's Bishop is good by our earlier definition. Using our rules for bad Bishops, we can see that White got his Bishop outside the pawn chain (Earlier in the game White's Bishop stood on d3 and his c-pawn was on c3. White played Bc4-d5 and only then c3-c4), turning a potentially terrible piece into a monster.

Though we have noted that White is winning the battle of the Bishops, we still have to figure out the rest of the imbalances. Let's go through the imbalance and thinking technique list (given in Part Two) in relation to the position under discussion:

1) Material is even.

2) White has the superior minor piece due to its greater activity. The fact that it is technically bad doesn't mean anything here. Accordingly, Black would be happy to trade Bishops.

3) Black has a weak pawn on b6 (backwards on an open file) while White has a weak pawn on a3 (isolated on an open file).

4) White has a space advantage on the kingside thanks to his advanced pawn on f5.

5) White can take control of the b-file (which usefully attacks the backward b-pawn) while Black will have more difficulty in taking control of the a-file because the a8 square is controlled by the White Bishop.

It should also be noted that Black's Bishop gets in the way of his Rook. The greater mobilization of White's forces gives him good chances of creating concrete threats and putting Black on the defensive. This is called taking the initiative. These facts lead us to the conclusion that White's game is superior.

Next we must figure out which side of the board we will base our play on. To do this we must remember that we can only play on the side of the board where a favorable imbalance or the possibility of creating one exists. In the diagrammed position we have chances for queenside play (weak pawn on b6 plus the superior White Bishop aims in that direction) and also possibilities for a kingside offensive (kingside space plus the White Bishop aims in that direction also). The center (normally the most important part of the board) is not to be considered since it is permanently blocked. It always amazed me that many students thought that 1.Rd1 followed by 2.Qd3 was good since then 3.Bxf7+ is a threat, winning the d8 Rook. The futility of such a 'plan' is clearly seen by the following sequence: **1.Rd1 Pass** (Black makes no move. This is illegal but allowable for our purpose—just think what Black could do if he bothered to do something useful!) **2.Qd3** And now after 2...Kh8, 2...Kf8, or even 2...Rd7 White's trap has failed and his pieces serve no real purpose on the blocked d-file.

This result forces us to acknowledge a very important rule that is actually more of a state of mind: *Don't play for traps! Don't hope that your opponent does something stupid!* If you develop the attitude where you expect your opponent to always make the best move, you will force yourself to do the same. You will not grow to depend on your opponent's mistakes—instead you will depend on your own good play. In other words, you always want to play a move that does something positive. Even if your opponent plays the best move in return you will still have improved your position in some fashion.

This is such an important point (meaning that almost everybody fails to follow it) that I will give the student a useful crutch. After deciding on the move you intend to play, ask yourself, "What wonderful thing does my move do for my position?"

Quite often you will find that your move actually creates weaknesses in your own camp. You may also find that, aside from some obvious (and easily defensible) one move attack, your move does nothing positive at all. Remember that if you can't answer this important question then *don't play the move!*

Now let's get back to our dissection by doing the next thing in our list of thinking techniques (that obscure mention of a fantasy position). It's time to set up fantasy (optimum) positions based on the imbalances and the side of the board where those imbalances exist. Since we have ascertained that we have chances on both sides of the board (but not the center) we must address these two sectors. First let's try the kingside. Probably the optimum way to attack Black's King with pieces is to place the Rook on g4 and the Queen on g3. This takes us to diagram #44.

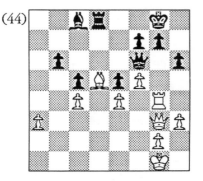

(44)

We are not yet concerned with how these pieces got to their

new homes. When you create fantasy positions just airlift them to whatever square you feel they would do the most good on. The idea is to see if the setup achieves anything concrete.

Does White threaten anything in diagram #44? Yes, the threat is 1.Rg6, utilizing the pin on the f7 pawn by the d5 Bishop. Can Black defend against this? Quite easily! Moves like 1...Kh7, 1...Kh8, or 1...Kf8 all stop the threat (by breaking a potential pin on the d5-g8 diagonal) and leave White without a good continuation. From my own experience I know that it is quite common to come up with a plan, finally get your pieces to where you want them, and to your horror find that your newly acquired setup does nothing at all! This technique of fantasy positions should prevent that from happening.

Since it is now clear that a piece attack on the Kingside fails to satisfy, we will discard the fantasy of diagram #44 and create another optimum position—this time based on a kingside pawn storm. See diagram #45.

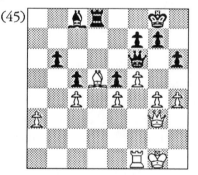

(45)

This position is certainly threatening and would allow White definite prospects (the immediate threat is g5 followed by g6). Having decided that it is a reasonable idea, White must determine if such a position is possible. Here there is little difficulty since by Qf2, g4, h4, and Qg3 White would achieve the desired setup. We must not forget, however, that Black will be going through these same stages also. Is our plan preventing Black from carrying out his? Is it going to prove stronger than Black's?

We must keep in mind that our pawn storm idea does not put

immediate pressure on Black. This allows him a large choice of possible plans. Such pawn storms also tend to leave the White King without cover—a fact that speaks of a certain amount of risk involved in its operation.

To be honest, I feel that White may do quite well with this idea. However, the element of danger entailed (lack of King cover) would make me think twice before doing it. With this in mind I would file it away for a moment and look to the queenside for a plan that might offer nice benefits with no particular risk. It's important to point out that even if we found that a kingside attack led to a strong position with no hazards attached, we would still look at our queenside possibilities—we must understand the *whole* position, not just half of it.

Back to our original position in diagram #43! For queenside operations our obvious target is the pawn on b6. Thus all our pieces must be placed in positions where they exert pressure on this pawn. Naurally, our Rook will go to the open b-file. But on what square? As funny as it may seem, many people think that the closer to a pawn a Rook gets, the more pressure it applies. Under that logic, b5 would be the best square and I have many students who recommend that post. The truth is that from b5 the Rook puts no extra pressure on the b6-pawn. In fact, its mobility is severly limited there! Compare the number of squares controled from b5 and then do another square count from b1. Simple addition will convince anyone that b1 offers the most square coverage and attacks b6 with the same force as on b5. The b1-square is good for another reason also: On b1 the Rook guards the first rank, thereby serving both an offensive (attacks b6) purpose and a defensive (guards the King) purpose. Clearly b1 is the superior square.

Now we must find a home for our Queen. Here some imagination is required. What is her very best square? If you said b2 you are not greedy enough. I use the word fantasy for a reason. If I asked you to draw your fantasy home would you create a shack or a mansion? The same gusto is required here. How about a7 (c7 is just as good and shows you are getting a feel for the subject. The only difference is that a7 is easier to reach)? There she does many things: attacks b6; ties the Black Queen down to the defense of f7 (meaning that the Queen and Bishop are working together); controls the a-file (the file leading to White's weakness on a3); and often threatens to play to the back rank. Sounds a lot better than a2, doesn't it?

Having transported our Queen to a7 and Rook to b1 we may now place Black's pieces in some sort of reasonable defensive formation. The idea is that if we can break down his defense then our setup has to be taken seriously. Black's Rook must obviously go to d6 if he is to retain his b6 pawn. His Bishop can be placed on e8 where it guards f7 and can be defended by his King if the need arises. We now have diagram #46.

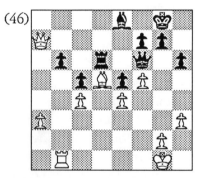

(46)

Most of you have probably heard that a pawn chain should be attacked at its base. While true, this is only half the story. What most don't know is that the idea is not necessarily to win the base pawn but to make it move or trade it. This will severely weaken the rest of the pawns in the chain. Thus in diagram #46 White can continue his attack on b6 by simply pushing his a-pawn to a4 and a5. Black would then be forced to trade with ...bxa5. After White recaptures with Qxa5 Black, whose whole army was devoted to guarding b6, will be unable to readjust to the new situation. As a result Black will not be able to defend c5. This means that White will win the c5 pawn and ultimately win the game.

Well—this whole plan certainly seems to lead to a positive

result! Can we achieve it? We now must go back again to the reality of diagram #43. We know that we want our Queen on a7 and the Rook on b1. For candidate moves we will only look at moves that accomplish (or aim to accomplish) those goals. With this in mind we can see that there are only two possibilities that make sense. One is 1.Rb1 and the other is 1.Qa4 (the only way to get to a7).

Normally you would now calculate out both moves and then choose the one you feel is best. Here we can take a shortcut by asking a simple question: Can Black prevent either move? Obviously 1.Rb1 is unstoppable. But Black can stop 1.Qa4 by 1...Bd7. This means that White must play 1.Qa4 first to avoid Black's preventing it altogether. Finally you can make your move and stop the clock.

At this point I can hear the exhausted reader screaming, "My God! I'd lose on time every game if I did all that!"

While I can understand your fears, I must say that this is quite untrue. Actually you will find youself using *less* time than usual.

Let's take a break with the following tale: I was once coaching a lady in the United States Women's Invitational Championship. She was thinking over her fourteenth move and, after taking fifteen minutes, made a horrible lemon. Another mistake or two followed and she was crushed without mercy.

After the game she explained that she could not find a good idea. Since she had used fifteen minutes in a fruitless search, she decided to do anything rather than risk getting into time pressure. Naturally, as her position worsened she used more and more time trying to save herself. Soon she was in time pressure *and* was the proud owner of a lost position!

Instead of going through the above she should have continued to break down the position until a reasonable plan had come to mind. In this way she might still end up in time pressure but she most likely would have enjoyed a good situation on the board.

Never pass in the hopes that an idea will come to you next move! As I stated earlier, *every move you make should strengthen* *your position in some way.* I remember when I was thirteen years old and my chess teacher asked me why I played a particularly useless move. I replied, "It was my move and I had to do something!" You can have all the talent in the world but laziness will still lead you to the well of defeat.

I did say though, that using my thinking method will help you save time. Let's demonstrate by going through the moves that arose from diagram #43.

For illustrative purposes we will say that White took twenty minutes to figure out the points covered earlier (practice will cut this down considerably). Having grown to understand the position, you confidently play **1.Qa4** and the game continues **1...Bd7 2.Qa7** White would play this without any thought at all. **2...Be8 3.Rb1** By simply following the plan you had mapped out earlier, this move should also come quickly. **3...Rd6 4.a4** Still following his plan. Let's say White took one minute here to double check his analysis. **4...Kh7** Black avoids 4...Qd8 5.a5 bxa5 6.Rb8 when White wins a piece. **5.a5 bxa5 6.Qxa5** Not 6.Qxc5? because 6...a4 holds on to the a-pawn. **6...Ra6 7.Qxc5** White's plan is at an end. He has won a solid pawn and, though he originally took twenty minutes to come up with the plan, the total time spent for its culmination averaged only three minutes a move.

To continue a bit further into the game, Black (after 7.Qxc5) played **7...Ra2**. Now White has to form a new plan. Here he has a material imbalance—an extra passed pawn on c4. He would like to push it. Unfortunately his Queen is in the way. We must also ask ourselves if Black has a threat. Yes, he threatens to actually win by 8...Qg5 when 9.g4 can be answered by the crushing 9...Qd2. Thus White would like to further his own plan (get the Queen out of the way of the passed pawn) and prevent Black's threat. Obviously a Queen move, but where can it go to prevent the threatened ...Qg5? It should not take long to find **8.Qe3!** when everything is in order for White. He went on to win without too much trouble.

I have broken the previous position (diagrams #43-46) down

into its component parts for you in a rather tedious and long-winded manner. This has been done to make sure everything was touched upon so that the method would be understood. Go over this example many times until you get a feel for the system of organized thought expounded.

As you can see, this method consists of you logically talking your way through a position. *All calculation is done with a goal already in mind!*

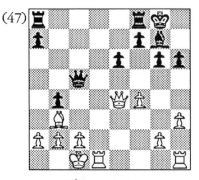

White to move.

Diagram #47 shows a situation with Bishops of opposite colors. In endgames, Bishops of opposite colors are known to be very drawish. In the middlegame, however, they take on a completely different significance. Here they are known as useful attacking pieces due to the fact that one can attack a point that the other cannot defend. At times it is almost like having an extra piece! Diagram #47 is such a case. White's Bishop guards a2 and c2 but is rendered inactive by the Black pawn on e6. Black's Bishop, on the other hand, is extremely powerful. Black simply intends to make use of his Bishop's power by ...Qe7 followed by ...Qf6 when White's b2-pawn is indefensible. Also plans like ...a5 followed by ...a4 and ...a3 would loosen the a1-h8 diagonal even further. If given time White would like to play g4 followed by f5 in order to activate his own Bishop. However, Black's threats come so fast that White's dreams never come to fruition. White's first move prevents Black's threat of ...Qe7. **1.Rd7 Rad8** Black challenges the open file and attempts to eradicate the d7 Rook so he can play ...Qe7. **2.Rhd1 Rxd7 3.Rxd7 Qg1+ 4.Kd2** White is not happy about this, but 4.Rd1 Bxb2+ is even less appetizing. **4...Qf2+** Black would also win after 4...Bxb2 but White could then put up a tough resistance by 5.Ke2 followed by 6.Rd1. **5.Kd3 Qf1+ 6.Qe2** After 6.Kd2 Bxb2 White can no longer play Ke2. **6...Qxf4 7.Qf3** Hoping to go into an ending where his active Rook and opposite colored Bishop would offer him excellent chances of a draw. However, why should Black turn White's centralized King, which is so bad in a middlegame, into an endgame strength? **7...Qe5** Black, with a material advantage *and* an attack, soon won.

Black's victory was due to his superior Bishop (favorable imbalance: superior minor piece) and the way he concentrated on making use of its power.

Another interesting example of Bishops of opposite color can be seen in diagram #48.

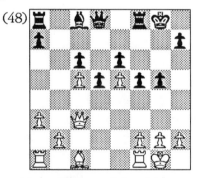

(48)

Keres-Konstantinopolsky, Moscow 1948.
Black to play.

Both sides have very bad Bishops, though Black's can gain a modicum of activity on a6. White has a space advantage on the queenside and in the center. Black owns more kingside space. Unfortunately for White the center is completely blocked, thereby negating any possibilities there. A queenside pawn break via b2-b4-b5 is also impossible since by ...Ba6, ...Bc4, and ...a6, Black would make the b5 square his own. Thus the queenside and center are useless for White. This leaves only the kingside as a source of play and that area belongs to Black.

If it were White to play, he would have the paradoxical 1.f4!, seemingly making his Bishop even worse. Actually the move 1.f4 poses Black some unhappy problems. If he captures by 1...gxf4, then 2.Bxf4 gives White's Bishop hopes of eventually reaching f6 where it would devastate the enemy position. 1...gxf4 also leaves Black's King too open and can be summarily rejected. This leaves 1...g4, a move that closes the kingside and leads to a drawn situation due to the absence of any breaks for either side. Note that if Black played ...g4 followed by ...h5 and ...h4, White would ignore Black's demonstration since ...h3 is answered by g3 while ...g3 is answered by h3. In both cases the position on the kingside would be completely blocked. It's clear then that 1.f4 does block White's Bishop (if Black avoids 1...gxf4) but it forces Black to give up his play on the kingside to do so.

It turns out, however, to be Black's move. Since Black has a space advantage on the only side where play is possible, it stands to reason that Black has the advantage. Naturally then, Black will strive to increase his kingside space advantage and prevent White from blocking things with f4. **1...f4! 2.Bd2** Unable to undertake anything active, the great Keres tries to set up a strong defensive formation. **2...Ba6** The Bishop activates itself with gain of tempo. **3.Rfe1 Rb8** It seems attractive to post the Rook on this open file. Actually the move has a much subtler purpose. As mentioned earlier, Black is playing for a kingside attack. This move fits into that scheme by following up with ...Rb7 and ...Rg7. Black will also post his Queen on the kingside via ...Qe8 to g6 or h5. Since the position is blocked, Black is justified in taking his time and slowly setting up the best attacking formation possible. This is clearly explained by the following well known rules:

1) In an open position one must react quickly—time is of great importance. Attacks are usually conducted by pieces due to the abundance of open lines.

2) In closed situations, attacks are initiated by pawn breaks. Slow maneuvering is quite all right.

In the present case Black is following the second rule. **4.Qd4 Bc4 5.Bc3 Qe8 6.Qd1 Rb7** Now the a7-pawn is defended and the Rook is ready to swing to the kingside. **7.a4 Qg6 8.Ra3 g4 9.Bd4 Rg7** Black's position now looks quite menacing. His threat is to kill White on the h-file by ...Rf5, ...Rh5, and ...Qh6. **10.f3** A bitter pill but White had no other way of preventing the threatened invasion down the h-file. Now 10...gxf3 11.Qxf3 leaves everything defended. **10...h5!** Konstantinopolsky was an extremely strong Soviet player who never became well known to the Western chess community. Here he follows Nimzovitch's famous axiom, "The threat is stronger than the execution." By holding off on the ...gxf3 capture, he forces White to constantly worry about it. It is also important to note that 11.fxg4 is out of the question since 11...hxg4 leaves White helpless against threats on the open h-file. This means that Black can place all his big guns on the g-file and only capture with ...gxf3 when he is fully loaded. Though 10...h5 is a strong move, White played 10.f3 to force it! He did this to prevent Black from making immediate use of the h-file. White succeeded in that goal but he will ultimately be drowned by the pounding pressure on the g-file. **11.Rc3 Rf5** Bringing the Rook to g5. Every piece calmly takes up its best position. **12.Kh1** Sidestepping a little trap. White could have played 12.Qc2? but this would have allowed various rules of combination to come into effect (see Part Three, Chapter Two). After 12.Qc2? Black would play 12...gxf3! when 13.Rxf3 leaves White with three undefended pieces (Queen on c2, Rook on e1, and Bishop on d4) and an over-worked Queen (the Queen must keep an eye on g2 to prevent mate). Black would finish matters with 13...Rxe5! (attacking two of the undefended pieces at the same time) when White must resign, since 14.Qd1 Rxe1+ 15.Qxe1 Qxg2 is mate, and 14.Qxg6 Rxe1+ 15.Kf2 Rf1 also ends the battle. Note that 14.Rxe5 or 14.Bxe5 hangs the Queen to 14...Qxc2. **12...Rg5 13.b3 Ba6**

14.Rg1 gxf3! Played with a clear purpose in mind. Almost every Black piece is aimed at g2. The only piece not doing its best is the Bishop. Now that the pawn on f3 is gone, the Bishop's optimum square (in relation to an attack on g2) is e4. This means that Black will devote all of his energy in placing his Bishop on that beautifully decisive square. **15.Qxf3** White loses after 15.gxf3 Rxg1+ 16.Qxg1 Qf5 17.Qe1 (17.Qf2 Qb1+) 17...Qh3 18.Qf2 Bf1 followed by 19...Bg2+. **15...Qe4!!** As said earlier, Black wants to place his Bishop on e4. However, the quickest route (via d3) is well guarded. The purpose of 15...Qe4 is to chase one of the guardians of d3 away, thus making the Bishop's trip possible. Normally (if you're trying to win) you would try to avoid a Queen exchange with Bishops of opposite colors. In this case however, the endgame would be won for Black after 16.Qxe4 dxe4 followed by 17...Rd8 since all of Black's pieces would be superior to their White counterparts. **16.Qf2** Defending his piece on d4. A Bishop move would hang the e5 pawn and 16.Rd1 hangs the pawn on g2. Since we have already mentioned that a Queen trade would lead to a very unhappy ending for White, he feels compelled to move his Queen to f2. Of course this is just what Black wanted since now the d3 square is 'legal' for Black's Bishop. **16...Bd3 17.b4 Qf5 18.b5 Be4** Black's plan has come to fruition and he has a winning game. The finish was: **19.bxc6 Rxg2 20.Rxg2 Rxg2 21.Qxg2+ Bxg2+ 22.Kxg2 Qe4+ 23.Kf1 f3** Not 23...Qxd4 24.c7. **24.Be3 Qg6 25.Ke1 Qb1+ 26.Kd2 Qb2+ 27.Rc2 Qxe5 28.c7 Qxh2+ 29.Kd1 Qxc7 30.c6 e5 31.Bxa7 d4! 32.Bb6 d3! 33.Rc1** If 33.Bxc7 then 33...dxc2+ and ...f2 wins. **33...Qxb6 34.c7 Qxc7 35.Rxc7 f2**, 0-1.

(49)

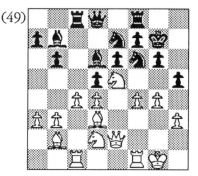

Alekhine-Rosselli, Zurich 1934.
White to play.

Diagram #49 illustrates how one can gain other advantages through the mere threat of activating a Bishop.

White has a space advantage and Black's kingside position is weakened by the unfortunate move ...h5. Some may feel that White's Bishop on b2 is poor but this would show a lack of understanding about this position. While it *is* true that the b2 Bishop is bad (by definition), it serves some highly useful functions. Its first order of duty is to guard the d4-pawn. More importantly, however, it prevents Black from undertaking anything serious in the center. For example 1..dxc4?? 2.bxc4 leaves the once 'dead' Bishop on b2 a powerhouse after an eventual d4-d5 push. It is with this in mind that White conceives of his next move. **1.c5!** Extremely strong! Black cannot capture since that would unleash the sleeping monster on b2: 1...bxc5?? 2.dxc5 Bxc5+ 3.Rxc5! Rxc5 4.g5 with a quick win for White. **1...Bxe5** Or 1...Bb8 2.b4 with a crushing space advantage, chances on the kingside and a strong passed pawn for White. **2.fxe5 Nd7 3.b4** With pressure on the open f-file, a huge space advantage that covers the board and a shaky Black kingside, White can be considered to have a winning position. Alekhine coverted these advantages into a win without any difficulty. The rest of the moves are not given simply because they no longer illustrate our theme.

(50)

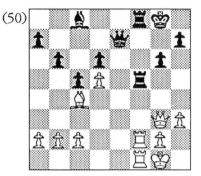

Tsvetkov-Smyslov, Moscow 1947.
Black to play.

I could readily imagine a draw being agreed from the position in diagram #50. Even the Rooks are going to be traded, which seems to further accentuate the position's drawish character.

Now for a moment let's imagine you are Black and your opponent is rated three hundred points below you. Clearly, a draw under those conditions would not make you very happy! What would you do as Black? Would you set as many traps as possible and hope he falls into one? Would you play on forever and hope he grows so tired that he makes some basic oversight?

How about another scenario. Black wants to watch the big football game and offers his opponent a draw. White looks indignant and refuses, making it clear that he would rather sit there all night and bore you to death in a never-ending effort to win. How do you react to this? Do you trade everything you can and then move your remaining pieces back and forth in an effort to demonstrate the uselessness of your opponents actions?

It turns out that it doesn't really matter what the situation is— you should play this (and every) position the same way if your opponent was your best friend or worst enemy.

In this and any position all you can do is find the imbalances and attempt to make them favorable for you. Once you have something in your favor you must nurture it and make it grow. You also have to point out the drawbacks in your opponent's position and strive to make these negatives more pronounced.

You will find that tricks are not necessary if you play in this restrained but logical fashion.

It's time to break down the position in diagram #50. First, a Rook trade actually suits Black since his King is more open than White's. Getting those dinosaurs off the board can only make Black's King breathe easier.

The one imbalance that allows play to continue is once again attributed to the minor pieces—White has a bad Bishop. "That's all?," asks the reader. "Surely that simple fact is not enough to make White lose the game. After all, the Bishop doesn't look so terrible."

The truth is that White should be able to hold this position. However the defense is not as easy as one might think and it only takes one or two small mistakes by White to hand the victory to Black on a platter.

Since the Black King is open and his one favorable imbalance would serve him well in an endgame, Black will first visualize trading all the pieces (this means the Queens and Rooks. The Bishops must be retained if Black is to have any chance at winning since that is where his advantage lies) to see if he can win a pure Bishop endgame. It turns out that he can't win such an ending at the moment (if it *were* a win then you would search for a way to effect these trades—that would be your plan).

Since that particular endgame is not a win, Black will look for ways to create an ending that *does* offer winning chances. To accomplish such a goal Black will trade Rooks (for King safety) but keep the Queens on. He will then centralize his Queen (maximize its potential and try to make it stronger than its counterpart) and attack White's queenside pawns in an effort to lure more of them onto light squares. Only when White's Bishop becomes extremely bad (a direct result of White placing his pawns on light squares) will Black trade Queens and go into a (hopefully) winning King and Bishop endgame.

This whole plan is very logical. You *always* play in accordance with the imbalances. If your opponent has a weak pawn you play to weaken it further and eventually win it. If he has a Knight, you play to take away all its advanced support points, thereby relegating it to the first few ranks and relative inactivity. If your only advantage is your opponent's bad Bishop (as in this case), you play to make it consistently worse and your own consistently better. **1...Rxf2** Getting rid of the Rooks is the first part of the plan. **2.Rxf2 Qe1+ 3.Bf1** Threatening 4.Rxf8+ winning the Black Queen. **3...Rxf2** Forcing White to recapture with his Queen and thus relinquish his hold on the central e5 square. **4.Qxf2 Qe5!** The Rooks are gone and now phase two is also complete—Black's Queen is powerfully centralized and thus superior to its White counterpart. **5.Qe2** To answer 5...Qxb2?? with 6.Qe8+. **5...Qd4+ 6.Kh2 Kf8** Stopping the White Queen from penetrating to e7 or e8. **7.c4?!** This plays into Black's hands, though his desire to guard his pawns is quite understandable. However, White should avoid placing his pawns on light squares, and a more logical attempt (considering his Bishop) is 7.Qf3+ Kg7 8.c3 Qe5+ 9.Kg1 Bb7 10.Bc4 when the Bishop still has a measure of activity. **7...Bf5** The comparison between armies is clear. Both of Black's pieces are much more active than their White counterparts.

Let's take a moment here and pretend that you have the White pieces. It's your move and you're not happy. Instead of getting emotional or panicking, you have to figure out what's wrong with your game. Whenever you are in trouble you must ask, "Why am I suffering? What's wrong with my position?" The answer here is obvious: the White Bishop is garbage!

If we now go back to our Bishop rules we will see that we are supposed to do one of three things with a bad Bishop. Let's look at each:

1) Can we get our pawns off the white squares? No. That means that we *must* —

2) Trade it, after which our problems would be solved. Or...

3) Get it outside the pawn chain. Let's do a quick fantasy position. Where is the best possible square for our Bishop? Does e6 look good? Definitely! If our Bishop got to this square than it would turn into an active powerhouse that would threaten the Black King.

Now we know what has to be done. The hard part is finding a way to do it.

Allow me to lecture for a moment. When I say that we *must* do one of these things, I mean it. If you just sit around and do nothing Black will probably beat you. If you're in trouble you have to identify the problem verbally and then find a way to cure the problem. You can't just analyze since it is difficult to cure an unknown disease. *First verbalize, then analyze.*

Going back to our defensive problem we must find a way to trade the Bishop or get it to e6. Since e6 lies on the h3-c8 diagonal we must get to that line. Going to g4 is difficult since e2 is not available and even if it were Black could stop us with ...h7-h5. If you look hard and long you will eventually find the three move series 8.g3!, 9.h4, 10.Bh3 when Black must either trade or allow the Bishop to go to e6. White's mission would then be accomplished and he would hold the game. If such a situation arises you should take as much time as necessary to solve the problem. Don't be lazy and just give up. Chess is part knowledge mixed with lots of *willpower!*

Thus, thinking in terms of imbalances will also help you defensively. The line of play beginning with 8.g3! was perhaps White's last hope of saving himself.

In the actual game White played the terrible **8.g4?** White places more pawns on light squares, further restricts his own Bishop, and weakens his King. Black surely smiled when he saw this. This move also illustrates another common weakness in the play of the amateur. Since 8.g4 threatens a piece, White obtains a sense of security for one move. Feeling unhappy about his position, White lashes out—this makes him feel better. However you must learn to give your opponent some credit. You know that he's not going to leave his Bishop hanging! If you intend to play a move like g4 you must first ask, "After he moves his Bishop, is g2-g4 a move that really helps my position?"

Play with the calm light of reason and avoid emotional reactions! **8...Bb1 9.a3** Avoiding 9.b3? which would leave every pawn on a light square. After 9.b3? Black would go into a Bishop ending with the surprising 9...Qe5+!. This gives White a protected passed pawn but leaves the White queenside pawns helpless before the attack of the Black Bishop: 10.Qxe5 dxe5 11.a3, and now Euwe's recommendation of 11...Bc2 12.b4 cxb4 13.axb4 a5 actually loses to 14.c5!. However, the simple 11...a5 followed by 12...Bc2 would win a pawn for Black. **9...Be4! 10.Kg3 Qe5+ 11.Kf2 Qf4+ 12.Ke1 Kg7 13.Qd2 Qe5 14.Qc3** White finally forces a trade of Queens, but this allows Black to fulfill the final part of his plan—a winning King and Bishop ending. **14...Qxc3+ 15.bxc3 g5!** Fixing White's pawns on the cursed light squares. This is an important concept to know. Now White's pawns will always be vulnerable to Black's Bishop while Black's pawns, all standing on dark squares, will be invulnerable to White's ineffectual counterpart. **16.Kf2 Kf6** Rushing the King towards the center—something you should always do in an endgame. **17.Ke3 Ke5 18.Be2** Hopeless for White is 18.Bd3 Bxd3 19.Kxd3 Kf4 20.a4 h6 21.Ke2 Kg3. **18...Bc2** Not falling for 18...Bg2 19.Kf2 Bxh3?? 20.Kg3 when the Bishop is trapped. **19.Kd2 Bb1 20.Ke3 h6 21.Bf3 Bc2 22.Be2 a6!** Black will employ the usual method of combatting pawn chains: He will play for ...b5 and destroy the base at c4. When this is done the d5 pawn will fall. **23.Kd2 Ba4 24.Ke3** White cannot allow Black's King to get to f4. **24...b5 25.cxb5 axb5 26.Bf3** Guarding the d5 pawn. 26.c4 would lose the d5 pawn after 26...bxc4 27.Bxc4 Be8! and 28...Bf7. **26...Bb3 27.Be2 Bc4** Winning material. **28.Bxc4 bxc4 29.a4 Kxd5 30.a5 Kc6 31.Ke4 d5+ 32.Ke5 d4 33.cxd4 c3 34.d5+ Kd7 35.a6** Perhaps White has some chances after all? **35...c2 36.a7 c1=Q 37.a8=Q Qf4 mate**! A cruel end to White's rising excitement.

UNDERSTANDING KNIGHTS

Without a doubt Knights are the hardest piece for the non-master to understand. This is because they are short-range pieces and can't sit back and do an aggressive job from the rear as Bishops can. However, with the right knowledge and effort Knights can be one of the strongest of men.

First Rule Of Knights

Knights need advanced support points to be effective! A support point is a square that acts as a home for a piece. A square can only be considered a support point if it cannot be attacked by an enemy pawn, or if the pawn advance would severly weaken the enemy position.

(51)

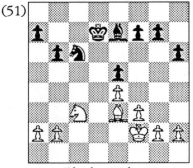

Black to play.

Diagram #51 illustrates what a support point is and is not.

Both sides have support points for their Knights on d4 and d5. At the moment White can jump into d5 at any time. However, Black must be more careful since, after 1...Nd4, White has the option of capturing the Knight by 2.Bxd4. To further weaken this square so that it can eventually be safely utilized, Black plays the excellent move **1...Bg5!**. After the trade of his bad Bishop for White's good one (see Part Four, Chapter One for an explanation of bad Bishop), Black will finally be able to hop into d4. Note that b4 is *not* a support point for Black's Knight since after 1...Nb4 White can chase the beast away via a3 whenever it suits him.

As I mentioned earlier, Knights are not long range pieces. The further advanced a Knight is, the more it starts to exert pressure on the opponent's position. Because of this, Knights gain in strength as they advance down the board. The following rules should prove useful for less experienced players:

1) Knights on the first and second ranks are purely defensive and are usually on their way to greener pastures;

2) A Knight on the third rank is useful for defense and is ready to take a more aggressive stance by jumping to the fifth;

3) A Knight on the fourth rank is as good as a Bishop and is well poised for both attack and defense;

4) A Knight on the fifth rank is often superior to a Bishop and constitutes a powerful attacking unit;

5) A Knight on the sixth rank is often a winning advantage. It spreads disharmony in the enemy camp to such a degree that the opponent will sometimes feel compelled to give up material to rid himself of it.

Keep in mind that when I speak of Knights on the fourth to sixth ranks, I refer to their being placed on unassailable support points.

One other piece of advice: A support point is only useful if it is in an area of the board where action is taking place. A Knight on the sixth rank in an unoccupied corner of the board is not a well placed piece!

With this information in mind, we can see that it is not enough to just get our Knights developed to any old square in the opening—we must endeavor to create advanced squares for them and then find a way to maneuver them to these 'homes.'

The following game features one of the main lines of the Ruy Lopez and shows both players fighting to get their Knights to the promised land.

Kavalek-Karpov, Caracas 1970. **1.e4 e5 2.Nf3 Nc6 3.Bb5 a6 4.Ba4 Nf6 5.0-0 Be7 6.Re1 b5 7.Bb3 d6 8.c3 0-0 9.h3 Na5** Black tries to capture White's active Bishop or at the very least chase it to a less attractive post. **10.Bc2** White retains his piece but temporairily places it on a rather inactive square. However, experience has shown that this Bishop can easily become strong if the center opens up. **10...c5** Black sees that placing his Knight on the fifth rank is useless since the post is not permanent. After 10...Nc4 White just chases it away by 11.d3 or 11.b3. **11.d4 Qc7** Avoiding 11...exd4? 12.cxd4 since then White's c2 Bishop would get very active after an eventual e4-e5 advance. By keeping his e5 pawn well defended, Black makes sure that White's Bishop stays bad. **12.Nbd2 Nc6 13.dxc5 dxc5** So far the Knights have not really played a major role in the strategy of the game. From here on out, though, the horses take center stage. **14.Nf1!** White sees two holes in the enemies camp: d5 and f5. With Nf1 White steers his Knight for e3 where it will eye both of these potential homes. **14...Be6 15.Ne3 Rad8 16.Qe2** It's clear where White's Knights are going, but what about Black? Can his Knights find any advanced posts? **16...c4!** Excellent! Black sees a hole on d3 and immediately makes a claim on it with his pawn (which backs up his d8 Rook). Now Black intends to play ...Nd7-c5-d3. **17.Nf5** (see diagram #52 on the next page).

(52)

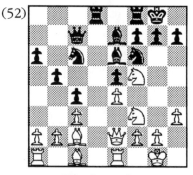

Black to play.

Now that the horse is on the fifth rank it starts to make Black uncomfortable. What can the second player do? Let's look at the possibilities:

1) He can chase it away with 17...g7-g6?, but then he has weakened the dark squares around his King and White would have the pleasant choice of 18.Nh6+ or 18.Nxe7+! followed by 19.Bg5;

2) He can take it by 17...Bxf5. However, after 18.exf5 Rfe8 (indirectly defending the e5 pawn) 19.Ng5! (heading for the new support point on e4) 19...h6 20.Ne4 Nxe4 21.Bxe4 White has the two Bishops and the once bad piece on c2 is now a tower of strength on the central e4 square;

3) Black can refuse to panic and just develop with 17...Rfe8. This is the choice Karpov made in the actual game.

17...Rfe8 18.N3h4 White takes a firm hold of f5 and guarantees that his Knights will make a positive contribution to the game. **18...Kh8 19.Nxe7 Qxe7 20.Qf3 Nd7** Starting the journey to d3. **21.Nf5 Qf8 22.Be3 Nc5?** A tactical mistake in an inferior position. **23.Nxg7!** It seems fitting that this Knight should deliver the decisive blow. The idea is that 23...Qxg7 24.Bxc5 leaves White a pawn up for nothing (the old inadequately defended piece rule) while 23...Kxg7 24.Bh6+! Kxh6 25.Qf6+ leads to eventual mate. White went on to win the game.

This game showed the efforts one goes through (starting right in the opening!) to place a Knight on an advanced post and the good things a Knight can do once it gets there. It is also a good illustration of a plan involving minor pieces: You start by recognizing that you have Knights. You next decide to make them better. You find or create weak squares in the opponent's camp. You finally find a way to get your Knights to these weak squares.

Second Rule Of Knights

Knights are very useful pieces in closed positions.

When the central pawns get locked together, Bishops tend to become inactive and devalued. However, Knights are very happy in such a climate. This is due to their ability to jump over other pieces and pawns.

(53)
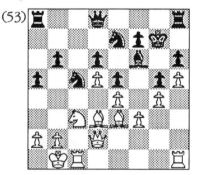

Silman-Czerniecki, US Open 1979.
White to play.

Here we have a position in which the kingside and the center is completely blocked. As is usual in such situations, the Knights take on great significance. In this case Black's Bishop on f6 is horrible. He also has holes on b5 and f5 that White's Knight can make use of. The one thing holding Black together is his strong Knight on c5. White's plan is to chase away this Knight with an eventual b2-b4 advance. Before doing this there are two other things he must take care of: 1) Bring his King to safety on the kingside; 2) Stop all Black counterplay by planting a piece on the b5 square. **22.Kc2!** This looks strange, but White has the time to move his King about like this because the position is closed. *In closed positions tempi are not so important and play often takes on a slow pace.* **22...Nc8 23.Kd1 Na7 24.Bb5!** Since the position is closed, White is happy to get rid of his Bishops—it's the Knight that he wants to retain. **24...Nxb5 25.Nxb5 Qd7 26.Qe2** White is obviously much better. His Bishop is superior to its very bad Black counterpart and his Knight has taken up a post on the fifth rank, a better place than the Black Knight's placement on the fourth. **26...Rhc8 27.Ke1 Bd8 28.Kf2 a4 29.Bd2** Black threatened to chase away White's Knight by 29...Ra5. **29...Be7 30.Kg2 Bd8 31.Rc2** White is not in any hurry to play b2-b4 so he first decides to double Rooks on the c-file. When you have a helpless opponent, take your time and place all your pieces on their best squares. **31...Nb7 32.Rxc8 Rxc8 33.Rc1** White doesn't mind trading the Rooks since his advantage in space and his superior minor pieces—the two things that make up his advantage—will still remain. **33...Rxc1 34.Bxc1 Nc5 35.Be3 Be7 36.Bxc5!** It turns out that the b2-b4 advance is no longer necessary. By swapping the Bishop for the Knight White wins the advanced Black a4 pawn and leaves himself with a powerful horse versus a rather sickly looking Bishop. **36...bxc5 37.Qc4 Qb7 38.Qxa4** The finish was: **38...Qb6 39.Qc4 Bf8 40.a4 Qa6 41.Kf2 Be7 42.Ke2 Kf8 43.Kd3 Bd8 44.Nc3 Qa7 45.Qb5 Qe7 46.a5 Qa7 47.a6 Ke7 48.Qb7+ Qxb7 49.axb7 Bc7 50.Kc4 Bb8 51.Nd1!** The Knight heads for the juicy f5 square. **51...Kd7 52.Ne3 Kc7 53.Nf5 Kxb7 54.Nxh6,** 1-0.

Third Rule Of Knights

Knights are the best blockaders of passed pawns. The reason for this is that while Bishops and Rooks are blocked by pawns, Knights can stop a passed pawn and remain active owing to its ability to jump over other men.

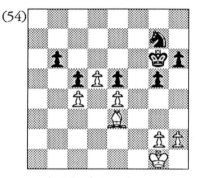

(54)

Black to play.

The position in the diagram looks good for White because he has a protected passed pawn and a very good Bishop. However, Black actually wins after **1...Ne8!** followed by 2...Nd6 when the strength of the Knight as a blockader becomes clear: not only does it stop the passer, it also attacks both its defenders.

Fourth Rule Of Knights

Knights are usually superior to Bishops in endings with pawns on only one side of the board due to their ability to go to either color!

This rule makes a good deal of sense. What makes a Bishop effective is its long range abilities. However, with pawns on only one side of the board these long range powers become useless. Instead, the Knight's advantage over a lone Bishop becomes evident: While a Bishop is forever trapped on one color, a Knight can go anywhere it wishes. What this means is that no pawn is safe from the hungry horse and the enemy King can always be checked away from any square it tries to sit on.

(55)

In diagram #55 Black is a pawn up but he has no chance to win because White's King is impregnable on e3. However, if we were to replace Black's Bishop with a Knight the picture would be quite different!

(56)

Now White is in check and his King immediately has to give ground. After 1.Ke2 Kd4 Black can continue to gain ground whenever he wants because his Knight can attack any square it wishes to. The comparison between diagrams 55 and 56 clearly shows the superiority of the Knight in such positions.

Now that we are thoroughly familiar with Knights and their habits, we can examine other examples where the battle centers around these interesting animals.

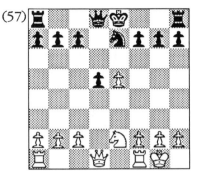

Norwegian Amateurs-Nimzovich, Oslo 1921.
Black to move.

The opening moves **1.e4 e6 2.d4 d5 3.Nc3 Bb4 4.exd5 exd5 5.Nf3 Bg4 6.Be2 Ne7 7.0-0 Nbc6 8.Bf4 Bd6 9.Ne5 Bxe2 10.Nxe2 Bxe5 11.Bxe5 Nxe5 12.dxe5** led to the diagrammed situation.

The position is quiet and both players can calmly try to formulate some sort of plan of action. Here the big imbalance is the mutual pawn majorities. Black's pawn majority (his c-pawn and d-pawn) can advance easily enough, but White has a problem—Black will play to control the f5 square, thereby freezing White's pawns. An attempt to play g2-g4 and fight for control of f5 would severely weaken the White King's position. Put simply, Black intends to advance his majority while simultaneously limiting White's.

Also important, but subtler, are the Knights. *Don't forget about your minor pieces!* Black will constantly try to create useful support points for his Knight while simultaneously (again!) limiting its White counterpart. Play continued: **12...Qd7** Preparing to castle queenside so that he can safely advance his kingside pawns in an effort to curtail White's. The Queen is well placed on d7 where it controls the critical e6, f5, and g4 squares. **13.f4** Trying to get his majority rolling, but it never really gets any further. The negative side of f4 is the weakening of the e3 square—a factor that gains in importance later in the game. **13...0-0-0 14.c3 Kb8 15.Qb3 c5** Black's majority is on the roll. Note how the d4 square is now no longer available to the White Knight. In doing this Nimzovich emulates Steinitz, who was the first to realize that the way to combat Knights is to take away their advanced squares, thereby relegating them to less active squares without hope of improvement. **16.Rae1 h5!** A very logical move! This adds to Black's dominance of the g4 square and as a result strengthens control of f5 and e6 also. The pawn will soon go to h4 where it will take the g3 square from the White Knight. In this way the White Knight will be unable to challenge Black's when it finally lands on the fine f5 square—an artificially created support point! **17.Kh1 Nf5 18.Ng1** Black would get a powerful attack after 18.Ng3 Nxg3+ 19.hxg3 h4. **18...h4** Threatening 19...Ng3+ 20.hxg3 hxg3+ 21.Nh3 Rxh3+ 22.gxh3 Qxh3+ and mates. **19.Nh3** There is no doubt whose minor piece is superior! **19...d4** Creating a passed pawn (the logical result of a pawn majority) and also creating a new and even stronger support point on e3. **20.cxd4 cxd4 21.Qd3 Ne3 22.Rf2 Qd5** The situation is growing steadily worse for White. Black's Knight dominates the board and the Black Queen radiates energy from its powerful central location. **23.a3 f6** Opening up new files so that the Black Rooks can join in the fight. **24.exf6 gxf6 25.f5!** An excellent move. White fights to activate his Knight. Now Nimzovich recommends 25...Rhe8! with a totally centralized position. Play might then continue 26.Rfe2 (26.Nf4 Ng4!) 26...Nxg2! 27.Rxe8 Nf4+ 28.Qe4 Rxe8 with an immediate win. Analysis by Nimzovich.

So everything turned out quite nicely for Black. The second player succeeded in every strategic operation he tried: stopped White's majority, activated his own, found a strong support point for his Knight and relagated White's to an obscure post on h3. Such a lopsided result must be partly due to some failing on White's part—White *must* be able to do better than that! Let's go back to diagram #51 and try to create a more balanced strategic struggle. We will allow the first few moves: **12...Qd7 13.f4 0-0-0 14.c3 Kb8**

(58)
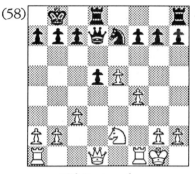

White to play.

Look closely at diagram #58. In the actual game White played 15.Qb3, but what does this do to stop Black's pawns or get his own going? Nothing whatsoever. Much stronger is **15.b4!**. This prevents ...c7-c5 and creates a fine post on d4 for the White Knight. Play might continue **15...Nf5 16.Qd3** Stopping ...Ne3 and eyeing the important f5 square. **16...h5 17.Nd4** And now Black is the one who faces a dilemma. If he retreats his Knight to h6 or e7 then 18.f4-f5 leaves White with all the trumps: active majority and superior Knight. If Black captures with 17...Nxd4 then 18.cxd4 leaves Black with a strategically lost position: White's majority is strong and he has plenty of play on the queenside also. Remember, the idea for both sides is to activate their respective majorities, place their Knights on strong posts, and prevent the opponent from achieving the same goals. With this in mind, Black *must* play **17...g6!** Now f5 remains in Black's hands. Though White should keep the status quo in the middle and strike out on the queenside with a2-a4, let's see what happens if White is tempted into doubling Black's pawns: **18.Nxf5 Qxf5! 19.Qxf5 gxf5** Black has a good position. White must always take a ...d5-d4 advance into account and if allowed, Black will play ...Kb8-c8-d7-e6 (the central King defends f7,f5, and d5) followed eventually by ...b6 and ...c5 when Black's majority of pawns is finally making itself felt while White's majority is completely blocked. The play from diagram #58 was more indicative of a balanced battle of ideas. Also note how the use of the majority of pawns remained a priority right into the endgame.

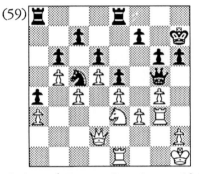

Guimard-Euwe, Groningen 1946.
Black to move.

In diagram #59 we have a blocked position. Such pawn configurations are always quite nice for Knights and here Black's steed is the better of the two. This is explained by the fact that White's Knight has no useful support points while Black's has c5, b3, and d4. At this point I can hear the reader saying that I am mistaken and that White's Knight has a nice home on c6 (obtainable by Nc2-b4-c6). Though c6 *is* available, it would be rather useless to go there since nothing is happening on the queenside. It is like having a million dollars worth of gold in the desert—who wants to lug that much metal around when you are dying of thirst? Here the queenside is a desert, while the sixth rank (normally gold) is visually pleasing but totally lacking in effect since it does not attack any weak points and does not work with the other pieces.

What else is going on? Well, it is an important fact that *in closed positions pawn breaks on the wings take on great importance* simply because this is the only way that the Rooks can be brought into play. Here the queenside and center are totally blocked. This leaves both sides slavering at the kingside. Given time, White will play h2-h4-h5 which could easily lead to a completely blocked position (if Black closed things up by ...g6-g5) and a resultant draw. Since a Black advance based on ...f7-

f5 is suicidal (opens the g-file for White and is impossible anyway because of White's iron control of that square), that leaves him only one possibility: Black must play for ...h6-h5 and subsequent play on the h-file. With this in mind Black's only logical candidates are 1) 1...h5; 2) 1...Kg7; 3) 1...Rh8, all of which aim to break open the h-file.

Let's look at each one:

1) 1...h5? fails to 2.gxh5 Qxh5 3.Qg2 when nothing is to be done about 4.Rh3 winning the Black Queen.

2) 1...Kg7 This walks into 2.Nf5+! when 2...gxf5?? 3.gxf5 wins the Queen again. Best is 2...Kh7 when White can trade Queens or return to the original position by 3.Ne3.

3) **1...Rh8!** Correct—the Rook immediately situates itself on the desired file. Now Black's King can go to g8 without blocking the Rook's path to the h-file. **2.Qe2** Getting out of the bothersome pin on the c1-h6 diagonal. **2...Kg7** Now this is good since 3.Nf5+ is met by the calm 3...Kf8 and White must retreat. There is an important lesson here. *Don't be afraid of ghosts!* Make sure that a move like 3.Nf5+ really does something for White before you bother to prevent it. Many players would avoid 2...Kg7 for fear of 3.Nf5+, thereby missing the best move and not allowing White the chance to go wrong. Another way of putting it would be: Deal in facts, not in paranoia! **3.Ng2** Preparing to try to close the kingside with h2-h4. **3...h5** Black beats White to it by one move! In the original position (diagram #59) some players might have been tempted to move the Knight to d4 (via ...Nb3-d4) before undertaking any other action. This lazy approach takes the Knight into account but ignores every other consideration. Don't get so engrossed in a single piece that you ignore what the rest of your army needs. **4.h4 hxg4** Just in time. A Queen retreat would have been met by 5.g5 with a blocked position. **5.fxg4**

Rxh4+! A sound sacrifice. Materially Black gets a pawn and Knight for his Rook. With it, though, he also gets an attack and control of the open h-file. Black's Knight will also gain in power since it can no longer be challenged by its now nonexistant counterpart. **6.Nxh4 Rh8!** Getting the other Rook into play as quickly as possible. Obviously 6...Qxh4+? 7.Qh2 would end Black's initiative. **7.Kg2** Or 7.Rh3 Rxh4 8.Rxh4 (8.Qh2 Rxg4 9.Rh7+ Kf8 10.Rf1 Rf4 also favors Black) 8...Qxh4+ 9.Kg2 Nd3! 10.Qxd3 (Black threatened ...Nf4+) 10...Qxe1 with a winning ending for Black. **7...Qxh4 8.g5 Nb3** The immediate 8...Qh2+ 9.Kf3 would not accomplish anything. Now, however, 9...Qh2+ 10.Kf3 Nd4+ is a disturbing threat! **9.Rg1** Making f1 available for his King. **9...Nd2!** Surprising but very logical. White had two squares to run to with his King (f1 and f3). Now both squares are off limits and the threat of ...Qh2 mate looms. Of course the Knight cannot be captured because the Queen would hang after ...Qh2+. This combination is made possible by a weakened White King and a hanging Queen.

A final point to consider: When attacking the King, don't just check a King here and there. First cover the squares that it can run to. This way your checks will become mate. This technique is called building a *mating net*. **10.Kf2** A horrible move to play, but there was no defense. **10...Nxe4+** White resigned, since he loses everthing. The Knight became very busy at the end by using its support points as jumping off squares for an attack.

DOGS VS. CATS/
BISHOPS VS. KNIGHTS

The battle between Bishops and Knights is one of the most interesting, and at times subtle, in chess. Games are often won or lost because of the superiority of a given minor piece and this section should be studied carefully if a mastery of the game is ever to be obtained.

As you have probably heard before, Bishops tend to be superior to Knights in open positions. Conversely, a closed, blocked position is more often than not going to see a Knight triumph over a Bishop. It is important to realize that a Bishop or Knight are not of themselves superior to each other. So many players feel that a Bishop is superior, but this is simply not true. It is what you do with a position, how you form it and its pawn structure, that makes one piece stronger than another. The poor maligned Knight must no longer be thought inferior—there is no room for bigotry on the chessboard.

In this chapter I have interspersed superior Knights with superior Bishops and have not divided them. I have done this so that you can look at each diagram and decide for yourself which minor is better—any other layout would rob you of the chance for this extra training. Before we look at specific examples though, a discussion of Steinitz's anti-Knight rule might prove informative.

The Anti-Knight Technique

It was Steinitz who first demonstrated the correct technique for battling Knights. *He showed that if you take away all their advanced support points the Knights will be ineffective and the Bishops will have an excellent chance of winning out.* Because of this you must make some decisions *before* you trade off into a Bishop vs. Knight position. Ask yourself the following questions whenever you face the possibility of creating this type of imbalance:

1) Is the position open or closed? If it's closed I may prefer to own the Knights. If it's open the Bishops may be a good bet.

2) Will there be support points available for his Knights? If there are, then other questions arise:

   a) Can his Knights get to them?

   b) If the Knights do get to these squares, does it matter? In other words, if his support point is on the queenside but all the play is taking place on the kingside then you would actually *encourage* him to stick his Knight on that far away post!

   c) Can the Bishops reach similar or superior squares?

Once again, it's very important to answer these questions before you make the trade! Don't make the mistake that so many players do and unconciously make a trade only to discover that the opponent's Knight is a dominant force. If you're going to give him Knights make sure that you can take away all his advanced squares (*a la* Steinitz) and slowly create an atmosphere in which your Bishops will thrive.

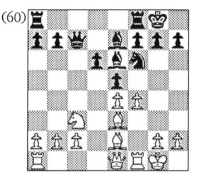

Smyslov-Rudakovsky, Moscow 1945.
White to move.

We will begin our examination of the battle between Bishops and Knights by looking at a typical situation in the Sicilian Defense (diagram #60). White has a nice support point on d5 but he is not able to make use of it since it is well guarded by the Bishop on e6 and the Knight on f6. His next few moves revolve around getting rid of the Black defenders of this square. **1.f5 Bc4??** This seemingly active move is in reality a terrible mistake. As stated earlier, this Bishop is needed to guard the d5 square, and now Black is offering to trade it for a piece that is not influencing d5 at all! Correct was 1...Bd7 followed by 2...Bc6 keeping an eye on d5 and putting pressure on White's e4 pawn. **2.Bxc4** White happily obliges! **2...Qxc4 3.Bg5** White hurries to get rid of the final defender of d5. In doing so he will be giving up a Bishop for a Knight, but the Bishop Black will be left with will be much inferior to the powerful White Knight which will permanently establish itself on d5. **3...Rfe8 4.Bxf6 Bxf6 5.Nd5! Bd8** White wins the Exchange after 5...Qxc2 6.Rf2 Qc5 7.Rc1 followed by 8.Nc7. **6.c3** The imbalance of minor pieces weighs decisively in White's favor. **6...b5 7.b3 Qc5+ 8.Kh1 Rc8 9.Rf3** With everything in control on the queenside and with the center in White's iron grip, White is ready to start a kingside attack. **9...Kh8 10.f6 gxf6 11.Qh4 Rg8 12.Nxf6 Rg7 13.Rg3 Bxf6 14.Qxf6 Rcg8 15.Rd1 d5** Black could do nothing about White's threat of Rxd6 followed by Rxg7 and Rd8. **16.Rxg7** Black resigned since after 16...Rxg7 17.Rxd5 there is no answer to Rd8+.

(61)
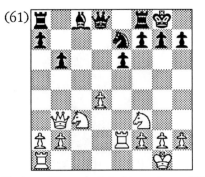

Blohm-Silman, San Francisco 1981.
White to move.

In diagram #61 Black threatens to play simply 1...Bb7 when his Bishop would be much superior to either White Knight. Add to this Black's use of the fine d5 square and the weakness of White's pawn on d4 and you come to realize White's sad plight. To counter this, White played **1.d5!?** A very interesting idea. White sacrifices a pawn but hopes to make his Knight better than the Black Bishop. **1...Nxd5 2.Nxd5 exd5 3.Nd4** Things have changed! White's weak pawn on d4 is gone and Black is now the one who must defend a weak d-pawn. Previously Black had use of the d5 square. Now that square is blocked while White has a very nice post on d4. Finally, White's sacrifice has turned Black's active Bishop into an inactive, bad piece—White's once inferior Knight now sits securely on d4 where it radiates power over the board. **3...Qf6!** Well, perhaps White's Knight isn't so securely placed after all! Black nips at the Knight and offers the pawn back since it only gets in the way of his Bishop anyway. To the untrained eye it might seem that both players are madly giving away pawns, but in reality neither player is overly concerned with material at the moment. They are more concerned with the activity of their respective minor pieces. It is clear that a vicious battle for minor piece superiority has been waged over the last few moves. This type of thing is typical of what the fight between imbalances is all about: Once you figure out the differences in the position, you must do everything you can to make your imbalance outweigh your opponent's. *Don't get distracted from this directive!* **4.Qxd5?** White has re-established material equality and even gotten rid of his weak d4 pawn. Unfortunately for him the board is now wide open. This means that the swift footed Bishop will prove its superiority over the more ponderous Knight. White must also face the fact that his Knight, while nicely placed on d4, is not defended by a pawn. This spells trouble since a Black Rook on the d-file could easily leave White's panic stricken pieces hanging. **4...Ba6** Gaining a critical tempo on White's Rook. **5.Re5** Blocks the Black Queen's access to d4 and intends to meet 5...Rad8 with 6.Qe4. **5...Bb7!** It turns out that White's Rook on e5 is as poorly protected as the Knight on d4. **6.Qb5 Rad8** The Knight must move since 7.Rd1 just walks into a pin. **7.Nf3** A very unhappy decision. White defended his Rook with the Knight because he saw that 7.Nb3 Ba6! picks up the poor Rook on e5. **7...Bxf3** As soon as the Bishop claims permanent superiority it trades itself away! In this case, however, a new imbalance is created: an extra, healthy pawn and a weakened King position. **8.gxf3** 8.Rf5 Bc6 loses a piece. **8...Qxf3 9.Rae1 Rd2 10.Rf5 Rxb2!** White is hopelessly lost because his Queen is overworked. **11.Qd7 Qg4+ 12.Kh1** Hoping that Black falls into 12...Rxf2?? 13.Qxf7+! Rxf7 14.Re8+ Rf8 15.Rexf8 mate! Before making any move always ask yourself: "Am I hanging anything? Does he have any checks?" This may seem silly but I guarantee it will save you crucial points and painful losses. Surely this is worth the few seconds it takes to do this! **12...Re2! 13.Rd1 Qe4+ 14.Kg1 Re1+** and Black easily converted his material advantage into a win.

In diagram #62 (see next page) Black's Bishop appears fairly active while the White Knight is not doing a lot. The big point is this: While the Black Bishop has reached its peak of activity, the White Knight has 'not even begun to fight.'

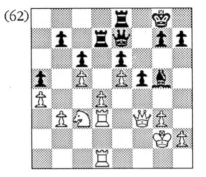

Botvinnik-Flohr, Moscow 1936.
White to move.

What is the Knight's optimum square? Those of you who said d6 can put a star on your forehead. On that post it eats the board alive and blocks Black's access to the weak pawn on d4. Can it get there? To answer this you must work backwards. The only uncovered square leading to d6 is c4. Our Knight can reach c4 from e3, d2, b2, and a3. Since d2 or e3 would allow the Bishop to exchange itself for our Knight, we must find our way to b2 or a3. The b2 square can only be reached from d1 or d3 but Rooks stand on both those points at the moment. The a3 square, however, can easily be reached from b1. Thus our move is obvious! **1.Nb1!** The Knight starts its journey towards greatness. **1...Qf8 2.Na3 Bd8 3.Nc4 Bc7** Black had to defend his a5 pawn. **4.Nd6** The Knight now constitutes a crushing advantage. Black does not want to take it since a powerful passed pawn would take its place. However, such a Knight cannot be tolerated for long, and Black will eventually feel compelled to hack it off. **4...Rb8 5.Rb1** White prepares to open the b-file and bring pressure to bear on Black's b7 pawn. *The Knight alone will not win the game. Only by creating a target can White hope to finish Black off.* You can do all the right things in chess but without a point of attack you won't find yourself winning many games. **5... Qd8 6.b4 axb4 7.Rxb4 Bxd6** The Knight had to go! **8.exd6!** Opening the e-file and thus exposing a new weakness on e6. Black is completely lost because White has a long range endgame advantage in his pawn on d6 (this pawn also cramps

Black's pieces) plus immediate targets on b7 and e6. The remainder of the game was marred by a big mistake on White's part, though his advantage is so large that he still gained the victory. For the curious, the finish was: **8...Qa5 9.Rdb3 Re8 10.Qe2 Qa8 11.Re3 Kf7 12.Qc4??** 12.Kg1! would have prevented the following counterplay. **12...b5! 13.Qc2 Rxd6 14.cxd6 c5+ 15.Kh3 cxb4 16.Qc7+ Kg8 17.d7 Rf8 18.Qd6 h6 19.Qxe6+ Kh7 20.Qe8 b3 21.Qxa8 Rxa8 22.axb5 Rd8 23.Rxb3 Rxd7 24.b6**, 1-0.

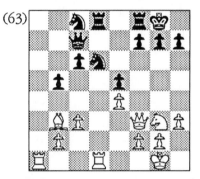

(63)

Alekhine-Junge, Warsaw 1942.
White to move.

Diagram #63 is not so easy to judge. No one has any really weak pawns, material is even, and space is also not much of a factor. The main imbalance is Bishop vs. Knight, but who does this favor? Black's Knight on d6 is doing a good job by challenging White's for the f5 square. This leaves a comparison to be made between the Black Knight on c8 and the White Bishop. The Bishop is bad since its e4 pawn stands on a white square. If the Bishop were chased back to c2 it would be a poor piece. As it stands though, it is quite active. On b3 it affects some central squares and aims at Black's kingside.

Now let's take a look at Black's c8 Knight. Knights in general are poorly placed on the first rank and should only go there if they are in transition to a nicer post. This means that at the moment the c8 Knight is inferior to White's Bishop. To counter this minor piece inferiority Black must place this Knight on a square where it will overshadow the Bishop—that square is c4.

On c4 the Knight blocks the Bishop and attacks the pawn on b2. Once it reaches c4 it would obviously no longer be inferior to White's Bishop. Indeed, White might be well advised to chop it off at that point. However, this Knight is not there yet. Fortunately for Black, c4 can easily be reached by ...Nb6-c4. This means that White's superior minor piece is only a temporary advantage—White must react quickly to take advantage of it.

Now that we know what Black is going to do (...Nb6-c4), let's figure out a plan for the White army. Which side of the board should White play on? Doubling Rooks on the a-file accomplishes nothing since Black would just trade pieces by ...Nb6 and ...Ra8 (doubling Rooks also has nothing to do with the imbalance—any plan must work with the Bishop on b3). Central action also fails since it doesn't take Black's plans into account. For example: 1.Rd2 Nb6 2.Rad1 Ndc4 when White's strategy can be seen as a complete bust. The logical place for White to seek play is the kingside. The reason for this is rather straightforward: White has three pieces pressuring the kingside (Queen, Knight, and Bishop) while Black has no pieces there at all (other than his King). It is important for the student to realize that White's Bishop on b3 resides on the queenside but exerts no real pressure there. Its influence, the muzzle of its gun, is pointed at the kingside. To repeat: *YOU MUST MAKE USE OF YOUR FAVORABLE IMBALANCES!* In this case that imbalance aims at the kingside. When the Queen and Knight join with the Bishop they can all work together towards a single goal. Note that the Rooks perform a prophylactic funtion: they eye the open files and prevent Black from getting counterplay there.

Now that we know that White is going to play on the kingside, we must determine which kingside point White will choose to attack (f7, g7, or h7). It is not my intention to give an in-depth explanation on how to attack a King here. A fantastic book that does this to perfection is Vukovic's *Art Of Attack In Chess*. Suffice it to say that one does not rush madly at the enemy King like a berserker. Instead you should pick one point and apply pressure to it in an effort to induce a weakening. In the present case it is clear that f7 is too well defended. The h7 point can be attacked by our Queen only—hardly sufficient to do anything wicked. That leaves g7, a point that can be attacked by both Queen and Knight.

To sum up: So far we know that Black intends (or should intend!) ...Nb6 followed by ...Nbc4. We also know that we will start a kingside attack and that g7 is our main target.

Only at this point, when we know exactly what both sides need to do in the position, do we decide on our candidate moves. Which moves attack our target (g7)? The only reasonable choices are: 1) 1.Qg4; 2) 1.Nf5; and 3) 1.Nh5. To cut down on our workload we can reject 1.Qg4 because it can always be played and we might prefer (after a Knight move) to move it to g3 instead (with a double attack on e5 and g7). At this point you should analyze 1.Nf5 and 1.Nh5 and choose the one you deem superior. In the game Alekhine played **1.Nf5!** Many players would reject this because of 1...Nxf5 when after 2.Qxf5 the attack seems to have ended before it ever got started. However 1...Nxf5 is an error since White can play the surprising and strong 2.exf5!. The doubled pawns don't hurt White's position at all; in fact the f5 pawn is an attacking force that threatens to push on to f6 and continue the strike against g7. The Bishop helps this attack by preventing ...f7-f6 due to the pin on the a2-g8 diagonal. Actually, after 1...Nxf5? 2.exf5! Black would be unable to stop the pawn's advance to f6 since 2...Qe7 3.Qxc6 hangs a pawn, while 2...Rd6 3.Rxd6 Qxd6 4.Rd1 Qf6 5.Rd7 leads to a winning bind for White.

Over and above all of this however, comes a subtler fact. With the clearing of the e4 square the White Bishop gains a permanent superiority over the Knight. Even if it gets chased back to c2 it will have the fine e4 square to sit on. This makes it apparent that White is not just attacking the King and hoping for mate. He is also trying to make his temporarily advantageous Bishop a permanent advantage. In this way he can carry his advantage into the endgame if a middlegame knockout punch eludes him. **1...Nb6!** Black wisely avoids getting distracted from his logical plan of posting a Knight on c4. **2.Qe3!** A very hard move to find, and stronger than 2.Qg3 g6 3.Nh6+ Kg7 4.Ng4 f6. After the text move White threatens both 3.Nxd6 winning a piece and 3.Qg5 Nxf5 4.exf5 Nd7 5.Rxd7! Rxd7

6.f6 and mates. **2...Nxf5?** Black panics. He should have calmly
played 2...Nbc4 when the final point of 2.Qe3 is shown: 2...Nbc4
3.Bxc4 Nxc4 4.Qg5 g6 5.Nh6+ Kg7 6.Ng4 and unlike 2.Qg3, the
Queen now stands in front of the Knight and threatens 7.Qf6+ Kg8
8.Nh6 mate. After the further 6...f6 7.Qh6+ White would retain just
a small edge. So White started with a small edge and perfect
defense by Black would keep it at that. Let me tell you a secret—
very few people defend perfectly! **3.exf5 c5** If 3...Nd5 then 4.Qf3
Nf6 5.g4 with a permanently superior minor piece and a strong
attack. **4.f6!** A wonderful thrust! White has been constantly trying
to accomplish two goals: to attack g7 and to make his Bishop
permanently better than the enemy Knight. This does both with
one move! Now the Black King is weakened and after 4...gxf6
White's Bishop will breathe fire down the b1-h7 diagonal. **4...gxf6**
Obviously 4...g6 5.Qh6 must be avoided. **5.Qh6** At the moment
the Bishop is still doing a great job on b3. Now the threats are
6.Qxf6 and 6.Bc2. **5...f5** Here White, realizing that all the rules for
a combination were present (weakened King, hanging piece
[Black Queen], inadequately guarded pieces) played **6.Bxf7+!!**
and completely destroyed Black. For the conclusion see Part
Three, Chapter Two (rules of combination), diagram #34.

(64)

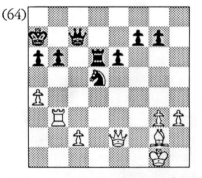

Poletayev-Flohr, Moscow 1951.
White to move.

A glance at diagram #64 gives a very favorable impression for
Black's cause. He is a solid pawn ahead, his Knight is well placed
in the center, and White's pawn structure is inferior to Black's. To

make matters worse, Black is the superior player! Surprisingly though, Black is dead lost! White's pawn minus *is* a negative, and his pawn structure *is* inferior. The factor that changes everything is the fight between the Bishop and the Knight. In this case the Bishop will prove to be far superior. **1.c4** If this pawn had stood on b2 (thereby 'improving' his split pawn structure), then White would indeed have been lost because the d5 square would be a permanent support point for Black's Knight. However, after 1.c4 the Knight must move and the newly opened diagonal for the Bishop quickly turns out to be decisive. **1...Ne7** Black also loses after 1...Nf6 2.Qf3 Rd8 3.a5 with a quick decision. **2.Qf3** Immediately making use of the Bishop's power by threatening mate on a8. In is now clear that Black's advantages (pawn structure and material) were static. White's superior minor piece and the initiative it confers is an active or dynamic advantage. It's important to state that dynamic advantages are not necessarily better than static ones; the individual position will determine which one will win out. If the dynamic (immediate) advantage can be nullified, then the static (long range) plusses of the defender should lead to eventual victory. In this case Black is not able to set up a successful defense, and so his static advantages will prove useless. A similar life situation is that of a person who puts all of his money away for his old age—only to die at thirty-five! **2...Qc6** Black would suffer after 2...Nc6 too: 3.a5! bxa5 4.Qe3+ Ka8 5.Rb6 followed by 6.Qc5. **3.Qxf7** So much for material disparity. **3...Qc5+ 4.Kh2 Rd1** Black actually threatens to mate by ...Qg1. White's King would be too open after 5.g4, and 5.h4 g5 complicates matters. The move White plays activates the only piece that is not carrying its load. **5.Re3!** Intending to simply guard it next move by 6.Qxe6. This capture would also open the e-file for the Rook, win a pawn, and create a double attack on the e7 Knight. The Rook cannot be captured by 5...Qxe3 because after 6.Qxe7+ mate would follow. **5...b5** Trying to give the King a runaway square on b6. **6.Qxe6 Nc8** Now a less experienced player might get excited by 7.Qf7+ Kb6 8.Qb7+ Ka5, but it is wrong to just check without a clear purpose in mind. Black's King is very unhappy on a7 since it is tormented by White's Bishop, Queen, and Rook. Allowing it to run to a5 would get it out of the Bishop's influence. **7.a5!** Very strong. As mentioned in an earlier chapter, this technique is known as 'building a mating net.' The idea is to close the doors of the King's escape routes and only *then* chase him. Of course—now he doesn't have anywhere to run to. **7...Qc7** Stopping 8.Qf7+. **8.Qe4** Threatening mate on a8. **8...Qb8 9.Qg4** A sadistic move. The Rook on d1 hangs, and 10.Qxg7+ would be a bone-crusher. Since 9...Rd7 still leaves the Rook *en prise* and 9...Qd6 hangs the Knight on c8, Black resigned. Instead of 9.Qg4, White could also have won more brutally by 9.Qe7!+ Nxe7 10.Rxe7+ Qb7 11.Rxb7+ (setting up the famous *Windmill* theme) 11...Ka8 12.Rxb5+ Ka7 13.Rb7+ Ka8 14.Rb1+ or 14.Rd7+ and Black has been cleaned out!

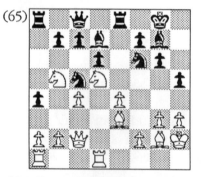

(65)

O'Kelly-Najdorf, Dubrovnik 1950.
Black to play.

Many of my students think that position #65 is quite nice for White. He has a space advantage and two powerfully advanced Knights. The bad Bishop on g2 is also serving a useful function guarding the pawns on h3 and e4, and can always become active by an eventual e4-e5 advance. Though Black has pressure on the e4 pawn, he cannot capture it because a catastrophe is threatened on c7. Thus, Black's first consideration must be a way of dealing with this threat. Retreats by ...Na6 or ...Ne6 are passive and displace Black's best piece (the Knight on c5). This leaves Black having to capture one or both of the bothersome Knights—don't allow your opponent to keep such fine looking beasts on the board!

If Black takes on b5 with his Bishop it will create an imbalance of Bishop vs. Knight. However, before doing so, Black must decide if such an imbalance would be favorable to him. He can't forget that taking on b5 opens up the c-file for White. This means that if White can chase the c5 Knight away by an eventual b2-b4 advance, then the pressure on the backward c7 pawn might prove to be unbearable.

After taking in all the factors of the position, Black hits upon the following long-range plan: He will capture on d5 first. This will force White to recapture with his e4 pawn (since cxd5 would hang the b5 Knight and Rxd5 would lose the e-pawn to ...Bc6). By making White's e-pawn go to d5 he has made White's Bishop on g2 *permanently bad* (it can no longer free itself by e4-e5). Next Black will capture the other Knight on b5, creating a Bishop vs. Knight imbalance. The Knight on c5 will then be strong, but can still be chased away by the pawn on b2 or captured by the Bishop on e3. These two *public enemies* must be dealt with or the position could turn against Black—if White succeeds in chasing the Knight from c5 and opening up the c-file, White would gain a clear advantage. To prevent this Black will play ...a3!, pinning the pawn on b2 by the Bishop on g7. White will then be forced to defend by Bd4 or Bc1, whereupon Black will trade first the pawns and then the Bishops, thus getting rid of both public enemies and leaving himself with a great Knight on c5 (completely unassailable and permanent) versus a terrible Bishop on g2. This advantage should be decisive.

Let's see how Black accomplished these goals: **1...Nxd5!** The correct move order. 1...Bxb5 allows 2.Nxf6+ Bxf6 3.cxb5, and White's Bishop on g2 can eventually become active by an e4-e5 advance. Now this Bishop will become bad without any active potential. **2.exd5** As stated earlier, 2.Rxd5 Bc6 wins material for Black. **2...Bxb5** Creating the imbalance of Bishop versus Knight. Black only did this because he realized that he could make his Knight permanently superior to White's Bishop on g2. Note that the alternative 2...Bf5 was very tempting. However, after 3.Qd2 Black has an active position but no way to cash in. This is a case of the static, long term advantage (superior Knight initiated by 2...Bxb5) being much better than the dynamic, short term advantage (2...Bf5). **3.cxb5 a3!** The pawn is attacked and cannot move because the Rook on a1 would hang. It appears that White has to guard it with his Bishop (if he doesn't want to lose material), thereby allowing Black to trade the only two pieces that could bother his Knight. **4.Bd4?** Since this leads to a positionally lost game with no active potential whatsoever, White should have sacrificed the Exchange by 4.b4! Bxa1 5.Rxa1. This would force Black's Knight to leave its great post on c5. True, Black would enjoy an extra Exchange; but White would be left with pressure on the c-file, two Bishops, and threats against Black's King on the a1-h8 diagonal. In this way White would have had several favorable imbalances to play with. Whether this would have offset Black's material advantage is a moot point—*never leave yourself with no favorable imbalances or no chances to create them.* If you do you will surely lose. It is much better to sacrifice material for some sort of compensation (in this case both long range [target pawn on c7 and two Bishops] *and* short term [chances against Black's King]) than to sit around passively with nothing whatsoever to crow about and lose like a dog (as happens in the game). Note that I say that you must sacrifice for *compensation*—don't sacrifice for one or two cheap shots and then resign if your opponent doesn't fall for your traps.

After the Exchange sacrifice Black would have to play very well to win and the slightest slip could easily lead to a White victory! For more information on material imbalance vs. various forms of compensation, see Part Nine, Chapter One. **4...Bxd4** There goes enemy #1. **5.Rxd4 axb2** And there goes enemy #2. **6.Qxb2 b6!** An unassuming but very important move! It gives additional support to the Knight, fixes the b5 pawn on a light square (thereby further limiting the scope of the g2 Bishop), and prevents White from gaining counterplay with b5-b6. In positions of this kind it is always a good idea to take time out and limit the opponent's active possibilities. **7.Rd2 Qf5** Black has a strategically won game thanks to his superior minor piece. Now many players in Black's position would be tempted to triple the Rooks and Queen on the a-file and try to win White's a2 pawn. However, this would fail to take into account possible White counterplay down the e-file or on the kingside. *If center files are open it is rarely a good idea to decentralize one's forces.* It must be realized that Black's advantages in this position are of a lasting nature. His Knight will always be better than the useless creature on g2. White's pawns on a2, b5, and d5 are all a little loose, while Black's queenside pawns are very secure. It's also important to note that the Bishop versus Knight ending would favor Black since no White pawn is safe from the Knight (which can go to any color). This means that Black is in no hurry; his advantages are not going away.

Because of this Black decided upon the following plan: He will play to take control of the open e-file. When this is done he will effect a penetration into White's position along the seventh or eighth ranks. This, combined with his superior Knight, should lead to larger gains. The beauty of this plan is it keeps the Black pieces centralized and thus offers White virtually no counter chances! **8.Re2 Nd3** The Knight does not intend to permanently leave c5, it is just snipping at White's heels and inducing him to give up the e-file. **9.Rxe8+ Rxe8 10.Qc2 Qe5!** Getting out of the pin by attacking the Rook on a1. Now the e-file is firmly in Black's hands. **11.Rd1 Nc5 12.h4 Qe2** The decisive penetration. White now loses material by force. **13.Qd2** 13.Qxe2 Rxe2 is also completely hopeless. **13...Qxb5** The first fruits of his positional concept. The immediate threat is14...Re2. **14.Re1 Rxe1 15.Qxe1 Qb2 16.f4** Or 16.Qe8+ Kg7 17.Qc8 Qxf2 18.Qxc7 Ne4 with a quick decision. **16...Kf8** Preventing the Queen from entering on e7 or e8. **17.f5** A desperate bid for counterplay. **17...Qe5 18.Qf1** Also easy for Black is 18.Qxe5 dxe5 followed by ...Ke7 and ...Kd6. **18...Qxf5 19.Qxf5 gxf5 20.Bf3 Ne4** With the heavy pieces gone, it is no longer important to keep the c-file blocked. Now the Knight can roam in search of food. **21.Bxh5 Nc3 22.Bf3 Nxa2**, 0-1.

Though every good player must be willing to make use of any imbalance that comes his way, a certain amount of favoritism lurks in the minds of most people. The great Chigorin thought Knights were superior to Bishops while David Janowsky had such a love for Bishops that he would often go out of his way (worsening his position in the process) to avoid trading them. His predilection for Bishops was so well known that for a couple of decades a pair of Bishops was usually referred to as the 'Two Jans'.

We find examples of minor piece preferences with modern players also: Petrosian had a known fondness for Knights while Fischer enjoyed making use of the long range powers of a Bishop. Personally, nothing makes me happier than a frisky Knight running rings around a hemmed in Bishop. I will end this chapter with a classic game that features a plan based on Knights winning out over Bishops.

Schlechter-John, Barmen 1905. **1.d4 d5 2.c4 e6 3.Nc3 f5 4.Nf3 c6 5.Bf4 Bd6** Black is playing the solid Stonewall Dutch. The one problem with this opening is the weakness created on e5. White will try to dominate that post and Black will do his best to keep the pressure on e5 under control while fighting for domination of e4. However, the e4 square is not a permanent outpost for Black since White always has the option of playing f2-f3. **6.e3!** A very good move. White would be happy if Black doubled White's pawns since that would give the first player an iron grip on e5. **6...Nf6 7.Bd3 Qc7 8.g3!**

(66)

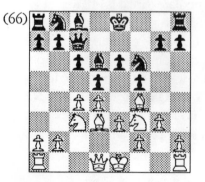

White makes sure his Bishop stays put, only allowing Black to exchange if he is willing to increase White's control of e5. **8...0-0 9.0-0 Ne4 10.Qb3 Kh8 11.Rac1 Bxf4** Finally giving White what he wants. **12.exf4 Qf7?! 13.Ne5 Qe7 14.Bxe4!** White sees that the position is closed and that Knights will become very valuable. Since Black's e4 Knight might eventually challenge White's control of e5 with ...Nd6 and ...Nf7, White snaps it off, leaving Black with a useless piece on c8. **14...fxe4 15.f3** Forcing open the e-file and exposing Black's weak, backward pawn on e6. This once again illustrates the importance of creating an attackable target. **15...exf3 16.Rce1!** Threatening 17.cxd5 cxd5 18.Nxd5! exd5 19.Ng6+ winning Black's Queen. **16...Qc7 17.Qa3 Kg8** On 17...Nd7 18.Qe7 leaves Black badly tied up. **18.Rxf3 Na6 19.b3 Qd8 20.c5** Continuing to grab more space and cramp Black. **20...Nc7 21.Qb2 Bd7 22.Qc2** If you wanted to play 22.Nxd7 here then shame on you!! White's Knight on e5 is an exceptionally strong piece. To trade it off for the pathetic thing on d7 would be criminal. **22...Qe7 23.Ref1** Since Black has managed to defend his backward pawn on e6 several times, White prepares to grab more space on the kingside and create new weaknesses in that sector. **23...Rae8 24.g4 Bc8 25.Rh3!** Creating new holes in Black's camp. Never be satisfied with what you have— chess is a game for greedy people! Leave the opponent with as many weak points as possible and his game will eventually disintegrate. **25...g6 26.b4** Aside from other things, Black must also worry about a potential queenside breakthrough via a4 and b5. **26...Qf6 27.Rhf3 Re7 28.a4 a6 29.Nd1!!** White intends to play g5 when he will plop his Knight into the newly acquired holes on f6 and h6 by Nd1-e3-g4. Don't just leave your Knights on reasonable looking squares. Place them on advanced posts even if it takes several moves to get them there. **29...Rg7 30.Ne3 Qe7 31.g5 Bd7 32.N3g4 Be8 33.Nh6+ Kh8 34.Qe2** Black has three major holes in his camp: e5, f6 and h6. White plans to occupy all three with Neg4, Qe5 and Nf6. **34...Qd8 35.Neg4 Bd7 36.Qe5 Ne8 37.Rh3 Qc7** Black is running out of moves. 37...Qe7 38.Qb8 would lead to the loss of a pawn. **38.Nf6!**

(67)
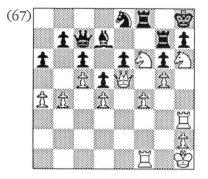

Black is completely overrun. Owning Knights doesn't get much better than this! **38...Qxe5** Not a happy choice but 38...Nxf6 39.Qxc7 drops the Queen, and 38...Qd8 39.Nxh7! is also hopeless. **39.fxe5 Re7 40.Rhf3 Nxf6 41.Rxf6 Rxf6 42.exf6!** Much better than 42.gxf6 since now White regains control of the e5 square and is able to use this square as an eventual entrance for his King. While it is true that most books tell you to capture with your pawns towards the center, it is correct to capture away from the center at least thirty-five percent of the time! This tells you that these rules are just basic guidelines. Every situation requires independent and original thought. **42...Re8 43.Nf7+** Bringing the Knight back to the center. **43...Kg8 44.Ne5 Rd8 45.Kg2 Kf8 46.h4 Be8 47.Kf3 Bf7 48.Kf4** Following a simple but important rule: *When you reach an endgame bring your King towards the center!* **48...Ke8 49.Rb1** Finally White prepares the long-awaited queenside pawn advance. Once the White Rook enters the Black position the game will come to an end. **49...Kf8 50.b5**, 1-0 due to 50...axb5 51.axb5 Be8 52.bxc6 Bxc6 (52...bxc6 53.Rb7 leaves Black completely helpless) 53.Nxc6! (White finally exchanges this piece so that his King and Rook can penetrate) 53...bxc6 54.Ke5 Re8 55.Rb7 and Black will lose all his pawns.

THE POWER OF THE TWO BISHOPS

As we know, a Bishop's weakness is that it is stuck on one color complex of squares. However this is not a factor if a player owns two Bishops. Two Bishops working together are a very powerful force because they have all the long range powers intrinsic in Bishops and also control both colored diagonals.

Let's take a look at how the two Bishops can make Knights look silly:

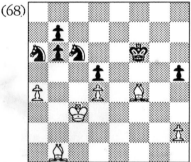

(68)

Botvinnik-D.Bronstein, World Championship Match, 1951.

Black is a pawn ahead but his Knights are tied down to the defense of his pawns and are not able to do any aggressive acts. White's speedy Bishops however, not only attack the enemy pawns but also tie down Black's King and restrain the Knights.

1.h4 Fixing the Black pawn on h5. Now it's just another weakness that White can attack. **1...Nab8 2.Bg5+ Kf7 3.Bf5** It's obvious that White's Bishops are dominating the board. **3...Na7** Hoping that White will allow him to advance his pawn to b5. **4.Bf4 Nbc6 5.Bd3** Preventing the ...b6-b5 advance. **5....Nc8 6.Be2 Kg6 7.Bd3+ Kf6 8.Be2** White is gaining time on the clock. **8...Kg6 9.Bf3 N6e7 10.Bg5** and now Bronstein thought for forty minutes and resigned. He is in zugzwang and must lose material: If the King moves the h5 pawn will fall; the c8 Knight can't move since that would hang the e7 Knight; any move with the e7 Knight would hang the d5 pawn. The real problem is that once he loses a pawn he will still be in the same unpleasant two Bishops vs. Knights situation, only with one pawn less than he started with! Nevertheless, I would person-ally have played it out and made him prove the win. As the old saying goes, "Nobody ever saved a game by resigning."

It is clear that this type of Bishop domination is no fun! If you find yourself in a position with Bishop and Knight (or two Knights) vs. two Bishops you should follow this useful strategy: *trade a pair of Bishops (or a Knight for one of his Bishops) and leave a more manageable Bishop versus Knight situation.*
The following game is an excellent illustration of this.

Glicksman-Silman, Software Toolworks 1988. **1.d4 Nf6 2.c4 e6 3.Nf3 Bb4+ 4.Nc3 c5 5.e3 Nc6 6.Bd3 Bxc3+** Black gives up the two Bishops without provocation! His strategy is to compro-mise White's pawn structure and play for a locked center. This will block the White Bishops and hopefully lead to a situation where the Knights will prove superior. **7.bxc3 d6 8.0-0 e5 9.Nd2 0-0** Black refuses to win a pawn by 9...cxd4 10.cxd4 exd4 11.exd4 Nxd4 since after 12.Bb2 White's Bishops would be very strong on their wide open diagonals. **10.d5 Ne7 11.f4** White is still trying to open up some lines for his Bishops. Now the threat is 12.f5 followed by 13.e4 when the c1 Bishop would be freed and White would obtain a crushing space advantage. **11...exf4 12.exf4 Bf5!**

(69)

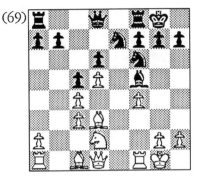

Excellent! Black prevents White from gaining space with f4-f5 and also trades off White's more active Bishop, thereby destroying the Bishop pair. Now White will be left with only one Bishop (and a bad one at that)—a situation that should make the Knights quite happy. **13.Qc2** If 13.Bxf5 Nxf5 14.Nf3 Black would make sure that the f5 square remains in his hands by 14...h5!. Black's Knights would then clearly dominate the White Bishop. **13...Qd7** Still fighting for control of f5. Bad would be 13...Bxd3 14.Qxd3 Qd7 15.f5 when Black's Knights don't have good squares and White's Bishop has been freed. **14.Ne4** If 14.Nf3 g6 15.Nh4 Black would play 15...Bxd3 16.Qxd3 Qg4! (By forcing White to place another pawn on a dark square he insures that the Bishop will be blocked in for a long time) 17.g3 Nf5! 18.Nxf5 Qxf5 19.Qxf5 gxf5. At this point many players will start screaming about Black's doubled pawns. Keep in mind that 'doubled' is just a word. The real question is "are they weak?" Since White has absolutely no way of attacking them the answer must be no. In the meantime Black has an excellent support point on e4 and has succeeded in entombing White's Bishop. **14...Nxe4 15.Bxe4 Rae8 16.Bd2 Bxe4 17.Qxe4 f5** Blocking the position. Now the f4 pawn will never be able to move and Black has created a nice support point on e4. **18.Qd3 Nc8!** (see diagram #70, next page)

(70)

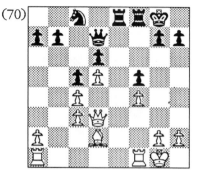

This move has two points. First Black intends to double Rooks on the e-file by ...Re4 and ...Rfe8. Because of this White will have to challange Black on that file and the Rooks will be traded. However, Black has determined that the trade of Rooks benefits him since with the absence of the big guns White would only be left with an ineffective Queen and Bishop vs. Black's Queen and excellent Knight. This highlights a little rule: *In general, a Queen and Knight is a better combination of pieces than a Queen and Bishop.* This is because the Queen already has the powers of a Bishop but the Knight is something completely new and tends to complement the Queen nicely.

The second point of 18...Nc8 is that the Knight will play to b6 where it pressures the very weak pawn on c4. This, in conjunction with ...Qa4 will eventually win that pawn. This demonstrates the importance of targets. You should always be trying to attack the weak points in the enemy camp. If none exist, it's up to you to create some. **19.Rfe1 Nb6 20.a4** Preparing to chase the Knight away from its threatening post. However, this creates a new problem: after White plays a4-a5 Black will eventually be able to play ...b7-b6 and create a passed a-pawn. **20...Rxe1+ 21.Bxe1 Re8 22.a5 Nc8 23.Bh4 g6 24.Re1 Rxe1+ 25.Bxe1 Qe7** Grabbing the only open file. Black does not fear a possible Queen trade since he sees that the resultant Bishop versus Knight ending would be bad for White. In this case Black would play the same plan as in the game. **26.Bf2 Kf7 27.Qb1 a6!** White is lost. Black's unstoppable winning plan is to bring his King over to the queenside and then to play ...b7-b6. When White captures, Black will obtain a mighty passed a-pawn and Black's Knight will reappear on b6. The c4 pawn will fall, the a-pawn will Queen and White will have to resign! The rest is easy to understand. **28.h3 h5 29.Qc2 Ke8 30.Qb1 Kd8 31.g4 hxg4 32.hxg4 Qf7 33.gxf5 gxf5 34.Bh4+ Kc7 35.Bg5 Qd7 36.Kg2 b6 37.Qa2 Kb7 38.axb6 Nxb6 39.Qe2 a5 40.Kg3 a4 41.Kf2** White's time pressure makes things even easier for Black. **41...a3 42.Qa2 Qa4 43.Bd8 Nxc4 44.Qe2 a2 45.Qe7+ Ka6 46.Qc7 Qb5,** 0-1.

This game made it appear that Bishops are easy creatures to contain. However, nothing could be further from the truth. Their potential power must never be underestimated—even if dormant, they can spring to life at any time and dominate the action. Our next example shows what can happen if two Bishops break loose.

Smyslov-Botvinnik, Moscow 1948. **1.e4 c5 2.Nf3 Nc6 3.d4 cxd4 4.Nxd4 Nf6 5.Nc3 d6 6.Bg5 e6 7.Be2 Be7 8.0-0 0-0 9.N4b5 a6 10.Bxf6 gxf6 11.Nd4 Kh8 12.Kh1 Rg8 13.f4 Bd7 14.Bf3 Rc8** In this position Black has two Bishops compared to White's Bishop and Knight. Unfortunately for Black, these Bishops are not very active at the moment. Still, Black has a solid position with play on the g and c-files and control of the critical c5, d5, e5, and f5 squares. This control of central squares in turn makes White's Knights ineffective since they don't have the use of any advanced support points.

White's usual plan in this type of position is to force Black to advance his e6 pawn to e5 by moves like f4-f5 and subsequent pressure on e6. If successful in this, then (after Black plays e5) Black's Bishops remain inactive while White will be able to use the excellent d5 post for his Knights, thus making the Knights better than the Bishops.

To accomplish this White might consider 15.f5 when 15...Ne5 can be met by 16.Nce2 followed by 17.Nf4 with pressure on e6. At any rate, this plan would logically continue the fight for the superior minor piece which the opening started. Instead White starts to play for a superior pawn structure but forgets to take into consideration the effect this will have on the minor pieces.

15.Nxc6? bxc6! It may seem silly to some that Black has blocked his open c-file and even placed a pawn in the way of the d7 Bishop. However, 15...bxc6 considerably strengthens Black's central situation, and thus allows him to play for a ...d6-d5 advance. **16.Ne2** White intends to play 17.c4, thereby making any central advances for Black undesirable. **16...d5!** Of course Black does not intend to wait for White's plans to congeal. If Black had allowed White to quell this central break by c4, then Black's Bishops would have remained blocked for a long time while White's advantage in space might have amounted to something. **17.f5?!** White's plan is to break down Black's pawn structure. Black allows White to get away with this, but only at the cost of freeing his Bishops. This gives us an excellent illustration of accepting static weaknesses for dynamic chances (initiative). **17...Qc7 18.c4** Still hacking away at Black's pawn formation. **18...dxc4 19.Qd4 c5 20.Qxc4 Bd6** The dark squared Bishop takes up an active post and theatens to gobble the h2 pawn. **21.g3 Bb5** This Bishop also begins to show alarming signs of activity. **22.Qc2 exf5!** Finishing the ruin of his own pawn structure. More importantly though, Black completely opens the position for his Bishops and also opens the e-file for his Rooks. **23.exf5 Rce8** The pressure on the e-file is already uncomfortable for White, who must have been wishing that he could start the game over again! **24.Rf2 Re3** The player with the initiative must always strive to increase the scope of his pieces. By playing actively and creating various threats, his opponent is kept off balance and is usually unable to consolidate his position. The text move keeps a threat of ...Rxf3 and ...Bc6 in the air and intends to double on the e-file. **25.Bg2 Qe7** Threatening to eat the Knight on e2. **26.Ng1** A horrible place for the Knight, but 26.Nf4 or 26.Nc3 are both mashed by 26...Re1+. **26...Bd3** The Bishops keep getting stronger. **27.Qd2 c4** Giving support to the d3 Bishop and further activating the Bishop on d6. **28.Rf3 Re8 29.Rd1** After 29.Rxe3 Qxe3 30.Qxe3 Rxe3 the Bishops' activity would carry over into the endgame. Actually, such an endgame would be an easy win for Black since White's b2 pawn would fall after ...Be5. If White tries to safety it by playing b2-b3, then ...c4-c3 would give Black an irresistable passed pawn. **29...Bc5** This position deserves a diagram!

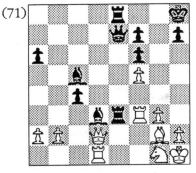

(71)

White to play.

Every Black pawn is either doubled or isolated. This would terrorize many players. Yet a comparison between White's pathetic Knight on g1 and the proud Black Bishops does not inspire confidence in White's game. **30.b3** 30.Rxe3 Bxe3 is also clearly in Black's favor. **30...Re1 31.bxc4 Bxc4** The calm reply. It would be bad to rush matters by 31...Bxg1? since White would survive after 32.Qxd3 Bf2+ 33.Rxe1 Qxe1+ 34.Qf1. **32.Bf1** There is no other defense to ...Bxg1. **32...Rxd1 33.Qxd1 Rd8 34.Qc2 Bd5** White can resign. The imediate threat is ..Bxg1 winning a whole Rook. **35.Qc3 Bd4!** Guarding the f6 pawn and thus freeing the Queen. Black is in no hurry to take the Rook—its defense keeps White off balance. **36.Qd3 Qe3!** Very simple. A material advantage is usually best exploited in the endgame. Thus Black forces the trade of Queens. **37.Qxe3 Bxe3 38.Bg2** Now the Rook must be taken. 38...**Bxf3 39.Bxf3 Rd2 40.Ne2** Or 40.a4 Ra2 thretening the a-pawn and Ra1. **40...Rxa2**, 0-1.

We have seen that the usual way to combat two Bishops is to do one of these three things:

1) Create a blocked position.

2) Create advanced support points for your Knights.

3) Trade off one of your opponent's Bishops and obtain a more manageable Bishop vs. Knight situation.

If these things cannot be accomplished, then the advantage will usually lie with the two Bishops. Of course, if you are the one who owns the two Bishops then you will be trying to avoid these three counters and will instead be going out of your way to nullify the enemy Knights. Steinitz was the first to discover the correct way to go about this: *The way to battle Knights is to take away all their advanced support points.* In this way the Knight would be relegated to the first few ranks, and, since it is not a long-range piece, it would be ineffective.

The next example shows Steinitz using this technique to turn his two Bishops into a decisive advantage. It is an historic struggle since this was one of the first times that this type of plan was ever executed.

(72)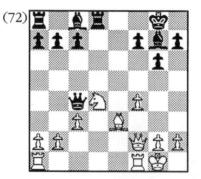

Rosenthal-Steinitz, Vienna 1873.
Black to play.

Black has the two Bishops but White's Knight is, at the moment, superior to either of them. Actually, if Black's c7 pawn were somehow exchanged for White's a-pawn, then White would have a huge advantage since his Knight would be permanently entrenched on d4 and any attempt to capture it by ...Bxd4 would lead to a fatal weakening of the dark squares around Black's King. Reality, though, has the pawn on c7, and this gives Black the capacity to force the Knight away from its fine post.

At the moment the only imbalance is the two Bishops vs. Bishop and Knight. Instead of trying to create anything else,

Black must clarify this imbalance in his favor. His plan is to take away the Knight's central post and place his light-squared Bishop on the strong a8-h1 diagonal. Since White has nothing to challenge this light-squared menace, he will be hard put to hold the equilibrium. Only after nullifying White's pieces and activating his own will Black form a new plan. **1...c5** Go away! **2.Nf3 b6** Guarding the c5 pawn and allowing the c8 Bishop to go to a6 or b7 as necessary. **3.Ne5** The stubborn Knight finds a new home. **3...Qe6 4.Qf3 Ba6** Guards the a8 Rook with tempo. **5.Rfe1 f6** Scram! **6.Ng4** 6.Nc6 looks more active, but after 6...Rde8 7.Bf2 Qd7 8.Rad1 Qc7 the Knight is trapped deep in enemy territory and after Black plays ...Bb7 it will never get out alive! **6...h5** The poor Knight must feel picked on at this point. **7.Nf2 Qf7** White threatened 8.Bxc5 with a discovered attack on the Queen. **8.f5?** A big mistake. The pawn will be very weak on f5. **8...g5 9.Rad1 Bb7** White cannot combat the power of this piece; the knight on f2 is certainly no match for it. **10.Qg3** Hoping for the greedy 10...Qxa2? 11.Qc7 when White will gain a certain amount of active play. **10...Rd5!** Black refuses to bite. Keeping the initiative is more important than rushing your pieces onto the sidelines—even if it does win a pawn. Pawn grabbing *is* fine as long as you don't throw away most of your other advantages along the way. The text threatens to gobble the f5 pawn. **11.Rxd5 Qxd5 12.Rd1 Qxf5** A pawn has been won, but his time Black's centrally placed Queen will help beat off any temporary activity White may get. **13.Qc7 Bd5** Blocks the d-file. **14.b3 Re8** Black does not keep his Rook passively guarding his a7 pawn. Instead, it enters the battle by attacking White's Bishop. Note how Black has kept his pieces nicely placed in the center. **15.c4 Bf7** The Bishops cluster around their King. Black's Queen and Rook will retake the initiative with threats on White's Bishop and weakened back rank. **16.Bc1 Re2 17.Rf1 Qc2** Now 18...Rxf2 19.Rxf2 Qxc1+ is the threat. **18.Qg3 Qxa2**, and Black's two pawn advantage quickly proved decisive.

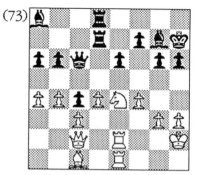

Longren-Silman, Santa Barbara 1989.
Black to play.

Black has the two Bishops and there is little doubt that the one on a8 is very powerful—the combined might of the Queen and light-squared Bishop creates a lot of mating possibilities. However, the Bishop on g7 is not really a factor for Black. How can Black break through White's position? A mistake is 1...f5? since 2.Nd2 followed by 3.Rf2 and 4.Nf3 leaves the e5 square very weak. Instead of a one move threat to White's Knight, Black should follow the basic rules pertaining to Bishops; e.g. When you have two Bishops you must open up the position! With this in mind, Black's decision to rip open the center is easy to understand. **1...f6! 2.h4 e5 3.dxe5 fxe5 4.h5 Rd3** Now the Bishop on g7 and the Rook on d3 are starting to drool on the pawn at c3. **5.b5** White tries to draw Black's Queen off of the a8-h1 diagonal and away from the defense of the g6 pawn. **5...axb5 6.axb5 Qe6!** The Queen temporarily leaves the diagonal, but she keeps a frim hold on g6. Now 7...Qg4 is a threat. **7.Nf2 Qd5 8.hxg6+ Kg8 9.Ne4 exf4 10.Bxf4 Qh5+ 11.Kg1 Qxg6** The combined might of Black's two Bishops raking down on their respective long diagonals makes a nice impression. With White's King so vulnerable and threats always hanging over the pawns on c3 and g3, White should not expect a long life. **12.Qa2 Bd5 13.Qc2 Rf8!** Threatens ...Rxf4. White's game is just about to crack. **14.Qc1 Bxc3!** The Bishops have their way. Since 15.Nxc3 Rxg3+! 16.Kf1 Rg1+ 17.Kf2 Qg3 is mate, White resigned.

CHAPTER FIVE

THE TWO KNIGHTS VICTORIOUS!

As already mentioned, to combat two Bishops you need a blocked position, good support points for the Knights, or a trade of a Knight for a Bishop leading to a favorable Knight versus Bishop situation.

The usual superiority of two Bishops over two Knights is logical; two Bishops work together very well, while two Knights tend to run into each other and are much harder to manage.

Still, many positions come about where the Knights clobber the Bishops, and a prejudice towards either must be avoided so that a player can keep an open mind and make an objective appraisal of each different situation.

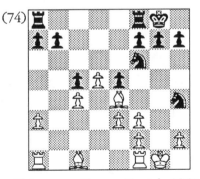

Taimanov-Euwe, Zurich 1953.
Black to play.

Diagram #74 is a typical situation which favors the two Knights. To quote Bronstein: "One Bishop is locked in a cell measuring a3 by c1 by e3; the other is chained to the pawn at f3. Both Bishops are absolutely impotent, and White has no useful moves."

Black's plan here is based on a favorable transition to a Knight versus Bishop position. He will play 1...Rae8 followed by ...Nxe4 when Black's remaining Knight is far superior to the poor Bishop on c1. For example: **1...Rae8 2.a4 Nxe4 3.fxe4 f5! 4.exf5 Nf3+ 5.Kg2 e4** with 6...Rxf5 to follow. The Knight on f3 would then clearly dominate the play.

(75)

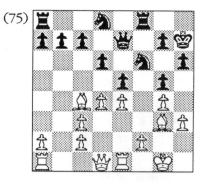

Wolf-Rubinstein, Teplitz Schonau 1922.
Black to play.

Black is doing well because of the closed nature of the position and the fact that the f4 square constitutes a great support point for the Black Knights. Black's plans include:

1) Placing a Knight on f4;

2) Keeping his pawn on e5 at all costs! This is of the utmost importance! If Black were to capture on d4 via ...exd4??, then White would answer with cxd4 when theats like e4-e5 will allow White to open up the center, activate his Bishops, and wipe Black out. Once again, Black *must* keep the position as closed as possible!

Since Black's first order of business is getting a Knight to f4, he must determine the best route to that square. 1...Ne6?? hangs the e5 pawn, so best is **1...Nf7** Heading for h8, g6, and finally f4. Closed or semi-closed positions allow for lengthy maneuvers like this, and a player should not feel that it takes too long to get there and start looking for another idea. It is important to understand that *Black has no choice!* He has Knights, and Knights need to land on advanced support points—it's as simple as that. **2.Qf3** White begins to play for tactical tricks. He should have given serious consideration to 2.Bxf7 Rxf7 3.f3, getting rid of his bad Bishop and simplifying things somewhat (the e4 pawn is stuck on white, so the light squared Bishop is bad. Since the d4 pawn can easily move from d4, the dark squared Bishop is not really blocked and is therefore good). The problem with White's game is that he has no real point of attack. If White is unable to generate some play and distract his opponent, then a Black Knight will reach f4 where it will be stronger than either White Bishop. When that happens White will feel compelled to trade it for the g3 Bishop, leaving himself with a bad Bishop versus a Knight. **2...Rae8!** White threatened Bxf7 followed by dxe5 and Qf5+ winning the e5 pawn. The text gives added support to this pawn, thus spoiling White's threat. Since this allows White another chance to get rid of his bad Bishop by Bxf7, Black could also have considered 2...Nh8 when 3.dxe5 dxe5 4.Qf5+ is safely met by 4...Ng6. Why didn't Black play this way? The answer is that he didn't want to let White trade Queens after 2...Nh8 3.Qf5+ Ng6 4.Qe6. The Rook on e8 stops this type of thing once and for all. **3.Qe3** Another trick, threatening 4.dxe5 followed by 5.Qxa7. Such planless one-movers will rarely lead to a good result and should be avoided. Remember: *Expect your opponent to see your threats.* Every move you make should be a strengthening of your position, not just the setting of a cheap trap. **3...b6** Guarding the a7 pawn and blocking the open b-file. Absolutely terrible would be 3...a6??, since after 4.a4 and 5.Rb1 Black's queenside would be under great pressure. **4.Bb5?** He should have played 4.Bxf7. The Bishop looks threatening here but it is actually poorly placed. **4...Rd8 5.a4 Nh8!!** A surprise that shows the depth of Rubinstein's vision. Most Grandmasters would hold off on this Knight maneuver for one move and answer White's 'threat' of a4-a5 with 5...a5. In this case though, Rubinstein doesn't fear the a4-a5 advance since he sees that this will eventually enable him to create a passed pawn on the queenside. **6.a5 Ng6 7.f3 Nf4 8.Bf1 Kh8!** Intending 9...Nh7 followed by ...Rf6 and ...Nf8-g6. **9.Bxf4** Otherwise, after ...Nh7 Black would be able to recapture on f4 with the Rook. **9...gxf4 10.Qf2 g5 11.d5??** A miserable move that every reader of this book should know to avoid. White further blocks the position (an action that can only favor the Knight), gives the Knight the fine c5 square, and makes his Bishop as bad as possible by placing another pawn on a light square. **11...h5** Playing to open the h-file for his Rooks. **12.Bg2** The Bishop stands horribly here, but it is needed for future defensive efforts. 12.axb6? is a mistake, since after 12...cxb6! Black would have a passed a-pawn and could attack White's doubled c-pawns by placing a Rook on the open c-file. **12...Kg7** Making way for the Rooks. **13.Qe2 Rh8 14.Kf2 Ra8 15.Reb1 Nd7** Finally heading for the great c5 square. **16.Qb5 hxg4 17.hxg4 Nc5** Black's Knight is so much better than the Bishop that Black must be considered to have a decisive advantage. Winning though, is easier said than done. Watch how Rubinstein plays on both wings and virtually surrounds his opponent! **18.Rh1 Rh4!** Blocks the file and allows Black to double his Rooks. **19.Rxh4 gxh4** Now White must watch out for ...h3! followed by ...Qh4+ with a decisive kingside penetration. **20.Bh3 bxa5!** The point of his fifth move (5...Nh8!!). This opens the b-file and gains a passed a-pawn. The next dozen moves are devoted to advancing his a-pawn, dominating the b-file, and solidifying his position on the kingside. **21.Qxa5 Qd8 22.Rb1 Rb8 23.Rb4** Black's two passed pawns and superior minor piece give him a winning endgame after 23.Rxb8 Qxb8 24.Qb4 Qb6 followed by 25...a5. **23...a6 24.Ke2 Rb6** Intending to break White's blockade by ...Nb7 and ...a5. **25.Qa1 Kg6** Black is in no hurry, and first gives support to his pawn on h4. **26.Kd2 Kg5** Black makes all of his pieces earn their keep. **27.Rb1 Qb8 28.Rh1** Trying to scare Black with threats against the h4 pawn. **28...a5!!** Black wants to advance this pawn—isn't it undefended? **29.Bg2** White does not take the 'gift.' After 29.Qxa5 Rb2 (threatening ...Nb3+) 30.Qa3 Nb3+ 31.Kd3 Qb5+ 32.c4 Qb6 Black's pieces succeed in penetrating to the White King. **29...a4 30.Qe1 Qh8 31.Qc1 Ra6 32.Bf1 Ra8 33.Bc4 a3 34.Ba2 Qh7** Now Black begins a series of strange moves that were undoubtedly a result of time pressure. If one enjoys an impregnable position, it is common for that player to make a few 'do nothing' moves in order to gain time on the clock. **35.Rh3 Nd7 36.Qf1 Qh8 37.Rh1 Nc5 38.Qc1 Rb8!!** Time pressure must be over and Black switches back into a positive mode. This surprising move threatens 39...Rb2 and forces White to take the a3 pawn. What does Black accomplish by this pawn sacrifice? He ties the enemy Queen down on the queenside, which allows his own Queen to decisively penetrate on the other side of the board. **39.Qxa3 Ra8 40.Qb2 h3** Intending ...Qh4. If White's Queen still stood on c1, he could play Qe1 and prevent this. Now, thanks to the deflecting sacrifice of the a-pawn, this defense is no longer possible and White is without a satisfactory answer. **41.Bc4 Qh4 42.Be2 Qf2!** Giving his other passed pawn away as well! **43.Rxh3 Qe3+ 44.Ke1 Na4**, 0-1. The threat of ...Nxc3 will end matters quickly.

A slow but fascinating struggle that won Rubinstein a brilliancy prize. The manner in which he played on both wings deserves close study.

Though Knights are known to be strong in closed positions, they can also prove to be a force in open positions where support points exist. In the game Ogaard-Flesch, Oslo 1974, the position that interests us came about after some typical moves in a Nimzo-Indian: **1.d4 Nf6 2.c4 e6 3.Nc3 Bb4 4.e3 c5 5.Bd3 0-0 6.Nf3 d5 7.0-0 cxd4 8.exd4 dxc4 9.Bxc4 Bxc3 10.bxc3 Qc7 11.Qe2 Nbd7 12.Bd2 b6 13.Bd3 Bb7 14.c4 Rac8 15.Rac1** (see diagram #76, next page).

(76)

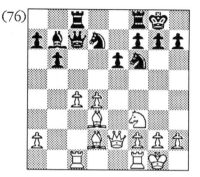

Black to move.

White has more space and the two Bishops. In addition, he is using the usual formula of battling Knights by taking away all their advanced squares; in this case c5, d5, and e5. One is led to believe that this position should favor White. **15...Bxf3!** A real shocker. Black voluntarily gives up his powerful Bishop and creates a two Bishop vs. two Knight scenario. He does this because he sees that he will be able to forge a new and favorable climate for his Knights. **16.Qxf3 e5!** The point. Black changes the central pawn structure and, aside from leaving White with a weak pawn on c4, gives himself a fine support point on c5. Once a Knight reaches that square it will be at least as good as either White Bishop. Keep in mind that support points for Knights rarely just happen; you must actively pursue their creation. **17.Be3** Not what White wanted to do, but 17.dxe5 Nxe5 18.Qg3 Nxd3 eradicates White's two Bishop advantage and leaves him with an isolated pawn on c4. Also in Black's favor was 17.d5 e4! 18.Bxe4 Ne5. **17...exd4! 18.Bxd4 Ne5 19.Qf5 Nxd3** So the two Bishop vs. two Knight imbalance did not last long, but this does not detract from the point of this example—if you can find a way to create support points for your Knights, then there is no reason why they should not prove just as good if not better than the enemy Bishops. In this case the creation of a pawn weakness on c4 is just icing on the cake for Black. **20.Qxd3** At first it looks as though White has the strong *zwischenzug* (Turn to the Glossary if you are unfamiliar with the term) 20.Bxf6, but Black would then play 20...Qf4! 21.Qxd3 Qxf6 when White's weakness on c4 gives Black all the winning chances. **20...Rfd8 21.Qc3 Ne4** Ending the threat of Bxf6 and heading for the promised c5 square. **22.Qb2 Nc5 23.Qc3** Bad is 23.Bxg7? Nd3 24.Qa1 Nxc1 25.Rxc1 Re8 26.Rc3 Re6 winning for Black. **23...Ne6 24.Be3 Rd6 25.Rc2 Qd7 26.Qb4 Rd3 27.a4** It seems as if White has made progress. He threatens a4-a5 when Black's queenside pawns will become targets. However, Black is able to start an attack against White's King by rushing forward with his f-pawn. Note the Knight's usefulness in helping the pawn march forward. **27...f5! 28.g3 f4 29.gxf4 Nd4 30.Bxd4 Qg4+ 31.Kh1 Qf3+ 32.Kg1 Rc6 33.f5 Rxd4 34.h3 Rg4+**, 0-1, since 35.hxg4 Qxg4+ 36.Kh2 Rh6 is mate.

A few years after this game was completed the following game between Portisch and Karpov, Bugojno 1978, was played: **1.d4 Nf6 2.c4 e6 3.Nc3 Bb4 4.e3 0-0 5.Bd3 c5 6.Nf3 d5 7.0-0 dxc4 8.Bxc4 cxd4 9.exd4 b6 10.Bg5 Bb7 11.Re1 Nbd7 12.Rc1 Rc8 13.Bd3 Bxc3 14.bxc3 Qc7 15.c4 Rfe8 16.Qe2 h6 17.Bd2**

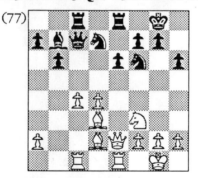

(77)

Black to play.

Look familiar? It's almost identical to the Flesch game (diagram 76). Though Black's usual strategy in this system is to put pressure on White's pawns on c4 and d4, Black was delighted to see that he had been given the opportunity to create homes for his Knights! **17...Bxf3! 18.Qxf3 e5! 19.Qg3?!** White decides to sacrifice a pawn in an effort to activate his Bishops. The problem with this is that Black will retain several advantages also, namely an extra pawn, a target on c4, and two extremely useful Knights. One of the beasts will sit on the dominating c5 post, while the other will stay back for defense. **19...exd4 20.Rxe8+ Nxe8 21.Bf4 Qc6 22.Bf5 Rd8** Black calmly steps out of the pin and places his Rook behind his passed pawn in anticipation of pushing it. **23.h3 Nc5 24.Rd1 Qf6 25.Bb1 Qe6 26.Kh2 Kf8 27.Be5 Qxc4 28.Qf4 Ne6!** Showing that Knights have a grace all their own. On e6 the hopper guards g7 and d4, and attacks the Queen on f4. **29.Qe4 Qd5 30.Qe2 Nd6 31.a4 Nc4** Now both Knights are well posted, and the end is near for White. **32.Bg3 Nc5**

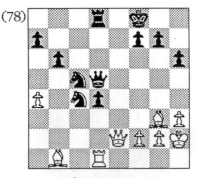

(78)

White to move.

A case of two Knights looking more coordinated and more threatening in an open position than two Bishops! **33.Ba2 d3 34.Qe1 Qd4 35.f3 Ne3** The Knights keep coming forward, and it becomes increasingly clear that the poor Bishops are no match for them. **36.Rd2 Re8 37.Qc1 Nxa4** Like all hard working animals, they need to feed as they labor! **38.Kh1 Nc5 39.Bf2 Qe5 40.Bb1 Kg8**, 0-1.

Never let anyone tell you that Knights are inferior to Bishops! We have seen that it's not the individual Knight or Bishop that is inferior or superior—it's the way you handle them.

Solve These Problems

(79)

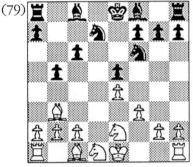

Black to play.

How can Black create a static imbalance that can be nurtured and used through out the game?

(80)

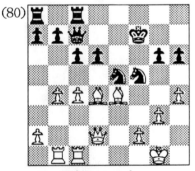

White to play.

What minor pieces rule in this position—the advanced Black Knights or White's two Bishops?

(81)

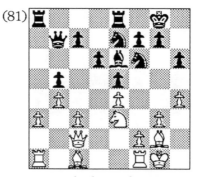

Black to play.

How can Black play for a superior minor piece?

(82)

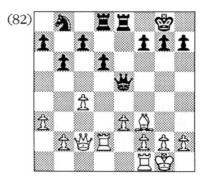

White to play.

What is his correct move?

PART FIVE

SPACE AND PREVENTIVE MEDICINE

The 1800's was a fun time for chess—sparkling combinations, sacrifices (their soundness didn't matter); everything and anything in the hope of a pretty mate. Those innocent days were shattered when Steinitz discovered that victory could be had by other means as well. He offered the chess playing public its first taste of scientific chess principles and, when Siegbert Tarrasch joined the bandwagon and started raving about the joys of a territorial advantage, the game had been completely transformed.

With the turn of the century came a new breed of chess masters. No more striving after attacks with reckless abandon! Instead players such as Maroczy, Schlechter, Teichmann, and Rubinstein took on a style of trench warfare. Their idea of a good time was to squeeze their opponents to death. No muss, no fuss, no risk—just a nice boa-like crush.

THE BIG SQUEEZE

What is space and why is it important? A player's territory is usually determined by the positioning of one's pawns. If we look at a line of pawns as a fence, we can see that the area behind these foot soldiers is their property—they have claimed it and put up borders that announce that claim. This extra property is an advantage for a very simple reason: if you have more territory you also possess more room to move around in.

Can someone really lose just because he has less territory? Our first example will make the answer abundantly clear!

(83)

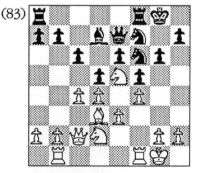

Capablanca-Treybal, Karlsbad 1929.
White to play.

In the diagrammed position both sides have an equal stake in the center, but White's superior Bishop and his space advantage on the queenside give him a clear advantage. **1.Ndf3** Strengthening his control of the e5 square. **1...Rfd8 2.b4**

White's control of the queenside grows, and Black must constantly be on guard for a breakthrough there by b4-b5. **2...Be8** Black avoids placing his Knight on e4, since aside from ignoring it, White could obtain a crushing Knight versus a pathetic Bishop: 2...Ne4? 3.Nxf7 Qxf7 4.Ne5 followed by 5.Bxe4. **3.Rfc1 a6 4.Qf2 Nxe5 5.Nxe5 Nd7** Following the rule that *the side with less space should __initiate__ exchanges so that he will have more room to move about in.* **6.Nf3** And White follows the opposite rule: *The side with more space should __avoid__ exchanges.* **6...Rdc8 7.c5** Increasing the space advantage and further restricting Black's pieces. Now White will play for a breakthrough by a4 and b5. White will also attempt to play for a kingside expansion with g2-g4 (In positions with this type of pawn structure on the kingside [White pawns on e3 and f4 versus Black pawns on e6 and f5], whoever gets to advance his g-pawn to the fourth rank first [g4 for White and g5 for Black] will usually take the advantage on that side of the board) since if White can take the initiative there too, then Black will not be able to consider action on that side of the board himself. In that case White would control the whole board and Black would be condemned to complete passivity. This means that a kingside expansion by White is not only an aggressive plan, but also defensive! **7...Nf6 8.a4** Not fearing the upcoming one move attack on his Queen since the enemy Knight can easily be chased away. Don't waste time and stop someone from making an attacking gesture if it turns out to be a dead end street for him. **8...Ng4 9.Qe1 Nh6 10.h3 Nf7 11.g4** So White was the first to advance his g-pawn. This means that he is now in control on the kingside also, which leaves Black passively stewing in his own juices. **11...Bd7 12.Rc2** Preparing to switch the Rook over to the kingside. **12...Kh8 13.Rg2 Rg8 14.g5** More space! Black's pieces are trapped on the first two ranks, and he can only wait and prepare himself for White's eventual breakthrough. Now White will play for both the b4-b5 and h4-h5 breaks. **14...Qd8 15.h4 Kg7 16.h5** By expanding his territorial limits on the kingside, White takes the first step in his plans to dominate the board. Now Black must worry about White tripling his heavy pieces (Rooks and Queen) on the h-file and breaking through there. **16...Rh8 17.Rh2 Qc7 18.Qc3 Qd8** Note how Black's lack of space leaves him completely helpless. He can only go back and forth and hope that White is unable to effect a breakthrough. **19.Kf2** With the position closed, White can maneuver as slowly as he wishes. He now intends to double Rooks on the h-file. When the opponent is helpless (as in the present case) you can and should take as many moves as you wish in setting up a desired position. What's the hurry? By not letting the opponent know what you intend to do and when you intend to do it, you keep him off balance. Here White will only play hxg6 if and when it suits him. **19...Qc7 20.Rbh1 Rag8 21.Qa1** Black has set up a solid defense on the kingside, so White maneuvers a bit before initiating his long awaited break on the queenside. **21...Rb8 22.Qa3** A subtle tactical move that helps make his b4-b5 advance possible. **22...Rbg8 23.b5!** Now the greedy first player annexes more territory on the queenside as well. **23...axb5** The point of Qa3 is revealed if Black plays 23...cxb5?? 24.h6+ Kf8 25.c6+ winning a piece. **24.h6+!** Going all out for a queenside decision! Black would gain a little counterplay after the automatic 24.axb5 gxh5! 25.Rxh5 Ra8. This closing of the kingside also accomplishes two other goals:

1) Traps the Black Rooks on the kingside long enough to enable White to obtain complete control of the soon to be opened a-file.

2) Takes even more space away from the Black pieces.

24...Kf8 Now the King interferes with the action of both Rooks. **25.axb5 Ke7 26.b6!**

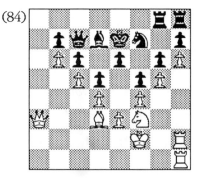

(84)

Black to play.

Setting up one of the unique positions in chess literature. White has a crushing spatial bind and has effectively taken over the whole board. Now that White has succeeded in his plans of spatial conquest, what does he need to do to actually win the game? The first thing he needs is a target. He also needs a way to penetrate into the Black position. The role of target is taken up by the base of Black's pawn chain—the pawn on b7. White's plan is to dominate the open a-file (the means of penetration) and bring a Rook to a7 where it attacks the b7 pawn. Once this is done White must bring more pressure to bear on b7. What other White pieces can do this? If you saw that you could bring the White Knight to a5 (fantasy position: White Rooks on a7 and a1, Knight on a5) then you are doing very well indeed! **26...Qb8** The attempt to grab the a-file by 26...Ra8?? fails to 27.Qxa8!. **27.Ra1 Rc8 28.Qb4 Rhd8 29.Ra7 Kf8 30.Rh1 Be8 31.Rha1 Kg8 32.R1a4 Kf8 33.Qa3** The a-file is obviously White's, but where is the breakthrough? **33...Kg8 34.Kg3** White is well aware that he wants to bring his Knight to a5 and apply pressure to the b7 pawn. Before doing that, however, he wants to place his King on its safest possible square in case of an eventual desperado ...Nxg5 sacrifice (after White moves his Knight). The fact that he takes several moves to do this merely highlights the fact that Black is completely helpless. **34...Bd7 35.Kh4 Kh8 36.Qa1 Kg8 37.Kg3 Kf8 38.Kg2 Be8 39.Nd2** Finally the Knight begins its journey to a5. **39...Bd7 40.Nb3**

Re8 Or 40...Be8 41.Na5 Rd7 42.Nxb7 Rxb7 43.Ra8 winning the
Black Queen. **41.Na5 Nd8** Can Black hold on? No, White has
one more piece that is capable of assaulting b7. **42.Ba6!** White
places everything but his King on the a-file. Now b7 goes and
the game comes to an abrupt end. **42...bxa6 43.Rxd7 Re7**
Quiet moves like 43...Kg8 lose the a-pawn to 44.Nb3 and
45.Rxa6. **44.Rxd8+ Rxd8 45.Nxc6**, 1-0.

In the game we just saw, Capablanca obtained an enormous
advantage in space on the kingside and queenside. Gaining
territory on the wings is wonderful if the center is closed, but if
the middle is not blocked by pawns then central space will
usually be boss.

(85)

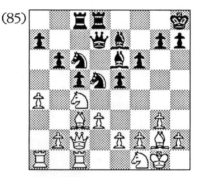

G.Lisitsin-Botvinnik, USSR 1932.
Black to play.

Diagram #85 shows a typical Maroczy Bind situation in which
Black has a comfortable central space advantage. White's problem is compounded by the fact that he has no way to get
counterplay on the wings: a b2-b4 advance just loses material,
and a4-a5 allows ...b6-b5, depriving White's Knight of the fine
post on c4.

White is also unable to generate kingside play because any
pawn advance there would simply weaken the pawn cover
around his own King. For example, f2-f4 weakens the e3
square, aside from simply dropping a pawn to ...exf4; it's clear
that g3-g4 is atrocious, and h2-h4 has no purpose at all.

By now it should be apparent that Black has a clear advantage. Black's plan is to post his Knight on the advanced d4 square. From there it will dominate the board. If White eventually chases it away by e2-e3, Black will have a nice target to attack in the form of a weak pawn on d3. If White captures on d4, then Black will recapture *away* from the center via ...exd4. This opens up the e-file and allows Black to put pressure on White's pawn on e2. **1...Nd4 2.Qd1 Bg4** Forcing White to capture on d4, since 3.f3 would leave White with many weak points and no active play. **3.Bxd4 exd4 4.Qd2 Bf8** Black now clears the e-file in anticipation of doubling on it. **5.Re1 Re8 6.h4** This weakens the pawn position in front of White's King; but he was already without good moves, since 6.e4 dxe3 e.p. would leave the d3 pawn deathly weak. **6...Bh3 7.Bf3 Re7 8.Nh2 Rce8 9.Kh1 Be6 10.b3 Nb4** Black hopes to play ...Bd5 and trade off White's important defensive Bishop. Note that 10...Nc3? would have been an error due to 11.e4!. **11.Bg2 Bd5 12.Nf3 Rf7** Intending to bring his dark squared Bishop into active play. **13.Kh2 Bd6 14.Bh3 Qd8 15.Rab1 Rfe7 16.Ng1** The poor 16.Nxd6? would trade off White's most active piece for Black's bad Bishop. **16...Bc7 17.Na3 Bb7!** With a bind in the center, Black turns his attention to the kingside (the threat is ...Qd5). This is the beauty of a space advantage in the middle: centrally placed pieces can strike out at the wings as they sit smugly on their central posts. **18.Bg2 Bxg2 19.Kxg2 Nd5 20.Nc2** Hoping to play b3-b4 with some counterplay. **20...Qd6!** Black intends to throw his Knight onto the strong but seemingly defended e3 square. Why? Because he sees that its capture would lead to a mate after ...Qxg3. This would not be possible if White's pawn still stood on h2, since the pawn on g3 would then be more solidly defended. **21.Na3** 21.b4 would have run into the same reply. **21...Ne3+! 22.Kh1 Ng4 23.Qf4** An admission of defeat, but 23.Rf1 Qd5+ 24.f3 Bxg3 or 23.Kg2 Nxf2! 24.Kxf2 Qxg3+ 25.Kf1 Re3 26.Nf3 Qh3+ 27.Kg1 Bh2+ are both hopeless possibilities for White. **23...Qxf4 24.gxf4 Nxf2+ 25.Kg2 Nxd3**, 0-1.

Now that we have seen what a space advantage can do we must address the question of how and when one creates such a state of affairs. A territorial edge usually comes about from the opening, but this tends to be minor and can be challenged if one plays actively and makes sure that some sort of counterplay exists. However, if a player does not repond in a proper manner, then the 'tiny' space disadvantage can come back to haunt him.

Tarrasch-Schlechter, Leipzig 1894. **1.e4 e5 2.Nf3 Nc6 3.Bb5 d6** This system was very popular in the late 1800's and early 1900's. Black ends up with a somewhat cramped but solid position. **4.d4 Bd7 5.Nc3 Nf6 6.0-0 Be7 7.Re1 Nxd4** Black follows one of the most important rules relating to cramped positions: *When you have less space, exchange some pieces.* This will give you more room and make the cramp less critical. Naturally, the other side of the coin is this: *If you have more territory, trade as few pieces as possible!* **8.Nxd4 exd4 9.Bxd7+ Qxd7?!** The cause of future problems. In later years it was realized that 9...Nxd7 was stronger. In that case Black's pieces would find good squares: his Knight can go to c5 or e5, his Bishop will be moved to f6 or to f8 and eventually g7, and his Rooks will find play on the e-file with pressure against White's e4 pawn. **10.Qxd4 0-0 11.b3** Avoiding Bg5 because White sees that at some time this could lead to more exchanges when the f6 Knight moves. As stated in the note to Black's seventh move, White wants to avoid exchanges because he is the one with more space. **11...Rfe8 12.Bb2 Bf8 13.Rad1 Qc6 14.Rd3 Re6 15.Rde3 Rae8 16.h3!** A good move. White takes away the g4 square from Black's Knight and prepares a later g2-g4 advance. **16...Qb6 17.Qd3** Still refusing to trade! **17...c6** Threatening to liberate himself by ...d5. **18.Na4 Qc7 19.c4!**

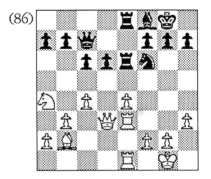

(86)

White's plan, based on his advantage in space, is the following:

1) Make his one attackable point (the pawn on e4) invulnerable.

2) Prevent any pawn breaks by Black that would free his pieces or give him any kind of counterplay.

3) Once all of Black's pieces have been relegated to passive posts, White will use his greater mobility by starting an attack against Black's King.

White's last move (19.c4) follows point two—he prevents Black from playing the freeing ...d6-d5 advance. **19...Nd7 20.Kh1** White sees that at some time Black will threaten to gain some space by ...f7-f5, so he prepares to discourage this by g2-g4 and Rg1. By taking away all of Black's active options, White knows that Black will eventually choke to death in the folds of his own constricted position. **20...f6 21.Qc2?!** Moving his Queen away from danger in view of the upcoming ...Nc5 or ...Ne5. However, it turns out that 21.Qb1! was more accurate. The unprotected state of the Queen on c2 allows Black his longed for chance of a ...d6-d5 break. See the note to Black's twenty-third move for a demonstration of this. **21...Ne5 22.Nc3** White's Knight is no longer doing anything on a4 so he moves it to a better location. It is now heading for the fine f5 post via e2 and g3 (or d4). **22...Nf7** This stops 23.Ne2 due to 23...f5!. **23.g4?** A good idea since it kills Black's ...f6-f5 advance. However 23.Qb1!

should have been played first, with g2-g4 following after that. **23...Qa5?** Missing his big chance! He should fight to break his chains by 23...d5! when 24.cxd5 cxd5 25.Nxd5 loses to 25...Qxc2. If the Queen had stood on b1 (see note to White's twenty first move) then Black's ...d5 advance would never have been possible. After 23...d5 24.exd5 Rxe3 25.Rxe3 Rxe3 26.fxe3 Qg3 Black's pieces would jump to life.

This shows that a space advantage is like having an enemy under control. While he is bound and gagged everything is fine. However, if you relax your attention for just a moment he may find a way to escape his bonds and jump all over you! **24.Rd1 Qb6 25.h4 Ne5 26.Rg3 Nf7 27.f3** Now the e-pawn is well defended and all of Black's pawn breaks have been permanently stopped. White has only to play Ne2-d4-f5 before starting his final assault. **27...Nh8 28.Ne2 Qc7** Black would find his Queen is in over her head after 28...Qf2?? 29.Bd4. **29.Rdg1** Not 29.Nd4 at once due to 29...d5!, taking advantage of the hanging Rook on g3. **29...Qf7 30.Nd4 R6e7 31.g5 fxg5 32.Rxg5 g6 33.Nf5** All of a sudden White's Rooks, Knight, and Bishop are all jumping on the Black King! Aside from the mundane 34.Nxe7+, White also threatens 34.Qc3. once again we see how an advantage in central space translates to an eventual attack on one of the wings. **33...Re5** Desperately trying to block the a1-h8 diagonal. **34.f4!** White is without mercy. He will answer 34...Rxe4 with 35.Qc3. **34...Rxf5 35.exf5 Bg7 36.fxg6**, 1-0.

THE DARK SIDE OF SPACE

An advantage in space has been shown to be a nice thing to have because it gives its owner greater room for maneuvering while simultaneously restricting the opponent. However, it can also be a double-edged sword. Since a space advantage is created by far advanced pawns, you can easily lose control of critical squares as the pawns advance. *The further a pawn advances the less squares it can potentially control.* This means that at times these forgotten squares can fall ito the hands of the enemy, and instead of being an advantage the space edge becomes a curse. It should also be noted that the advanced pawns themselves can often become targets, as can the ones in back since they no longer have support from the front runners.

(87)
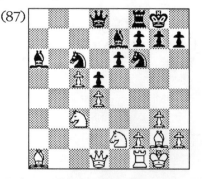

E.Osbun-Silman, San Francisco 1981.
Black to play.

In diagram #87 the advanced pawn on c5 gives White a clear

queenside space advantage. However, this same advanced pawn has lost potential control of the b3, b4, and b5 squares and it can no longer give support to the pawn on d4 (as it would if it stood on c3). Also, the absence of a b-pawn and the fact that White's d-pawn stands on d4 leaves the c4 square unguardable.

To sum up: White has various weakened squares on the b-file, a weakened c4 square, and a d-pawn that can no longer be supported by other pawns. As for the minor pieces, White has two Knights that are going nowhere, a terrible Bishop on a1, and a 'good' Bishop on g2 that is completely inactive.

Black, on the other hand, has a tight, very safe, pawn formation, a Bishop on a6 that slices across the board, and Knights that aim at such useful squares as b4, d4, and e4.

After a few moves it will be apparent that Black is making use of the weak squares on the queenside. Why is White unable to play on that side of the board himself? The answer lies in the realm of target conciousness: *Black has a target to attack on d4 while White has nothing to attack at all.* As is so common, the person with the weakness or target (White) is off balance and forced onto the defensive. **1...Qa5** Making way for the Rook and taking control of the a-file. **2.Re1 Rb8 3.Bf3** Preparing Qa4 which fails right away to 3.Qa4?? Qxa4 4.Nxa4 Bxe2 5.Rxe2 Rb1+, etc. **3...Bc4** Black's active pieces, control of queenside squares, pressure on d4, and more compact pawn structure combine to give him a clear advantage. **4.Qa4 Qxa4 5.Nxa4 Nd7** Keeping White out of b6 and intending to intensify the pressure on d4 by ...Bf6. **6.Bc3 Bf6 7.Rd1 Bb3** Winning material. **8.Ra1 Ra8 9.Nb6 Rxa1+ 10.Bxa1 Nxc5 11.Bc3 Na4 12.Nxa4 Bxa4**, 0-1, since Black will also win the d-pawn after ...Bb5.

When we read Nimzovich's comments about a pawn's "lust to expand," we might find it difficult to see how the advance of a pawn could contribute towards a player's downfall. The following example must be understood if you are to gain an appreciation of this concept.

(88)
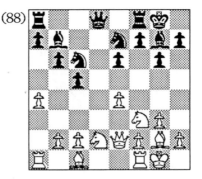

White's pawn on c2 may not seem important to some players but it is actually the one of the most important pawns White has! From c2 it potentially controls the squares from b3 to b8 and d3 to d8. As it advances it starts to lose some of its potential. For example, if it goes to c3 it would lose control of d3 and b3. For this reason a player must be very careful when he advances pawns because they can't move backwards and what they give up is *forever*. In this case the c2 pawn is important because it *will* play to c3 (White is willing to give up d3 and b3 since Black is not in a position to make use of them) and, aside from blocking the diagonal of the g7 Bishop, it keeps Black's pieces out of d4 and b4. However, a beginner might try c2-c4, reasoning that he is making a gain in territory. In reality though, c2-c4 would only accomplish a bunch of negatives. It would take away the useful c4 square from White's Knight and it would permanently give Black use of the b4 and d4 squares. This shows us that you can't just rush your pawns down the board in an effort to gain space. You must carefully weigh each pawn move you make.

Our next example is from Grandmaster play and shows White playing for and gaining a large edge in territory. Unfortunately for him, he did not take into account the weaknesses he was creating and Black was able to enter White's position on these 'soft' spots.

Csom-Korchnoi, Hungary 1965. **1.d4 Nf6 2.c4 g6 3.d5** A highly unusual move at this stage. White makes it clear that he intends to grab all the space he can. The problem with 3.d5 (aside from the loss of time in moving a pawn twice) is that it opens up the h8-a1 diagonal for Black's dark squared Bishop and also allows Black to post pieces on the newly weakened c5 and e5 squares. **3...Bg7 4.Nc3 0-0 5.e4 d6 6.Be2 c6 7.Be3 a6** Intending to gain space on the queenside and chip away at White's pawn chain with ...b7-b5. **8.a4** White prevents Black's advance and takes over some territory on the queenside himself. The trouble is that White has left a hole on b4. **8...a5** Grabbing b4 and also preventing a later b2-b4 advance. By doing this Black has also permanently annexed the c5 post. White may be wishing that his a-pawn could go back to a3! **9.g4** White's next few moves start to take over kingside territory as well. **9...Na6!** Eyeing b4 and c5. **10.f4 Nd7** Unleashing the g7 Bishop and pointing another eye to c5. **11.h4**

(89)

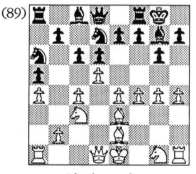

Black to play.

To the non-master, things probably look very good for White. He has more space in the center and he seems to be overrunning Black on the kingside. However, this is not really the case. Black's next few moves show that White's pawns on b2, e4, c4, and g4 are all in need of a defender or two. Aside from this, the c5, b4, and b3 squares are about to fall into the hands of the enemy. This was made possible by the indiscriminate advance of the White pawns. **11...Ndc5!** Threatening 12...Bxc3+ followed by 13...Nxe4. **12.Bf3 Qb6!** Intending to eat the b2 pawn. Now 13.Rh2 is answered by ...Qb4! with a double attack on c3 and c4. **13.Qe2** A disguised trap. He is hoping that Black will take on b2 and fall for his trick. **13...Qxb2!!** Black promptly 'falls.' At this point White got very excited. He was sure that Black had overlooked something! **14.Qxb2 Nd3+ 15.Kd2 Nxb2 16.Be2** It appears that Black's Knight on b2 is stranded. According to Flesch, Csom left his seat and was congratulated by the spectators. However, a surprise awaited him when he returned to the board. **16...Bxg4!**. On seeing that 17.Bxg4 is met by 17...Nxc4+ 18.Kd3 Nxe3, White resigned. 0-1. A tragic end. He built a nice big house (filled with lots of space) and it all fell on his head!

It can be seen that control of squares (which give one's pieces nice homes which, in turn, leads to enhanced activity) is just as important (if not more so) as an edge in space. Of course, in general superior space *does* constitute an advantage. I mention the disadvantages because I want the student to remember that nearly every rule or formula has exceptions, and all must be judged in relation to the other imbalances and according to each individual situation. Saying that any one imbalance will give you an advantage to the exclusion of every other consideration is, to say the least, naive. Dogma and blind faith in rules will stunt the growth of any player—be it in chess or in other areas of life.

BLOCK BEFORE YOU PUNCH!

We have seen that a space advantage can be very effective if you can prevent the opponent from making use of any weakened squares or other avenues of counterplay. It's very important to spend a few moves and stop him from getting anything started—when you finish killing his play your advantage in territory will still be there. Once your opponent's options have been silenced and his army is groveling before you, then and only then should you look for a way to break down his last defences and penetrate into the heart of his position.

(90)
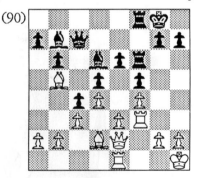

Kupchik-Capablanca, Lake Hopatcong 1926.
Black to play.

Diagram #90 shows a mutual wing attack situation. The center is completely locked. Black has a sizeable space advantage on the queenside and will advance his pawns there—there is nothing White can do to stop this. White, for want of anything better, should play for a g2-g4 advance and a subsequent kingside attack. It seems that 1...a6 would be the logical move for Black. However, Capablanca comes up with another idea. Since space is about equal on the kingside, he will play on that side of the board first in order to prevent White from gaining any chances there. Only when he has killed White's kingside hopes will he steamroll on the queenside. **1...h5! 2.Ref1 Rh6!** A successful g2-g4 advance for White is now a long way off. **3.Be1 g6 4.Bh4 Kf7! 5.Qe1 a6** Though White has followed the basic rules and gotten his bad Bishop outside the pawn chain, he is unable to generate open lines on the kingside. Now Black starts his queenside offensive and White will discover that he has no adequate counter to this plan. **6.Ba4 b5 7.Bd1 Bc6 8.Rh3 a5 9.Bg5 Rhh8 10.Qh4** An impressive display that accomplishes nothing. *In closed positions with locked centers you must attempt to get open lines on the wings by breaking with pawns.* If your opponent accomplishes this before you do, you will usually be at a marked disadvantage. **10...b4 11.Qe1** White suddenly realizes that his 'attack' on the kingside is dead in the water, and so he rushes back for defense. **11...Rb8 12.Rhf3 a4 13.R3f2 a3** Blasting open the queenside. **14.b3** Black would dominate the open b-file after 14.bxa3 bxa3. **14...cxb3 15.Bxb3 Bb5 16.Rg1 Qxc3** With all the play and an extra pawn, Black won without difficulty.

Capablanca has just showed that when you have a permanent advantage in one sector, you should not just allow the opponent to get counterplay in other areas of the board. We are not after a race! We want a risk free victory! Some people have the mistaken impression that if they control one area of the board the opponent has a right to another area. Why? If you can take over the queenside, center, and kingside then you should do so. Greed pays in chess—you can be nice *after* the game.

Our next example is a rarity: White makes spatial gains in every sector and, after stopping all his opponent's attempts at counterplay, blows Black off the map.

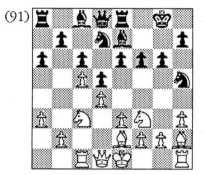

(91)

Silman-Barkan, US Open 1981.
White to play.

The idea of taking the initiative in an area of the board where the opponent is making threatening gestures is a useful one. In the position from diagram #91 White has an obvious space advantage on the queenside, and the usual plan is queenside expansion by b4, a4, and b4-b5. However, Black has his plans also. He intends to gain space in the center by ...e6-e5, which could easily lead to a kingside attack if Black is allowed to push on to e4 followed by ...f6-f5. So, if White plays a natural move like 1.0-0, Black will create messy complications by 1...e5 (since 2.dxe5 would leave the c-pawn undefended). With this in mind White takes the initiative in the center himself, thus depriving Black of his dreams of central activity. **1.e4!** Now 1...dxe4 2.Nxe4 is very good for White, since the d6 square is a nice home for White's e4 Knight and h2 Bishop. **1...Bf8 2.0-0 Bh6 3.Rc2 Kh8 4.Re1 Nf4 5.Bf1 Rg8 6.b4** With the center under control, White resumes his queenside expansion. **6...Nf8 7.a4 g5** Black can no longer just move to and fro waiting for his execution, so he goes on a desperate bid for kingside play. This is a sensible decision—White owns the queenside and center, so Black tries to lay claim to the only area still not in his opponent's possession. **8.Bxf4 gxf4 9.Nh2!** An extremely greedy idea! Already in charge of the queenside and the center, White decides to attack Black's King also! If he can get away with this, then Black will be totally without counterplay. White's justification is his central control (which allows his forces to rush to any side of the board with great speed), and his lead in development. **9...Ng6** An attempt to prevent Qh5 by 9...Qe8 fails to 10.exd5 cxd5 11.Nxd5, etc. **10.Qh5 Bf8 11.exd5 cxd5** Now White has a permanent endgame advantage due to his beautiful queenside pawn majority. However, at this point White has bigger gains in mind. **12.Bd3 f5 13.Nf3** White's forces flow very quickly to the center and kingside. **13...Be7 14.Rce2 Bf6 15.Rxe6!** Completely decisive. The f5 pawn will also fall now, and White's Bishop will come strongly into play. This type of thing cannot really be considered a sacrifice since White will get at least two pawns for the Exchange. Material will actually be equal, while Black's other weak pawns, shaky King, and inactive pieces will decide the game in White's favor. **15...Bxe6 16.Rxe6 Be7 17.Bxf5** Threatening to simply capture a free piece on g6. **17...Nf8 18.Ne5!** All of White's pieces now join in the romp. 19.Nf7+ is the immediate threat. **18...Qe8 19.Nf7+ Kg7 20.Nxd5!** A true joint effort—all the pieces work towards the extinction of the Black King. **20...Nxe6** The Queen would be lost after 20...Qxf7 21.Rxe7. **21.Qh6+ Kxf7 22.Bxe6** mate.

We finish our discussion about space with a game that warns us not to forget about targets. If you have space on one side but it doesn't come with any attackable target then you will eventually run into a brick wall.

(92)
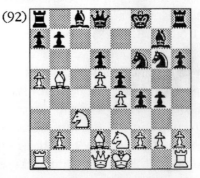

Silman-C.Lakdawala, Los Angeles 1989.
White to play.

A glance at diagram #92 suggests that the chances are evenly balanced. After all, both sides have a lot of space on their respective sides. The truth, though, is that White enjoys a significant edge. White reasons that his queenside chances are not going away and if he can stop Black from getting too far on the kingside he will be able to eventually take over the game. Since Black threatens to play ...Nh4, White takes time out to contain the Black pieces on that side of the board. **1.g3! f3 2.Nc1** Now Black's c8 Bishop and his f6 Knight are blocked by the pawn on g4, while his Knight on g6 can't go to either f4 or h4 due to the pawn on g3. Black is already reaching a dead end, so he quickly plays to open the h-file. **2...h5 3.Qa4 h4 4.Rf1 hxg3 5.hxg3 Bh6** So far, Black has played quite logically. He controls the open h-file and now gets to trade off his bad Bishop for White's good one. The problem with Black's game is that he only has one real target—the pawn on f2, and that little pawn is amply guarded by White's Rook on f1. All right, the student may say, but what's so special about White's game? What does he have?

Aside from his obvious advantage in queenside space, White will also be able to put pressure on Black's d6 pawn via Qb4 and a later Nb5. If Black ever plays ...a7-a6, then his b6 square becomes weak and can easily be invaded by Na4-b6. Black must also watch out for a White advance based on a5-a6, when the reply ...b7-b6 allows Bc6 followed by Nb5 with pressure on both d6 and a7. White's final idea is quite simple: if given time, he will play a Rook to the open c-file and penetrate into Black's position.

We can now see that Black's play is: 1) centered around his control of a useless file far away from the action on the queenside and in the center, and 2) pressure against a pawn that is easily defended. White, on the other hand, has many long term ideas and several potential points of attack. **6.Nb3 Rb8 7.Qb4!** An excellent move. Now Black can't play a piece to d7 because d6 will hang. Note that 7...a6 now fails to 8.Bxa6. **7...Kg7 8.Bxh6+ Rxh6 9.Nd2 Nh8 10.Nc4 Nf7 11.Ne3** A great square for this Knight. Black must always worry about the

Knight crashing through to f5. **11....Qh8 12.0-0-0 Rh2 13.Kb1** Seeing what Black has in mind, White gets his King off the c1-h6 diagonal. If given a chance, White intends to play Rc1 with penetration down the c-file. **13...Qh6** Threatening to sacrifice the Exchange with 14...Rxf2! 15.Rxf2 Qxe3 with strong play. Naturally, White stops this idea dead in its tracks. **14.Rde1! Nh7 15.Qc4!** This wins by force. The threat is 16.Qc7 Ra8 17.a6 bxa6 18.Bc6 winning material. **15...a6 16.Qc7 Ra8 17.Bd7!** Winning the battle for the f5 square. **17...Bxd7 18.Qxd7 Nf6 19.Qxb7 Qh8 20.Nf5+ Kg6 21.Nh4+ Kg7 22.Nf5+** White was a little low on time, so he repeats moves to get that much closer to the time control. This is a useful thing to do, but you must be careful not to allow a three time repetition! **22...Kg6 23.Nh4+ Kg7 24.Rh1!** Very strong. White takes away the h-file from Black and gets rid of the opponent's active piece on h2. **24...Rxh1 25.Rxh1 Qd8 26.Nf5+ Kg6 27.Rh6+!** , 1-0. If 27...Nxh6 28.Qg7+ Kh5 29.Qxh6 mate.

Solve These Problems

(93)
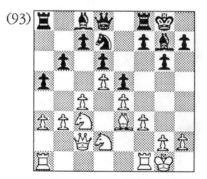

White to play.

White can gain space on the queenside with 1.b2-b4 or he can gain space on the kingside with 1.f3-f4. Which idea is best?

(94)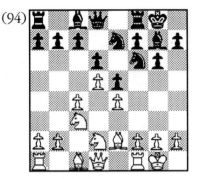

Black to move.

Though Black's pawns are pointing towards the kingside (in positions with closed centers you should usually play in the direction your pawns point), he chooses to play on the opposite wing with **1...c5**. Is this wise?

PART SIX

THE MYSTERY
OF THE CENTER

In the 1800's and early 1900's most players felt that a large pawn center bestowed an instant advantage on its owner. This view dominated the chess scene until upstart hypermoderns like Reti and Nimzovich claimed that a pawn center could be viewed as an object of attack also.

Nowadays we know that owning an imposing pawn center is both a boon *and* a responsibility. The positive side of the pawn center is that it restricts the enemy pieces and gives its owner a spatial plus. However, like any artificially built edifice, it may easily turn into a liability which will be in need of constant defense.

The first responsibility of the owner of a big center is to make it indestructible. If this can be done, then the opponent will be without play and will smother to death in the folds of his own position.

Conversely, *the responsibility of the player facing the pawn center is to apply constant pressure to it, and try to prove it to be a weakness instead of a strength.*

THE CENTER UNDER SIEGE

Creating a full pawn center is an act of war! Once you push your pawns to the middle and start to annex space, you are announcing your intention of entombing your opponent in its prison-like walls. This threat of death by asphyxiation forces the opponent to fight and destroy this central monolith before it becomes too strong. He *must* throw everything he has at the offending line of pawns before it destroys him. A typical example of the center's birth in the opening and the concentrated effort the other side makes to dismantle it can be seen in the following popular variation of the French Defense: **1.e4 e6 2.d4 d5 3.Nd2 Nf6 4.e5 Nfd7 5.f4** White establishes a space advantage on the kingside and gives extra support to his pawn on e5. He hopes to make his center so strong that Black will be unable to threaten it. Then White will be able to attack Black on the kingside at his leisure. **5...c5** Losing no time in starting countermeasures against White's center. **6.c3 Nc6** All of Black's moves will now revolve around White's center and the pressure that Black hopes to build against it. **7.Ndf3!** In turn White realizes that he has built a large center (at a certain cost in time) and he must do everything he can to protect his investment. The more natural 7.Ngf3 fails to bring as many defenders to d4. Now (after 7.Ndf3) White's Queen eyes d4 and the other Knight can go to e2 where it will also hold onto d4. **7...Qb6** Continuing to strike at the White central pawns. **8.Ne2 f6**

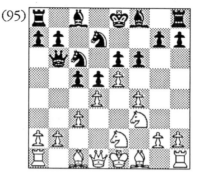

(95)

The battle is already in full swing and Black will not stop attacking d4 and e5 until something cracks. The further course of the game shows that the intensity of a central war tends to grow rather than lessen. **9.g3 cxd4 10.cxd4 Bb4+ 11.Nc3 0-0** White still has his advantage in space but all the pawn moves have allowed Black to take a lead in development. Since White's King is still in the middle, Black will do his best to knock White's center aside in an attempt to reach the enemy monarch. **12.a3 Be7 13.Na4 Qc7 14.Be3** Black gets a strong attack after 14.Bh3 fxe5! 15.Bxe6+ Kh8 16.dxe5 Ndxe5 17.Bxd5 Nxf3+ 18.Bxf3 Bh3. This is not surprising—White's greed (via 14.Bh3 and 15.Bxe6+) has helped Black to rip the White center open and break through the middle. **14...g5!?** Black is willing to do anything to push White's center pawns aside! **15.exf6 Nxf6 16.Nxg5 e5!!**

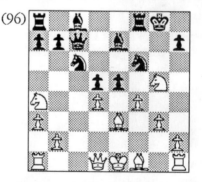

(96)

White's center finally gets ripped apart and Black's pieces get the chance to try and chase down the White King. **17.Qc2?!** Worse is 17.fxe5? Ng4, but 17.dxe5! Ng4 18.Bc5 still leaves the burden of proof on Black. So far we have been following Shamkovich-Brown, London 1981, now Black should have played **17...exf4 18.Bxf4 Qa5+ 19.b4 Nxb4 20.axb4 Bxb4+** with tremendous complications in which Black's attack gives him compensation for the sacrificed piece.

Our next game explores a similar theme: White is allowed to litter the center with pawns and Black does his best to sweep them away.

Scheichel-Adorjan, Hungary 1981. **1.d4 Nf6 2.c4 g6 3.Nc3 d5 4.cxd5 Nxd5 5.e4 Nxc3 6.bxc3** White already has a huge center. Black must start immediate operations against it or risk being squashed. **6...Bg7 7.Bc4 0-0 8.Ne2 c5 9.0-0 Nc6 10.Be3 Qc7 11.Rc1 Rd8**

(97)

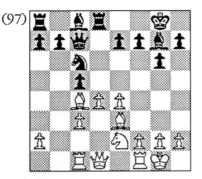

The ideas being used by both sides are easy to follow: White is doing his utmost to uphold the integrity of his center. Black has assigned an armada of pieces to attack White's d4 pawn. **12.h3** White wants to take even more of the middle with f2-f4 but he is worried about ...Bg4 when one of White's d4 defenders would be chopped off. 12.h3 ends this possibility. Another way of defending the center is by 12.Qd2 followed by 13.Rfd1 when White's entire army is backing up his pawns. How can Black hope to destroy the White center in this case? Haik-Kouatly, Cannes 1986 shows us a useful strategy; instead of destroying the center he forces it to advance. This leaves weak squares in its wake: 12...a6 (after 12.Qd2) 13.f4 b5 14.Bd3 f5!

15.exf5 (15.e5 leads to the same type of light square domination for Black) 15...c4! 16.Bb1 gxf5 17.Ng3 e6 18.Nh5 Bh8 19.Rf3 Ne7 20.Bf2 Bb7

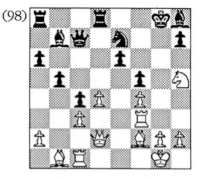

(98)

Black has won the central battle without destroying the White center! How is this possible? By getting rid of the e4 pawn (forcing the pawn to e5 would have created the same situation) Black created a terrible weakness on d5 and along the a8-h1 diagonal. This shows us that there are two ways to defeat a center: 1) Destroy it; 2) Force it to advance, thereby creating weak squares that can be occupied by the opposing forces. Remember—*a center is only good because it restricts the opponents pieces. If it has to advance and give the enemy pieces good squares then its whole purpose has been negated!* After the further 21.Re3 Kf7 22.Rce1 Rd6 23.Bh4 Ng6 24.Bg5 b4! the remains of White's center was falling apart and Black enjoyed a big advantage. **12...b6** Since the Bishop can no longer go to g4, Black places it on b7 where it will pose a threat to White's pawn on e4. **13.f4** White grabs more space and has possibilities of starting a kingside attack with an f4-f5 advance. **13...e6 14.Qe1 Na5 15.Bd3 f5!** Hoping for 16.e5 when 16...c4 17.Bb1 Bb7 gives Black all the squares. **16.g4** White is hoping that his center will hold up long enough for his kingside attack to get some momentum. **16...Bb7**

(99)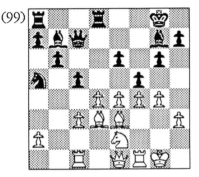

Quite a picture! White's central pawns on d4 and e4 are both under attack by the enemy pieces and pawns. **17.Ng3** Black's pieces get too active after 17.exf5 gxf5 18.gxf5 Re8. **17...Qd7 18.Rd1 cxd4 19.Bb1? Nc4 20.Bxd4 e5!** The central battle reaches its peak. **21.fxe5 fxg4 22.Qe2 Qc7 23.Qxg4 Nxe5** The only things that remain of the once proud White center are two weak pawns on c3 and e4. It is also important to note that all of White's minor pieces are inferior to their Black counterparts. The rest of the game needs no comment: **24.Qg5 h6 25.Qe3 Rf8 26.Kg2 Ba6 27.Rxf8+ Rxf8 28.Bxe5? Qxe5 29.Bc2 Bc4 30.Bb3 Bxb3 31.axb3 Qxc3 32.Qxc3 Bxc3 33.Rd7 Rf7**, 0-1.

THE INDESTRUCTIBLE CENTER

We have seen how a center can fall apart if its owner doesn't take meaures to insure that it remains intact. Lest the impressionable reader think that a full pawn center is nothing to fear, here are two games that show it in a positive light.

M.Botvinnik-M.Yudovich, USSR Championship 1933. **1.c4 Nf6 2.d4 g6 3.Nc3 d5 4.Nf3 Bg7 5.Qb3 c6 6.cxd5 Nxd5 7.Bd2 0-0 8.e4 Nb6 9.Rd1!** White immediately starts to defend his center. This not only means that he will guard each pawn, it also means that he will attempt to prevent Black from attacking the center with the usual breaks (...e7-e5 or ...c6-c5). **9...N8d7** 9...Bxd4 loses material to 10.Bh6. After the more active 9...Bg4 10.Be3 Bxf3 11.gxf3, White's center would be very solid. **10.a4** Threatening to capture more territory with a4-a5. **10...a5** Black stops White's threat but weakens the b6 square. **11.Be3** Black is already in a desperate situation. He is unable to attack White's center with ...c5 or ...e5 because of the unfortunate position of his b6 Knight (11...e5 12.dxe5 uncovers White's e3 Bishop on the b6 Knight). **11...Qc7 12.Be2 Qd6** Black hopes to play 13...Qb4 when the pressure is off his Knight on b6. **13.Na2** Since White has more territory he has no interest in allowing exchanges unless it leads to some particularly favorable situation. Note how White's center restricts all of Black's pieces and leaves him with no active play at all. **13...e6 14.0-0 h6 15.Rc1 f5**

(100)
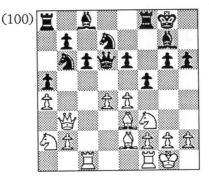

Finally Black gets to kick at the White center a bit! Unfortunately this leaves the g6 and e6 pawns weak. This is a typical metamorphosis—one type of advantage may dissappear but it usually leads to the creation of another. In this case Black will succeed in gaining a square or two but he now must contend with a weakened King position and a weakling on e6. **16.Nc3 Kh7 17.Rfd1 fxe4 18.Nxe4 Qb4** Black goes after White's a4 pawn but forgets that his King is in danger. Better was 18...Qe7, though even then 19.Qc2 Nd5 20.Ng3 leaves the g6 pawn in need of careful defense. **19.Qc2 Qxa4 20.b3 Qa3 21.Nh4** Now g6 crumbles. **21...Qe7 22.Nxg6 Kxg6 23.Bh5+!**, 1-0. Both 23...Kh7 24.Nf6+ and 23...Kxh5 24.Ng3+ lead to mate.

Black died without a fight simply because the White center deprived him of any kind of play. It's amazing how strong an uncontested pawn center can be!

In our final example we see Black mistakenly allow White to build up an imposing center. After this error, though, he starts to attack it with gusto. However, one lazy moment on Black's part ends his counterplay and soon the pawn center rolls over the enemy position.

Leonhardt-Burn, Carlsbad 1911. **1.e4 e5 2.Nf3 Nc6 3.Bc4 Bc5 4.c3 d6?** White threatened to take over the center when he played c2-c3 and Black ignored him. If your opponent wants something good for himself, don't let him have it! More purposeful is 4...Nf6 (counterattacking White's e4 pawn) 5.d4 cxd4 6.cxd4 Bb4+ 7.Bd2 Bxd2+ 8.Nbxd2 d5! 9.exd5 Nxd5 followed by

...c6 and ...0-0 when White's once proud center has been blown to bits. **5.d4 exd4** Gives White a strong, mobile center. However, 5...Bb6 loses a pawn to 6.dxe5 when 6...dxe5 7.Qxd8+ forces Black to abandon either the f-pawn or e-pawn. Even worse is 6...Nxe5 7.Nxe5 dxe5 8.Bxf7+!. **6.cxd4 Bb6 7.Nc3 Nf6 8.0-0 0-0**

(101)

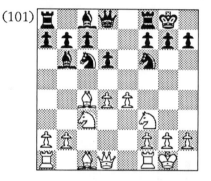

Now that White owns the lion's share of the center, he must see to its preservation. How should he go about this? Should he play the aggressive 9.d5? No, that only weakens the e5 square and blocks the Bishop on c4. How about 9.e5? After 9...dxe5 10.dxe5 Qxd1 Black has succeeded in trading pieces (always desirable for the cramped side) and opening up the diagonal for his b6 Bishop. White's correct plan is to attempt to make his center indestructable—not to push it and create weaknesses!

Is Black able to place any pressure on White's center? Yes, 9...Bg4 is a threat. The logical reaction to this is 9.h3, and this would be an excellent move if Black was not threatening something even worse, namely 9...Nxe4! 10.Nxe4 d5 when White's proud center is gone, and only a weak, isolated d4 pawn remains. It's clear that the threat of 9...Nxe4 is the first that White must address. **9.Bb3!** Stopping ...Nxe4 but allowing the pin. **9...Bg4** Otherwise White would play h3 and deprive Black of all counterplay. **10.Be3 h6?** Black is at the point where he has to find a suitable plan. With 10...h6? he fails dismally! If you have followed our theme you will realize that Black *must* initiate an attack on the White center. The only two attackable points are d4 and e4 so those are the targets. Since the e4 pawn is standing on an open file and is vulnerable to Black's Rooks, it is the main point of attack. With this bit of knowledge we can see that 10...Bxf3 11.gxf3 actually helps White since it makes the e4 pawn rock solid (White can also make use of the open g-file with Kh1 and Rg1). The correct play is 10...Re8! 11.Qd3 (still hoping Black will capture on f3) 11...Bh5! (The real point of ...Bg4 is revealed—the Bishop will play to g6 where it will join the rest of the Black army in an attack on e4) 12.Nd2 Bg6 and White can easily go wrong: 13.a3? d5! and the White center disintegrates. Best is 13.d5! Ne5 14.Qe2 when White still keeps an edge, though he has been forced to play d4-d5 against his will. With 10...h6? Black wastes precious time and allows White to consolidate his center. This results in Black getting no play at all and falling into a hopelessly passive position. **11.Qd3 Re8 12.Nd2 Qe7** Now 12...Bh5 no longer has the desired effect after 13.f4 Bg6 14.f5. **13.Rae1** Note how all of White's moves are devoted to making his center unattackable. **13...Rad8 14.a3 Qf8 15.f4!** Gobbling up even more territory and threatening to trap the g4 Bishop with f5 and h3. **15...Bc8 16.h3** White's center is an indestructible monster that prevents Black from doing anything anywhere. The luxury that such a center provides is that White is now able to play on either wing under cover from his central umbrella. **16...Kh8 17.g4! Ne7 18.Kh1 d5 19.e5 Nh7 20.f5 f6 21.e6** White owns the center and kingside so he soon will turn his attention to the queenside. He reasons that if he can also control that zone he will rule the world! **21...c6 22.Bf4 Ng8 23.Na4** Threatening to win a pawn by 24.Nxb6 axb6 25.Bc7. **23...Ba5 24.Bc2 Qe7 25.Qg3 b5 26.Nc5 Bb6 27.b4 Nf8 28.a4 a5** He didn't like 28...bxa4 29.Bxa4 and 28...a6 29.a5 Ba7 (or 29...Bxc5 30.dxc5 followed by Bd6) 30.Bc7 is also an unhappy affair. **29.Ndb3 bxa4 30.Nxa5 Bxc5 31.Nxc6! Bxd4 32.Nxe7** and White won without difficulty.

Solve This Problem

(102)

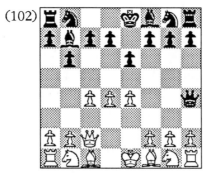

After **1.d4 e6 2.c4 b6 3.e4 Bb7 4.Qc2 Qh4** we reach the position in diagram #102. Is Black a beginner or does he have a method in his madness?

PART SEVEN

WEAK PAWNS— STRONG PAWNS

Most amateur players brought up on a diet of Reinfeld and various 'instructive' manuals know that weak pawns are isolated, backward, or doubled. This often gets drilled into the poor student to such an extent that the mere thought of such pawns will fill him with unholy dread.

While it is true that such pawns *are* often weak, it is also true that sometimes they are not; or that other factors outweigh their potential weakness. This is another case where dogmatism ("doubled pawns are always bad") can easily lead the chess aspirant down the road to folly.

The Smyslov-Botvinnik game from the two Bishops chapter (Part Four, Chapter Four, diagram #71) is an excellent example of doubled and isolated pawns being overshadowed by other factors. However, this is just one of many cases where so called weak pawns rule the day. In this section we will see when a weak pawn is *really* weak and when a suspected weakness is more illusion than reality.

DOUBLED PAWNS

Though despised by most players, the doubled pawn is not all bad, and often it can be an actual advantage. First, a doubled pawn gives its owner an extra open file for his Rooks; second, (if the pawns are central) they allow for coverage of critical squares that would not be possible if the pawns were undoubled and 'healthy'.

(103)

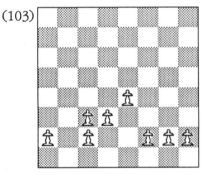

Diagram #103 is a simple example of these things. The doubled pawns give White many interesting possibilities. For example, the open b-file is a result of the doubling. Even more important is their fine central influence. The c3 pawn guards d4 while the c2 pawn gives d3 support. White can also switch into another central position: by playing c4 he gets greater control of d5, and c2-c3 re-establishes control of d4. Normally a c4, d3, e4 pawn formation leaves d4 very weak. Here that is not the case—thanks to the trusty doubled pawns!

(104)

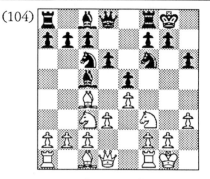

White to play.

Diagram #104 shows a common situation—one which beginners find very puzzling. Both sides have developed their pieces in a solid but unimaginative fashion. Now White plays **1.Be3!** offering Black the chance to double his pawns. Black replies with 1...Bb6, refusing to comply, and instead allows White to double Black's! Have they both gone mad? The answer, of course, is no. It just so happens that their moves are all based on very logical considerations. With 1.Be3 White actually dreams of having his pawns doubled! After 1...Bxe3 2.fxe3 White would have gained a lot: an open f-file plus added control of d4 and f4. In particular, the d4 square was a potential home for Black's pieces. Now it is taboo. With all this in mind, Black retreats by 1...Bb6 and welcomes 2.Bxb6 axb6 since then Black would have use of the a-file while his pawns are all quite sturdy (none of the weakness that one associates with doubled pawns). In fact, it is also possible for Black to simply leave his Bishop on c5: 1...Re8 2.Bxc5 dxc5 after which Black would enjoy play down the newly opened d-file plus greatly increased control over the d4 square.

In the following game Black plays an opening where he actually begs White to give him the added central control and extra open file that only doubled pawns can bestow. Kaplan-Larsen, San Antonio 1972. **1.e4 c6 2.d4 d5 3.Nc3 dxe4 4.Nxe4 Nf6 5.Nxf6+ gxf6**

(105)
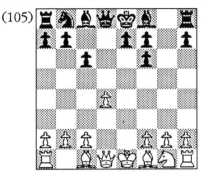

In the Caro-Kann, White usually has control of the useful e5 square—a square that often turns into a juicy home for a White Knight. In this line however, Black's doubled pawn on f6 keeps unwanted visitors out of e5 and also gives Black use of the newly opened g-file. Later in the game this same pawn on f6 may decide to advance to f5 where it gains control of e4. True, Black's pawn on h7 is doubled, but he hopes that the dynamic potential inherent in his pawn structure will more than make up for this minor weakness. **6.Nf3 Bf5** This Bishop steps outside the pawn chain before ...e7-e6 is played. **7.Be2 Qc7 8.0-0 Nd7 9.c4 e6 10.Bd2 Bd6** Since White's pieces have no footholds in the center (thanks to the doubled pawns!), Black decides to make use of his open g-file and play for a kingside attack via ...Rg8 and ...0-0-0. **11.Kh1 Rg8 12.c5?** Chasing the Bishop from its strong diagonal is nice, but giving up the critical d5 square is too high a price to pay. **12...Be7 13.Qc1 Be4 14.Bf4 Qa5 15.Bg3 h5!** All of a sudden the 'weak' h-pawn joins in the fray. **16.Rg1 f5 17.Nd2 h4! 18.Bd6? Bd5 19.Bxe7 h3!** Who would have guessed that the once despised h-pawn was destined for such great things? **20.f3 hxg2+ 21.Rxg2 Rxg2 22.Kxg2 Kxe7** Black understands that he probably won't be able to mate his opponent. However, he has new things to crow about: White's pawn structure is now inferior to Black's—with targets on d4, f3, and h3, Black can look forward to an endgame with confidence. **23.Nc4 Bxc4** White's Knight can't be allowed to jump into d6. **24.Bxc4 Nf6** Adding a superior minor piece to his list of positional advantages. Aside from d5, this Knight has designs on the attractive f4 post. **25.Qf4** Else Black would have played ...Qc7, ...Nh5, and ...Nf4. **25...Rd8 26.a3 b6 27.b4 Qa4 28.Ra2 bxc5 29.dxc5 Qd1** Black allowed White to get rid of his weak d-pawn in exchange for complete domination of the open d-file. It's instructive to see how Black keeps trading his positive imbalances in for other, but no less useful, advantages. **30.Bf1 Rg8+** White's King is not looking very healthy. **31.Kf2 Nd5 32.Qd2** 32.Qd6+ Kf6 leaves Black with a decisive attack. **32...Qb3** Since White's King is so unhappy, Black no longer has any desire to trade Queens. **33.Rb2** Giving up a pawn in a desperate bid for counterplay. **33...Qxa3 34.Ra2 Qxb4** Only now, with material in Black's pocket, will the second player take the heat off the White King and trade into an endgame. **35.Rxa7+ Kf6 36.Qxb4 Nxb4 37.Rb7 Nd5 38.Bc4 Rc8 39.Kg3 f4+** The doubled pawn continues to play a useful role in the game. Now it gives the Knight an excellent post on e3. **40.Kf2 Ne3 41.Bd3 Rh8 42.Rc7 Nd5! 43.Rxc6 Nb4** Forcing a decisive simplification. **44.Rd6 Nxd3+ 45.Rxd3 Rxh2+ 46.Kg1 Rc2 47.Rd4 Rxc5 48.Kf2** Sadly for White, 48.Rxf4+ Rf5 is completely hopeless. **48...Rc2+ 49.Kf1 Kg5 50.Rd8 Kh4 51.Rg8** Black's King cannot be allowed into g3. **51...f5** The f7 pawn played a useful but quiet role throughout this game by defending e6. Now it takes a more active interest in events and prepares to turn the e-pawn into a monster. **52.Rg6 e5 53.Re6 e4 54.fxe4 fxe4 55.Rxe4 Kg3 56.Re8 Rc1+**, 0-1. Funnily enough, the once doubled f-pawn will soon turn into a Queen.

Larsen put it well when he said, "In this variation, many endings are won with the aid of the seemingly humble [doubled] center pawns."

In our next example we see a case of ugly doubled and isolated pawns taking back seat to more important considerations.

Fischer-Euwe, Leipzig Olympiad 1960. **1.e4 c6 2.d4 d5 3.exd5 cxd5 4.c4 Nf6 5.Nc3 Nc6 6.Nf3 Bg4 7.cxd5 Nxd5 8.Qb3!** White doesn't mind that Black will give him doubled-isolated pawns on f2 and f3. He expects to get a lead in development that will more than compensate for this structural flaw (a common case of Black's favorable imbalance—pawn structure—battling White's—initiative based on development). Never allow yourself to believe that any one imbalance will always beat out another—they are all of equal value and only take on special significance in relation to other factors in the position. **8...Bxf3 9.gxf3 e6 10.Qxb7 Nxd4 11.Bb5+ Nxb5 12.Qc6+ Ke7 13.Qxb5 Nxc3?!** An error that allows White's lead in development to take on menacing proportions. Today it is known that 13...Qd7! 14.Nxd5+ Qxd5 15.Qxd5 exd5 leads to an endgame where Black's isolated d-pawn is weaker than White's doubled pawns simply because the d-pawn is situated on an open file (*a pawn is only weak if the enemy forces can get to it*). However, White's advantage is so slight in this endgame that a draw is the usual result. **14.bxc3 Qd7 15.Rb1!**

(106)
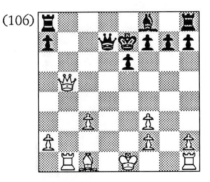

Fischer's comment on this move: "Upon looking deeper I found that, horrible as White's pawn structure may be, Black can't exploit it because he'll be unable to develop his kingside normally." **15...Rd8?** Better was 15...Qxb5 16.Rxb5 Kd6! though Fischer points out that White would still retain a clear advantage after 17.Rb7 f6 18.Ke2 Kc6 19.Rf7 a5 20.Be3. **16.Be3 Qxb5 17.Rxb5 Rd7 18.Ke2** White feels that he can win the Black a-pawn any time he wants to, so he first hurries to get his remaining Rook into the game. **18...f6 19.Rd1!** Getting rid of Black's only active piece. **19...Rxd1 20.Kxd1 Kd7 21.Rb8!**

Black's pieces would gain some measure of freedom after 21.Bxa7 Bd6 22.Rb7+ Kc6 23.Rxg7 Bxh2. **21...Kc6** Stopping the threatened Bc5. **22.Bxa7 g5 23.a4 Bg7 24.Rb6+ Kd5 25.Rb7** and White went on to win the ending.

It may appear that doubled-isolated pawns are never useful and may at best be offset by some other advantage (as in the Fischer-Ewue game). However, this is by no means the case. The following game presents a sound argument against this opinion. Hammie-Silman, San Francisco 1975. **1.e4 c5 2.Nf3 Nc6 3.d4 cxd4 4.Nxd4 g6 5.Nc3 Bg7 6.Be3 Nf6 7.Bc4 Qa5 8.0-0 0-0 9.Nb3 Qc7 10.f4 d6 11.Be2 b6 12.Bf3 Bb7 13.Rf2.** We seem to be in the middle of a typical Sicilian Defense—the amateur may think that Black is supposed to play on the queenside with ...b6-b5, while White will try for a kingside attack with g2-g4. However, Black upsets the apple cart with an insane looking move. **13...Na5!!**.

(107)

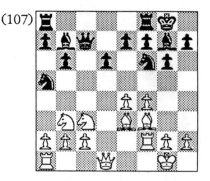

This offers to accept doubled-isolated Rook pawns! Naturally, White couldn't resist the temptation to chop on a5; stopping Black from jumping into c4 and simultaneously destroying his opponent's pawn structure. **14.Nxa5 bxa5 15.Bd4 Nd7 16.Nd5 Bxd5** Playing for a superior Knight versus a bad Bishop. **17.exd5 Bxd4 18.Qxd4 Qc5** Believe it or not, even though Black has those horrible looking a-pawns he realizes that his advantage will increase if he can trade the Queens. Why? Black allowed his pawns to be doubled in the first place because he saw that he would be able to use the open c-file and b-file to pressure White's pawns on c2 and b2. Since the presence of the Queens gives White some chance for kingside counterplay, Black welcomes their exchange. This leaves White with only one point of attack—the pawn on e7—but Black can easily defend it with a Rook on b7 and a King on f8. **19.Rd1 Rab8 20.c3 Rb7!** This prepares to defend e7 with the Rook and also to double on the b-file. Black enjoys an active position.

At this point I can hear the sharp reader say that though the doubled pawns did indeed give Black play on the b-file, they themselves are not serving any dynamic role in the game. This assumption is shown to be false when we look at diagram #108.

(108)
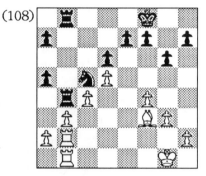

Black to move.

This is the type of position that could have arisen from our previous game. With White's Bishop looking useless and the e7 pawn solidly defended, Black is ready to play for a decisive break-through. He can only do this with the help of his dynamic a-pawns: **1...a4!** Now we see that the a-pawns are being used as battering rams. Black knows that if he can destroy the base of the pawn chain on b3, then c4 will be deprived of protection and die. **2.Bd1 a3!** Usually Black plays 2...axb3 followed by ...a7-a5-a4. However, he sees another idea in the position. **3.Rc2** Not 3.Re2 Rxc4 and the pin on the b-file leads to the win of a pawn. **3...a5** Here comes the other one! **4.Rc3 a4** when after 5...axb3 the doubled pawn has been transformed into a powerful passed pawn on a3.

We have seen that doubled pawns defy any absolute label of good or bad; however, sometimes their lack of flexibility can turn potentially useful doubled pawns into weak targets.

After **1.d4 Nf6 2.c4 e6 3.Nc3 Bb4 4.a3 Bxc3+ 5.bxc3 0-0 6.f3** we have a situation where White's doubled pawns give him a strong center and more space. Fortunately for Black, he can develop his pieces in such a way as to make the doubled pawn on c4 the object of a 'search and destroy' mission. **6...b6!** If Black just developed by 6...d6 7.e4 Nbd7, the White center would be unassailable after 8.Bd3. Instead, Black wisely takes note of the potential target on c4 and does everything he can to attack it. **7.e4 Ne8** Black can defend his kingside with ...f7-f5 and this Knight can also go after c4 with ...Nd6. **8.Bd3 Ba6 9.Ne2 Nc6!** followed by ...Na5 with strong pressure against c4.

This last example shows us that if your opponent has doubled pawns, you must strive to take advantage of their inherent weaknesses. If you fail to do this then your opponent may make use of the dynamic possibilities that they provide; the position will then turn against you.

(109)

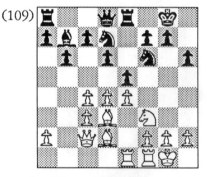

Janowsky-Nimzovich, St.Petersburg 1914.
Black to play.

The type of position in diagram #109 can easily favor White. After all, he has more space, a strong pawn center, and his pieces are fully mobilized. On top of that, his potential weakness on c4 is completely safe since Black's pieces are unable to get to it. Seeing that White would cement his advantage if he succeeds in moving his Knight and playing f2-f4, Black begins a plan to control the f4 square himself and stop White from expanding on the kingside. **1...Nh7!** A deep move that prevents Nh4 and prepares to bring the Knight to e6 where it will eye both f4 and d4. **2.h3** Still hoping to play Nh2 and f2-f4. It should be noted that White has no intention of every playing d4-d5 since that would give Black use of the c5 square and allow Black to open the c-file by ...c7-c6. In general, White will only play d4-d5 if Black plays ...c7-c5 first. Then the c5 square will be blocked by a Black pawn and ...c7-c6 will no longer be possible. **2...Nhf8 3.Nh2 Ne6!** The point of Black's play. The White Knight had to move to make f2-f4 possible, but this took the Knight away from the center and weakened d4. **4.Be3** The space gaining f2-f4 advance is still threatened. **4...c5! 5.d5 Nf4!** Black forced White to push his pawn to d5 since now 6.Bxf4 exf4 gives Black use of the e5 square. **6.Be2 Nf8** and Black has effectively stopped White from gaining ground on the kingside. The closed position makes the Knights more valuable than the Bishops.

How did White's doubled pawns influence the play in the Janowsky-Nimzovich game? Were they a negative factor or was White simply outplayed? While White *was* clearly outclassed, the doubled pawns also played a part in the direction the game followed. The reasoning for this goes as follows: If White's pawn on c4 stood on b2 (as it would in non-doubled pawn positions), White would have the option of playing on the queenside by d5, c4, b4, and c5. However, the fact that the c-pawns were doubled meant that White was not able to play anywhere but the kingside (the center was for all intents and purposes locked—any advance by d4-d5 would only help Black). In other words, the inflexibility of the doubled pawns left White with fewer options than normal. In view of this, Black came up with a plan that stopped White's kingside play and, as a result; left White with nothing to do anywhere.

(110)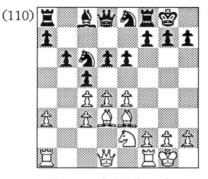

Botvinnik-Reshevsky,
World Championship Tournament 1948.
Black to play.

This position, like the previous one, seems nice for White, who has a lead in development, atacking chances on the kingside, two Bishops, and more space. Yet the truth is that Black's game is preferable. The reason is that Black has no weaknesses in his camp and he is well positioned to defend himself on the kingside. Black's main trump however, is the very weak pawn on c4 (easily attacked by ...Na5 and ...Ba6); a pawn that White will have great difficulties in defending. **1...Na5** Though behind in development, Black moves an already developed piece. As strange as it may seem, the move makes perfect sense.

Black has two main concerns: 1) attack the pawn on c4; 2) defend his kingside. The move chosen (1...Na5) starts to address the first problem. In contrast, a developing move like 1...Bd7? has nothing to do with the position— it does not attack c4 and it has nothing to do with kingside defense. **2.Ng3 Ba6 3.Qe2 Qd7!** A wonderful dual-purpose move. The Queen can now go to a4 and increase the pressure on c4. The other point of ...Qd7 is that it allows Black to play ...f7-f5. This advance would stifle White's aggressive intentions down the b1-h7 diagonal. **4.f4 f5!** Black does not rush to win the c4 pawn. He reasons that if he can form an unpassable defensive shield around his King, then he can later win the c4 pawn (and the game with it) without risking an unhappy kingside debacle. **5.Rae1** Black would only increase his pressure on c4 after 5.d5 g6! 6.dxe6 Qxe6 7.exf5 gxf5. **5...g6!** Here we have an interesting battle of ideas: White attacking on the kingside, Black on the queenside. Happily for Black, his targets on the queenside are ready made and permanent (weak pawns on a3, c3, and c4). White's plan is more wishful thinking. He has no clear object of attack and thus he finds himself in a state of desperation; for if he fails on the kingside, he will surely perish on the opposite wing. Black then merely has to strike a balance on the kingside for an eventual win. **6.Rd1 Qf7 7.e5 Rc8** So that after 8.exd6 Nxd6 the c5 pawn will be defended. **8.Rfe1 dxe5! 9.dxe5 Ng7** Now Black's kingside is as solid as a rock. **10.Nf1 Rfd8** Reshevsky shows great patience. His last move ends any White fantasies of play down the open d-file. **11.Bf2 Nh5! 12.Bg3** and not 12.g3, which would lead to death along the a8-h1 diagonal after 12...Qe8 followed by 13...Qc6 and 14...Bb7. **12...Qe8 13.Ne3 Qa4** White was left without prospects while Black's play on the queenside was just getting started. Black eventually won.

THE ISOLATED PAWN

An isolated pawn is potentially weak because no other pawn can help defend it. Since no pawns can stand by its side, the square directly in front of it also tends to be vulnerable. If we want to see such a pawn at its worst, then a glance at diagram #111 will suffice to make us avoid iso's like the plague.

(111)

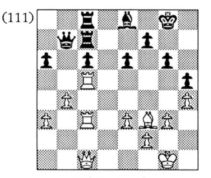

White to play.

Without a doubt, Black is suffering. His pieces are passively placed and his isolated pawns on a6 and c6 are both very weak—they are targets and nothing more.

However, this position didn't paint a complete picture—the lowly isolated pawn has some good points as well: it controls squares that might turn out to be useful homes for your pieces; there are open files on either side of an isolated pawn—place your Rooks on them and strive for activity.

It should also be mentioned that an isolated pawn doesn't

have to remain on a sickly square. If you can advance it, then the once spurned foot soldier might turn into a powerful battering ram (diagram #108 in the chapter on doubled pawns is an excellent illustration of this battering ram idea). Our next example shows aspects of all these positive features.

(112)

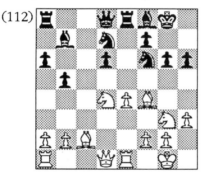

Fischer-Spassky, Return Match 1992.
Black to play.

In this game the dynamic potential of the isolated pawn more than compensates for its slight weakness. It gives Black control of the c5 and e5 squares (excellent posts for the Knights) and offers the Black Rooks nice files on c8 and e8. **1...Ne5** If White plays 2.Qd2 then 2...Nc4 is bothersome. Note that the 'weak' d6 pawn is defended twice and attacked by nothing! **2.b3** Keeping the Knight out of c4. **2...d5!** Demonstrating an important rule: If you can advance and subsequently trade your isolated pawn, then the supposed weakness was nothing more than an illusion. **3.Qd2** White had probably counted on 3.Bxe5 Rxe5 4.f4 Re8 5.e5 but then realized that 5...Ne4! is strong: 6.Bxe4 dxe4 7.Nxe4 Bxe4! 8.Rxe4 Qd5 and the threat of ...Bc5 gives Black a winning advantage. According to Sierawan, White's best move was 3.exd5 Qxd5 4.Ne4 Ned7 5.Nxf6+ Nxf6 6.Rxe8 Rxe8 7.Nf3 with a likely draw. **3...dxe4 4.Nxe4 Nd5!** and Black's threats of ...Nxf4 and ...Bb4 gave him the better game.

A mirror image of this last example can be seen in diagram #113 (next page).

(113)
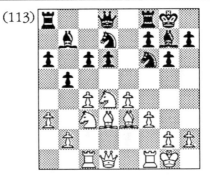

Karpov-Kasparov, World Championship Match 1990.
White to play.

White played **1.cxb5**, expecting that after the obvious 1...axb5 he would have some pressure on Black's pawns on d6, c6, and b5 (if the c-pawn ever advanced). Surprisingly, Black recaptured away from the center with **1...cxb5!** and gave himself an isolated pawn on d6. He had several reasons for doing this: 1) His pawns on a6 and b5 are now completely safe; 2) As is common in these situations, Black has use of the c5 and e5 squares, plus chances on the open 'c' and 'e' files. It's important to note that the e5 square is almost like a permanent support point for Black since if White ever tries to contest it with f3-f4, his e-pawn will become quite weak; 3) He opens the diagonal for his Bishop on b7; 4) The isolated pawn on d6 is not really a weakness since he can trade it off by ...d6-d5 anytime he wants to.

Kasparov's concept was proven correct after the futher **2.Re1! Ne5 3.Bf1 Re8 4.Bf2** and now instead of 4...d5?! 5.exd5 Nxd5 when White could have taken advantage of the newly weakened c5 square by 6.Ne4 (showing that the d6 pawn *does* play a significant role in controlling the c5 and e5 squares), Black should have kept building with 4...Rc8 followed by ...Nc4 with a dynamic position.

The most common type of isolated pawn tends to be a d-pawn, and several opening systems exist where White or Black willingly allow themselves to be stuck with one in the hopes that the pawn's dynamic potential will offer ample compensation for its static weaknesses.

In diagram #114 we see a quiet position from the Tarrasch Defense to the Queen's Gambit.

(114)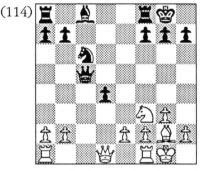

Nilsson-Stolz, Stockholm 1950.
White to play.

Black has an isolated d-pawn, but can such a pawn be considered weak? Not at all! At the moment the d-pawn is solidly defended and can be given extra support by a Rook if the need arises. The real weakness in the position is White's pawn on e2, a pawn that is stuck on its original square due to the cramping influence of the d-pawn. If you add to this Black's obvious advantage in space, you come to realize that instead of being worried about his pawn on d4, Black is actually delighted with it! **1.Rc1 Qb6 2.b3 h6** By taking time out to keep White out of g5, make h7 available for his Bishop, and stop any future back rank mates, Black is saying that he has a comfortable game and is in no hurry to prove anything. **3.Qd2 Bf5 4.Rfd1 Rad8 5.Rc4 Rfe8** Black exerts an uncomfortable amount of pressure on his opponent. The centralized Black Rooks are particularly attractive. **6.Bf1 d3!** Allowing every Black piece to reach a high level of activity. **7.exd3? Be4 8.Ne1 Bd5 9.Rf4 g5! 10.Ra4 Nd4!** The d-pawn is gone but the Black army is starting to overrun the White position. **11.Rxd4** White saw no other way to contend with the threat of ...Rxe1 followed by ...Nf3+. **11...Qxd4** and Black's material advantage led to an eventual win.

Piece activity is the key word when trying to make use of an isolated pawn. Often this can translate into a direct kingside attack.

(115)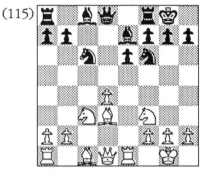

Keene-Miles, Hastings 1975/76.
White to play.

As is so common with isolated d-pawn positions, White has kingside attacking chances due to his pressure down the half open e-file and use of the e5 square. In return Black has the d5 square as a home for his Knight and lasting pressure against the d4 pawn. However, White's threats against Black's kingside are more pressing at the moment. It's important to realize, though, that as the minor pieces get traded off (thereby reducing White's attacking potential), the weakness of the d4 pawn becomes more noticeable. This means that while White's immediate chances are preferable, Black has the better long range possibilities. The diagrammed position is very common in modern practice, and White is considered to have a slight edge, with the smallest mistake swinging the balance in favor of the opponent. In the present case the dynamic potential of the 'iso' overcomes its long term static weakness. **1.Bg5 Nb4?!** Better is 1...b6 with ...Bb7 to follow. **2.Bb1 b6 3.Ne5 Bb7 4.Re3!** White is not in a subtle mood. He wants to mate the Black King before the isolated pawn becomes a problem. **4...g6 5.Rg3 Rc8?** Ignoring the danger! According to Keene, Black should sacrifice the Exchange by 5...Nc6 6.Bh6 Qxd4! 7.Qxd4 Nxd4

8.Bxf8 Kxf8 with only a slight advantage to White. **6.Bh6 Re8 7.a3 Nc6 8.Nxg6!** Black's King position is torn asunder. **8...hxg6 9.Bxg6 fxg6 10.Qb1 Ne5** Instead of resigning, Black tries to make the game last longer so that it will look better on 'paper'! **11.dxe5 Ne4 12.Nxe4 Kh7 13.Nf6+ Kh8 14.Bg7+ Kxg7 15.Qxg6+**, 1-0. Better to resign than to get mated!

We have seen that a central 'iso' grants its owner active piece play, but as these pieces get traded it becomes more of a liability. In general, an isolated pawn reaches its peak of vulnerability when all the minor pieces are gone and only a couple of Rooks (or Queen and Rook) remain. In that case, the heavy pieces can double up and bring great pressure to bear against it.

With this in mind, the owner of the isolated pawn does well (if his attacking potential has been spoiled and most of the minor pieces have been traded) to swap Rooks. In this way, his isolated pawn will be more tolerable.

(116)
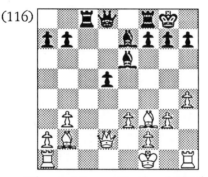

Silman-Minev, Portland 1984.
Black to move.

Diagram #116 illustrates this defensive idea nicely. Black does not have enough activity to compensate for the isolated pawn. Because of this he comes up with the following simple but effective plan: Black will double Rooks on the c-file. This will force White to challenge this file in order to prevent Black's Rooks from penetrating there. Black will then trade Rooks. In the resultant position, White will not be able to generate enough pressure against Black's d5 pawn to gain serious winning chances. **1...Rc6! 2.Kg2 Qd7 3.Rac1 Rfc8 4.Rhd1 Rxc1 5.Rxc1 Rxc1 6.Qxc1 f6 7.Bd4 a6 8.Qd2 Bg4 9.Bxg4**, 1/2-1/2.

It is obvious that White should avoid such a massive trade of Rooks if he wishes to achieve something positive against the isolated pawn.

Our next position is a classic example of how to turn a seemingly healthy isolated pawn into a glaring weakness.

(117)

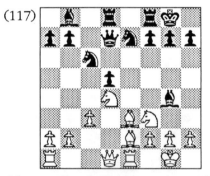

Silman-Filguth, San Francisco 1977.
White to play.

Black has an isolated pawn, but his pieces are very active and the isolated pawn itself is extremely well guarded. First on White's list is to trade as many of the minor pieces as possible. The Bishops are the first to go since they are less active than their Black counterparts. **1.Ng5!** Getting rid of the light squared Bishops. **1...Bxe2 2.Qxe2 Nxd4?!** A mistake. Black should not be in such a hurry to trade pieces. The simple 1...h6 2.Ngf3 was better, though White would enjoy some advantage here also. **3.Bxd4 Nf5 4.Qd3 h6 5.Nf3 Rfe8 6.Rad1** White is in no hurry and just continues to build his position. Remember, White's advantage (Black's weak pawn on d5) is permanent. All he has to do is prevent Black from gaining too much active play or from trading both Rooks. **6...Rxe1+ 7.Rxe1 Ne7 8.g3** Creating luft for his King and blunting the activity of Black's remaining Bishop. **8...Nc6 9.Kg2** By guarding the f3 and h3 squares,

White continues to quietly improve the placement of his pieces.
9...Re8 10.Rd1 White is aware that a trade of Rooks would kill
his winning chances. At least one Rook (working with the
Queen) must be retained if White hopes to place any real
pressure on the d5 pawn. **10...Qe6** And not 10...Re4? 11.Be3!
Ne7 12.Qxe4. **11.Re1** Stopping Black from playing ...Qe4.
11...Qd7 12.Be3 Still refusing to swap Rooks. Now 12...Qe6 is
answered by 13.Rd1. **12...Rd8 13.Rd1 Qe7 14.Nd4** Heading
for f5. **14...Nxd4** Avoiding 14...Qe4+ 15.Qxe4 dxe4 16.Nxc6
Rxd1 17.Nxb8 Rd8 18.Bxa7 **15.Qxd4!** Intending to trade the last
minor piece by 16.Bf4. **15...a6 16.Bf4 Bxf4 17.Qxf4** The
position White was dreaming about. The isolated pawn has
been turned into a weakness with no redeeming virtue. White
now intends to double by Rd4 (it is very important to place the
Rook in front of the pawn so that it can't advance) and Qd2,
when an advance by c3-c4 will take advantage of the pin on the
d-file and win the d5 pawn.

If, as the defender, you were going to be left with only one
major piece, it is better to be left with a Queen. The reason for
this is that a Rook could still cause trouble by playing to d4
followed by a c3-c4 advance. White's King could also march to
the center and take up a dominating position on d4. However,
with just Queens remaining, White's King will not be safe in the
center, and any c4 ideas fail because no d-file pins will exist
(Black's Queen will guard the pawn from e6 or c6). Basically
put: Rooks are more cumbersome defenders than Queens.
17...Qc5 18.Rd4 Qc6 19.Qd2 b5 White threatened Kg1 followed by c3-c4, so this was more or less forced. Now, however,
White will be able to create new weaknesses to attack. **20.Kg1**
Getting off the unpleasant a8-h1 diagonal. **20...Qg6** Threatening to win the a-pawn with ...Qb1+. **21.a3** Also good was the
immediate 21.a4, but White is in no hurry. Such tactics often
frustrate an opponent who must sit and calmly wait in a passive
position. **21...Kf8? 22.h4** Still taking his time and improving his
position. Now White's King has two squares (g2 and h2) to run
to. **22...Qb1+ 23.Kg2 Qf5 24.a4!** Creating a new weakness.

24...Qe6 Or 24...bxa4 25.Rxa4 with pressure on a6 and d5. **25.axb5 axb5 26.Qd3** Threatening both the b5 pawn and Qh7. Even without this trick, White, if he so desired, could have eventually won the d-pawn by b3 and c4. **26...Kg8** Giving up the pawn rather than allow the penetration to h7. Such lines as 26...Qc6 27.Qh7 Qg6 28.Qxg6 fxg6 29.Rb4 hold out longer for Black, but are just as certainly lost. **27.Qxb5 Rd6 28.Qd3 g6 29.c4** So it turns out that White gets to use this theme anyway! **29...dxc4** Black had the choice of accepting the loss of the d-pawn or rushing into a hopeless King and pawn ending. **30.Rxd6 cxd3 31.Rxe6 fxe6 32.Kf3 e5 33.Ke3 e4 34.f3 exf3 35.Kxd3 g5 36.hxg5 hxg5 37.g4**, 1-0.

BACKWARD PAWNS

A backward pawn's weakness or strength depends on the following questions:

1) Is it sitting on an open file?

2) How well it is defended?

3) Is the square directly in front of it adequately defended by pieces? See diagram #60 (Smyslov-Rudakovsky, Moscow 1945) for a nice example of such a square falling into the hands of the opponent.

4) Is it serving a useful purpose defending the pawns that have gone ahead of it?

5) Can it successfully advance, thereby ridding itself of the 'backward' label?

As with an isolated pawn, if a backward pawn can safely advance then its weakness will turn out to be more illusory than real. A typical case of a backward pawn that is only temporary comes about after the following opening moves: **1.e4 c5 2.Nf3 a6** O'Kelly's rather rare variation. **3.d4** White's only real chance for advantage lies with 3.c4 or 3.c3. **3...cxd4 4.Nxd4 e5!** Black weakens the d5 square and creates a backward d-pawn just so he can attack the enemy Knight. Why? Black knows that White will move the horse to safety, so what has Black really gained? The reason 4...e5 is so good in this position is that the White Knight is chased back to an ineffective post while the e5 pawn guards the two critical squares on d4 and f4. These points alone do not justify the weaknesses that were created, but Black also sees that the negatives are just temporary—by playing ...Bb4 he will be able to advance his pawn to d5 and get rid of his problems all at once. **5.Nb3** The more aggressive 5.Nf5 is well met by 5...d5! when the Knight on f5 is shown to be a little loose. **5...Nf6 6.Nc3 Bb4** Threatening to capture the e-pawn with ...Nxe4. **7.Bd3 d5** With this advance Black eradicates his backward pawn and gains control of d5. After 8.exd5 Nxd5 Black would enjoy an excellent position.

Compare the active play of this last example with the following mess: **1.e4 c5 2.Nf3 Nc6 3.d4 cxd4 4.Nxd4 g6 5.Nc3 Bg7 6.Be3 e5??** A common amateur mistake. Black is tempted to attack the White Knight and forgets all other considerations. In this case ...e7-e5 blocks the fianchettoed Bishop and creates disasterous holes on d6 and d5. **7.Ndb5!** Suddenly it's clear that the back-ward d-pawn will be backward for a long, long time. Remember: you only attack an enemy piece if you succeed in chasing to an inferior square. Even then you won't do this if it means creating too many weaknesses in your own camp. Never allow yourself to think that he may leave his piece hanging—train yourself to *always* expect your opponent to play the best move. In the present case Black destroyed his position to chase the enemy Knight to a crushing position—doesn't make much sense, does it? After 7.Ndb5 the Black position is absolutely awful.

We have just looked at two opening sequences that led to very different results: In one, Black accepts a backward pawn but sees that he can get rid of it at will. In the other, Black creates a bunch of weaknesses and gets nothing in return. Let's make these ideas clearer by looking at one more opening variation from the Sicilian. After **1.e4 c5 2.Nf3 Nc6 3.d4 cxd4 4.Nxd4 Nf6 5.Nc3 e5 6.Nbd5 d6** Black once again gets a backward pawn that may remain backward for the rest of the game. However, this time he hopes to get something in return. White's Knight on b5 is offside and, after it is chased to a3 (via ...a7-a6), will need several moves to get back into play. While White is horsing around with his Knight, Black hopes to take control of d5 with his pieces and either force a ...d6-

d5 advance or gain active piece play as compensation. Note that Black's d6 pawn is never in any real danger since White is not able to direct a concentrated attack on it. Instead the battle rages around the hole on d5. **7.Bg5** If 7.Nd5 Nxd5 8.exd5 Nb8 the White pawn has plugged up the hole on d5 and the backward d-pawn no longer stands on an open file. **7...a6 8.Bxf6 gxf6** 8...Qxf6 is not possible due to 9.Nc7+. **9.Na3 b5** Threatening to win a piece by ...b5-b4, and also denying the a3 Knight access to c4. **10.Nd5** and now Black can fight for d5 with 10...Bg7 followed by 11...Ne7, or he can undouble his pawns by 10...f5 and attempt to make use of his two Bishops; the open 'c' and 'g' files might also prove useful. The position after 10.Nd5 is quite rich and this Sveshnikov Variation has been popular at all levels for many years. I will give one quick taste of the type of play that can follow: **10...f5 11.exf5 Bxf5 12.c3** Preparing to recycle the Knight to e3, where it will eye the important d5 and f5 squares. **12...Bg7 13.Nc2 Be6 14.Nce3 Ne7** Fighting for d5. **15.Nxe7** Giving Black the chance to advance his pawn. However, the Black position is also fully playable after 15.g3 Nxd5 16.Nxd5 0-0 17.Bg2 Kh8 18.0-0 a5 19.Qe2 Rb8. **15...Qxe7 16.g3 d5!** This is possible due to the series of pins that follow. **17.Nxd5 Qb7 18.Bg2 0-0-0 19.0-0 Bxd5 20.Qg4+ f5 21.Qxf5+ Kb8** and Black had the preferable position, A.Kuzmin-Goryelov, Moscow 1984.

By now it should be clear that the dynamic possibilities springing from active pieces often compensate for weak pawns. Our next game is just one more illustration of this 'active' principle.

(118)

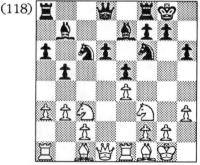

Unzicker-Taimanov, Stockholm 1952.
Black to play.

Black has a backward pawn on d6, yet here it can hardly be considered a weakness. Aside from it being well defended, White is quite unable to bring any more pressure to bear on it. The position favors Black, since he will attack White's e4 pawn and bring great pressure to bear down the open c-file. The backward pawn defends the e5 pawn and the c5 square, and White must be continually on guard for its advance to d5. The e5 pawn (the seeming cause of the backward pawn) is also very useful, as it takes away the f4 and d4 squares from White's pieces, blocks White's dark squared Bishop when it goes to b2, and fixes White's e-pawn on e4. White's problem is that he has no real target to attack and is thus having difficulty finding a plan. **1...Rc8 2.Bb2 Rc7** A multi-purpose move, preparing to double on the c-file and also preparing to exert more pressure down the a8-h1 diagonal by ...Qa8. **3.Nb1** White would be left with a weak backward pawn on c4 after 3.Nd5 Nxd5 4.exd5 (note that Black's backward pawn is a thing of the past— White's d5 pawn blocks the d-file and covers up the hole on d5) Nb8 5.c4 bxc4 6.bxc4 Nd7. **3...Qa8 4.Nbd2 Nd8!** Opening the c-file and preparing to bring the Knight to e6, where it will have a choice of several nice squares. **5.Bd3 Ne6 6.Rc1 Rfc8 7.Nh2 Nd7 8.Nhf1 Ndc5 9.Ng3 g6** Following Steinitz's rule of taking away advanced posts from the enemy Knights. **10.Ne2** Hoping Black will bite with 10...Nxe4 11.Nxe4 Bxe4 12.Bxe4 Qxe4 13.Nc3, when it is true that White has lost a pawn, but he has gained use of the d5 square. Black avoids this and lets White continue to suffer from a lack of constructive ideas. **10...Bg5** White is bound hand and foot. **11.Nc3 Nd4 12.Ncb1 d5** The backward pawn is no longer backward! Now Black's pieces reach a peak of activity. Note that 13.Bxd4 loses to 13...Nxd3. **13.exd5 Nxd3 14.cxd3 Rxc1 15.Bxc1 Bxd5 16.f3 Rc2** White is without moves. The e5 pawn is untouchable: 17.Rxe5? Qc6 18.Re1 Rxc1 19.Qxc1 Qxc1 20.Rxc1 Ne2+. **17.a4 b4 18.Kh1 Qc6**, 0-1. White is unable to prevent ...Nxb3.

So far we have seen that a backward pawn is not necessa.
the nightmare that it is often made out to be. However, since a
backward pawn is undefended by other pawns and is usually
fixed in its position, it tends to be vulnerable to attacks if it is
placed on an open file. Whenever you see a backward pawn
you must ask: Can the owner of the pawn generate enough
active play to compensate for the potential weakness? If that
compensating play is not there, then the pawn will indeed turn
into a target.

(119)

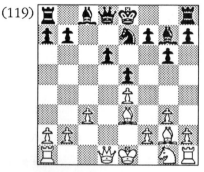

Smyslov-Denker, USSR vs. USA Match 1946.
White to play.

Aside from suffering from a weakness on d6, Black's d5
square is also very weak and vulnerable to an eventual White
occupation. These weaknesses are permanent unless Black can
successfully play a ...d6-d5 advance, which would cure him of
most of his ills. Thus, the first part of the battle consists of
White's attempts to prevent such an advance by controlling the
square directly in front of the backward pawn. **1.Ne2 0-0 2.0-0
Be6 3.Qd2!** Threatening 4.Rfd1 when Black would have to
defend his d-pawn by the very passive ...Nc8. **3...Qc7** The
dreamed of advance 3...d5 fails to 4.Bc5! when White wins a
pawn due to the unstoppable threat of 5.Bxe7 and 6.exd5. After
4.Bc5, 4...dxe4?? drops a piece to 5.Qxd8 and 6.Bxe7. **4.Rfc1!** A
very fine move! White realizes that the only way to definitely
prevent a d5 advance is to play c3-c4. To prepare this advance
by 4.b3 fails to 4...b5, when White's pawn on c3 is as weak as

Black's on d6. Black's reply of 4...b5 would also follow 4.Rac1. Note that the obvious 4.Rfd1 is answered by 4...Rfd8, when nothing could stop Black from playing ...d6-d5. **4...f5** A desperate bid for counterplay. 4...b5 would no longer work: 5.a4! a6 6.Rd1! and now Black can try: 1) 6...Rfd8 7.axb5 axb5 8.Rxa8 when White wins the d6 pawn; 2) 6...Rad8? 7.axb5 axb5 8.Ra7; 3) 6...Bb3 7.Qxd6 Qxd6 8.Rxd6 Bxa4 9.Nc1 threatens 10.b3 winning the Bishop. Variations one and two make it clear why the Q-Rook had to stay on a1. **5.c4 fxe4** Of course not 5...Bxc4 6.b3. **6.Nc3! Nf5** Or 6...Qxc4 7.Nxe4 followed by a capture on d6 when White has a clear advantage. Also bad is 6...Bxc4 7.Nxe4 d5 8.Ng5 when the threats of 9.Ne6 and 9.b3 are hard to meet. **7.Nxe4 Nxe3** The support point on d4 is only illusory after 7...Nd4 8.c5! d5 9.Ng5 Bf7 10.f4!, etc. **8.Qxe3 h6 9.Rd1!** More pressure on d6 and d5. White is not afraid of 9...Bxc4, since 10.Rac1 leaves Black unable to get out of the pin: 10...d5 11.Rxd5!. **9...Rfd8 10.Rac1 Rac8 11.b3 b6 12.Nc3** The first stage of White's plan is complete—the d5 square is completely in his hands. The second phase is to trade off light squared Bishops (which further weakens d5 and leaves Black with a bad Bishop vs. a good Knight) and to triple up on the d-file and clobber the pawn on d6. **12...Qe7 13.Bd5 Kh7 14.Bxe6 Qxe6 15.Rd3 Rc7 16.Rcd1 Rf7 17.Ne4** Some players might be tempted to play 17.Nd5 here, since it was stated earlier (in the section on Knights) that a Knight on the fifth is stronger than a Knight on the fourth. Once again, though, the whole picture is more important than one or two basic rules. In this case, the Knight on e4 guards the f2 pawn and works with the Rooks in attacking the d6 pawn. On d5 the Knight forms a pleasing picture, but does not complement any of the other White pieces—it just selfishly does its own thing. Remember: *All your pieces must work together towards a common goal.* Don't make a move because it looks good or because it goes along with a basic rule. **17...Bf8 18.Rd5 Qg4** Passive defense by 18...Rfd7 would eventually lose to 19.Qd3 followed by 20.b4 and 21.c5, when the d6 pawn falls just the same. **19.R1d3** Keeping Black out of f3. **19...Be7 20.Nxd6** The harvest! **20...Bxd6 21.Rxd6 Rdf8 22.Qxe5 Rxf2 23.Rd7+ R2f7 24.Rxf7+ Rxf7 25.Rd8! Rg7 26.Qe8 g5 27.Qh8+ Kg6 28.Rd6+ Kf7 29.Qxh6** Poor Black still has no checks! **29...Qf5 30.Rd1! Qc5+ 31.Kg2 Qe7 32.Rf1+ Kg8 33.Qf6** and White, with two extra pawns, soon won. An extremely well played game by Smyslov!

CHAPTER FOUR

PASSED PAWNS

Passed pawns are usually thought of as huge assets, offering great chances in an endgame. The truth of this statement can be seen in the following diagram.

(120)

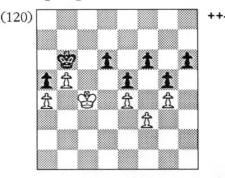

++-

Black to play.

Black is a pawn ahead and has the move, but he is completely lost. The reason for this is that he can't stop the White monarch from strolling into the heart of the Black position and devouring all of his pawns. This sad state of affairs is due to the fact that Black's King is forced to nursemaid the belligerent enemy pawn on b5. For example: 1...Kc7 2.Kd5 Kd7 3.b6 and Black will lose quickly. Just as bad is 1...Kb7 2.Kd5 Kc7 3.Ke6 when White's King is beginning to look like a frenzied shark.

It certainly appears that a passed pawn is a useful thing to have, but the fact of the matter is that passed pawns can also be a disadvantage.

"How is such a thing possible?", the reader may ask. Our next example lends credence to this seemingly outrageous statement.

(121)
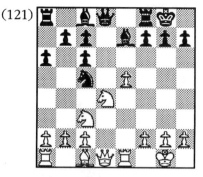

Vesely-Pachman, Prague 1951.
Black to play.

This position (reached after the moves **1.e4 e5 2.Nf3 Nc6 3.Bb5 a6 4.Ba4 Nf6 5.d4 exd4 6.0-0 Be7 7.e5 Ne4 8.Nxd4 0-0 9.Re1 Nc5 10.Bxc6 dxc6 11.Nc3**) was once thought to be very nice for White. Black has doubled pawns, and White's kingside majority is ready to roll via f2-f4-f5 with good attacking chances. This line's popularity died out, however, when Black's correct strategy was discovered. **11...f5!** At first this looks like a ridiculous move. In one swoop Black has blocked his own Bishop on c8 and given White a passed pawn! How can such a move be correct? Aside from the fact that it blocks White's f-pawn (which can no longer advance all the way to f5), the passed pawn White gets is a liability instead of a strength. The trouble with a passed pawn is that it can often be blockaded. In that case the pawn acts as a traitor, since the piece that blocks it is safely hidden by White's own pawn; in other words *Black is using the White pawn as a shield!*

Let's take a look at the further course of the game and see how Black used this strategy. **12.Nce2** Black's strange pawn move to f5 is met by this strange Knight retreat by White. An amateur might think that both players had a bit too much to drink before the game!

After 11...f5 most players would triumphantly play 12.f4,

creating a protected passed pawn. This would be a mistake however, since it does nothing to prevent the blockade of the pawn: 12.f4 Ne6 13.Be3 Nxd4 14.Qxd4 Qxd4 15.Bxd4 Be6 and White's positive imbalance (the kingside pawn majority) has reached its zenith (the creation of a passed pawn), leaving White with no more play. Black, on the other hand, has two well placed Bishops aiming at the queenside and a pawn majority there that can advance and conquer space. This means that White's play is over while Black's play is just beginning.

After 12.f4 Ne6, White could also try 13.Nf3, when Black's plan is to stop White from ever challenging the blockade: 13...Bb4 14.Be3 Bxc3 15.bxc3 c5 (White's Knight can no longer go to d4) 16.Qd3 Qe7 17.Rad1 h6 (and now White's Knight can no longer challenge Black by going to g5) 18.h3 b6 19.Kf2 Bb7 (Black's Bishop is obviously superior to all the White minor pieces) 20.Qd7 Qxd7 21.Rxd7 Be4 22.Re2 Rad8 23.Red2 Rxd7 24.Rxd7 Rd8 25.Re7?? Kf8 26.Rxe6 Kf7 and the Rook is trapped, Darga-Ivkov, Hastings 1955/56.

The idea of 12.Nce2 is to be able to play the Knight to f4 or d4 and challenge the blockade on e6. **12...Ne6 13.Nxe6 Qxd1 14.Rxd1 Bxe6 15.Nf4** Better was 15.Nd4, but Black would still stand very well after 15...Bc8 (15...Rad8? 16.Bg5!) followed by ...c5, ...g5, and ...Be6. **15...Rad8! 16.Be3 Bc8 17.Nd3** White saw that his Knight would be pushed away by ...g5, so he checks out the waters on the queenside and heads for c5. White could also have waited for Black to play ...g5, but his game was bad in any case, and this would not have changed the overall result. **17...b6** Black has won the battle for e6 with his ability to play ...b6 (keeping the Knight out of c5), ...g5 (keeping it off of f4), and ...c5 (keeping it out of d4). **18.b4!** Stopping Black's intended ...c6-c5 expansion and threatening a4-a5 when Black's doubled pawns are proving to be a real weakness. For example: 18...h6? 19.a4 g5? 20.f4 g4 21.a5 b5 22.Bc5! (getting rid of Black's pair of Bishops and leaving him with the bad one) 22...Bxc5+ 23.Nxc5 and White's crushing Knight and powerful passed pawn give him a won game. Naturally Black does not allow White to get away with this plan. **18...f4!** Playing for the activation of the Bishops. **19.Nxf4** Bad is 19.Bxf4 Rxd3!, while 19.Bd2 f3 20.g3 Bf5 is also in Black's favor. **19...Bxb4 20.Ne2 Bf5** Black's Bishops are extremely active now, while White's passed pawn has had no say in the game at all. **21.c3 Ba5 22.Rac1 c5 23.f3 Be6** White is completely tied up and must guard three weak pawns on a2, c3, and e5. The finish was: **24.Kf2 Bc4 25.Nf4 Rfe8 26.Rxd8 Rxd8 27.a3 Re8 28.e6 Bxe6 29.Nxe6 Rxe6 30.c4 Kf7 31.Bf4 b5! 32.Be3 Bb6 33.cxb5 axb5 34.Rb1 c4! 35.Bxb6 Rxb6 36.Ke3 c5 37.Ke4 Ke6**, 0-1.

This game shows that you don't really want a passed pawn if it can be blockaded, *unless* you have play elsewhere and the passed pawn acts as endgame 'insurance.'

Naturally, you should only allow such a pawn if you can successfully blockade it. In relation to this, it's important to know that the best blockader is a Knight. The reason for this is that a Knight's strength is not diminished by having a pawn or a wall of pawns in front of it.

(122)

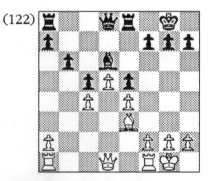

In diagram #122 White has a passed pawn that is blocked by a Bishop. Note how the poor Bishop, which is not really suited to this task, looks more like a tall pawn than a real piece. If we were to switch Black's Bishop on d6 with a Knight, then the whole situation would be very different. Now Black's blockading piece is, aside from stopping the pawn, attacking the White pawns on c4 and e4, plus eyeing important squares on b5 and f5. Quite a difference! It's clear that a Knight enjoys the role of blockader.

(123)

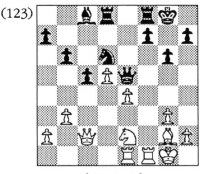

White to play.

Our next example (diagram #123) shows a major battle against White's passed pawn. At the moment the d5 pawn is firmly blocked and the e4 pawn appears to be a target. However, White realizes that if he can advance his e-pawn to e5 then the blockade will be broken, the Bishop on g2 will be freed, and Black's forces will be cast out of the wonderful posts on e5 and d6.

These considerations should enable White to find the subtle **1.Kh1**, threatening 2.Ng1 and 3.Nf3. If White plays 1.Kh1 the ball would be in Black's court—he has to find an answer or the position will turn against him and the passed pawn will change from a dead lump to a dynamic force. It should not take long for Black to play **2...Ba6!**, pinning the Knight. Black will gleefully snap it off next move since White's horse is the only thing that can break Black's hold on the blockading e5 square. Black would then enjoy an iron grip on the position.

Now that I've pointed my finger at passed pawns and insulted them, it's time to take the other side and discuss some of their plusses. We have already seen a passed pawn's power in a King and pawn endgame (diagram #120). In the middle game a passed pawn can be just as effective. Aside from acting as a juggernaut of doom that marches down the board and forces the enemy to run before its might, a far advanced pawn can also be used to offer support points to one's pieces.

(124)

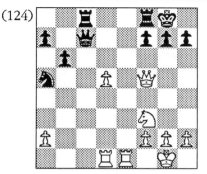

Spassky-Petrosian, World Championship Match 1969.
Black to play.

The passed pawn is very strong in diagram #124. All White's forces are behind it and the threat of its advance is very real. Black could consider blockading it by putting the Knight on d6, but this would allow White to use the pawn as a support for his own Knight. Thus, after 1...Nb7 2.Nd4 Nd6 3.Qf3 followed by 4.Nc6, White would have a dominating position. With this in mind, Black goes pawn hunting, but in doing so he allows the pawn to grow into a giant. **1...Qc2 2.Qf4!** Refusing the Queen trade and taking control of the square in front of the pawn. **2...Qxa2 3.d6** Black has won his pawn and now has two connected passed pawns. White's lone pawn is much superior, however, because it is acting as an immediate irritant to the Black position. Black's queenside passers are just sitting around and doing nothing.

It is also very important to explain why White was so careful not to trade Queens. One reason is that the Queen gives added support to the pawn and has the power to control the square directly in front of it. The other reason is that the Queen keeps a hungry eye on Black's kingside; with Black's forces thrown off balance by the advance of the passed pawn, White can, at any moment, begin an attack against the Black King. It must be remembered that one positive imbalance is usually not enough to win by itself. Two points of attack, though, will often be more than a poor defender can handle. **3...Rcd8 4.d7 Qc4 5.Qf5 h6 6.Rc1** In such positions the passed pawn will win if

White can break the final blockade on d8. **6...Qa6 7.Rc7 b5 8.Nd4 Qb6 9.Rc8 Nb7** Of course not 9...Qxd4 10.Rxd8 Rxd8 11.Re8+ and mates. **10.Nc6** The d8 blockade is creacking. **10...Nd6 11.Nxd8!** The blockade is finally destroyed—it only costs White a Queen! **11...Nxf5 12.Nc6**, 1-0. Black cannot prevent 13.Rxf8+ followed by 14.d8=Q.

Once a passed pawn is created, even in the opening, one must develop one's army around that fact in an effort to create an advantageous situation around the passer. The following game is a classic example. Unzicker-Donner, Goteborg Interzonal 1955. **1.e4 e6 2.d4 d5 3.Nc3 dxe4 4.Nxe4 Nd7 5.Nf3 Be7 6.Bd3 Ngf6 7.Qe2 Nxe4 8.Bxe4 c5 9.d5! e5** Black allows White a passed pawn because he thinks it will not amount to much. **10.Bf5!** If White plays casually, Black will play ...Bd6, ...0-0, ...f5, etc., when White's pawn is firmly blocked while Black's majority is very strong. To avoid this, White goes on a campaign to make his passed pawn a dynamic part of the game. White must do everything in his power to disrupt Black's pieces and to control the square directly in front of the d-pawn. The immediate threat is Bxd7 followed by eating the e5 pawn. **10...0-0 11.0-0** It is unwise to take the pawn since his King is still in the center. Now White will dine if allowed. **11...Bf6** Not the ideal square, but 11...Bd6 allows 12.Ng5! g6 13.Bxd7 followed by 14.Ne4, when there are some holes around Black's King and the blockade is already being challenged. **12.Nd2!**

(125)

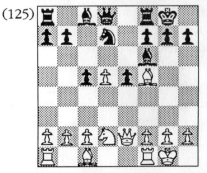

Black to play.

Few would play this move. White is not yet fully developed, yet he retreats his Knight and blocks his undeveloped Bishop! The reason for this is that White has no interest in just developing his pieces. He intends to make immediate use of his d5 pawn; thus the Knight is heading for e4, where it will control the critical d6 blockading square. **12...g6 13.Bxd7 Qxd7!** After 13...Bxd7? 14.Ne4 b6 15.Nxf6+ Qxf6 16.c4 White will change plans, and will instead crush Black on the weakened a1-h8 diagonal by b3, Bb2, and eventually f2-f4. This is a good case of Bishops of opposite colors giving the side with the initiative attacking chances. **14.Ne4 Bg7 15.Rd1** The natural 15.c4 guards the pawn, but does nothing to help in its advance. **15...b6 16.Bh6!** When one has a passed pawn, it is usually a good idea to trade as many minor pieces as possible. A situation with Queen and two Rooks vs. Queen and two Rooks is excellent, though Queen and one Rook may be even better, since that leaves the opponent with less chance for counterplay. The idea of trading the minor pieces is that a Queen and Rook are poor blockaders, and would be inferior to their counterparts who would not be hampered by such considerations as blockading passed pawns. **16...f5** Naturally 16...Bxh6?? 17.Nf6+ must be avoided. **17.Bxg7 Qxg7 18.Nc3 Bb7 19.a4!** The pawn on d5 will shortly advance, but first White will create another weakness on b6 by a5 and axb6. The combination of blocking the d-pawn and trying to guard a weak pawn on b6 will prove too much for Black. **19...a5?** Aiding White, though it must be admitted that Black had a bad game anyway. **20.Qb5 Qc7 21.d6 Qd8** A good example of the disruptive value of a passed pawn is 21...Qc6 22.Qxc6 Bxc6 23.d7! Rfd8 24.Rd6! Bxd7 25.Rad1 Ra7 26.Nd5 and Black is suffering. **22.Nd5** Forcing the trade of the last minor piece. Naturally, 22...Qxd6 23.Nxb6 is hopeless. **22...Bxd5 23.Rxd5 e4 24.Rad1** Every piece comes to the aid fo the passed pawn! **24...Kg7 25.d7** Black cannot live through a pawn like this. **25...Rf6 26.h3** With such a dominating position, it is always nice to put an end to all back rank problems. **26...Re6 27.Qc4 Re7 28.Rd6** Tightening the noose. To win, White must break the final blockade on d8. **28...Ra7 29.Qc3+ Kg8 30.Qf6 Ra8 31.Qxe7!** Breaking the blockade and simultaneously breaking Black's resistance. 1-0, since 31...Qxe7 32.d8=Q+ Rxd8 33.Rxd8+ Kf7 34.R1d7 leaves White a Rook ahead.

Solve these Problems:

(126)

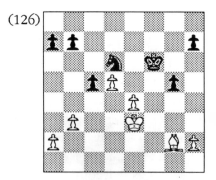

White to play.

Who stands better?

(127)

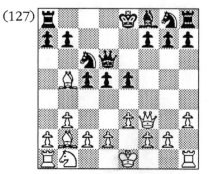

White to play.

The position in diagram #127 was reached after **1.Nf3 d5 2.b3 c5 3.e3 Nc6 4.Bb2 Bg4 5.h3 Bxf3 6.Qxf3 e5 7.Bb5 Qd6** White now has the opportunity to give his opponent doubled pawns by 8.Bxc6+. Is this a good idea?

(128)

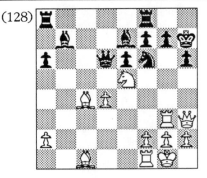

Black to play.

The position in the diagram was reached after **1.d4 d5 2.c4 dxc4 3.e3 Nf6 4.Bxc4 e6 5.Nf3 c5 6.0-0 a6 7.Qe2 b5 8.Bd3 cxd4 9.exd4 Be7 10.Nc3 Bb7 11.Bg5 0-0 12.Rad1 Nbd7 13.Ne5 h6 14.Bc1 Nb6 15.Qe3 Nbd5 16.Qg3 Nh5 17.Qg4 Nhf6 18.Qh3 Nxc3 19.bxc3 Qd5 20.c4 bxc4 21.Bxc4 Qd6 22.Rd3 Kh7 23.Rg3** It has become obvious that White wishes to smash Black. Is he justified to desire this? Do the positional factors back him up? Black has many defenses; analyze them all and give what you feel is best.

(129)

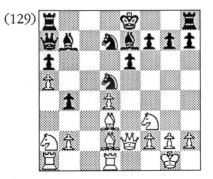

White to play.

Explain this position.

(130)
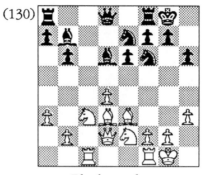

Black to play.

In this position, play continued **1...Ng6 2.Bxg6 fxg6 3.Nf4**. Was Black's decision to play 1...Ng6 an intelligent one? Explain the diagrammed position and also the position after 3.Nf4.

PART EIGHT

WEAK SQUARES

Playing for dominance of one single little square is a hard concept for many amateurs to fully understand. Nevertheless, the idea of fighting for squares instead of material or attack is extremely important and *must* be appreciated if the student wishes to improve his/her game.

The reason one plays for control of a square (an undefended square is also known as a 'hole') is that it will usually prove to be an excellent home for a Knight or a Bishop (though other pieces can also gain from laying claim to such a hole). In return, this piece will inevitably be more valuable than its counterpart on the other side of the board. In a sense then, the gain of a square allows you to gain materially also, simply because your pieces become more valuable then the opponent's.

THE CREATION
OF A WEAKNESS

Though anyone can plop a Knight down on a square that has suddenly become available (usually through a blunder by the opponent), very few players actually make an effort to create these gaping holes. Diagram 109 shows how a weak square can be created by using your pawns to force his to give up control of a desired spot.

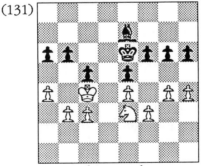

(131)

White to play.

This endgame is very favorable for White. His King is well posted on c4 and will wreck havok on the Black position if it succeeds in penetrating to d5. White also enjoys a superior Knight versus a very poor Bishop. Since the nice square on d5 has been claimed by the White King, that leaves the Knight in need of a home. This is easily created by **1.h5!** forcing the

Black pawn on g6 to give up control of the f5 sqaure. **1...gxh5 2.gxh5 Bf8 3.Nf5** and Black is in *Zugzwang*. The Bishop must stay on f8 to defend the h6 pawn, 3...a6-a5 allows 4.Kb5, and 3...Kd7 4.Kd5 b5 5.a5 b4 6.c4 Kc7 7.Ke6 is also hopeless since Black's pawns are starting to fall.

(132)

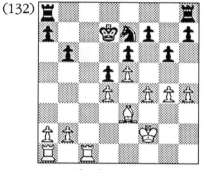

Black to move.

In diagram #132, White appears to stand well—he enjoys more space on the kingside and has a Rook posted on the only open file. In the meantime the Black Knight is without any advanced support points (if the Knight heads for c4 via a5, White can deny the horse access by b2-b3). This is all an illusion though, since Black has a pawn move that gains the mighty f5 square for his Knight. **1...h5! 2.g5** Else Black would play ...hxg4 and start to attack the White h-pawn. **2...Nf5** and suddenly the White position is clearly inferior. His pawns on d4 and h4 need constant attention and after 3.Rh1 Rac8 Black is the one who can initiate play on the c-file.

We have seen how pawn advances can give us control of a square. However, piece exchanges that double the enemy pawns or trade off a square's defenders (see diagram #60, Smyslov-Rudakovsky, Moscow 1945, for an excellent illustration of this theme) can also lead to the creation of a hole. The game Karpov-Browne, San Antonio 1972, shows us how doubling an enemy pawn can pull that pawn away from the defense of our target square: **1.c4 c5 2.b3 Nf6 3.Bb2 g6 4.Bxf6!**

(133)

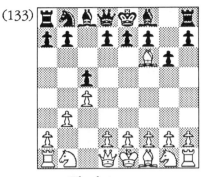

Black to move.

White gives up his fine b2 Bishop in order to take the Black e-pawn away from the defense of d5. Now White will develop his whole army around the d5 square. The trade of imbalances (giving Black two Bishops for control of d5) favors White, since Bishops by themselves are nothing special, and once a White Knight lands on d5 it will dominate the game. **4...exf6 5.Nc3 Bg7 6.g3 Nc6 7.Bg2 f5 8.e3** This pawn fixes Black's pawn on f5 (thereby blocking the c8 Bishop) and keeps any Black pieces out of d4. The White Knight on g1 will fit in very nicely on e2, where it can always move to f4 with additional control of d5. **8...0-0 9.Nge2 a6 10.Rc1 b5 11.d3** White's Rook moved to c1 to give the c3 Knight more support and to get off the dangerous a1-h8 diagonal, thus making a ...b5-b4 advance harmless. **11...Bb7 12.0-0 d6 13.Qd2 Qa5 14.Rfd1 Rab8 15.Nd5** Since White has a static advantage in structure, his edge will last right into the endgame. **15...Qxd2 16.Rxd2 b4** Black avoids 16...bxc4 17.dxc4! when White's control of d5 has been increased and a file has been opened to Black's weak pawn on d6. **17.d4** Karpov feels that White has a strategically won game thanks to his better pawn structure, control of d5, more active pieces, and potential control of the d-file. **17...Rfd8** And now Karpov feels that 18.dxc5 dxc5 19.Rcd1 (threatening Ne7+) would have been very strong. Instead he played 18.Rcd1?! cxd4 19.exd4 Kf8 20.c5? (20.Ne3 was still good for White) when 20...Na7! demonstated that White had just given up the critical b5 and c3 squares. White ended up winning anyway after a long fight.

The final way to induce a weak square is to make a threat that forces the opponent to create a hole in order to counter it. Our next example shows this theme in a simple way.

(134)

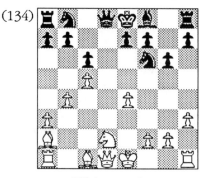

White to play.

White—who has more space, a lead in development, and the two Bishops—has a clear advantage. He makes this even more tangible by **1.Qb3!** with the obvious threat of 2.Qxf7+. Of course, White knows that Black will defend his f-pawn by ...e7-e6, but that is just what White wants since the advance of Black's e-pawn leaves two big holes on d6 and f6. After **1...e6** White is willing to give up d5 to increase his control of the newly created weaknesses: **2.e5! Nd5 3.Ne4** and the holes on d6 and f6 leave Black in bad shape.

MAKING USE OF A WEAK SQUARE

If you are lucky enough to get a useable square due to an opponent's bad play, or if you create one by dint of hard work, it won't do you any good if you can't get a piece to nest on it. It doesn't matter if getting to the square is difficult or takes several moves, the reward is usually so great that you get more than enough for your effort!

(135)

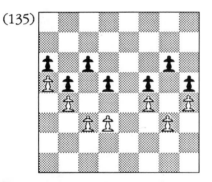

In diagram #135 we see a bunch of pawns with no pieces. This may appear to be nonsensical to the amateur, but the professionel's trained eye immediately notes the holes on g5, e5, and c5. Defensively, only the weak square on g4 would give White any worries. If White had a dark-squared Bishop on a3, he would hasten to bring it into the game by Ba3-c1-e3-d4 when it stands actively and hits both c5 and e5. If White had a Knight on b1, he would head for the post that would bring the most rewards (depending on what other pieces existed and the placement of the Kings). If c5 were his goal (with an attack on a6), he would play Nb1-d2-b3-c5. If e5 (attacking both c6 and g6) or d4 (attacking c6) turned out to be superior, White would play Nb1-d2-f3, etc.

Note that if White saw this structure coming earlier in the game, he would avoid owning a light-squared Bishop (on f3 for example) since it would have no say over the weaknesses in Black's position.

If Black was helpless then White would not care how long it took for his pieces to reach these wonderful squares. If Black had threats of his own, White might play to defuse his opponent's plans and only then bring his pieces to their desired homes. Diagram #136 illustrates this theme.

(136)

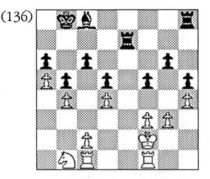

White to play.

Having decided that his Knight must reach the tasty squares on c5 or e5 to be effective, White starts the journey with **1.Nd2 Rhe8** Black doubles Rooks and creates a threat of ...Re2+. This forces White to stop his plans for a moment and kill off Black's counterplay. **2.Rfe1 Kc7 3.Rxe7+ Rxe7 4.Re1!** By getting rid of the Rooks, White allows his King to march up the board and try to take up residence on e5 or g5. The Knights are not the only pieces that like to sit on weak squares! **4...Rxe1 5.Kxe1 Kd6 6.Ke2 Ke6 7.Ke3 Kf6 8.Kf4 Be6 9.Nb3** With his King in its best possible position, White is free to resume his Knight's journey. **9...Bd7 10.Nc5 Bc8 11.c3** Zugzwang! Black is forced to let the enemy King advance. **11...Kf7 12.Ke5** A beautiful sight. White's two remaining pieces take up residence on the target holes. **12...Ke7 13.f4** Zugzwang again. Now White's King goes deep into the Black position and wins material. **13...Kf7 14.Kd6**, 1-0.

(137)

Mitchel-Nimzovitch, Berne 1931.
White to play.

I must confess that this is one of my favorite positions. Though it appears to be a hopelessly boring game that is heading for a draw, it is actually a fantastic illustration of a battle for one little square (revolving around the minor pieces) waged by almost every piece from both armies.

Let's break the position down in an attempt to understand it: With the pawn structures almost identical, many pieces traded off, and no real weakness in either camp, things would seem to be pretty equal. To see if this assessment is true though, we must carefully weigh the only two imbalances that exist here; namely Black's temporary lead in development and the very important difference of Bishop vs. Knight.

As stated earlier in the book, if a Bishop vs. Knight is the only imbalance or the major imbalance in a position, then you must strive to make your individual piece superior to the one your opponent has. In this case we have a wide open position—the type of thing that usually favors a Bishop. If White's Bishop can get to c3, it will dominate the Black Knight and would then show its superiority over the unfortunate horse. Clearly, Black cannot allow this! Additionally, Black must find an advanced support point for his Knight. How is this possible? No central pawns exist that can be used to anchor the beast. This is where willpower comes into play. Conceptually, Black knows what he needs to do. Now he must insist on its becoming a reality! Black's plan is as follows:

His fantasy square for his Knight is d3. It is clear that the Knight will be extremely powerful on this post; but if he is to keep it there he will need the aid of his army, since no pawns can help. To accomplish this, Black will need to place his Rooks on the d-file and move the Knight from c6 to e5 to d3. This plan will be aided by Black's lead in development. Black knows that a development lead is only temporary and he wishes to convert it into a permanent advantage, namely a superior Knight versus a less active Bishop. This leaves us with the unusual case of Black playing to win neither a pawn nor space. The apple of his eye in this case is a seemingly useless, disembodied square!

White's first move, a big mistake, allows Black to bring his plans to fruition. **1.Re1? Rfd8!** Making immediate use of his development lead. Since White can neither move his Queen nor take Black's, he is forced to place his Bishop on d2 and into an unfortunate pin. **2.Bd2 Qf5** Black devotes his whole existance to the control of d3. A big mistake would be 2...Qd5? 3.Bc3 when White's minor piece would be the one to claim dominance. **3.Rac1 Ne5** Heading for the promised land. **4.Qc2** A blunder would be 4.Rc5?? Nf3+ winning the loose Rook. **4...Nd3 5.Rf1** Forced, since 5.Re2? Nxc1 6.Qxf5 Nxe2+ 7.Kf1 Rxd2 wins easily for Black. **5...Qg4 6.Rcd1 Qe2** Black's Knight is fantastic! It blocks the d-file and also prevents White from placing Rooks on the e-file and c-file. However, great care must now be used. Black must not think that he has won the fight—the battle for d3 has only just begun! **7.Qb1 Rd5!** Many players would be tempted to play something like 7...Rac8. This would be very pretty, but it would have nothing to do with Black's plan of dominating d3. By playing his Rook to d5 he prepares to give added (and much needed) support to d3. Also note how the d5 Rook can swing over to the kingside in some variations. Naturally a light square was chosen; it is always a good idea to avoid possible contact with White's Bishop. **8.Be3** Under the present circumstances, White decides to play his Bishop to e3, where it prevents the Knight from eventually going to f4 with chances of a kingside attack. **8...Rad8 9.Rd2 Qh5 10.Rfd1**

(138)

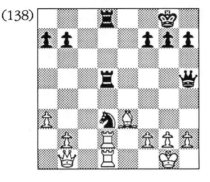

A very rare situation has arisen. Both sides are devoting all their forces to the capture of this one little d3 square! White knows that if the Knight can be made to move, then his Bishop will take over as the superior minor piece.

I should mention that White avoided the greedy 10.Bxa7 because he feared 10...Nf4 11.Rxd5 Rxd5 when the threat of 12...Ne2+ 13.Kh1 Qxh2+! 14.Kxh2 Rh5 mate is rather irritating. **10...b6!** Black leaves his Knight hanging, and instead guards his pawn! Has he gone mad? No, this is based on an *X-Ray combination*. If 11.Rxd3??, then 11...Qxd1+! wins outright: 12.Qxd1 Rxd3 13.Qf1 Rd1 and Black will be up a clear Exchange in the endgame.

Another question: wouldn't it have been preferable to play 10...a6, placing the pawn on the opposite color of White's Bishop? The answer to this is a resounding no! The reasoning is as follows: If we were to take off all the Rooks and Queens, we would have a Bishop vs. Knight endgame. Since the position is an open one and there are pawns on both sides of the board, the Bishop would be superior here (especially since the White King could walk to e2 and chase the Knight away). If such an ending were reached, Black would indeed prefer his pawn on a6. However, since Black's advantage can only be maintained in a middlegame (where the pieces can keep the Knight on d3), he will avoid any trades and play for the restriction of the Bishop. Thus, instead of the endgame strategy of putting the pawns on safe squares, Black follows a middlegame strategy of putting his pawns on the identical color of the enemy Bishop in an effort to restrict it. **11.f3 Qg6 12.Qc2 h6 13.Kf1** The battle for d3 is reaching a climax. White has decided to bring his King to e2 and force the Knight to move away! To do this, though, White must first guard the g2 pawn by g2-g3. This will obviously weaken White's kingside. What we are going to end up with is a case of trading advantages. Black is willing to give up his superior minor piece and move it away if White ends up with an insecure King. **13...Kh7 14.Qc3** Avoiding the tactical mistake 14.g3 Qf5 15.Ke2 Nf4+!. **14...R8d6** Black takes his time and just keeps improving the position of all his pieces. **15.b4 h5 16.g3 Qf5 17.Ke2** White has finally succeeded in chasing away the irksome Knight, but only at the cost of a weakened King position. **17...Ne5 18.Bf4** And not 18.Rxd5 Qxf3+ followed by 19...Rxd5, which wins material for Black. **18...Rxd2+ 19.R.xd2 Rc6!** Since Black's chances are now based on attacking the White King, it is logical for him to keep as many pieces on the board as possible. **20.Qd4** Avoiding the blunder, 20.Qxe5? Re6. **20...Ng6 21.Bd6** Quite funny—the minor pieces' roles are now reversed! Black's Knight is now clearly inferior to White's Bishop, but White's King has no safe home to go to. **21...Qh3 22.Ke3 Qfl 23.Rd1 Qg2 24.Qd2 Qh3 25.Qd5 Rc2 26.Rd2** And not 26.Qxf7 Qg2 with a winning attack for Black. **26...Rc3+ 27.Rd3 Rc1 28.Qxf7 Qxh2 29.Qf5 Rc4** Threatening 30...Qgl+. Though Black has the initiative, it is by no means easy to demonstrate a clear win. **30.Rd1 Rc3+ 31.Kd4!** The obvious 31.Rd3 loses to 31...Qg1+ 32.Ke4 Rxd3 33.Qxh5+ (or 33.Kxd3 Qb1+ picking up the White Queen) 33...Kg8 34.Kxd3 Qd1+ winning the Bishop on d6. **31...Rxa3 32.Kd5 Rc3 33.Ke6??** White had to play 33.Kd4 with chances to hold on. The text is the start of a death march. **33...Qe2+ 34.Kf7 RcT+!** and White resigned, since 35.Bxc7 Qe7 is mate.

I strongly recommend that the student play over this game several times until the concepts it demonstrates (Bishop versus Knight and the fight for a square) are firmly etched in his mind.

Our final example of weak squares shows several of the phases that we have discussed in this section: Creation and domination of a weak square, the journey to get to it, and finally occupation of the hole.

Silman-Shapiro, World Open 1990. **1.d4 Nf6 2.c4 e6 3.Nc3 Bb4 4.Qc2 c5 5.dxc5 Bxc5 6.Nf3 Qb6** Black is willing to waste a bit of time with his Queen in order to force White to play e2-e3 and block in his dark-squared Bishop. **7.e3 Qc7 8.Be2 0-0 9.0-0 b6 10.b3** Since the c1-h6 diagonal is blocked, White prepares a new diagonal for the Bishop. **10...Bb7 11.Bb2 a6 12.Rac1** Though this defends White's Queen, it is basically a prophylactic move. The placement of the Rook opposite the Black Queen discourages ...d7-d5 by the opponent. **12...Be7 13.Ng5!** White tries to make use of his lead in development (a temporary advantage) by creating weaknesses in the enemy camp (weak squares are a permanent advantage). **13...g6** Forced, since White threatened to initiate a tactical attack against h7 by 14.Nd5! exd5 15.Bxf6. **14.Nge4!** Fishing for holes in the Black structure. Both f6 and d6 are a little loose but they are not too serious at the moment. **14...Nxe4 15.Nxe4 f5 16.Qc3!** The point. The threat of mate forces Black to play advance his e-pawn and weaken the important d5 square. **16...e5 17.Nd2 d6**

(139)
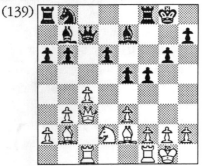

White has achieved his first goal—the d6 pawn is backward and the d5 square is a potential home for a White piece. The second part of White's plan is to gain control of d5, thus making it habitable for a piece and also preventing Black from ever advancing his backward pawn to d5. **18.Rfd1 Bc6 19.b4 Bf6 20.Qb3 Kg7 21.Bf3!** Black's main defender of d5 was his light-squared Bishop so White hastens to trade it off. **21...Nd7** The exchange could have been prevented by 21...e4 but after 22.Be2 Black's King position would be slightly looser than before due to the open a1-h8 diagonal, his light-squared Bishop would be blocked by his own pawn, and the d4 square would be added to White's list of acquisitions. **22.Bxc6 Qxc6** With the light-squared Bishops gone and White's Queen, c-pawn, and d1 Rook all eyeing d5, White has clearly taken control of that square. Now it's time for the final part of the puzzle: bring a minor piece around so that it can use the hole as a home. **23.Nb1!** Heading for the promised land. **23...e4 24.Nc3 Be5 25.Nd5 Rae8** Everything has gone White's way. All he has to do now is find a way to break into Black's position. **26.b5!** It appears that White is giving Black use of the c5 square. However, White has correctly judged that Black's Knight is needed on d7 to defend the pawn on b6. **26...Qc5** Naturally, 26...axb5 must be avoided since 27.cxb5 allows White's pieces to flood into Black's position via the c-file. Note that 26...Qb7 27.bxa6 Qxa6 also fails to 28.Nc7. **27.Ba3 Qc8 28.bxa6** White has coverted his positional advantage into a material one. **28...Nc5 29.Qxb6 Nd3** White doesn't fear this Knight (even though it's on the dreaded sixth rank) since it is cut off from the rest of Black's army. **30.Rc2 Rf7 31.f4 Bf6 32.Rb1** With a two pawn advantage, White is not after any adventures. Instead he simply grabs more squares, keeps control of critical files, and improves the placement of all of his pieces. This type of tight play prevents counterplay. **32...Bd8 33.Qb5 Re6 34.Bb2+ Kh6 35.Bd4**, 1-0.

Solve These Problems

(140)

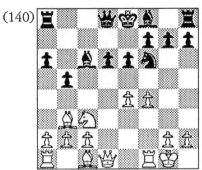

White to play.

The position in the diagram came about after **1.e4 c5 2.Nf3 d6 3.d4 cxd4 4.Nxd4 Nf6 5.Nc3 a6 6.Bc4 e6 7.Bb3 b5 8.0-0 Bb7 9.f4 Nc6 10.Nxc6 Bxc6**. Black threatens both 11...Nxe4 and 11...b5-b4. What is White's best move?

(141)

White to play.

Should White double Black's pawns with 1.Bxf6, pin the other Knight with 1.Bb5, or calmly develop with 1.Be2?

PART NINE

MATERIAL LOSS AND SACRIFICE

One of the most important types of imbalance is inequality of material, and one must be very careful before giving material away. All the same, it must be realized that *material inequality is an imbalance and not some mindless goal unto itself.* This means that a player's plan, his potential for active play, and the opponent's plans always come into consideration before winning or sacrificing material.

A material advantage influences all phases of the game. In the opening and middlegame the side with extra material possesses more units of force—his army is larger. Another influence of material is that the 'down' side is always afraid to go into an endgame where a material disadvantage is usually decisive. Due to this his possibilities in the middle game are severely curtailed. One might even go so far as to say that the side with a material deficit is giving endgame odds!

All this makes one think that winning material is an end unto itself and that a huge appetite for wood can become a winning philosophy of chess. While many games are won in just this way, such a view turns out to be shallow. There is a lot more to this subject than meets the eye!

I have already said that material is just one of several possible imbalances. Whenever you plan to win material and stir the pot of imbalances, you must ask the following question: *are you paying a price to win this material and is that price too high?*.

EXCHANGING MATERIAL FOR OTHER IMBALANCES

Though we all can sacrifice material if we see a forced mate, many of us are less likely to part with our men if the return is just 'positional.' However, I must once again remind the student that material is just an imbalance like pawn structure, space and all the others. Does it make sense to create one imbalance in your favor (material) while giving the opponent several others (space, better minor pieces, superior pawn structure, initiative, etc)? Simple math gives us a clear answer.

The irrational fear of losing material (or the thrill of winning it) can often make us lose sight of the realities on the board and leave us with blinders on.

Our first example shows a case where positional considerations are suddenly interrupted by the siren call of materialism.

A.Ivanov-Silman, New York Open 1991. **1.e4 c5 2.Nf3 Nc6 3.d4 cxd4 4.Nxd4 g6 5.Nc3 Bg7 6.Nde2 Nf6 7.g3 b5 8.Bg2 Rb8 9.0-0** White's opening goal is to play Nd5, force Black to capture, and then (after exd5): 1) Make use of the weakened c6 square (by Nd4-c6). 2) Build pressure against the e7 pawn by placing the Rooks on the half open e-file. **9...0-0 10.Bf4 d6 11.Qd2 b4 12.Nd5 Nxd5** Normally Black would not be in a hurry to capture this Knight and open the e-file for White. However, he decides that his queenside play will be faster than the plans that White has outlined in the note to his ninth move. **13.exd5 Na5** The White pawn on b2 hangs and

...Nc4 will prove uncomfortable for the first player. **14.b3!!**

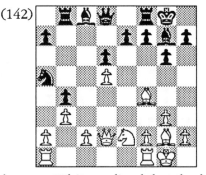

(142)

A wonderful move. White realized that the battle was turning against him and offers material to deaden the Black Knight and regain the initiative. Now Black is forced to make a mental readjustment to the changing situation on the board. **14...Ba6!** Keeping a clear head and refusing to be overwhelmed by greed. If 14...Bxa1 15.Rxa1 White would get ample play on the weakened a1-h8 diagonal and also torment Black with threats of Nd4-c6. The point of 14...Ba6 is to destroy the White Knight and end all fears of an invasion on c6. **15.a3!** By continuing to offer material, White gets rid of Black's immediate pressure down the c-file and fights for the initiative. **15...Bxe2 16.Qxe2 Bxa1 17.Rxa1 bxa3 18.Rxa3** White's two Bishops and pressure down the a-file gave him plenty of compensation for the sacrificed exchange. The game was eventually drawn after a sharp fight: **18...Qc7 19.Qa6 Nb7 20.Qc6 Qb6 21.Qd7 Rfe8 22.Be3 Nc5 23.Qxa7 Qxa7 24.Rxa7 Ra8 25.Rc7 Rec8 26.Rc6 Nb7 27.Bh3 f5 28.Rb6 Nd8 29.g4 fxg4 30.Bxg4 Rxc2 31.Bg5 Rc7 32.Rb4 h5 33.Bh3 Rb7 34.Re4 Rxb3 35.Kg2 Nf7,** 1/2-1/2.

The widely celebrated game that follows shows that the strategic potential in a position can easily transcend mere material considerations.

(143)

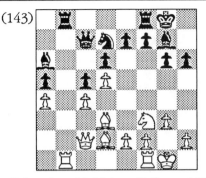

Selesniev-Alekhine, Triberg 1921.
Black to play.

A look at the diagram gives one a very favorable impression of White's chances. His Bishops and Queen aim menacingly at Black's kingside, he has a central space advantage, and he can eventually play for a central break via f2-f4, e2-e4, and e4-e5. The queenside is in a state of balance though, to be honest, Black's a5 pawn is under more pressure than either of White's on c4 and a4. As I said earlier, it looks bleak for Black—we could not find one favorable thing for Black to play with.

With this in mind, Alekhine realized that he had to create a favorable imbalance or he would most likely lose the game. Extreme measures are called for, so: **1...Rb4!!** Hanging his Rook to White's Bishop! If White does not take it, Black will play 2...Rfb8 and 3...Rb2 with active play. **2.Bxb4 cxb4!** Inferior is 2...axb4. By capturing with the c-pawn, Black creates instant pressure on White's c4 pawn and a fine support point for the Knight on c5. Add to this Black's strong passed pawn on b4 and increased King safety due to the absence of White's dark squared Bishop, and you get a dynamic Black position full of potential.

White is now unexpectedly thrown on the defensive, and his only favorable imbalance now is his advantage in material. Unfortunately, his material advantage is made up of Rook vs. Bishop; but the White Rooks have no open file for activity.

Hopefully, this list of favorable imbalances will override the student's materialistic prejudices and make him realize the importance of giving oneself something (an imbalance or the creation of one) to use. **3.Nd2!** An excellent move. White will blockade Black's b4 pawn with that finest of blockaders, the Knight. **3...Nc5?** A big mistake that loses a lot of time. Black should have increased the pressure on White's c4 pawn by ...Rc8 followed perhaps by ...Nb6. **4.Nb3!** Another fine reply. White is willing to give back the material to retake the initiative. **4...Nd7** A sad retreat, but 4...Nxa4 5.Ra1! Bxa1 6.Rxa1 Nc5 7.Nxa5 Kg7 8.Nc6 favors White. **5.c5!** Very sharp. White gives away a pawn but creates some favorable imbalances for himself, namely the trade of his bad Bishop on d3 plus the loss of his target pawn which was on c4. Soon Black's pawn will be on c5, and will be weak and in need of defense. Note how both players are not so much interested in material as they are in the creation of favorable imbalances. **5...Bxd3 6.exd3!** White happily doubles his own pawns. The idea of this move is to control c4 so that after ...dxc5 Black's c5 pawn will not be able to advance. Furthermore, now White has an open e-file to use for his Rooks, and, as a result, he can put pressure on Black's weak e-pawn. **6...dxc5 7.Rfe1** Now White has a material advantage plus pressure against c5 and e7. Black eventually won a long battle, but this position favors White.

So far we have seen that material sacrifices leading to positional gains can fight for the initiative and force the opponent to go through a difficult mental readjustment that can easily lead to errors. The play in diagram #144 highlights these points.

(144)

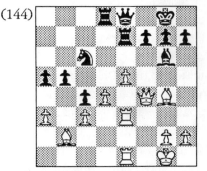

Reshevsky-T.Petrosian, Zurich 1953.
Black to play.

In this position White has the game under control. His center restricts Black's pieces and threats like h4-h5 or e5-e6 are always in the air. Seeing that his pieces are not effectively posted, Black makes a startling decision. **1...Re6!!** A tremendous defensive move. The idea is to create a blockade on the light squares by stopping e5-e6 and following up with ...Nc6-e7-d5. White would probably have done better to ignore the Rook and continue his attack on the kingside with Rg3 and h4. **2.a4 Ne7!** Logically following his plan and avoiding 2...b4? 3.d5 Rxd5 4.Bxe6 fxe6 5.Qxc4 with advantage to White. **3.Bxe6** White, feeling that his position was so good that he deserved some sort of reward, takes the material (a somewhat emotional decision) but soon finds that the position has turned against him. **3...fxe6 4.Qf1 Nd5** It's time to take stock. White's kingside attack no longer exists. He does have an extra Exchange but that's the best we can give White. On the other hand the White Rooks are no longer active and the b2 Bishop is bad. Add to this Black's dominating central Knight, his active Bishop, and queenside majority, and you will begin to see that White's material advantage is of secondary importance. **5.Rf3 Bd3 6.Rxd3** White, to his credit, realizes that he's been outplayed and brings his mind (and expectations) back to reality. Here he is using one of the finer points of material gain: The ability to sacrifice it back for defensive purposes. He must return his ill-gotten gains if he is to avoid being overrun by Black's minor pieces. **6...cxd3 7.Qxd3 b4 8.cxb4** 8.c4 Nb6 9.Rc1 Nxa4 is also fine for Black. The play is now about even and peters out to a draw. **8...axb4 9.a5 Ra8 10.Ra1 Qc6 11.Bc1 Qc7 12.a6 Qb6 13.Bd2 b3 14.Qc4 h6 15.h3 b2 16.Rb1 Kh8 17.Be1**, 1/2-1/2.

By now the student will have noticed that these material offers are all positional in nature. Unlike a combination, which is quite a different thing, a true sacrifice can't be calculated to the end. The student is advised to look up the terms *Sacrifice* and *Combination* in the glossary. A review of *Part Three: Calculation and Combinations*, will also clarify the differences between the two terms.

Diagram #145 is our final example of a sacrifice for purely positional returns.

(145)

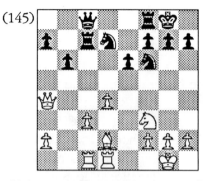

Taimanov-Karpov, Moscow 1973.
Black to play.

White intends to play c3-c4 with a good game, since then the Black Knight's would be contained (due to control of c5, d5, and e5) and White would enjoy a space advantage. To prevent this, Black is willing to part with a pawn. **1...Rc4! 2.Qxa7 Qc6 3.Qa3** Black threatened to win the Queen by ...Ra8. **3...Rc8** For the pawn, Black has left White with a bad Bishop and weak pawns on c3 and a2. Black is now the one with a space advantage, and can also boast an iron grip on the c-file and a fine square on d5 for his Knight. Since White is unable to attack anything in the solid Black position, he is quite helpless and must quietly wait for Black to find a decisive plan. **4.h3 h6** Black is in no hurry, since White cannot do anything. Because of this, Black will slowly put all his pieces on their very best squares. **5.Rb1 Ra4 6.Qb3 Nd5 7.Rdc1 Rc4 8.Rb2 f6** Black will not rush to win his pawn back if it leads to the loss of his other advantages. 8...f6 restricts White's Knight by taking the e5 square away. The immediate 8...Nxc3 9.Rxc3 Rxc3 10.Bxc3 Qxc3 11.Qxc3 Rxc3 12.Ne5 would have led to a draw. **9.Re1 Kf7 10.Qd1 Nf8** The Knight guards all the vulnerable points on h7, g6, and e6. **11.Rb3 Ng6 12.Qb1 Ra8 13.Re4 Rca4 14.Rb2 Nf8 15.Qd3 Rc4 16.Re1 Ra3 17.Qb1 Ng6 18.Rc1 Nxc3** Seeing that he can retain the initiative even after some exchanges, Black finally takes his pawn back. **19.Qd3** Or 19.Bxc3 Raxc3 20.Rxc3 Rxc3 when the threat of ...Rc1+ leaves Black in charge. **19...Ne2+ 20.Qxe2 Rxc1+ 21.Bxc1 Qxc1+ 22.Kh2 Rxf3!!** A combination based upon the loose Rook on b2 and the weakened White King. **23.gxf3 Nh4** At this point White lost on time. Play might have continued 24.Rb3 Qg5 25.Qf1 Qf4+ 26.Kh1 Nxf3 27.Qg2? (27.Rxf3 is forced but hopeless) 27...Qc1+ 28.Qg1 Qxg1 mate.

MAKING USE OF EXTRA MATERIAL:
The Joys Of Eating Wood

If you happen to be in the enviable position of having an advantage in material you must first of all determine just what place this edge in wood has in the creation of a plan. If you have a healthy extra pawn on the queenside but your plan consists of mating the opponent's King on the kingside then the extra material may play no role other than as a kind of endgame insurance. If you are up two pieces for a Rook and are also playing for a mate, your two attacking units (Bishop and Knight) will very likely prove to be more than the enemy's one defensive unit (a Rook) can handle. In a case like this the extra material gives you an advantage in force that you can use to overpower your opponent.

In general, if you have an advantage in material you should base a plan around it (like you would any imbalance). To understand a plan in relation to a material advantage, and to be aware of the things we would like to avoid while trying to achieve it, we must make a study of the *Four Rules Of Material Gain.*

Rule One: If you have a material advantage, find a plan that enables you to use the extra wood (using the extra material to overpower the opponent or trade all the pieces and go into a winning endgame). Don't pat yourself on the back, create ballads in your honor, fall asleep, and expect the game to win itself.

(146)

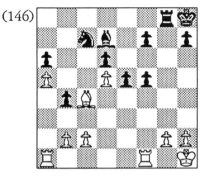

Silman-Delaune, World Open 1990.
White to play.

In this game White had a strong attack and Black was forced to sacrifice the Exchange to ward off White's threats. Black has just played 24...Rg8 and offered a draw. With a pawn for the Exchange, pressure against the White pawn on d5, and the possibility of mobilizing his pawns in the center, Black possesses a measure of compensation for his small material deficit. However White, who was still under the spell of his earlier attack, thought that winning material was his reward for earlier good play and that the game was going to be won without any further effort. Due to this terrible mental attitude White ceased to think, refused the draw offer, and coasted along mindlessly, making one awful move after another. The continuation was **1.h3?? f4 2.Rf2 Bf5 3.Ra4 Rb8 4.Kh2 Be4 5.Rd2 h5 6.Ra1?? h4 7.Ra4 f5 8.Kg1? Kg7 9.Kf2 Kf6** and White found himself in a position where he could not make a useful move. Notice how White played with no plan and allowed Black to strengthen his position in any way he liked. Black went on to win this game.

Now let's return to the position in diagram #146. How can White improve his play? Two factors stand out. White is an Exchange up, so he *must* create open files for his Rooks. Without open files his Rooks are no better than the Black minor pieces. The other critical factor is Black's pawn on f5. At the moment it is a potential target. However, if it can successfully march to f4 it becomes a thorn in White's camp and also frees the d7 Bishop.

White's plan is now clear. He must somehow open files for his Rooks which will allow an eventual penetration into Black's position and also fix the Black pawn on f5. The only way to do this is **1.c3!** Now 1...Rg4 2.Be2 Re4? 3.Bd3 is obviously bad and 1...Rb8 2.g3 leaves Black's pawn stuck on f5 and White always threatening to open up the c-file with cxb4. Note that 2...bxc3? 3.bxc3 Rb2 fails to 4.Rab1 when the threat of Rb7 will prove decisive. This example clearly shows the importance of coming to terms with the imbalances as quickly as possible. Black had various positive features while White's one plus was his extra material. In such positions you have to make use of your advantages or the opponent will take over the game.

Let's look at another example of an extra Exchange. In this case, White correctly makes a point of opening up a file and using his Rook to overpower the opponent.

(147)

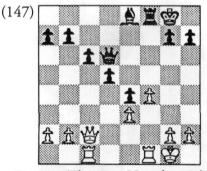

Kramer-Thomas, Utrecht 1949.
White to play.

Black has a Bishop and a pawn vs. a Rook. At the moment the White Rooks are not very active, while the Black center pawns make his position look attractive. Furthermore, if Black can play ...b6, ...c5, and ...Bb5-d3, he will stand very well.

White is winning, however, because he should be able to cope with these problems, when White's material advantage should be able to turn the game in his favor. White's plan is to keep Black's Bishop bad by preventing a ...c6-c5 advance.

White will centralize his Queen on d4 and play to open a file for his Rooks (you must make use of your favorable imbalance. In this case you have an extra Exchange so you have to find a way to get that Rook into the game). He will accomplish this by an eventual b4-b5 advance. Once an open file is established, the Rooks' penetration will be decisive. **1.Qc3** Preparing for b2-b4 and heading for the fine post on d4. **1...Bd7 2.b4 a6 3.Qd4** Black's queenside and center pawns are now stuck on white squares. **3...h6 4.Rfd1** Threatening 5.Qxe4!. **4...Qe7 5.a4 Kh7 6.b5!** Now a file gets ripped open, and the game is won for White. **6...axb5 7.axb5 Ra8 8.bxc6 Bxc6 9.Ra1** "That file belongs to me!" **9...Ra3 10.Rxa3 Qxa3 11.Ra1 Qb3 12.h3** Before the Rook leaves the back rank, White gives his King a comfortable hiding place on h2. Such positions (when the opponent has no counterplay) should never be rushed! King safety must always be taken into account. **12...Qd3 13.Qc5** Avoiding 13.Qxd3 exd3 when the advanced d3 pawn will tie White's pieces down. **13...Kg6 14.Ra8 Kh5** Also hopeless is 14...Kh7, since 15.f5 followed by 16.Kh2 and 17.Qf8 will lead to a quick mate. **15.Kh2!** Now if White's Queen moves in for the kill and leaves the e3 pawn undefended, it won't hang with check. **15...Qe2 16.Rg8, 1-0.**

Rule Two: When you make a successful strike into the opponent's camp and win material, you must often pull your army back towards the center and reorganize your forces. The reason for this is that once you fulfill a plan you often find that your pieces are out of balance and no longer work together. Since a shattered army rarely succeeds, it is of great importance to recentralize your men and get them to relate to each other again. This type of reorganization will prevent the enemy from launching a successful counterattack. With armies that are doing equal work, your advantage in material should prove decisive (you would then go to rule #1).

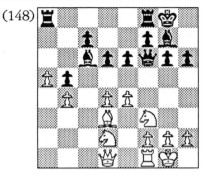

C. Powell-Silman, San Francisco 1981.
Black to play.

In diagram #148 White has lost the Exchange but has compensation in pressure down the open c-file, and Black's pieces have no clear point of attack. However, with an extra Exchange and two Bishops, Black realizes that if he can blast the position open (creating open files for the Rooks and open diagonals for the Bishops) he will have every reason to expect to win. The way to achieve this aim (to open the position) is by a ...c7-c5 advance.

The problem Black faces is that his pieces are not working together towards this goal. In fact, they are not working together towards any goal! With this in mind, Black reorganizes his whole army. He first defends his weak pawns on b5 and c7, then he posts all his pieces in such a way as to support the desired ...c7-c5 advance. The fact that he has to put all his men on the back rank should in no way discourage a player from carrying out the strategic mission that the position gives him. **1...Rfc8!** Guards the c-pawn and prepares an eventual ...c5 push. **2.Qe2 Rab8** Simply defending b5. **3.Nb3 Qd8** Brings the Queen back so it can work with the other pieces and stops any nonsense based on e4-e5 by White. **4.Ne1 Be8!** Clears the way for the c-pawn and gives extra support to Black's kingside structure on f7 and g6 (in anticipation of an f4-f5 attack by White). **5.Nc2 Bf8!** Completes the picture. Black is finally ready to play ...c7-c5. **6.d5 exd5 7.exd5 Qg5** Now White's center is gone, and Black's Queen and dark squared Bishop leap to activity. **8.Ne3 Bg7 9.f4 Qe7 10.f5** A last ditch effort to complicate matters. **10...c5!** The big break finally comes, and with it Black's other pieces decisively enter the game. **11.dxc6 e.p. Bxc6 12.Qf2** After 12.fxg6 fxg6 13.Bxg6 Rf8 Black's active Bishops and material edge will bring about a quick decision. This shows another nice thing about a material advantage: *you can always sacrifice something back and not be down anything.* Kind of like ballast in a hot air balloon. **12...Be4!** Getting rid of White's attacking Bishop. **13.Bxe4** No better is 13.f6 Bxf6!. **13...Qxe4 14.Nd2** White also gets nothing after 14.fxg6 fxg6 15.Qf7+ Kh8. **14...Qxb4 15.Nf3** Also hopeless is 15.fxg6 fxg6 16.Qf7+ Kh7 17.Nd5 Qd4+ 18.Kh1 Rf8 19.Nf6+ Kh8. **15...Qc5** White could have hung it up here. The remaining moves were: **16.fxg6 fxg6 17.Kh1 Kh7 18.h4 Re8 19.Re1 Re7**, 0-1.

> **Rule Three:** When you take material, you put pressure on your opponent to justify his sacrifice! This induces a certain element of panic which can easily send his brain spinning off into the void. A good basic rule goes as follows: if you are in an uncomfortable position (or just want to go all out for the win) and you are offered an unclear sacrifice, you should contain your fear and scarf up the offered meal! By doing this you are saying, "Give me proof or lose!"

Gorman-Silman, Ervin Memorial/San Francisco 1987. **1.e4 c5 2.Nc3 Nc6 3.Nge2 d6 4.d4 cxd4 5.Nxd4 Nf6 6.Be3 Ng4 7.Bg5 Qb6 8.Bb5 Bd7 9.Bxc6?! bxc6 10.0-0**

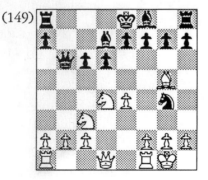

(149)

Black to play.

White has a lead in development and hopes to be able make use of this by opening the position up and attacking the Black King. Black has the two Bishops and has no real weak points. The calm method is to catch up in development and castle when his pair of Bishops should grant him an excellent game (once he is as well developed as White, any opening of the position would favor the side with the Bishops). However, rather than play in such a restrained manner, Black (who was in a must win situation) decides to put real pressure on White by capturing the pawn on b2. All of a sudden White is faced with a major problem: if he doesn't get compensation quickly he will be down a pawn for nothing and a loss will be staring him in the face. **10...Qxb2 11.Qd2 h6!** Black must now get his pieces out as quickly as possible. If he can catch up in development (thereby negating White's one favorable imbalance) he will most likely win the game. **12.Bh4 g5 13.Rab1 Qa3 14.Rb3 Qa5 15.Bg3 Bg7 16.h4?** A mistake that is easy to understand. White feels compelled to start a fight and so he lashes out at Black's kingside. However, this fails because it allows Black to trade off some pieces. *Simplifications to an endgame almost always favor the side with more material.* **16...gxh4 17.Bxh4 Bxd4! 18.Qxd4 Qe5** The dual threats of 19...Qxd4 and 19...Qh2 mate force White to trade Queens. **19.Qxe5 Nxe5** Now Black need only solidify his position and his extra pawn will tell. **20.Rb7 f6 21.f3 Bc8 22.Rb4 Rg8 23.Kh1 Kf7,** White's pressure has been blunted and Black went on to win a long endgame.

Rule Four: When up material you have the added defensive resource of giving material back to stop his attack. While the opponent scrambles to regain his lost wood, you quietly improve your position. When he finally recreates a material balance, you should have succeeded in either equalizing a difficult position, grabbing the initiative, or gaining some sort of positional advantage that will serve you well in the later stages of the game.

(150)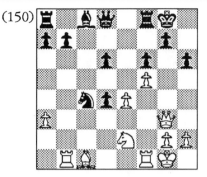

Remlinger-Silman, San Francisco International 1987.
Black to play.

Black is a couple of pawns ahead but matters are not so clear. The d4 pawn is doomed and the pawn on d6 can eventually become weak. To top this off, Black's pieces are not yet developed and his King may come under an attack. Black comes up with a plan based on centralization, i.e. putting his pieces in a centrally located position where they can work together towards a single goal. He gives back his extra material but by doing so is able to develop his remaining forces and put pressure on White's weaknesses on a3 and e4. This brings us to a good general rule: *When in doubt play in the center!* A plan based on centralization will rarely lead you astray because your pieces can quickly go to any area of the board where they may be needed. **19...d5! 20.Bxh6 Rf7 21.Nxd4 Qd6!** It becomes clear that White has misplaced his pieces when he regained his material. Now 22.Qxd6 Nxd6 would leave Black with a double threat of 23...gxh6 and 23...Nxe4. **22.Bf4 Qc5 23.Rfd1 Bd7! 24.Kh1 dxe4 25.Rxb7 Qd5** A look at the respective armies shows an interesting thing: White no longer has a plan. His pieces are thrown here and there, one is attacked and another is pinned. When you take into account Black's beautifully centralized army and the sorry state of White's pawns on a3 and f5, you begin to see the troubles White has. **26.Rb4 a5 27.Rbb1 Ba4 28.Nb3 Qxf5** Black has once again won a pawn but this time he also retains a positional advantage. **29.Rf1 Rd7 30.Be3 Qe5 31.Bf4 Qh5 32.Rfc1 e3 33.h3 Bxb3**, 0-1.

Solve these problems:

(151)

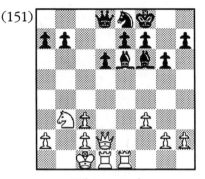

White to play.

After **1.e4 c5 2.Nf3 d6 3.d4 cxd4 4.Nxd4 Nf6 5.Nc3 g6 6.Be3 Bg7 7.f3 0-0 8.Qd2 Nc6 9.Bc4 Bd7 10.Bb3 Rc8 11.0-0-0 Ne5 12.Bg5 Nc4 13.Bxc4 Rxc4 14.Nb3 Rxc3 15.bxc3 Be6 16.e5 Ne8 17.Bh6 Bxe5 18.Bxf8 Kxf8 19.Rhe1 Bf6** we reach the position in the diagram. Black has two Bishops, a pawn, and attacking chances against White's King in exchange for two Rooks. How should White handle this situation?

(152)

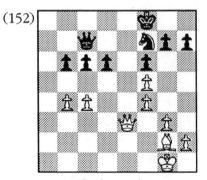

Black to play.

The game has just been adjourned with White sealing 1.b3-b4. White thought he had excellent chances to win. Is this true or was Black able to find resources that his opponent missed?

(153)

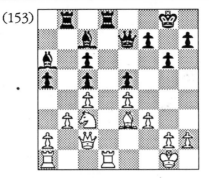

Black to play.

Assess this position and figure out what Black should do.

PART TEN

TEMPORARY IMBALANCES
Initiative and a Lead
in Development

The initiative and a lead in development are important imbalances that are largely misunderstood. Many players getting a lead in development, for example, *will* note that they possess it but won't have any idea how they can take advantage of it.

The initiative is even more insidious. Though top players are always fighting to obtain it, the average tournament warrior wouldn't be able to recognize the initiative if it bit him on the nose!

Why are these imbalances so difficult to grasp? The reason is that they are invisible to the untrained eye! They are based on dynamic considerations instead of static ones. Since we must understand the relationship between dynamics and statics if we are going to fully appreciate development and initiative, I strongly recommend that the serious student make a detailed examination of the concepts presented in this part of the book.

SLOW PLAY
VERSUS FAST PLAY—
STATIC VERSUS DYNAMIC

One of the great philosophical battles on the chess board is when a permanent (static) advantage (space, material, superior pawn structure, etc.) runs head-long into a temporary advantage based on active piece play, a lead in development, threats against the enemy King, or some other sort of pressure on the opponent's position. This type of temporary advantage is considered to be *dynamic* .

Our first example features a game where White is willing to give a static advantage to his opponent; in return he hopes to create threats against Black's King. White is hoping that his dynamic possibilities will compensate for the static plusses that his opponent obtains.

This type of tradeoff is very common in modern chess, but it must be understood that such a war of ideas can lead to victory for either side—a static advantage will not always be of much use against the power of a dynamic assault. On the other hand, if the dynamic potential of the enemy position can be contained and eventually negated, the trusty static advantage will be around to claim the win.

Rohde-Silman, American Open 1989. **1.d4 Nf6 2.c4 e6 3.Nf3 Bb4+ 4.Bd2 Qe7 5.g3 Nc6 6.Nc3 d5 7.cxd5 exd5 8.Bg2 0-0**

9.0-0 Bg4 10.Bg5 Bxc3 Ending the immediate threat against d5.
11.bxc3 h6 12.Bxf6 Qxf6 13.h3 Bxf3 A big decision. Black
hopes to show that the following Bishop versus Knight battle is
all right for him. The move also had some psychology attached
to it: Rohde is a well known attacking (dynamic) player and
Black hoped that the resulting quiet strategic situation would not
be to his opponent's taste. **14.Bxf3 Rad8 15.Qd3** Threatening
both 15.Qb5 with a double attack on b7 and d5, and 15.e4, when
the Bishop would clearly be more active than the Knight.
15...Qe6! Defending d5 and also eyeing the undefended pawn
on h3. **16.Rab1** Not best, since the Knight wanted to head for c4
anyway and after ...b7-b6 this Rook won't have much future on
the b-file. However, even after the calmer 16.Kg2 Black would
prevent e2-e4 and attempt to keep the position partially closed
by 16...f5. **16...Na5 17.e4?!** Bored with the goings-on, White rips
the center open and activates his Bishop. Though Black would
not normally allow this, he decides that the pawn (a permanent
static advantage) he will get in return is more valuable than
White's dynamic compensation.

(154)

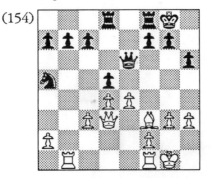

Black to play.

17...dxe4 18.Bxe4 b6 Taking time out to defend his guy on
b7. White won't be able to guard both his hanging pawns on a2
and h3. **19.Rbe1 Qxa2** Black doesn't want to get his Queen in
trouble after 19...Qxh3 20.Bf5. Besides, now Black has a passed
a-pawn. **20.Qf3** Threatening to win his pawn back by 21.Qf5 g6
22.Qf4 with a double attack on h6 and c7. **20...Rd6!** Keeping the

White Queen out of f6 (if Black ever plays ...g7-g6), defending g6 (which will be important later in the game), and blocking the diagonal to his pawn on c7. **21.Qf5** White keeps working with threats, but Black knows that if he can hold on then his extra pawn will eventually give him great winning chances. In other words: Black is willing to be pushed around for awhile for a tasty pawn. It seems that everyone *does* have his price! **21...g6 22.Qf4** Yet another threat! On 22...Kh7 White envisions moves like 23.h4 followed by 24.h5. **22...Nc4!** Enough grovelling; it's time to counterattack! Black will meet 23.Qxh6 with 23...Qd2! when 24.Qxd2 Nxd2 picks up the Exchange and 24.Qh4 Qxc3 is also bad for White. **23.Bd3 Qb3!** Still drooling over the target on c3. **24.Be2?** White cracks and sticks his Bishop on a terrible square. He had to swallow his pride and play 24.Rc1. It's clear that White's initiative is starting to dry up. It's important to point out that the static advantage of the extra pawn on a7 is not what's killing White; instead he is being tortured by the static weakness of his pawn on c3! **24...b5** Refusing to hang his Knight by 24...Qxc3?? 25.Rc1, Black instead takes some time to firmly guard his fine steed on c4 (which, funnily enough, is now superior the the enemy Bishop). **25.Rc1** White finally admits that the c-pawn had to be defended. **25...Kg7** Taking care of his loose pawn on h6. Now Black intends to turn his a-pawn (once an insignificant static plus) into a dynamic force by advancing it. **26.d5** Knowing that he is hopelessly lost, White tries to confuse the issue. **26...Rxd5 27.Qxc7 a5** The rest of the game does not require comment: **28.Qb7 Re5 29.Bd1 Qa3 30.Rc2 Qe7 31.Qc6 Qc5 32.Qd7 Rd5 33.Qb7 Rfd8 34.Bg4 Rd2 35.Rxd2 Rxd2 36.Qe4 Nd6 37.Qf4 Qxc3 38.h4 a4 39.Re1 Qd4 40.Qf3 Rd3**, 0-1.

Our next game shows how a 'dynamic versus static' battle can be part of opening theory. One side is willing to take on a weakness (in this case an isolated pawn) in return for active piece play (a fast play situation); the other side needs to calmly neutralize the enemy's activity (a slow play situation) and then make use of his static advantages.

T.Petrosian-Peters, Lone Pine 1976. **1.c4 Nf6 2.Nc3 c5 3.g3 Nc6 4.Bg2 e6 5.Nf3 Be7 6.d4 d5 7.cxd5 Nxd5 8.0-0 0-0 9.Nxd5 exd5 10.dxc5 Bxc5** In this opening Black willingly accepts an isolated d-pawn in exchange for active pieces and pressure down the e-file against White's e-pawn. **11.a3 a5 12.Ne1!** The Knight is heading for d3 where it eyes the c5 and e5 squares and can also jump to f4 and attack Black's d-pawn. **12...d4?!** Hoping to fix White's e-pawn on e2 and apply pressure down the e-file. The problem with the move is that it makes the Black Bishop a poor piece while simultaneously opening the diagonal for White's light-squared Bishop. 12...Be6 would have been preferable. **13.Nd3 Bb6 14.Bd2 Re8 15.Rc1 Bg4 16.Re1 Rc8** Peters thinks that White would also retain his advantage after 16...Qd7 17.Qb3! Ba7 18.Nf4 followed by 19.h3. **17.h3 Bf5 18.Qb3! Be4 19.Bxe4 Rxe4 20.Qb5** White is in no hurry and slowly builds up pressure against Black's weak pawns on a5, b7, and d4. He can afford to take his time (slow play) since the Black pawns will remain weak for the rest of the game. **20...Na7 21.Rxc8 Nxc8** White wins material after 21...Nxb5? 22.Rxd8+ Bxd8 23.Nc5 Re7 24.Nb3 b6 25.a4 Nd6 26.Nxd4. **22.Bg5 Qd6** Black must avoid an exchange of Queens. Why? Because a Queen trade would allow White to take the c-file with his Rook and use his King to attack the Black pawns without any fear of retaliation by the now non-existant big guns. With the Queens on, Black can keep the White King at bay and even attempt some counterplay by biting at e2 and h3. This is one of the plusses of slow play over fast play; the side in slow play mode can often expect his advantage to grow as the pieces disappear from the board. The fast play side needs to keep the pieces on. **23.Rc1 Na7 24.Qf5 Re8** Black would also be unhappy after 24...Rxe2 25.Qf3 Re8 26.Qxb7. **25.Bf4 Qd8 26.Rc2 Nc6 27.h4 h6 28.Qb5 Na7 29.Qf5 Nc6 30.Kf1! Re6 31.Qb5 Na7 32.Qb3 Nc6 33.h5!** A deep move. Gaining space on the kingside. However, White will eventually have to play g3-g4 to defend the h-pawn and f2-f3 to guard the g-pawn. Won't this ultimately leave his King exposed? **33...Ne7 34.Ke1!**

(155)

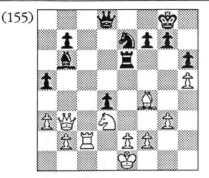

With Black's pieces unable to generate any activity because of their need to defend the many weak pawns, White realizes that he has all the time in the world. This allows him the luxury of running his King away from potential danger—it will be quite safe on b1. **34...Nd5 35.Qb5 Nf6** Taking the Bishop on f4 would leave White with a superior minor piece. **36.Kd1 Nd5 37.Be5 Ne7 38.g4** Since the King is no longer on the kingside, White can fearlessly move his pawns there. Now f5 has been taken away from Black's Knight and White's space advantage in that sector begins to grow. **38...Nc6 39.Bg3 Na7 40.Qb3 Nc6 41.Kc1!** Threatening Nd3-f4-d5. Black gets counterplay after the immediate 41.Nf4? d3! 42.exd3 Rd6. White should avoid anything that allows Black even a smidgeon of active play. **41...Re4 42.f3 Re3 43.Kb1 Ne7?** A mistake that hastens the end. However, if Black had remained passive then White would have eventually broken through on the kingside with Bg3-f2 followed by a kingside pawn storm. **44.Bh4** Jumping at the chance to obtain an active Knight versus a poor Bishop. **44...Qd6 45.Bxe7 Rxe7 46.Rc8+ Kh7 47.Rf8!** Qc7 White gets a winning endgame after 47...Qe6 48.Qxe6 fxe6 49.Ne5, while 47...Rxe2 48.Qxf7 Qe6 49.Qxe6 Rxe6 50.Nf4 followed by Ng6 weaves a mating net. **48.f4! Bc5?! 49.Qd5 Re5 50.Rxf7!**, 1-0.

Peters is a fine attacking player but he was never able to get anything going in this game at all. Petrosian's play was not exciting but proved very effective: all he did was restrict Black's activity and, when everything was just right, eventually capitalize on his long term (static) advantages (weak Black pawns at a5, b7, and d4, plus kingside space). White was never in any hurry because he knew that these plusses were not going to run away!

By now it may look like a static advantage will always triumph over a dynamic advantage if the static side plays with care. Nothing could be further from the truth! A superiority in dynamics (active piece play, more pieces in one sector that can lead to a brutal attack, combinative possibilities) is every bit as useful as a static advantage. In fact, it's not at all unusual to see the static side completely overwhelmed by a hard hitting opponent. In the end, the comparison between statics and dynamics comes to down one important question: Will the immediate force of dynamic potential destroy the enemy before the static influences can come into effect and take over the game? This means that if you can't unlock the position's dynamic potential and make use of it, you will definitely succumb to the opponent's static plusses. The following game illustrates this in a graphic way.

Kelson-Silman, Reno 1993. **1.e4 c5 2.Nf3 Nc6 3.d4 cxd4 4.Nxd4 g6 5.Nc3 Bg7 6.Be3 Nf6 7.Nxc6 bxc6 8.e5 Ng8 9.f4 Nh6 10.Qf3 0-0 11.0-0-0**

(156)
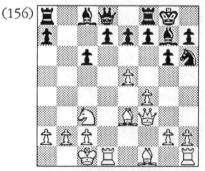

Black to play. When each side castles on opposite wings we usually see attacks against both Kings. In diagram #156, though, White enjoys certain static advantages that could easily drag Black down the dark tunnel of oblivion: White has a space advantage in the center thanks to his pawn on e5; Black's

Bishop on g7 is hitting a stone wall on e5; Black's Knight is out of play and will be entombed by h2-h3 followed by g2-g4. If White is allowed to advance these pawns and also play Bc4, Black will be squashed by his lack of mobility.

Realizing that the game is virtually hanging in the balance, Black starts a tactical operation designed to cure the ills of his position and tear down the plusses of the enemy camp. **11...d6!** Offering a pawn to destroy White's block on e5 and activate his g7 Bishop. Black also threatens to win the Exchange by 12...Bg4. **12.Qxc6** After a long think, White finally grabs the pawn. Now White has added a material advantage to his other static plusses. What has Black gained? First on the list is the gain of time Black will enjoy by attacking the White Queen. This gives him a lead in development. Second on the list is the fact that Black has gotten a new open c-file which can be used to bother the White King. Most importantly, though, by taking the pawn White has renounced his intentions of attacking Black's King simply because White no longer has the time to get anything under way. **12...Bd7 13.Qd5 Ng4!** White missed this tactical trick which allows Black to get rid of his inactive Knight. 14.Bg1 allows 14...Bh6! 15.g3 Nxe5! when the Knight triumphantly enters the game. Also poor is 14.exd6 (freeing the monster on g7) 14...Nxe3 15.dxe7 Qxe7 16.Qxd7 Qb4! and the threats of 17...Nxd1 and 17...Rab8 leave White in a bad way. **14.Qf3 Nxe3 15.Qxe3** We still have a static versus dynamic situation but now the dynamic end of the argument has a clear advantage. True, White owns an extra pawn. But Black's two Bishops and open queenside files give him strong pressure against White's queenside and King. Note that White will never be tempted to win another pawn by exd6 since that would allow the g7 Bishop to come powerfully into play. **15...Be6!** Not allowing White to place his Bishop on the c4 square. **16.Nd5** Tying Black's Queen down to the defense of e7 and once again threatening to move his Bishop to c4. **16...Rc8** Taking control of the c-file and still denying White's Bishop access to c4. **17.Ba6 Rc5!** White is lost. His extra pawn is playing no part in the game and he about to be swamped on the queenside. A Knight retreat allows ...Qa5 followed by ...Rb8 when Black's whole army is pounding down the gates to the White King. For a more detailed discussion of the position after 17.Ba6 see diagram #31 in Part Three, Chapter One (Calculation & Combinations). **18.c4 Bxd5 19.Rxd5 Rxd5 20.cxd5 Qa5 21.Bc4 Rc8 22.b3 Qxa2** Poor White has never been given a moment's rest since he took the pawn on move twelve! Now material is even and ...Qa1+ threatens to pick up a Rook. **23.Re1 dxe5 24.fxe5 Bh6!** A nice little combination. White has been trying to keep this Bishop blocked out of play for most of the game; now it strikes the decisive blow on a different diagonal! The finish needs no comment: **25.Qxh6 Qxb3 26.Re4 Rxc4+ 27.Rxc4 Qxc4+ 28.Kb1 Qe4+! 29.Kc1 Qxd5 30.Qe3 Qxg2 31.Qxa7 Qh1+**, 0-1. White loses his two remaining pawns.

It should be clear that a sense of urgency is often needed to make full use of one's dynamic possibilities. In the game we just saw, Black willingly chose an opening that allowed a sharp battle to come about. However, sometimes things go wrong and we are dragged into positions that may not be to our taste. Once you reach a certain type of position, though, style and taste no longer matter; you *must* figure out what positive imbalances you have going for you and make immediate use of them. It doesn't matter if you like taking or sacrificing material—you have to obey the board and do what the position wants you to do.

(157)

F.Frenkel-Silman, National Open 1992.
Black to play.

I had not been happy for several moves in my game with Frenkel. As a player who loves to take material and bore my opponent to death in an endgame, I found myself a solid pawn down. Instead of panicking, though, I calmly assessed the situation and made use of my lead in development to reach the position in diagram #157.

Still a pawn down, Black will certainly lose if he can't make use of his more active pieces and the vulnerable position of the White King. Here we have the sense of urgency that was alluded to earlier—White can't be given time to rest and develop the remainder of his forces. **1...Rh8 2.Qg1 Ng4!** Working with threats all the time. White must prevent 3...Rh2+ 4.Bg2 Nf3+ picking up the Queen. On 3.Qg3 Black can win the Exchange by 3...Nb3+. **3.Bg2 b5!** Opening up new lines of attack on the queenside and posing fresh problems for White to solve. **4.cxb5 Nxb5 5.Nfe2 c4!** Blasting the center open. 6.d4 or 6.dxc4 are both impossible due to 6...Nxc3 with a discovered attack on the g5 Bishop. **6.Bf4** White rejected 6.Bxe7 since that gave Black the added possibility of 6...Bh6+. **6...Rf8!** Overloading the Knight on e2, which must now guard c3 and f4. **7.d4 Nxd4 8.Nxd4 Rxf4** The pawn has been regained and White no longer has anything to boast of: Black has the superior pawn structure, more active pieces, safer King, and the two Bishops. In other words, White is hopelessly lost. **9.Nde2 Rf2 10.Ke1 Qb6 11.Bh3 Bxc3+ 12.bxc3 Qe3 13.Qxg4** White also loses after 13.Bxg4 Rxe2+. **13...Bxg4 14.Bxg4+ Kc7 15.g7 Rg2!**, 0-1.

White's extra pawn was never a factor because Black never allowed it to be. That's the whole philosophy of a dynamic advantage: By putting constant pressure on the opponent, you never allow his static plusses to become important.

The next two chapters on development and initiative delve into other aspects of statics and dynamics.

A LEAD IN DEVELOPMENT

A lead in development is definitely a useful imbalance—albeit a temporary, dynamic one. Since it tends to disappear after a few moves, the side with the extra development should try to use it quickly to create some type of static imbalance. For example, you might be able to double or isolate an enemy pawn, gain a space advantage in some area of the board, get a superior minor piece, etc. In this way your opponent may eventually get all his men out, but he will be permanently saddled with a weakness or face some other type of problem.

Of course, the ultimate ideal of a lead in development is to blast through the enemy lines of defense and chew him up before he can get all his forces into play.

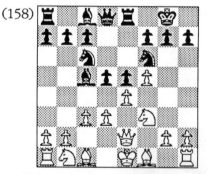

(158)

Tchigorin-Burn, Ostend 1906.
Black to play.

White possesses an advantage in space (static) on the kingside. However, Black enjoys a great lead in development (dynamic) and White's King is still sitting in the middle (dynamic inferiority). Clearly, if White is able to play Bg5, Nbd2 and 0-0-0, Black's lead in development will no longer exist while White's space on the kingside will remain. With this in mind, Black has to find a way to make use of his advantages while they still exist. As it turned out, Black was up to the challenge and played: **1...Bxf5!** Black starts an attack before White can get his men out. *If you can't open up the position, a lead in development will not prove effective.* **2.exf5 e4** and White is already lost. If he moves his Knight then ...exd3 picks up the Queen.

Do experienced players really forget that it's bad to leave the King in the middle and fall behind in development? No, all good players are well aware of these factors. However, sometimes they become so involved with winning material, gaining space, or creating a weakness that they take a chance and walk the tightrope—they fall off when they fail to judge the resultant position correctly.

Silman-Peters, Summit Match, 1989. **1.d4 Nf6 2.c4 e6 3.Nc3 Bb4 4.Qc2 d6 5.Bg5 Nbd7 6.Nf3 h6 7.Bh4 Qe7 8.e3 b6 9.Bd3 Bb7 10.0-0-0 Bxc3 11.Qxc3 c5 12.Kb1 cxd4?** Opening the e-file was certainly not necessary. However, Black noted that he could give White an isolated d-pawn and he gets so carried away with his plans that he fails to sense the danger until it is too late. **13.exd4 d5 14.Rhe1**

(159)

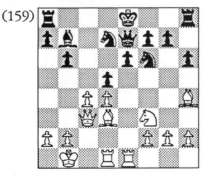

Black to play.

The White army is clearly more active than their Black counterparts. **14...Rc8** Still blinded by his plans. Better was 14...0-0, though 15.Ne5 would still favor White. **15.Qb3** At this point all thoughts of giving White an isolated pawn should have been thrown out the window! Unfortunately Black was unwilling to accept that things had turned out badly for him and so he continues to make threatening gestures that do nothing to make up for his lack of development. **15...g5?** The unpleasant pin is broken but the Black King will never find a truly safe haven. **16.Bg3 Ba6?** Another loss of time that Black won't recover from. Black had to castle and cross his fingers. **17.Ne5!** Virtually winning. Some sample lines: 1) 17...Nxe5 18.dxe5 and the threats of 19.Qa4+ and 19.exf6 kill Black; 2) 17...Kf8 18.Nxd7+ Qxd7 19.Qa3+; 3) 17...0-0 18.cxd5 Bxd3 19.Nxd3 Nxd5 20.Qxd5; 4) 17...dxc4 18.Bxc4 Bxc4 19.Nxc4 and White will hop into d6 with a Knight or a Bishop with great effect. **17...Nb8 18.f4** Following the rule that the side with more development should try to open the position. **18...0-0 19.fxg5 hxg5 20.h4!** Cracking the kingside open. Now 20...Ne4 is strongly answered by 21.cxd5!. **20...dxc4 21.Bxc4 Nh5 22.Bxa6 Nxa6 23.Qf3 Ng7 24.Nc6! Qb7 25.d5!** Every White piece joins in the attack. The end is near. **25...Rfe8 26.Qf6** Threatening to mate with 27.Be5. **26...exd5 27.Ne7+ Rxe7 28.Rxe7**, 1-0.

The fact that White tried so hard to open the position in the last example leads us to believe that one should never allow the opponent a signifcant lead in development if the position is wide open. This is a good rule to live by—in an open position I will never do anything that allows my opponent a big lead in development unless my King is safely castled and I am sure that I can catch up before major damage is done.

Our next game is a stern warning for the greedy at heart.

Browne-Quinteros, Wijk aan Zee 1974. **1.e4 c5 2.Nf3 d6 3.Bb5+ Bd7 4.Bxd7+ Qxd7 5.c4 Qg4?!** A bit too greedy since, aside from losing time, it also helps White to open up the position. **6.0-0 Qxe4 7.d4** White tries to rip it open as fast as he can. **7...cxd4 8.Re1 Qc6 9.Nxd4 Qxc4?**

(160)

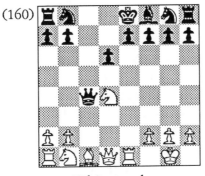

White to play.

Black's first capture was greedy but this is simply suicide. Not only does Black fall further behind in dvelopment (thereby increasing White's existing imbalance) but he also opens up more lines for White's pieces! **10.Na3 Qc8 11.Nab5** Threatening to win immediately with 12.Nxd6+. The obvious defensive move 11...e6 gets eaten alive by 12.Nf5 with an unstoppable disaster on d6. **11...Qd7 12.Bf4** Still threatening to break in on d6. Notice how White is able to make threats and bring out his final forces while Black has difficulty getting any pieces out at all. **12...e5 13.Bxe5!** With such a lead in development all White has to do is break through—how much material you have to give up to do so is not really a consideration. Now the Rooks join in the massacre, so we can say that White has not really given up a Bishop as much as he has gained two Rooks! **13...dxe5 14.Rxe5+ Be7 15.Rd5!** Not giving Black a moment's breath. By forcing Black to keep his pieces at home White is in effect material ahead. **15...Qc8 16.Nf5 Kf8 17.Nxe7 Kxe7 18.Re5+**, 1-0.

A significant advantage in development is not an easy thing to achieve. Usually such a situation comes about after one side sacrifices a pawn in the opening or makes some sort of positional concession. This creates the desired lead in development but it also places the attacker in the position of facing long-range static problems. This in turn creates certain psychological difficulties since the attacker is under pressure to justify his sacrificial decision.

T.Petrosian-B.Larsen, San Antonio 1972. **1.d4 e6 2.Nf3 f5 3.g3 Nf6 4.Bg2 b5 5.Ne5 c6 6.Nd2 Qb6 7.e4!?** White already has a lead in development and if he wished, he could calmly defend his d4 pawn and retain a good position. However Black's risky opening has left White with the desire to punish his opponent. In order to achieve that, White decides to sacrifice a pawn and increase his lead in development even more. **7...Qxd4 8.N5f3 Qc5 9.exf5 Qxf5 10.0-0** Let's let Petrosian himself tell us what is going on: "For the sacrificed pawn White has an appreciable advantage in development. If there were something to attack in Black's position, it might be possible to capitalize on this. Unfortunately, there are no vunerable spots in evidence. At the same time Black's position does not inspire confidence; his Queen will be forced to run about, and his queenside is very tied up due to the action of the Bishop on g2." **10...Nd5! 11.Nd4 Qf7 12.N2f3 Qh5!** Stops unpleasant moves like Ng5 and Ne5. **13.Re1 Be7 14.Re5 Qf7 15.Re2 0-0 16.Ne5 Qh5**

(161)

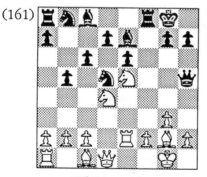

White to play.

Once again I think it's appropriate to let Petrosian become our teacher: "Now after the preparatory 17.Bf3 Qe8 18.Nxb5, 18...Rxf3 is a simple reply. The Queen continues to promenade fearlessly.

It was precisely this fearlessness, this immunity, which made me feel that somehow White's initiative had dried up, and that he had nothing for the pawn. But then I remembered an ancient truth: *many players, sacificing a pawn, lose because they play as if they had lost it, rather than deliberately parted with it.*"

This shows us that there is a difference in giving up material as a means of highlighting other imbalances in your position, compared to giving up wood to gain a temporary initiative, attack or lead in development. In the former, the sacrifice is logically based on the specific imbalances in a position; while in the latter case the decision is often emotional in nature and puts great psychological pressure on both sides—one player must defend with great care, the other feels the constraints of time, knowing that the material deficit may eventually catch up with him.

White eventually won the game after a back and forth battle.

Our next example demonstrates the type of pressure the attacker is under. By sacrificing a pawn in the opening, the attacker makes it clear that he is a gambler. He is taking a risk in order to wipe you out. However, if the defender gets everything in order, it is not uncommon for the once fearless attacker to panic and lash out in desperation. This typically leads to an even quicker demise.

C.Diebert-Silman, World Open 1989. **1.d4 Nf6 2.Nc3 d5 3.e4 dxe4** Diebert has played this gambit on many occasions with great success. **4.f3 exf3 5.Nxf3** White has a lead in development for his pawn but Black enjoys a solid position. The first thing Black wants to do is get his King to safety. **5...g6 6.Bc4 Bg7 7.Bg5 0-0 8.0-0 c5** Once the King is safe a counterattack in the center is called for. The idea is to gain a little space so his last couple of pieces can develop to good squares. **9.d5** Taking c6 away from the Black Knight. Black would keep his pawn after 9.dxc5 Qa5. **9...Nbd7 10.Qe2 Nb6 11.Rad1 Bf5** Black has managed to get his army mobilized and his King to safety. At this point White begins to doubt his compensation—the same psychological failing that Petrosian pointed out earlier. **12.Rd2** Black threatened to win the c2 pawn by 12...Bxc2 13.Qxc2 Nxc4. **12...Nc8!**

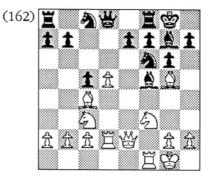

(162)

Heading for d6, which will give the f5 Bishop more support and also block White's d5 pawn. It should be noticed that White's pawn on d5 actually acts like a traitor since it gets in the way of White's Knight on c3, Bishop on c4 and Rook on d2. Seeing that it's about to be fixed in its location, White panics—the psychological specter of the pawn minus begins to show itself. **13.d6? Nxd6 14.Nd5 Nxd5 15.Bxd5 Qb6!** Aside from having two extra pawns, Black's pieces also enjoy great activity. **16.Bxe7** Getting one pawn back but running into other problems. **16...Rae8** All of a sudden White's pieces are pinned and he finds himself hopelessly lost. **17.Re1 Nc8 18.Bxf8 Rxe219.Rdxe2 Bxf8 20.Ne5 Nd6** Black's material advantage led to a quick victory.

CHAPTER THREE

INITIATIVE

The initiative is a term that denotes control of the game. When you have the initiative you call the shots and the opponent must take on the role of the defender. The initiative can be based on either dynamic or static factors. If you are attacking a weak pawn and your opponent is defending it, we have a case of the initiative based on static considerations. If you are beating up your opponent due to a lead in development, we have a case of a dynamic initiative (the game Browne-Quinteros in chapter two is a typical example).

A player can have the initiative if he is materially even, up or down. A typical case of a slight opening initiative is the following: **1.e4 c5 2.Nf3 Nc6 3.d4 cxd4 4.Nxd4 g6 5.c4 Nf6 6.Nc3 d6 7.f3 Nxd4 8.Qxd4 Bg7 9.Be3 0-0 10.Qd2** White has the initiative because his space advantage and Black's lack of counterplay allow White to dictate the tempo of the game. After the further **10...Qa5 11.Rc1 Be6 12.Nd5** Black must fight for the initiative by **12...Qxa2! 13.Nxe7+ Kh8** when Black has created certain imbalances that could turn out in his favor. In this case we would have a battle between White's superior pawn structure and advantage in space versus Black's lead in development and active pieces. In the 1970's, though, Black would usually answer 12.Nd5 with 12...Qxd2+? and suffer after 13.Kxd2 Bxd5 14.cxd5. Now the initiative is permanently in White's hands because all the imbalances are in his favor (space and two Bishops).

The example that we have just seen is the first hint that a large part of successful chess strategy revolves around the battle for the initiative—it starts in the opening and continues throughout the game. This struggle for the lead in the dance often takes on epic proportions—a good player will do almost anything to impose his will on the opponent.

(163)
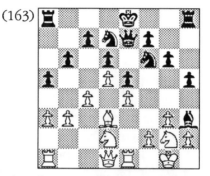

Saidy-Silman, Paul Masson Masters 1975.
Black to play.

In diagram #163 White intends to take the initiative with b4 followed by an eventual c4-c5 advance. Rather than bow to White's wishes and play a defensive game by castling and trying to hold on, Black decides to initiate a risky kingside counterattack. **16...h4!!?** Black sacrifices the Exchange so that his Knight can find a nice home on f4 and the White King position will be weakened. Perhaps the best thing about the move is that Black will retain the initiative for a long time to come because White will be too busy defending to make gestures on the queenside. **17.Nxh4 Rxh4 18.gxh4 Nh5** Picking up the h4 pawn and heading for f4. **19.Bf1 Qxh4 20.Bxh3 Qxh3 21.Qf3 Qh4 22.Kh1 Ke7!** Black can only hope for success if his whole army joins in the attack. **23.Rg1 Ndf6** Preventing Rg4. **24.Rae1 Rh8** Threatening 25...Qxh2+!! 26.Kxh2 Nf4+ 27.Kg3 Rh3 mate. **25.Nf1 g5!** Everything will play a part here. Black intends to continue with ...g4, ...Nh7-g5-f3. Notice that White's Rooks have not proven themselves superior to Black's minor pieces because they lack open files into the enemy camp. **26.b4 g4 27.Qe3**

axb4 28.axb4 Nh7 29.Qe2 Threatening not only Rxg4 or Qxg4 but also Nf1-g3-f5. Has White finally succeeded in retaking the initiative? **29...f5!!** A very nice blocking sacrifice. After 30.exf5 N5f6 Black would threaten ...Ng5-f3 and he would not have to worry about White's Knight settling into f5. **30.Ng3 Ng7 31.Nxf5+ Nxf5 32.Qxg4** Unfortunate, but 32.exf5 Ng5 33.Rg2 Nf3 34.Ra1 gets mated after 34...Qxh2+. **32...Nf6 33.Qxh4 Nxh4** The battle for the initiative has ended with Black getting two strong Knights for a Rook and two pawns. Black has all the chances but a last minute blunder allows White to get away with a draw: **34.Re3 Nh5 35.h3 Kf7 36.Kh2 Nf4 37.Reg3 Nhg6 38.Ra1 Ne2 39.Rf3+ Ngf4 40.Ra7 Rc8 41.c5 bxc5 42.bxc5 Kf6??** Black could have won with the obvious 42...dxc5 43.d6 Ke6. **43.c6 Rg8 44.Rxc7 Rg2+ 45.Kh1 Rg1+**, 1/2-1/2.

We have seen how a material sacrifice often enables a player to wrest the initiative from an opponent who seems to be in control. Knowing this, the player with the initiative might consider refusing such a gift. It's wonderful to win material, but don't accept a sacrifice if it means passing the initiative to the enemy.

Silman-Schroer, Southern California Action Championship 1990. **1.d4 Nf6 2.c4 c5 3.d5 b5** In the Benko Gambit, Black sacrifices a pawn and tries to take the intiative right away. **4.cxb5 a6 5.b6** Keeping the a-file closed. By doing this White renounces his extra pawn but limits the activity of the Black forces. White eventually hopes to take the initiative in the center. **5...Qxb6 6.Nc3 e6 7.e4 Be7 8.Nf3** Threatening 9.d6! when 9...Qxd6 10.Qxd6 Bxd6 11.e5 wins a piece. **8...exd5?** This reaction to the threatened 9.d6 allows White to take over the game. **9.e5 Ne4 10.Nxd5 Qa5+ 11.Nd2** Intending to win the Black Knight on e4 by 12.b4!. **11...Nxd2** Saves the Knight but falls further behind in development. You can tell that the initiative is firmly in White's hands because Black is reacting to White's moves and threats. **12.Bxd2 Qd8** Black expects to complete his development by ...0-0, ...Bb7, and ...Nc6. **13.Qg4!** Not giving his opponent the time to get his pieces out. 13...0-0 loses material to 14.Bh6 so Black is forced to weaken his kingsdie. **13...g6 14.Qe4** This looks strong. White threatens both 15.Nf6+ and 15.Nxe7, in both cases with a discovered attack on Black's a8 Rook. **14...0-0!** Played instantly! After 15.Nxe7+ Qxe7 16.Qxa8 Qxe5+ 17.Be3 Nc6 Black would be the one with a lead in development and the initiative. True, White would possess an extra Rook, but his King would be dangerously placed in the center and his Queen would be out of play on the queenside.

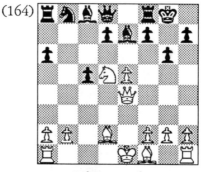

(164)

White to play.

15.Bc4! White likes material but the price was way too high. Instead he completes his development and hopes to make use of the weakened d5 square and the loose dark-squares around Black's King. **15...Nc6 16.0-0 Bb7 17.Bh6** Development is about even but White is still calling the shots. Note that White didn't start his attack until his King was safely castled. **17...Re8 18.Rfe1** Don't forget the Rooks! Now the e-pawn is defended and Black must worry about threats to his pawn on f7 via Qf4 or Qf3. **18...Na5** Getting rid of White's strong Bishop. However, Black's many weak points on the d-file and the kingside still leave White in complete control. This is a case of the initiative being fed by static considerations. **19.Rad1 Nxc4 20.Qxc4 Rb8 21.Qc3!** Defending b2 and staring at a potential mate on g7. **21...Bxd5** The pieces come off but Black's problems remain. This is because White has the initiative *and* long term static advantages. **22.Rxd5 Qb6?** Losing, but his position was very bad in any case. **23.e6! Qxb2 24.exf7+ Kxf7 25.Qc4!**, 1-0.

I will conclude this part of the book with a game that illustrates a battle for the initiative spanning the opening right into the endgame.

V.Pupols-Silman, Portland 1985. **1.d4 Nf6 2.c4 e6 3.Nc3 Bb4 4.Qb3 c5 5.dxc5 Nc6 6.Nf3 Ne4 7.Bd2 Nxd2** Black has gained the two Bishops and will now try to create a pawn structure where the Knights are inactive (using the Steinitz rule) and the Bishops are strong. **8.Nxd2 f5** Taking away the e4 square from White's Knights. **9.g3 Bxc5 10.Bg2 b6 11.0-0 Bb7 12.e4**

(165)

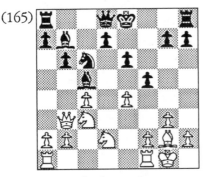

Black to play.

A critical moment in the game. White is trying to take the initiative by creating some squares for his Knights. For example, after 12...0-0 13.exf5 White will acquire either e4 or d5. **12...f4!** Black wants to be in control and refuses to give in to White's wishes! The pawn sacrifice weakens the White King and keeps all of White's minor pieces bottled up. **13.gxf4 Nd4 14.Qd1 0-0 15.f5** Seeing that the f4 pawn is going to fall, White sells it dearly by making Black give up one of those precious central squares. **15...Qh4!** Playing for the attack. Now 16.fxe6 dxe6 keeps control over d5 and opens up the f-file for Black's Rooks. **16.Nf3 Nxf3+ 17.Qxf3 exf5** The pawn has been regained and the Black Bishops are dominating the action. **18.Nd5? fxe4 19.Qxe4 Bxf2+** Black's initiative has resulted in the win of a pawn. **20.Kh1 Qxe4** By going into an endgame Black gives up on the initiative for a short while. Instead he concentrates on consolidating the advantages he has gained. This illustrates a rule set forth earlier in the book: *When you win material, stop rushing forward. Instead you must tighten everything up, defend your weak points, get your army to work together again, and only then start the final assault.*

The first order of business is to insure the safety of his main trump—the two Bishops. The extra pawn will not be activated for a long time. **21.Bxe4 Kh8** To prevent the loss of the b7 Bishop by Ne7+. **22.b3 Rae8 23.Bg2 Re2** With everything safe Black once again tries to seize control of the game. **24.a4 a5 25.Rad1 g6** Ending back rank mate problems. **26.Rd3 Rb2** The combination of the Rook on the seventh and the two Bishops on an open board leave White tied up and helpless. **27.Rfd1 Bc5 28.Rf1 Rxf1+ 29.Bxf1 Kg7 30.Bh3 Bc6 31.Bg4 h5 32.Bd1 d6 33.Bf3 Bd7** The other Bishop finally rears its ugly head. **34.Ne3 Bh3** Now White's King is in jeopardy. Notice how each of Black's pieces is superior to its White counterpart. **35.Nd1 Rb1** White is paralyzed and decides to shed another pawn for a bit of freedom. **36.Rd2 Rxb3 37.Be4 Ra3 38.Nb2 Ra1+ 39.Rd1 Rxd1+ 40.Nxd1 Bd4!** Black has retained the initiative from the opening to the endgame by utilizing the imbalances he created at the beginning of the game. Now White's Knight is trapped by a very dominant dark-squared Bishop and Black threatens to win it with 41...Bg4 since 42.Bc2 is answered by 42...Bf3 mate. **41.Bf3 Kf6 42.Be2 Ke5 43.Bf3 h4 44.Be2 Kf4 45.Bd3 Bg4** Threatening mate and the Knight. **46.h3 Bxd1**, 0-1.

Solve These Problems

(166)

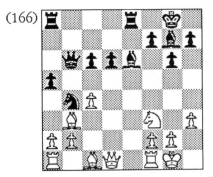

White to play.

Do you think White can get away with 1.Qxd6?

(167)

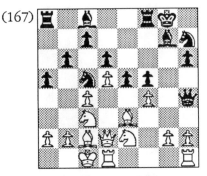

White to play.

White doesn't fear ...e4 or ...exf4 since both moves allow White's Knight to come to a powerful square on either d4 or f4. On the other hand, White does not wish to play 1.fxe5 since 1...dxe5 leaves the White minor pieces with no advanced posts and gives Black a mobile center. How should White handle this position?

(168)

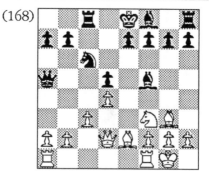

Black to play.

In the diagrammed position Black played for queenside space with 1...b7-b5. Is this a good move?

(169)

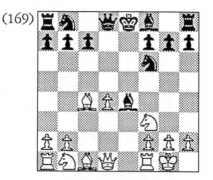

White to play.

The position in the diagram was reached after the following moves: **1.d4 d5 2.c4 dxc4 3.e3 e5 4.Bxc4 exd4 5.exd4 Nf6 6.Nf3 Bf5 7.0-0**. Black now tried **7...Be4**.

What is Black's idea? Is this move any good? What should White do?

PART ELEVEN

OPEN FILES

"The aim of all maneuvers on an open file is the ultimate intrusion along this file onto the seventh or eighth rank, i.e., into the enemy position."—Nimzovich.

Rooks need open files if they are to become a force in the game. However, if the open file does not fit in with the overall strategic plan, then it is not at all clear if you should play to control it—each position has its own answer. In particular, putting one's Rooks on a file often just leads to the opponent doing the same, and a subsequent massive trade down this file would then be a typical result. Of course, trades are not to be spurned, especially if you have prevented the opponent from dominating a file that could lead to an eventual unpleasant penetration.

Before you decide to fight for a file or simply give it to the opponent, you should answer the following questions:

1) Is a penetration along this file possible for my opponent or myself? If it turns out to be a dead end street then why bother with it in the first place?

2) Can I afford to take the time to place my Rooks on this file or do I have more urgent business to attend to elsewhere?

3) If I place my Rooks on this file will they work with the rest of my pieces and influence the imbalances in the position?

4) Do certain factors in the position call for me to retain at least one Rook? If so, I might want to avoid the file (and a possible exchange along it) altogether.

PENETRATION DOWN AN OPEN FILE

Like dogs to a bone, Rooks have a natural attraction to the seventh rank. Once on the seventh, a Rook usually attacks many pawns and often traps the enemy King on the back rank.

(170)

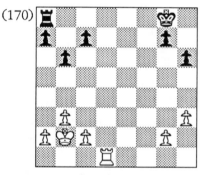

White to move.

Diagram #170 shows what may look like an equal position to the untrained eye. However, White actually has a won game because his Rook can dominate the seventh rank. **1.Rd7 Rc8** 1...c5 leads to the same type of thing. **2.Kc3 Kf8 3.Kc4** Simply intending Kb5 followed by Kc6. **3...a6** To prevent Kb5. 3...c6 hangs the a7 pawn. Ideas like 3...g5 4.Kb5 Ke8 lose to either 5.Kc6 or 5.Rh7. **4.Kd5 c5 5.Rd6 Rb8 6.Kc6** And Black must lose material. Loss of the game will follow.

Some books claim that control of the seventh rank is worth as much as a pawn. In the absence of more important considerations, this makes perfect sense: the seventh rank makes your Rook better, and therefore more valuable, than the opponent's piece.

(171)

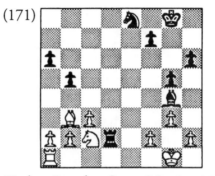

Fischer-Spassky, Santa Monica 1966
White to play.

White is a solid pawn ahead and has the move but the strong placement of the enemy Rook on the seventh makes a win impossible. **1.Ne3 Bf3 2.Bc2 Nd6** It's important that Black make use of all his pieces. **3.b3** This keeps the Black Knight out of c4 and makes the b-pawn immune from the Black Rook. **3...Kf8 4.a4** Getting the last queenside pawn off his second rank and preparing to open a file for his own Rook. **4...Ne4 5.Bxe4** Black's pieces get a little too active after 5.axb5 Nxf2 6.Bf5 (to stop ...Nh3+) 6...g4! 7.bxa6 Nh3+. **5...Bxe4 6.axb5 axb5 7.b4** Making the White b-pawn immune from attack and fixing its opposite number on b5. It looks like White has made progress but the poor position of the White King gives Black enough counterplay to hold the game. **7...Rb2** If White's Rook passively stays on the first rank then he will not be able to achieve anything. If it journeys down the a-file for an adventure then Black will get a check on the back rank. **8.g4 Kg7 9.Kf1 Kf6 10.Ra5** White decides to allow an immediate draw. **10...Rb1+ 11.Ke2 Rb2+ 12.Kf1**, 1/2-1/2.

Though the seventh rank is the ultimate goal of every Rook due to it's ability to attack pawns and tie down the enemy King, the sixth rank also has its virtues:

1) It attacks any enemy pawn on that rank;

2) Like a Rook on the seventh, it allows for domination of a file by bringing a Rook and/or Queen up behind it;

3) It is always ready to jump to the seventh.

(172)

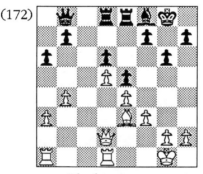

Black to move.

White stands better because his Bishop is much superior to its pathetic counterpart on f8. However, it doesn't seem like anyone will dominate the c-file because as soon as one player puts a Rook there the opponent will challenge and the result will be mass exchanges. Matters change, though, if Black were to play **1...b5??** since White could dominate the game immediately by **2.Rac1 Rc8 3.Rc6!** Now Black does not want to play 3...Rxc6 because after 4.dxc6 White would have a crushing passed pawn on c6 and the Black pawn on d6 would be very weak. After 3.Rc6! Black might try 3...Qb7 but then 4.Rdc1 followed by 5.Qc2 forces Black to either make the losing capture on c6 or to give White total control of the c-line.

This very useful idea of placing a Rook on a weak square on the sixth and then building up behind it was used to perfection in our next example.

(173)

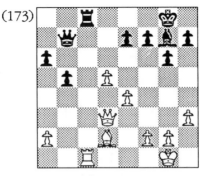

Karpov-Kasparov, World Championshiop Match 1990.
White to play.

It appears that the Rooks will be traded, when we would be left with a battle between mutual pawn majorities. However, Karpov finds a way to grab the file: **1.Rc6!** Kasparov must have missed this move. Taking the offered pawn loses to 1...Rxc6 2.dxc6 Qxc6 3.Qd8+ Bf8 4.Bh6. **1...Be5 2.Bc3!** Fighting to make everything he owns superior to Black's. Black can now take and bring White's Queen to c3, or retreat and allow White's Bishop to dominate the a1-h8 diagonal. **2...Bb8** Also hopeless was 2...Bxc3 3.Qxc3 Rxc6 4.dxc6 (this pawn dominates the game) 4...Qc7 5.e5 Kf8 6.e6 f6 7.Qc5 Ke8 8.Qd5 b4 9.Qd7+ Qxd7 10.cxd7+ and White wins by rushing his King over to the queenside. **3.Qd4 f6 4.Ba5!** Eyeing the critical c7 square, which is the target of the White Rook once it dominates the file, or a White passed pawn (created if Black ever captures on c6) that wants to avoid a blockade. **4...Bd6** Black would lose his Bishop after 4...Rxc6 5.dxc6 Qxc6 6.Qd8+ and 7.Qxb8. **5.Qc3** Building up behind the Rook and forcing Black to give White total control of the c-file. **5...Re8 6.a3** Knowing that he has a won game, he proceeds to kill all of Black's potential counterplay. This little pawn move stops ...b5-b4. **6...Kg7 7.g3** Ending all back rank mate worries. Now that everything is safe, White can calmly proceed with the execution. **7...Be5 8.Qc5 h5 9.Bc7!** The Rook wants to go to the seventh, so the Black Bishop must be removed. **9...Ba1 10.Bf4 Qd7 11.Rc7 Qd8 12.d6 g5 13.d7 Rf8 14.Bd2 Be5 15.Rb7**, 1-0.

We have seen what a Rook can do if it reaches the sixth or seventh rank. However, control of a file may turn out to have more visual appeal than bite if no means of penetration exists.

(174)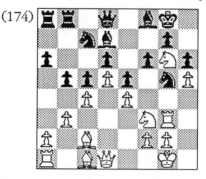

Karpov-Andersson, Stockholm 1969.
Black to play.

The weak f5 and g6 squares plus the eventual possibility of an f4 break by White don't speak well for the Black position on the kingside. Black was well aware of this and tries to open up the queenside as quickly as possible. **1...a5** Intending ...a4, when both the a-file and b-file would soon be opened. **2.a4!** Now Black will be left with only one open file. **2...bxc4 3.bxc4 Na6 4.Qe2** White stands much better because his play on the kingside is more real than Black's chances along the b-file. White's first goal is to take away any entry points there; then the file will be more or less useless. It should be noted that White is not worried about Black's Knight landing on b4, since the b-file would then be blocked by Black's own piece. **4...Ra7 5.Bd2 Rab7 6.Bc3** Now the Rooks cannot penetrate and White will be free to seek a kill on the kingside. This is a case of a dominated file being useless due to a lack of penetration points. **6...Nb4** Karpov feels that Black should sacrifice the Exchange by 6...Rb4, when 7.Bxb4 cxb4 gives Black a strong passed pawn, pressure against c4 and a4, and a nice support point on c5. Compare this with the Selesniev-Alekhine game in the section on Material Loss and Sacrifice (Part Nine). **7.Bd1 Na6 8.Nd2 Nb4 9.Re3 Be8 10.Nf1 Qc8 11.Ng3 Bd7 12.Qd2 Nh7 13.Be2** With Black in possession of a now useless open file, White is ready to set about his next plan—

trade the light-squared Bishops and dominate the f5 square. **13...Kf7 14.Qd1 Be7 15.Nf1 Bd8 16.Nh2 Kg8 17.Bg4 Ng5 18.Bxd7 Qxd7 19.Nf1** Now that the Bishops are gone, White moves his Knight back to strike at f5. **19...f5** This turns out poorly, but to allow White Ng3, Nf5, g3, and f4 was also hopeless. **20.exf5 Qxf5 21.Ng3 Qf7** White wins material after 21...Qc2? 22.f4!, since mate ensues if the f4 pawn is captured. **22.Qe2** Threatening 23.f4. **22...Bf6 23.Rf1** White is ready to create two open files by f2-f4. The difference between White's play along the e-file and Black's along the f-file is that all of White's pieces are combining to pressure the Black King, while Black's pieces are without that type of clear purpose. **23...Qd7 24.f4 exf4 25.Rxf4 Bxc3 26.Rxc3 Re8 27.Re3 R7b8 28.Qf2** Threatening 29.Re7! Rxe7 30.Rf8+. **28...Nh7 29.Nf5 Rxe3 30.Qxe3 Nf6 31.Nge7+ Kh8 32.Nxh6 Re8 33.Nf7+ Kh7 34.Re4! Rxe7** Hopeless, but 34...Nxe4 35.Qxe4+ leads to mate. **35.Rxe7**, 1-0. A great example of how to neutralize a file, create your own files, and play to dominate a particular square (f5). It also demonstrates how a kingside attack does not have to be a hurried or rushed affair; it can be prepared over a period of many moves before being unleashed (moves 13 through 19).

While it should now be clear that an open file has no worth if you can't penetrate on it, a file is also useless if it has nothing to do with the other imbalances in the position. Diagram #175 is an excellent illustration of this idea.

(175)

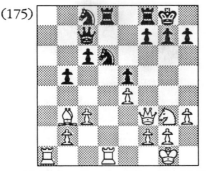

Alekhine-Junge, Warsaw 1942.
White to move.

Here we have a case where White can play on two open files—either the a-file or the d-file. Many players might be tempted by 1.Ra6 followed by Rda1 and others might like 1.Rd2 followed by Rad1. Both plans are completely incorrect however! It turns out that White should ignore both files and play elsewhere. The reason for this can only be found after we break down the imbalances. Since this position was deeply explored in Part Four, Chapter Three, we will only look at the features that cover the present theme. The main imbalance is White's active Bishop. At the moment it is clearly superior to Black's Knight on c8 (we can say that the Knights on g3 and d6 are evenly matched). We must also note that White has most of his pieces on or aimed at the kingside (the Bishop, Queen and Knight) while Black has nothing over there at all. Since our superior Bishop is aimed at the kingside and since our Queen and Knight are also working over there we can confidently say that we should play on that side of the board. Since this has nothing to do with either the a-file or d-file we can see that to play on them would be counterproductive to the needs of the position. Once again: *Only play where the imbalances tell you to play!* Following the general rule of playing on open files would not help us here.

Knowing how to use the imbalances and the rules that go with each type of situation will help us decide how to treat a file. For example, if our opponent has an isolated pawn we know that a Queen *and* a Rook are necessary to take complete advantage of the pawn's weakness (if you *don't* know this then go back and review the section on isolated pawns).

(176)

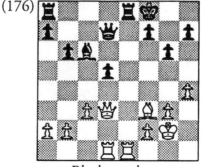

Black to play.

The only open file is the e-file, but that has little to do with the strategy that a player directs at a weak isolated pawn (it's a plus for the side who possesses the iso). Seeing that his pawn no longer has much dynamic potential left to it, Black seeks to get rid of all the Rooks. **1...Rxe1+ 2.Rxe1 Re8** Now White must allow the trade or give Black control of the file. It is correct to play **3.Rd1!** and allow Black possession of the e-file. This is proper procedure when battling an isolated pawn—the e-file carries less weight than the inherrent weakness of d5.

Often a file is no great prize but it still offers a Rook more activity than it would normally have. Our final example in this chapter demonstrates the potential that even the most unassuming file offers to a Rook.

Fischer-Gheorghiu, Buenos Aires 1970. **1.e4 e5 2.Nf3 Nf6 3.Nxe5 d6 4.Nf3 Nxe4 5.d4 Be7 6.Bd3 Nf6 7.h3** White has a bit more space so he tries to add to it by restricting Black's Bishop on c8. **7...0-0 8.0-0 Re8** So far both sides have developed their pieces in a straightforward manner. White is not playing for anything subtle; he just wants to get his pieces out and add to his edge in space. Black, on the other hand, has no weaknesses, but he is unable to get any kind of active play. Not being sure what to do, Black follows basic principles and places his Rook on the open file, hoping that it may prove useful there in the future. **9.c4 Nc6 10.Nc3 h6 11.Re1** Now White places his Rook on the e-file also. Does this really accomplish anything? White's idea is simply to challange Black's Rook on e8 and trade them if the opportunity arises. The point is that the Black Queen will not be able to stay on the e-file and eventually a White Rook will chase it away and take over possession of the file. The file itself offers no great rewards at the moment; however, the Rook is more active on e1 than elsewhere. **11...Bf8 12.Rxe8 Qxe8 13.Bf4 Bd7 14.Qd2** Matters are becoming clearer. With no real effort White has gained a considerable edge in territory and is now ready to take command of the e-file via Re1. **14...Qc8** Hoping to ease the pain with an exchange of Bishops by ...Bf5. **15.d5! Nb4 16.Ne4! Nxe4 17.Bxe4 Na6 18.Nd4** Now the threat of ...Bf5 has been nullified. **18...Nc5 19.Bc2 a5 20.Re1**

(177)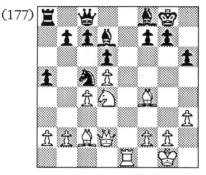

Black to play.

So White has ended up with the file. He also has finally developed all of his pieces and has prevented any kind of counterplay in the center or on the queenside. Since White's mobilization is complete and all his pieces aim at the kingside, it stands to reason that White should now direct his energies into a kingside attack. **20...Qd8 21.Re3!** The Rook is able to join in the attack due to the enhanced mobility that the e-file provided. **21...b6 22.Rg3 Kh8 23.Nf3 Qe7 24.Qd4! Qf6 25.Qxf6 gxf6** Fischer forgoes the kingside attack for the permanent advantage that comes with Black's shattered pawn formation. **26.Nd4 Re8 27.Re3!** White occupies the file simply to prevent the opponent from owning it. **27...Rb8** Black decides that a Rook exchange would do nothing to solve his structural problems so he retains his Rook in the hope that it may offer counterplay after a ...b6-b5 advance. **28.b3 b5 29.cxb5 Bxb5 30.Nf5 Bd7** The pawn would still fall after 30...h5 31.Ng3 h4 32.Nf5. **31.Nxh6 Bxh6 32.Bxh6 Rb4 33.Rg3 Ne4 34.Bg7+ Kh7?** Losing immediately, but 34...Kg8 35.Bxe4 followed by 36.Bxf6+ would also prove to be completely hopeless. **35.f3**, 1-0.

DOMINATION OF OPEN FILES

If there is no play elsewhere, the only open file will take on great importance and both sides will fight desperately for its favors.

(178)
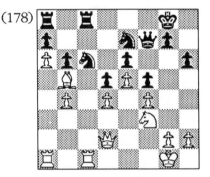

Alekhine-Nimzovich, San Remo 1930.
White to play.

In diagram#178 there is not much going on. The kingside and center are blocked, and the queenside is also tied up with pawns. It's apparent that the only way either side will penetrate into the hostile position is along the c-file. Because of this, White immediately begins operations that are designed to claim this file as his own. **1.Rc2 Qe8** Other moves don't help: 1) 1...Nd8 2.Bd7! leaves White in control of the file; 2) 1...Rc7 2.Ra3 Rac8 3.Rac3 is similar to the game. **2.Rac1** A bit more accurate was 2.Ra3! followed by Rac3 and Qc1. **2...Rab8 3.Qe3 Rc7 4.Rc3 Qd7 5.R1c2 Kf8 6.Qc1** The pressure White exerts on the file is crushing. After this game was played, this form of tripling on a file with both Rooks in the lead became known as *Alekhine's Gun.* **6...Rbc8 7.Ba4!** Threatening to win a piece by 8.b5. **7...b5 8.Bxb5 Ke8 9.Ba4 Kd8** Now c7 is adequately guarded. **10.h4!** *Zugzwang!* If Black moves either Knight, he instantly drops material. If he moves a Rook, the Knight on c6 would not have enough support. If the King or Queen were to move, then b4-b5. This leaves Black with only pawn moves, but when these run out he will be forced to move one of his pieces and accept heavy material loss. Because of these unpleasant facts, Black resigned. 1-0.

Though anyone can spot an open file and stick his Rooks there, real skill is necessary to create a useful open file from a file that was once cluttered with pawns and pieces. This is particularly important in cases of opposite side castling and the subsequent wing attacks that typically arise.

(179)

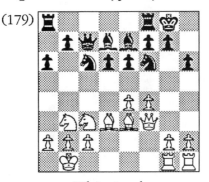

White to play.

Black is going to get routed after **1.g4!** because he is helpless to prevent 2.h4 and 3.g5 when at least one file will be opened to the Black King. It is interesting to note that if Black's h-pawn were moved back to h7 his King would be much safer since White would have more difficulties in opening up a file.

Our final game pushes home this point: you *must* open a file for your Rooks if you hope to be successful in an opposite side castling situation.

Karpov-Korchnoi, Moscow 1974. **1.e4 c5 2.Nf3 d6 3.d4 cxd4 4.Nxd4 Nf6 5.Nc3 g6 6.Be3 Bg7 7.f3** The popular Yugoslav Attack versus the Sicilian Dragon. The Kings will castle on opposite wings and each sides will try to storm the other's fortress with everything he has. **7...0-0 8.Qd2 Nc6 9.Bc4 Bd7 10.0-0-0 Rc8** Starting immediate play on the half open c-file. **11.Bb3 Ne5 12.h4!** White realizes that he needs an open file for his Rooks also. The d-file is available but has nothing to do with the Black King, so White rips open the h-file and goes for mate. **12...Nc4 13.Bxc4 Rxc4 14.h5** White is willing to sacrifice a pawn in order to lay claim to the newly opened h-file. In a game which featured a similar line of the Dragon Sicilian, Fischer wrote: "I'd won dozens of skittles games in analogous positions and had it down to a science: pry open the h-file, sac, sac...mate!" **14...Nxh5 15.g4 Nf6 16.Nde2 Qa5 17.Bh6 Bxh6 18.Qxh6 Rfc8**

(180)

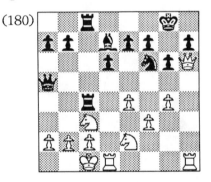

White to play.

The diagram shows a battle being waged almost entirely on the player's respective half open files. White is trying to break through to h7; Black is trying to get to c2. **19.Rd3** White takes a moment for defense—19.Rd3 prevents possibilities of a double Exchange sacrifice on c3. **19...R4c5 20.g5!** White now initiates an assault on f6—he knows that if he can induce the Knght on f6 to move, then h7 will fall and Black's King will die with it. **20...Rxg5** White's pawn sacrifice pulled one of the Black Rooks off the c-file. This enables the c3 Knight to move without fear of c2 falling. **21.Rd5! Rxd5** Of course, 21...Nxd5?? got mated to 22.Qxh7+ and Qh8 mate. **22.Nxd5** The White Knight will force the removal of Black's key defender on f6. **22...Re8 23.Nef4** After the tempting 23.Nxf6+ exf6 24.Qxh7+ Kf8 the Black King can run to safety via e7. Now this other Knight can come to d5 after an exchange on f6 and it also stops Black from blocking the h-file with ...Nh5. **23...Bc6 24.e5!!** A pretty move that blocks the Black Queen's access to h5. **24...Bxd5** The main point of 24.e5!! is revealed after 24...dxe5 25.Nxf6+ exf6 26.Nh5! and mates since 26...gxh5 27.Rg1+ leads to disastor along the g-file. If White had not thrown e5 in, Black could have answered Nh5 with ...Qxh5. **25.exf6 exf6 26.Qxh7+** The h-file finally becomes completely open and the Black King must flee in terror. **26...Kf8 27.Qh8+**, 1-0. After 27...Ke7 28.Nxd5+ Qxd5 29.Re1+ Black loses his Rook.

Solve These Problems

(181)

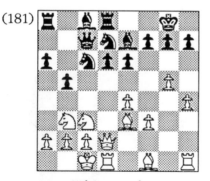

White to play.

The position in the diagram came about after **1.e4 c5 2.Nf3 Nc6 3.d4 cxd4 4.Nxd4 Nf6 5.Nc3 d6 6.Bg5 e6 7.Qd2 Be7 8.0-0-0 0-0 9.Nb3 Qb6 10.f3 a6 11.g4 Rd8 12.Be3 Qc7 13.h4 b5 14.g5 Nd7**. White is obviously going to attack Black on the kingside while Black will play for a counterattack on the queenside. Should White first prevent ...b5-b4 by a2-a3, or should he immediately continue with his own plans? Also say how White will attack Black's King.

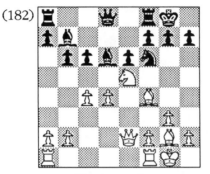

(182)

Black to play.

In the actual game Black stopped the threatened Nxc6 by chopping on e5 (1...Bxe5). Was this a good decision?

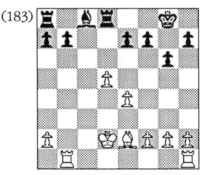

(183)

White to play.

Who stands better and how would the superior side make use of this advantage?

PART TWELVE

THREE KEYS TO SUCCESS

To succeed as a world class chessplayer takes natural talent, tremendous will power, an enormous fighting spirit, and the desire to study the game in a serious way. These servants of Caissa think of chess during every waking hour, dream of opening variations during the night, and travel the world from youth to dotage in a neverending attempt to play artistic games that will be scrutinized and, if they pass the tests of the critics, adored for hundreds of years to come.

For those who don't have the talent or the time to put into chess (or for the majority that would prefer the security of a job and a regular paycheck), three factors will make you a much better player than you might have deemed possible:

1) Learn to recognize the different imbalances and acquire a sense of which imbalance will dominate another in any given situation;

2) Always strive to prevent the opponent's counterplay;

3) Never give up. Defend as if your life were hanging in the balance!

MASTERING POSITIONS WITH MANY TYPES OF IMBALANCES

It is very rare to have only one kind of imbalance in a game. Usually many will exist, interacting with each other in ways that often make finding the correct idea far from easy. If this happens to you during a tournament game (and it will—it happens to everyone all the time), you must take on the attitude of a student and cultivate your will power. You must *insist* on finding a worthwhile path that blends in with the imbalances— if it takes twenty or thirty minutes to do so then so be it.

Never play a move because it was 'your move and you had to do something' (my original answer to my first chess teacher!). Never take five or ten minutes and then play 'any old thing in the hope that you will avoid time pressure and that the right idea will come to you in a move or two' (this is the reason a student of mine in the U.S. Women's Closed Championship played a series of useless moves. She lost badly, of course).

In diagram #184 (see next page) things are looking good for White. He enjoys a space advantage, two Bishops, and chances for a kingside pawn storm. Black has some pressure against White's b3 pawn but it can't be increased since 1...Rb7 runs into 2.e5 while 1...Rb6 2.Bd2 threatens 3.Ba5. Without any counterplay Black is in trouble, and I thought long and hard here. I realized that my play had to come on the queenside due to his weakened b-pawn and the fact that White controls the center and kingside. Unfortunately, there is no apparent way to continue.

(184)

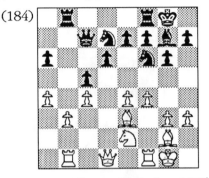

R.Ervin-Silman, Berkeley 1976.
Black to move.

After sixty minutes thought I finally hit upon the following plan: I will maneuver my d7 Knight to e6 (via f8) and place the other Knight on d7 (thereby unleashing the Bishop on g7). Then I will sacrifice a pawn by placing the e6 Knight on the very strong d4 square. This Knight obviously stands well here and serves to increase the pressure on b3. If White accepts the offer and captures on d4, Black will have succeeded in trading pieces (usually a good idea when you have less space), and will also have created a fine post on c5 for his remaining Knight. Black will then be a pawn down of course, but his chances on the queenside will be markedly increased because the remaining Knight will be clearly superior to White's bad Bishop. **1...Rfc8!!** A strange looking move that makes way for the Knight's 'suicidal' journey to d4 via f8 and e6. **2.Qd3** White does not see what Black is up to. **2...Nf8 3.g4 Ne6 4.g5 Nd7 5.Kh1!** Only now did White realize what Black's intent was. The point of the King moves will be clear in a moment. **5...Nd4! 6.Nxd4 cxd4 7.Bxd4 Bxd4 8.Qxd4** If White's King still stood on g1, Black would play 8...Qc5, trading Queens. Then White's kingside attacking chances would be completely gone, while Black could pile up on the b3 target at his leisure. **8...Rb4 9.Qd1 Rcb8**

(185)

White to move.

The situation has changed a great deal. Black now has great pressure on b3 and can increase it any time by ...Qb6 or ...Nc5. Obviously the b3 pawn is falling. Black's superior minor piece is also a concern for White. White's only plusses are his extra pawn (which is soon going to evaporate) and some nebulous kingside chances. The immediate 10.f5 Ne5 would leave Black's Knight in a dominant position and would end any real chances of a kingside success for White. **10.e5!!** A very fine pawn sacrifice which fights to activate his Bishop and to limit the scope of Black's Knight. **10...dxe5 11.f5!** The Knight can no longer go to e5, and the once bad Bishop on g2 is now breathing fire down the open h1-a8 diagonal. **11...gxf5 12.Rxf5 e6 13.Rf1 Nc5 14.Qh5 Rxb3 15.Rbe1** Black has crashed through on the queenside, and White is pinning all his hopes on his chances on the other wing. Black now plays directly for material gain. **15...Nd3!!** Extremely risky, since it allows White's Bishop to go to e4. 15...Rg3 was a simpler move. **16.Be4 f5! 17.gxf6 e.p. Nf4** Threatening the Queen and ...Rxh3+. **18.Rxf4** Black also wins after 18.Rg1+ Kh8 19.Rg7 Nxh5 20.Rxc7 Rxh3+ 21.Kg2 Rg3+ 22.Kf1 Nxf6, etc. **18...exf4 19.Rg1+ Rg3! 20.Rxg3+ fxg3 21.Qg5+ Kh8 22.f7** This seems to win for White, since 23.Qf6 mate is a threat and 22...Qxf7 loses the b8 Rook after 23.Qe5+. However, Black had prepared a surprise for White. **22...g2+!!** White resigned, since 23.Kxg2 Qxf7 24.Qe5+ Qg7+ is an easy win for Black, as is 23.Bxg2 Rb1+. Best is 23.Kg1

Qb6+! 24.c5 Qb2, and everything is defended while Black's counterattack by ...Qd4+ followed by ...Rb2 will soon begin.

Naturally, a lot of heavy calculation was involved here but don't let this distract you from the real point of the game—the tremendous battle for initiative (Black's pawn sacrifice which started with the Knight maneuver to f8-e6, and finally d4) and the fight to attain specific (favorable) imbalances (Black trying to get a good Knight vs. bad Bishop, and White's fine counter sacrifice 10.e5!, fighting to make his Bishop as active as possible).

Our next three examples of the subtle interplay between many types of imbalances all feature the ideas and moves of some of the finest players of all time. It will help the student if he studies each diagram carefully and writes his own analysis and assessments down before looking at what actually happened.

(186)

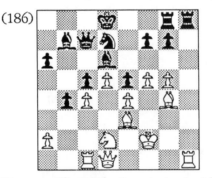

Karpov-Gligorich, San Antonio 1972.
White to play.

White has a space advantage and a passed pawn. Black has an advanced queenside majority. The fact that it is advanced is both a plus and a minus. The plus side is that Black can quickly create a passed pawn by ...a5, ...a4, ...b3, etc. Unfortunately for Black, this fact will not take on meaning until the endgame (which is still far away). The minus is that the advanced pawns have left many holes in their wake. The a4 square is an excellent entry point for White's Queen, and White can, at any time, open up lines on the queenside by a2-a3. Karpov began his exploitation of the virtues of the White position in a very subtle way. **1.Qg1!** Let's see what Karpov had to say about this move: "Such moves are very difficult to find! White has an obvious spatial advantage (on the kingside and in the center) plus the resultant positional gains. So as to increase them, he must find an exact plan for regrouping his pieces. Here are my basic thoughts about the position:

1) Black has only one weakness—the c5 pawn; White must quickly organize an attack on it since this will enable him to restict the maneuverability of the opposing pieces;

2) The best place for the King is at f3, where it is not liable to be checked; it overprotects the Bishop at g4, and opens the g1-a7 diagonal for the Bishop-Queen battery and the second rank for Rook maneuvers;

3) White must battle for possession of the h-file and to develop an initiative on the kingside. At an opportune moment he can initiate play on the opposite wing and transfer there the weight of the struggle utilizing the great mobility of his forces. White's last move meets all these conditions."

1...Nb6 2.Rh2 Qe7? Better was 2...a5. Naturally, 2...Rxh2+ 3.Qxh2 would leave White in control of the h-file. **3.Nb3 Kc7 4.Kf3! Nd7 5.a3!** Switching to the queenside. Black's game quickly falls apart, since he does not have room to set up a proper defensive crouch. **5...bxa3 6.Ra2! Rh4 7.Rxa3 Rgh8 8.Rb1 Rb8 9.Qe1 Rxg4** Desperation. **10.Kxg4 Bc8 11.Qa5+,** 1-0.

It was interesting to note how Karpov broke the position down into individual imbalances—he analyzed no moves at all but still explained the position's secrets in a very thorough way.

(187)

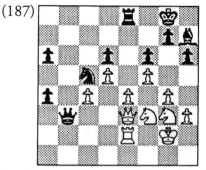

Capablanca-Bogoljubov, London 1922.
White to play.

In our next example (see diagram #187) of multiple imbalances, the author can take a rest and allow the legendary Capablanca himself to explain things: "Black's Queen, Rook, and Knight are aggressively placed, and compared to White's pieces, have greater freedom. All White's pieces are defensively placed and his c-pawn and e-pawn are subject to attack. The only way to defend both pawns would be Nd2, but then Black would reply ...Qb4 and he could then advance his a-pawn with no difficulty.

"So far everything has been in Black's favor and, if there were no other factors in this position, White's game would be lost. However, there is a feature which is very much in White's favor, namely, the position of the Bishop at h7. This Bishop is not only completely cut off from play but, even worse, there is no way of bringing it into the game. White is playing, as it were, with an extra piece."

White's plan then, is to trade or displace Black's Knight from c5. Then by a c4-c5 advance White will create a passed d-pawn. He can count on a success with this because he has an extra unit of force (a Knight vs. a dead Bishop) that is participating in the battle. **1.Nd4 Qxe3 2.Rxe3 Rb8 3.Rc3 Kf7 4.Kf3 Rb2 5.Nge2 Bg8 6.Ne6 Nb3** Also leading to a loss is 6...Nxe4 7.Kxe4 Rxe2+ 8.Kd3 Rh2 9.Kd4 h5 10.c5. **7.c5 dxc5 8.Nxc5 Nd2+ 9.Kf2 Ke7 10.Ke1 Nb1 11.Rd3 a3 12.d6+ Kd8 13.Nd4 Rb6 14.Nde6+ Bxe6 15.fxe6 Rb8 16.e7+ Ke8 17.Nxa6,** 1-0.

In a game of chess it is usual for certain imbalances to be present for both sides. However, a player must keep an open mind when utilizing his advantageous imbalances because they often mutate. In other words, you must often be willing to give up one advantage in order to create another.

(188)
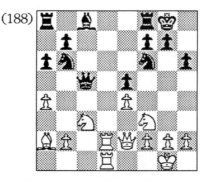

Botvinnik-Sorokin, USSR 1931. White to play.

In diagram #188 White has a lead in development (which is usually of a temporary nature) and control of the d-file. These things in themselves are not doing much for White—he needs targets. Unfortunately, moves such as a4-a5 and threats to the e5 pawn are all thwarted by Black's Queen, which is doing a superlative defensive job. Because the Black Queen is holding her position together, Botvinnik strives to rid himself of this female thorn in his side. **1.Qe3!** How many players would refuse to even look at this move because of the doubled, isolated pawns? To quote Botvinnik: "This far from obvious move is the strongest in the given position. With the exchange of Queens, which he cannot avoid, the defects of Black's position grow more perceptible. In view of the backwardness of his development, Black now certainly cannot oppose anything to the pressure along the d-file. His e5 pawn becomes very weak. To defend it, Black finds himself forced to exchange a Bishop for the Knight on f3, after which not only his queenside but his f7 square is weakened. The doubling of White's pawns on the e-file is of no essential importance."

1...Qxe3 2.fxe3 Bg4 3.a5 Nc8 4.Rc1 Taking control of both files, breaking the pin, and threatening Nxe5. **4...Bxf3 5.gxf3 Ne7 6.Nd5 Nc6 7.Nxf6+ gxf6 8.Rd7 Rab8 9.Kf2!** White's control of the d-file has now led to penetration of the seventh rank. The lead in development is gone, but in its place is a new imbalance: active Bishop vs. Knight. **9...Nxa5 10.Rcc7 Rbc8 11.Rxf7 Rxc7 12.Rxc7+ Kh8 13.Bd5 b5 14.b3** Black's Knight is now totally dominated by White's mighty Bishop. **14...Rd8 15.Kg3 f5 16.Kh4 fxe4 17.fxe4 Rd6 18.Kh5 Rf6 19.h3 Rd6 20.h4 Rb6 21.Kg4 Rf6 22.Ra7 Rb6 23.Re7** Black has been helpless for a long time (typical of a Rook on the seventh) and now loses material. White won the game without difficulty.

The truly great players have a talent for creating a series of problems that sap the energy and will of the opposition. One of the greatest exponents of this type of warfare was Bobby Fischer. In this chapter's final example we see him complicating the issue by changing the structure again and again to conform to the imbalances that he wants to achieve.

(189)

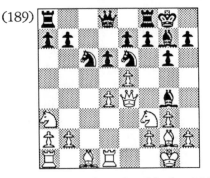

Bisguier-Fischer, Stockholm 1962.
Black to move.

White enjoys more central room and hopes to smother Black's pieces with his advanced center pawns. Instead of letting his opponent push him around, Fischer creates a position that is more suitable to his own tastes. **1...Bxf3!** Giving White the two Bishops. However, it appears that the position is open and that the threat of d4-d5 will force the Knights to retreat. **2.Bxf3 d5!** All of a sudden the position is closed and the Bishops are hemmed in. **3.Qe3** Avoiding 3.Qxd5? Nexd4 when the White e-pawn will also fall. **3...Rc8!** Threatening to win the d-pawn by 4...Qb6 since Nc2 will fail to ...Nxe5 with a discovered attack on c2. **4.Bg4 Qb6 5.Bxe6 fxe6** Black's dark-squared Bishop is locked in but his pressure on d4 and play on the c-file and f-file more than make up for this one failing. **6.b3 g5!** Gaining more space on the kingside. 7.Qxg5? fails to 7...Nxe5! 8.dxe5 Qxf2+. **7.Bb2 Rf5 8.Rd2 Rcf8** The pressure on the f-file gave White new problems to worry about. Black eventually won the game.

PREVENTING COUNTERPLAY

At times one's advantages might be clearly defined, but instead of proceeding to utilize them it may be a good idea to curtail all of the opponent's chances and only then proceed unhindered with your own plans.

One of the most common errors an amateur makes is to win a pawn or get some other type of long lasting advantage and then spoil his winning position by trying to force the issue. When you have a permanent (static) advantage you should solidify your position before striking out—if you equalize all other factors, your static advantage will give you a quiet, risk free victory.

Perhaps the greatest master of snuffing out the opponent's play before it even got started was the late World Champion Tigran Petrosian, and so it is logical to start with an example from his own praxis.

(190)
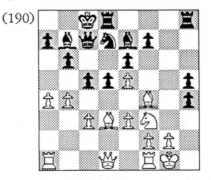

Spassky-Petrosian, World Championship Match 1966.
Black to play.

296

Black has an opposite attack on the kingside, while White will seek his chances on the opposite wing. Many people playing this position would throw themselves at White's King in the hope of being the first to land a punch. This race horse/boxer mentality is not necessary here, though, since Black already has open files leading to the White King—his play can't be stopped. Petrosian realized that all Black had to do was nullify White's play on the queenside; then he could attack on the kingside at his leisure without fear of any counterplay by the opponent. **1...c4!** Playing to close the queenside. The d4 square looks like a gift for White but in actuality it will prove to be useless. This is because a Queen or Rook on that square does nothing, while the Knight must stay on f3 to guard the e5 pawn. **2.Be2** A better defensive try was 2.Bf5! followed by Bh3, though this too would ultimately prove to be in Black's favor. In Spassky's words: "My Bishop would look like a pawn on h3!" **2...a6!** Killing all possibilities of a queenside breakthrough. Now 3.a5 b5 or 3.b5 a5 would both leave the queenside completely blocked. **3.Kh1 Rdg8** With the queenside safe, Black can now focus his energies on White's King. **4.Rg1 Rg4 5.Qd2 Rhg8 6.a5 b5** White has no play at all, and he eventually fell prey to Black's attack.

Our next game shows how a player can set up long term advantages in one area of the board and then win by preventing the opponent from generating counterplay elsewhere. After the moves **1.e4 Nf6 2.d3 e5 3.Nf3 Nc6 4.g3 Bc5 5.Bg2 0-0 6.0-0 d5 7.Nbd2 dxe4 8.dxe4 Be6 9.c3 a5 10.Qe2 Nd7 11.Nc4 f6 12.Ne3 a4!** we reach the position in diagram #191.

The strategic goals are clear: White will play for a kingside attack by placing a Knight on f5 and advancing his h-pawn. Black will pressure the light squares on the a2-g8 diagonal and tie down the a1 Rook to the defense of the a2 pawn. If this pawn ever advances to a3, then the b3 square will be severely weakened. Of course, an attack on the King is more dangerous in the short run, so Black mixes his queenside plan with the building of an impenetrable kingside fortress.

(191)

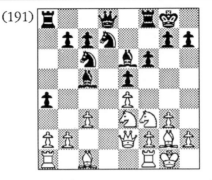

Z.Harari-Silman, San Francisco 1976.
White to move.

13.Rd1 Na5 Hitting c4 and getting ready to jump into b3 if White ever plays a2-a3. Black's targets, then, are a2 and all the light squares along the g8-a2 diagonal. Another point of ...Na5 is that the d5 square can now be covered by ...c7-c6, thus making that square a dubious (and very temporary) home for White's Knight. **14.Nf5?** More accurate was 14.Nh4 followed by Nhf5 and h2-h4-h5. **14...Rf7** Guarding both g7 and the Knight on d7. It also allows the d7 Knight to later go to f8, when Black's kingside pawns would all be securely defended against any White attacking scheme. **15.Bh3?!** It was better to first play h2-h4. **15...Qe8** Guarding the e6 Bishop and breaking the pin on the d-file. The Queen will also later switch to f7, where it will bring great pressure to bear on the a2-g8 diagonal. **16.N3h4 Nf8 17.Bf1 Kh8** Ending any chances for White to play Qg4 and Nh6+. **18.Qf3 Rd7** Challenging the d-file and freeing the f7 square for Black's Queen. **19.Rxd7 Qxd7 20.Ne3 Rd8 21.Nhf5 c6 22.h4 Qf7 23.Ng4** Hoping for 23...Bxa2 24.Nxg7! Kxg7 25.Rxa2! Qxa2 26.Qxf6+ Kg8 27.Nh6 mate. **23...Nd7!** Guarding f6. **24.Bh3 Bf8** Now—with f6 and g7 both well defended— Black can finally turn his full attention to queenside matters. **25.Be3** Or 25.a3 Nb3 26.Rb1 Nxc1 27.Rxc1 Nc5 with a clear advantage for Black. **25...Bxa2** White has been parried on the kingside, and now Black enjoys the fruits of his positional superiority on the other sector. **26.h5 Bb3** Staking further

claims. Now the d-file is Black's. **27.h6 g6 28.Ng7 b5** White's
e3 Bishop would gain some scope after 28...Bxg7 29.hxg7+.
Black already has enough advantages to win, so he prefers to
keep his kingside secure. **29.Kg2 Nb7 30.Re1 Nd6 31.Kh2**
White is helpless. **31...Ne8** Now Black threatens to win another
pawn *and* retain his useful dark-squared Bishop by capturing
on g7 with the e8 Knight. **32.Nxe8 Rxe8 33.Re2?** A blunder in
a lost position. **33...Bd1** And Black won on move forty.

In the battle that follows, Black appears to be in complete
defensive mode. Things are not always what they seem though;
I saw that White's attack led to a dead end street—once his play
ended, mine began.

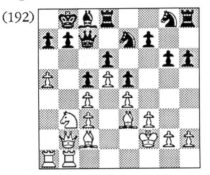

Spiller-Silman, National Open 1989.
Black to move.

Diagram #192 shows a typical situation in a closed position:
Both opponents are trying to generate play on their respective
sides of the board (one always plays on the wings when the
center is locked). Here we are shown the importance of
shutting down the opponent's play on his side of the board
before going ahead with action in your own area.

White has the two Bishops but the closed nature of the
position makes them no better than the Black Knights. However, it is clear that White is trying to generate an attack against
Black's King on the queenside. Though Black would love to
play ...f7-f5 and get his own plans started, he notices that White

has a strong threat to play Qa3 and then break though on the queenside by sacrificing a piece on c5. Seeing this, Black must swallow his pride, put off his kingside advance, and prevent White from realizing his plans. **1...Nf6!** **2.Qa3** Threatening 3.Nxc5! dxc5 4.Bxc5 (intending 5.Bxe7 or 5.d6) 4...Neg8 5.Bb6! or even 5.Be3 followed by 6.c5, in both cases with a winning attack. **2...Nd7!** Now White's plans have come to a standstill, and Black can once again give his attention to the kingside. **3.Qc1 Rh7!** Intending to meet 4.Bxh6 with 4...Rdh8 5.Bg5 f6 and 6...Rxh2. **4.Ra2 Rdh8 5.Kg1 f5 6.a6 b6 7.Na5 f4** Black's position is almost indestructible on the queenside, so he can now go full steam ahead on the kingside with little fear of reprisal. **8.Bf2 Ka8 9.Nb7 g5** Black has no interest in winning a pawn with 9...Bxb7, since that would open lines on the queenside for White's Rooks. *Don't allow yourself to be distracted from your correct strategic plan.* **10.Ba4 Nb8 11.Bb5 Rg7 12.Qa3 Rhg8 13.Rd1 g4** The long awaited break finally arrives and with it comes a decisive attack. Black went on to win the game.

Our final example illustrates the virtues of patience.

(193)

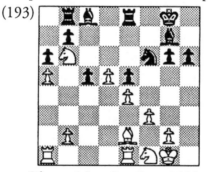

Silman-Mar, San Jose 1983.
White to play.

White has achieved a dominating position. His pawn on a5 and Knight on b6 eat up queenside squares while the passed d5 pawn gives White an advantage in central space. To make matters worse, Black has two inactive Bishop's and weak pawns on c5 and e5. All this would indicate that White should now go about executing Black. Not quite! Black threatens to get rid of White's super Knight on b6 via ...Nd7. Before undertaking any decisive action White must show a bit more patience and deal with Black's bid for a bit of breathing room. **27.Ne3! Nd7 28.Nec4 Nxb6 29.Nxb6 Bf8** So White has managed to retain a Knight on b6 after all. Only now, when Black's counterplay has been neutralized, can White search for a way to penetrate into the enemy position and finish the game off. **30.Rec1** Piling up on the weakness on c5 and hoping to eventually penetrate into Black's camp via the c-file. **30...Kf7 31.Bd1!** Since White's Bishop is bad he hastens to place it outside the pawn chain. White could have won a pawn by 31.Na4 but after 31...Bd7 32.Nxc5 Bxc5 33.Rxc5 Rbc8 followed by ...Ke7 and ...Kd6 Black's pieces would have broken free of their chains. **31...h5** Black hopes to get his Bishop into play on h6. **32.Ba4** Notice how White improves the position of each and every piece before initiating the final breakthrough. **32...Rd8 33.Kf2** Stopping a potential check on e3 by Black's dark-squared Bishop. **33...h4 34.b4!!** Since all of White's pieces are optimally placed he sacrifices a pawn so that he can force his way into Black's camp. The restricted Black forces will not be able to survive such an assault. **34...Bh6** Admitting defeat, but 34...cxb4 35.Rc7+ Kg8 36.Rac1 h3 37.g4 h2 38.Kg2 would lead to the loss of the c8 Bishop. **35.Rxc5 Bf4 36.Rc7+ Kf6 37.Bd7!**, 1-0. The restricted pieces on c8 and b8 led to Black's demise.

THE ART OF FIGHTING BACK

When I was just starting out in chess I thought that every chess book was something to drool over and cherish. Time and experience showed me that this was hardly the case, but one book did have a real impact on my development. This little, inexpensive book is called *The Art of the Middle Game*[1] and is by Keres and Kotov (a new edition has just been published). In its pages was a very simple but useful bit of advice about defending: When you find yourself in a very bad position *don't* set one final cheap trap and expect to resign if the opponent sees it! Instead, hold on as if your life depended on it. How to do this? Simple: *play the move that you would hate to see if you were in your opponent's shoes!* We all can identify with this; we all have been in wonderful positions where we know we *should* win but desperately hope the opponent doesn't play one particular move because it will make us work forever to score the full point. This type of grim goal-line stand unbalances the opponent psychologically. It tires him and can often lead to blunders that turn a hopeless cause into a victorious celebration. At the risk of dredging up memories best left buried, let's take a look at diagram #194.

---

[1] *The Art of the Middle Game,* by Paul Keres and Alexander Kotov, translated by H. Golombek Dover, New York, 1989.

(194)

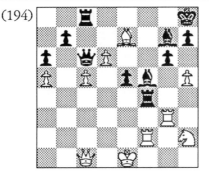

Silman-Ruth Haring, San Francisco 1981.
Black to move.

White's game is horrible. He is a pawn down, his pawn on c5 is ready to fall, and his King has nowhere to hide. Is it time to resign? No—White had actually made a major psychological gain a few moves ago when his flag had fallen and Black failed to notice as one move after another was played. Finally the time control was reached and a friend informed Ruth that she could have won just by pointing a finger! She was crushed by this news and now the task of having to work for the point sapped her will. Add this to the fact that she probably could have mated me earlier and you can understand the turmoil that my opponent was going through. **1...Qe4+** She decides to mate me. The safer 1...Rxf2 2.Kxf2 Qxc5+ 3.Qxc5 Rxc5 was also possible but the presence of the passed pawn on d6 scared her away from such endgame considerations. Surely she could get more than a mere winning endgame!? **2.Re3** Not much for White to do but hold body and soul together and hope to wear the opponent down! **2...Qb4+** 2...Qh1+ 3.Nf1 Qxh5 looks easy enough but she is starting to get tired and depressed. She feels that I should be dead by now and is having trouble adjusting to the reality of my continued survival. **3.Qd2 Qb1+ 4.Ke2 Rd4 5.Qe1 Qb5+ 6.Kf3 Qxc5** So my position has actually gotten worse! In such situations you must hang on and make the opponent *earn* the victory—right to the bitter end. **7.Kg3 Qd5** When she won the c5 pawn she relaxed a bit. I'm sure she thought the win would be easy now. However, by relaxing she has let down her sense of danger and her quiet Queen move has given White a free moment. I've learned from painful experience that you only relax when the game is over! **8.h6! Bxh6 9.Rxe5** All of a sudden a tired opponent starts to see counter-threats of Bf6+ followed by Re8+. I'm sure she was thinking, "Why won't this guy just die like he's supposed to in such positions?" **9...Rc3+ 10.Qxc3 Qxe5+ 11.Kg2** Here Ruth intended to win instantly by 11...Rg4+ 12.Nxg4 Qxc3 but noticed that 13.Bf6+ gets the Queen back with an extra Exchange for White! This is the point where a player's patience can easily disappear. **11...Be4+?** An emotional move. The check gives a sense of temporary security; it offers up a feeling of power and control. However, she is actually giving up control of the crucial c8 and d7 squares. **12.Nf3** All of a sudden there are no more useful checks and White actually threatens to win by 13.Qc8+ Kg7 14.Qf8 mate. **12...Bxf3+ 13.Qxf3** Now 13.Bf6+ is threatened and the disappearance of Black's light squared Bishop has made the d6 pawn very dangerous. Black—exhausted, in time pressure, and depressed—is unable to cope with the changed situation and completely collapses in the final moves. **13...Rf4 14.Qe2 Qd5+ 15.Kg3 Qb3+ 16.Rf3 Rxf3+ 17.Qxf3 Qe6 18.Qf6+**, 1-0. A far cry from good chess but an amazing comeback nontheless. It really is incredible what a dour defense can accomplish!

Though such a passive defense is called for on occasion, it is much better if you can start some sort of counterattack. To do this you must have a favorable imbalance to use. If you don't, you must do everything that is possible to create one.

(195)

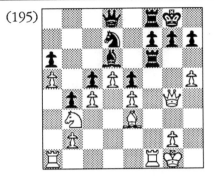

Tal-Petrosian, USSR ch. 1958.
Black to move.

In diagram #195 White has an obvious superiority. He has more kingside and central space, pressure against the Black pawn on c5 and chances for an attack against Black's King. The immediate threat is 1.Bg5 Rxf1+ 2.Rxf1 Qc7 (2...f6 3.Qe6+) 3.Bh6 winning the Exchange. If 1...Kh8 then Black would stop the threat but he would have a passive game with no hope of future activity. Does he have any choice? If there is no positive imbalance to use then he can't do anything but sit tight; in this case, though, Black does have the possibility of creating some chances for himself. **1...Rf4!** A major surprise! Black sacrifices the Exchange. *This is not a move of desperation!* Rather, it enables Black to create some positional plusses in return for a modest material outlay. **2.Bxf4 exf4 3.Nd2 Ne5** At this point White may have been reeling a bit. Just a couple moves ago he was expecting a nice slow crush and now Black has active pieces and counterplay. Psychologically such a change in momentum may pay huge dividends. **4.Qxf4 Nxc4 5.e5!** The ever aggressive Tal sacrifices a pawn to open a file for his Rooks and give his Knight a nice post on e4. **5...Nxe5 6.Ne4 h6 7.Rae1?** Not sensing Black's upcoming counterattack. 7.Nxd6 Qxd6 8.Rfe1 f6 9.Rad1 was better. Now Black is able to retain his dangerous Bishop. **7...Bb8 8.Rd1 c4** Activating his queenside majority and giving his Knight the d3 square as a home. **9.d6 Nd3 10.Qg4 Ba7+ 11.Kh1 f5** Hoping for 12.Rxf5 Rxf5 13.Qxf5

Qh4+ 14.Qh3 Qxe4. **12.Nf6+** An attractive counter-shot that doesn't quite have the desired result. **12...Kh8! 13.Qxc4 Nxb2 14.Qxa6 Nxd1 15.Qxa7 Qxd6 16.Qd7 Qxf6 17.Qxd1 Rb8.** We leave the game here as it no longer illustrates our theme. Obviously Black has taken over the driver's seat.

Aside from making sure that you always have some favorable imbalance to fall back on (in diagram #194 it was a passed pawn on d6; in diagram #195 Black created a queenside majority and activated his minor pieces), there are two other defensive themes we should address here:

1) The best reaction to an attack on the wing is a counter-attack in the center.

2) As explained in Part 5, if you have less space trade pieces—this will ease your cramped position. You should also trade pieces if you are under attack; this way you will eliminate his attacking forces.

(196)

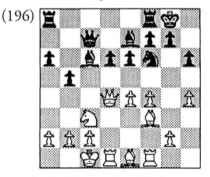

Averbach-Botvinnik, Moscow 1957.
White to play.

Diagram #196 illustrates our theme concerning a counterstrike in the center. White seems to have a powerful attack in the making. He will play g2-g4-g5 and smash Black quickly unless the second player can attract his opponent's attention in some way. **1.g4** White doesn't need an invitation. He wants blood. **1...b4 2.Ne2** Bad is 2.Qxb4? due to 2...d5 with a double attack on the White Queen and the pawn on f4. Besides, White doesn't want to open lines on the queenside anyway; he just wants Black to leave him alone for a move or two—that's all it will take for him to execute Black's King. **2...Qb7!** Not giving White time for g4-g5. Now the e4 pawn is hanging. **3.Ng3** A forced move that defends the e-pawn but potentially blocks the g-file from the White Rooks. **3...d5!** Striking a blow in the center. Now 4.g5 dxe4! 5.gxf6 Bxf6 is hopeless for White so he tries to close up the middle so he can get back on track on the wing. **4.e5 Ne4!** Keeping things alive in the middle. **5.Bxe4 dxe4 6.Qe3 Rfd8**, and Black has good chances due to the open lines in the center.

Though I have already mentioned that the best reaction to an attack on the wing is a counterattack in the center, I brought it up again because I think it is one of the most important general rules in chess. When someone is bringing their pieces to the wings for an attack they are simultaneously taking away their pieces from the center. This often gives the defender a chance to open things up in the middle and force the opponent to give up his attacking plans altogether. Remember: *the center is the most important part of the board. If you can gain influence there then by all means take it!*

Now let's address the rule that concerns exchanging off the enemy's attacking forces. It is really quite easy to understand: If the opponent is building up for an attack and you are not able to undertake a counterattack, then you must trade off his attacking units and reduce his army to a manageable level. This is particularly useful if you are up material. Then you can sacrifice some of your extra wood back to force the attack-stopping exchanges.

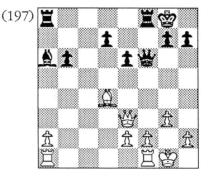

(197)

Kasparov-Karpov, 1985 World Championship Match.
Black to move.

Diagram #197 is a great example of an exchange of pieces getting rid of the opponent's attacking prospects. In this game White has a double attack on Black's Queen and b6 pawn—it's clear that this pawn is doomed but the presence of Bishops of opposite colors gives Black good chances in any kind of endgame. However, we have not reached an endgame. In fact, the White Bishop is stronger than the Black one. If we take into consideration the rule that tells us that Bishops of opposite colors are useful attacking tools (because one can't defend what the other attacks) but are often drawish in endgames, then we can understand Black's decision to get the Queens off and end any attacking possibilities once and for all. **1...Qh6!** This also saves the impending loss of a pawn because now White's Queen will not be defending the e2 pawn. Black is not concerned about the doubling of his kingside pawns; he knows that the opposite colored Bishops will enable him to draw now that an endgame will come about. **2.Qxh6 gxh6 3.Rfe1 Bc4 4.a3 b5** Now all is safe. **5.Rad1 Rf5 6.Bb2 Rd5**. Continuing the policy of exchanging. 1/2-1/2.

Solve These Problems

(198)

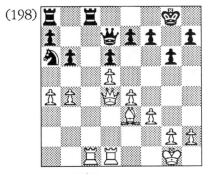

White to move.

List the components of White's advantage and figure out how
he should proceed.

(199)

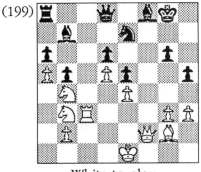

White to play.

Is White better, and if so, how much? How should White
continue here?

(200)

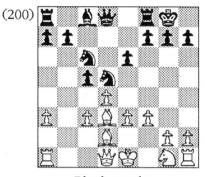

Black to play.

The position in the diagram was reached after the following opening moves: **1.d4 Nf6 2.c4 e6 3.Nc3 Bb4 4.a3 Bxc3+ 5.bxc3 c5 6.f3 d5 7.e3 0-0 8.cxd5 Nxd5 9.Bd2 Nc6 10.Bd3** Is Black doing well or will the advantages in White's position lead to difficulties for the second player?

(201)

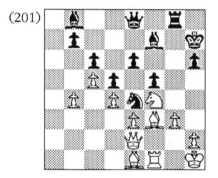

Is anything wrong with 1.Qd3?

PART THIRTEEN

USING IMBALANCES IN EVERY PHASE OF THE GAME

Many players look at the three phases of a chess game as separate parts that have little to do with each other. They see the opening as a place to develop all their pieces. Next (ideally!) they come up with some sort of plan for the middlegame that is based on the imbalances (only if they have read this book—otherwise they may simply make one or two move threats and try to checkmate the enemy King). The endgame is some sort of an enigma—queening a pawn is the only thing they can relate to.

If you wish to play good chess you must realize that every phase of the game is part of one homogeneous whole. The opening creates the imbalances that fuel the middlegame and these same imbalances often influence the play right to the end of the game.

So far we have mainly addressed middlegame considerations. Now it's time to tie everything together and show how these same imbalances that we use in the middle carry just as much weight at the beginning and end of a game also.

IMBALANCES IN THE OPENING

Most books will tell you that the purpose of the opening is to develop your pieces. However, it turns out that this is just a small part of the picture. *The true purpose of the opening is to create imbalances and develop your army in such a way that your pieces, working together, can take advantage of them.*

To prove our point, let's look at diagram #202.

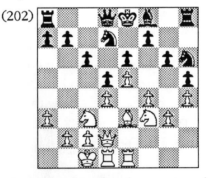

White has a huge lead in development and according to the established rules of the opening, White should have a large advantage. However, just the opposite is true! White is the one who is in trouble. This can be blamed in part on the fact that in closed positions development is not so important, simply because the opponent has no way to get through to you. Here White has no way to effect an entry into Black's position. Though his pieces seem active, he actually has no targets to strike at and, as a result, no plan. On the other hand, Black's plan is simplicity itself: He will play for a queenside attack via ...b5, ...Nb6, ...Nc4, ...Qa5, etc. It turns out that Black's undeveloped pieces are quite active while White is unable to challenge Black's coming assault. With this position in mind, we can meditate upon the maxim: *No development is better than a bad development.*

Allowing yourself to fall behind in development in the opening is all right as long as you are conforming to the strategic designs of the position. The *Czech Benoni* is a case in point: **1.d4 Nf6 2.c4 c5 3.d5 e5 4.Nc3 d6 5.e4 Be7 6.Bd3 0-0 7.Nge2 Ne8!** This funny looking move appears to break a couple of rules—namely, *Knights are poorly placed on the back rank* and, of course, our old *don't move the same piece twice in the opening.* However, the truth is that 7...Ne8 is very logical and nicely meets the demands of the position. In positions with closed centers, both sides must turn their attention to the wings, with play usually being initiated by pawn breaks. These pawn breaks serve two purposes: 1) opens files for the Rooks; 2) gains additional space on the side where you wish to make your conquest. The point of 7...Ne8 is to prepare for the thematic ...f7-f5 advance. For example, 8.0-0 g6 9.Bh6 Ng7 and Black will eliminate White's h6 Bishop by ...Nd7, ...Nf6, ...Kh8, ...Ng8, and will eventually play ...f5 with chances on the kingside. This time-consuming maneuver is made possible by the closed nature of the position, which makes extended maneuvers a typical sight.

It should be mentioned that there is another point to ...Ne8; Black intends ...Bg5, trading his bad Bishop for White's good one.

It's amazing how much a retreating, undeveloping move like 7...Ne8 can do!

Another example of a lead in development being allowed in the opening is: **1.e4 c5 2.Nf3 d6 3.d4 cxd4 4.Nxd4 Nf6 5.Nc3 a6 6.Bg5 e6 7.f4 Qb6 8.Qd2 Qxb2 9.Rb1 Qa3.** This position from the *Poisoned Pawn Variation* of the *Najdorf Sicilian* was once a favorite of Bobby Fischer. He was willing to allow White a huge lead in development and real chances for a successful attack in exchange for the extra pawn that White has sacrificed. The reasoning for this decision is simple: If Black can contain White's attack, his extra pawn will eventually lead to a win for him.

This is the whole point of successful opening play—don't just develop mindlessly; create some long term imbalance that you can build around and nurture for the rest of the game. A glance at a couple of contemporary opening lines in the *Nimzo-Indian Defense* should suffice to demonstrate this concept.

The Nimzo-Indian: **1.d4 Nf6 2.c4 e6 3.Nc3 Bb4** Black is willing to give up the two Bishops, but in return he will get an easy development and play against White's doubled pawns, though other types of imbalances can also be created, depending on White's choice of reply. One line goes: **4.a3** (called the *Saemisch Variation*) **4...Bxc3+ 5.bxc3 0-0 6.f3** White intends to play e4, get a big center, and play for an attack against Black's King. One of my favorite moves here is the ridiculous looking **6...Ne8!?** It looks like Black is trying to set his pieces up anew and start over, but there is a lot of common sense to this unprovoked Knight retreat. First, Black sees White's intentions and prepares a later ...f7-f5, blocking lines on the kingside. In the meantime, Black must find a point of attack and develop around it. With this in mind, Black eyes White's doubled pawns as objects to go after. In particular, the c4 pawn suggests itself as the main course, since the farthest advanced pawn in a doubled set tends to be the weakest. Black will continue: ...b6, ...Ba6, ...Nc6, ...Na5, with great pressure on c4. Note that this pressure can be further increased by ...c5 followed by ...Rc8, or even by the direct ...Nd6. There can be little doubt that c4 will fall, leaving Black with a queenside superiority and a material advantage. The big question is, can White achieve anything concrete on the kingside? The battle lines are drawn and the more determined and imaginative player will emerge as the victor.

Another popular Nimzo-Indian line (known as the *Hübner Variation*) is **1.d4 Nf6 2.c4 e6 3.Nc3 Bb4 4.e3 c5 5.Nf3 Nc6**

6.Bd3 Bxc3+ Done without any prompting by White! Black's aim is to set up a position which, due to the lack of elasticity of the doubled pawns and the closed nature of the position, will ultimately prove the Knights superior to the White Bishops. The famous game Spassky-Fischer, Reykjavik 1972, now continued **7.bxc3 d6 8.e4 e5** Playing to close it up. **9.d5 Ne7 10.Nh4 h6 11.f4 Ng6! 12.Nxg6 fxg6 13.fxe5?! dxe5 14.Be3 b6 15.0-0 0-0 16.a4 a5**

(203)

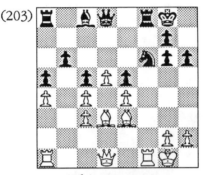

White to move.

It seems as if White must stand better. He has an advantage in central space, two Bishops, a protected passed pawn, and play against a backward pawn on b6. However, this is more an illusion than a reality. White's central space advantage is of no consequence since the center is blocked off. All the play will be on the wings and there the space is about equal. The White Bishops (in particular the light-squared one) are rather limited in scope, his passed pawn is not going anywhere, and the b6 pawn is easily defended.

So White doesn't really have anything, but what can Black boast about? Surprisingly enough, he can claim bragging rights to several different factors. Black can safely expand on the kingside by ...g6-g5 without opening up his own King; he can put pressure on White's a4 pawn by ...Bd7; and his Knight has hopes of eventually landing on the fine f4 post. This Knight excursion is a great idea since on f4 the horse is superior to either Bishop. Once the Knight reaches that square (via Nf6-h5-

f4), if White were to chase it away with g2-g3, he would weaken his kingside; if he takes it with his e3 Bishop he will be left with a bad Bishop vs. Black's good one.

Black also intends to trade Rooks on the open f-file. The point of this is to get rid of any potential pressure against b6. Black's King (yes, every piece must earn its keep!) will then be free to walk over to c7 where it will give support to the b6 pawn and stop the d-pawn from advancing. White turns out to be rather helpless against all of this. **17.Rb1 Bd7 18.Rb2 Rb8 19.Rbf2 Qe7 20.Bc2 g5 21.Bd2 Qe8! 22.Be1 Qg6** (the e4 pawn has turned into a target) **23.Qd3 Nh5 24.Rxf8+ Rxf8 25.Rxf8+ Kxf8 26.Bd1 Nf4 27.Qc2?? Bxa4!**, 0-1, since 28.Qxa4 Qxe4 threatens both the Bishop on e1 and mate on g2.

Though it is no problem to play good openings if you know all the book lines, most people have not taken the time to prepare themselves for every possible situation. Even if you have memorized a large amount of current theory, there is always some guy out there who will play a rare line that you are not familiar with. How are you supposed to react to this type of surprise? Panic is out of the question, and avoiding an in-depth breakdown of the position until all your pieces are developed is also unacceptable.

Instead of courting uncertainty, you have to sit back and size up the situation; make every effort to understand the logic of the opening that is being played and figure out the purpose of the variation that your opponent is trying to lead you into. Keep in mind that every move you make should lead to some sort of gain other than just development. Remember that your goal is to create at least one usable imbalance and then develop all your pieces around this difference!

At times it's not unusual for a major crisis to come up within a very short span of moves. The following innocent opening hides many difficulties that need to be solved: **1.d4 Nf6 2.Bg5 e6 3.e4** Black may well be confused after only three moves: after all, he hasn't done anything wrong, but White enjoys a space advantage, a large pawn center, and a lead in development (Black will fall behind in development because of the difficulties in getting his queenside pieces out). On top of everything else, White seems to threaten 4.e5. Is it already time for panic?

(204)

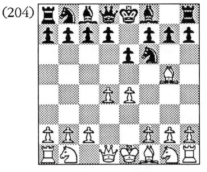

Black to play.

Actually, if Black assessed the position as we just did, then he is already exhibiting signs of panic—things are not nearly as bad as we just made them out to be. First of all, Black enjoys a solid position without any weaknesses. His only problem is the absence of positive imbalances. The question then is, how can Black create an imbalance that he can work with? Certainly 3...Be7 (to defend against 4.e5) is nothing for Black to be proud of. Sure, the move develops a piece and breaks the pin, but it does nothing to address the problems of White's space advantage, pawn center, and development plus. After 3...Be7 4.Nd2 White would enjoy the more comfortable position.

Clearly, Black must create something positive for himself or accept some degree of inferiority. If Black notices that White's pawn on e4 is unprotected, he might find the excellent **3...h6!**. Now 4.Bh4? g5 picks up the White e-pawn, so **4.Bxf6** is forced. After **4...Qxf6**, what has Black accomplished? White still has all the advantages that were mentioned earlier. However, now Black can also claim something; now Black can brag about his possession of the two Bishops! Of course, this is not necessarily an advantage, but he will do everything in his power to make it so. Black will proceed to develop his forces around this difference with moves like ...g6, ...Bg7, ...b6, ...Bb7 (placing both Bishops on their optimum diagonals), ...d6, ...Nd7, ...0-0, ...a6 (following the basic rule: *When combatting Knights, take away all their advanced posts*), and eventually ...c5, when White has nothing that is equal to the powerful Bishop on g7.

Our next game shows this plan being contested by two of the world's strongest players.

Spassky-Karpov, Montreal 1979. **1.d4 Nf6 2.c4 e6 3.Nf3 b6 4.Bf4** A bit of history here: Several months earlier, Spassky had tried the Black side of this position against Miles, who often played 4.Bf4. Miles won convincingly. Shortly thereafter, Spassky again played Miles, who again played 4.Bf4. Miles won another nice game. Now Spassky figures that "if you can't beat it, play it"! **4...Bb7 5.e3 Be7 6.Nc3?!** It's hard to believe that such a natural move is dubious, but it allows Black to grab White's Bishop. Better was 6.h3 and only then 7.Nc3. **6...Nh5! 7.Bg3 d6!** Seeing that he will have the two Bishops versus White's Bishop and Knight, Black immediately begins anti-Knight operations. This consists of making all the advanced squares unavailable to White's Knights.

Note that Black is in no hurry to capture the Bishop; it's not going anywhere and there is no reason to give White the open h-file right away. **8.Bd3 Nd7**

(205)
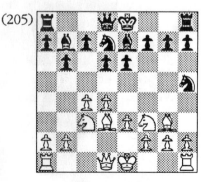

White to play.

9.0-0?! White is just developing his pieces and has no real plan in mind. Much more logical is 9.Qc2! g6 10.Be4! when White will trade one pair of Bishops and create a more acceptable Bishop versus Knight battle. **9...g6** A multi-purpose move. Black defends his Knight, blunts the d3 Bishop and prepares to place his e7 Bishop on the active h8-a1 diagonal. **10.h3 Nxg3** Before it can run away. **11.fxg3 0-0 12.Rc1 Bf6 13.Rc2 Bg7 14.Rcf2 Qe7 15.Kh2 a6!** Black is following the Steinitz formula beautifully! The first stage of Black's plan was to obtain the two Bishops. The second stage was to make the White Knights lame by taking away all their advanced squares. The next stage is to open up the position so that the power of the Bishop pair can be felt. **16.Qe2 Rae8 17.Bb1 c6 18.a3 f5 19.e4 c5!** Blasting open the center. All of a sudden the Black Bishops look like scissors cutting into the White position! The g7 Bishop in particular has nothing in the White camp that can challenge it. **20.exf5 exf5 21.Qxe7 Rxe7 22.dxc5 bxc5!** The only difficult concept in the game. Black is willing to sacrifice the bit on d6 in exchange for the destruction of White's pawn structure. **23.Rd1** 23.Nd5? Bxd5 24.cxd5 Rb8 allows Black to pick up the pawn on b2. **23...Bxc3!** This should cause a certain amount of confusion. Black fights to get the two Bishops and all of a sudden he just gives them up! What Black is doing is simply switching from one advantage to another. In the first phase of the game the inactivity of the White Knights and the threatened activity of Black's Bishops left White with very little to do. Now Black cashes his two Bishops in for the destruction of White's pawn structure and an eventual material advantage. **24.bxc3 Rf6 25.Rfd2 Re3 26.Ng1 Kf8! 27.Rxd6 Rxd6 28.Rxd6 Ke7 29.Rd3 Re1** It's time to add up the imbalances. True, White is a pawn ahead. However, all the Black pieces are superior to their White counterparts: Black's King is centralized and active, the b7 Bishop is obviously stronger than the thing on b1, White's Knight is useless and the placement of the Rooks speaks for itself. When we add to this list the dreadful state of White's pawn structure, we begin to understand why White is unable to put up any real resistance. **30.Ba2 Rc1** Threatening to win immediately with 31...Rc2. **31.Nf3 Bxf3!** Trading advantages again. Now Black is the one left with a Knight versus Bishop but in this case he has made sure that his horse has excellent squares. It certainly will have no trouble dominating White's inactive, bad Bishop. **32.Rxf3 Ne5 33.Re3 Kf6 34.Bb3 a5** Zugzwang! White has no reasonable moves left. 35.a4 completely entombs his Bishop. 35.h4 walks into a Knight fork and 35.g4 just hangs a pawn. White's King cannot move and 35.Re2 hangs the c3 pawn. Since 35.Ba2 Rc2 36.Bb3 Rb2 also drops material, White decides to give up the c-pawns in the hopes of activating his pieces. **35.Ba4 Nxc4 36.Re8 Rxc3 37.Rc8 Ne3** The Knight lands on the sixth. Now Black's plan is very simple: he will advance his passed c-pawn and Queen it! **38.Bb5 c4 39.Kg1 Rc2** Making sure that White's King doesn't escape its cage. **40.Bc6 c3 41.Bf3 g5 42.g4 f4**, 0-1. A wonderful game by Karpov in which he shows us how to develop around an imbalance and how to trade one imbalance for another.

Some Black opening systems (like the Petroff Defense with 1.e4 e5 2.Nf3 Nf6 3.Nxe5 d6 4.Nf3 Nxe4) are designed to keep the imbalances for both sides down to a minimum in the hope that a sterile equality can be reached and a draw obtained. This is perfectly acceptable. However, avoid openings which give your opponent one or two useful imbalances while leaving you with nothing to play for at all! *Leaving yourself with nothing to build on equals a failed opening effort.*

Silman-Gogel, U.S. Open 1981. **1.d4 Nf6 2.c4 g6 3.Nc3 Bg7 4.e4 d6 5.Be2 0-0 6.Bg5 c5 7.d5 e6 8.Qd2 exd5 9.exd5 Re8 10.Nf3 Bg4 11.0-0 Nbd7 12.h3 Bxf3 13.Bxf3 a6 14.a4 b6** (see diagram #206).

(206)

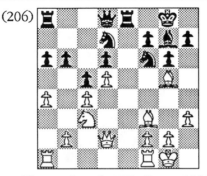

Silman-Gogel, U.S. Open 1981.
White to move.

Black has successfully developed his pieces, but he has gained no really favorable elements. White, however, has two Bishops and an advantage in space. This makes the opening a success for the first player. White's plan is to limit the scope of the Black Knights while posting his Bishops in such a way as to make any counterplay by Black impossible. Then White can play for a kingside offensive, or he can also consider a queenside break by a5 or b4. **15.Rae1** The immediate 15.Bd1! was more accurate. **15...Rxe1 16.Rxe1 Qf8 17.Bd1! h6 18.Be3 Rb8 19.Bc2** Eyeing Black's kingside and further controlling the e4 square. **19...Ne8 20.f4** Taking e5 away from Black's Knights. **20...Nc7 21.Bd3** Making Black's ...b6-b5 advance impossible. **21...Re8 22.Bf2 f5?** As a direct result of the opening, Black has no counterplay. Unhappy with his miserable status, Black lashes out for space but only succeeds in weakening his kingside. **23.Rb1!** The immediate 23.a5 is also possible, though Black might mix it up a bit by 23...Bxc3!? 24.Qxc3 b5. Besides, Black should have traded Rooks, and I did not intend to give him another chance. **23...a5** White threatened to play b2-b4, and 23...Qf6 24.a5! takes away Black's possibility of ...Bxc3. **24.g4! Qf6** Also bad is 24...fxg4 25.Bxg6. **25.gxf5 gxf5 26.Ne2!** Now there is a clear target on f5 and White hastens to attack it with everything he's got. **26...Qg6+ 27.Ng3 Rf8 28.Kh2 Ne8 29.Rg1 Qh7 30.Qc2**, 1-0. When f5 falls, the rest of Black's game will go with it.

IMBALANCES IN THE ENDGAME

Most endgame imbalances should be cultivated, nurtured, and used in much the same way as they are in the middlegame. For example, if the position is closed, a Knight, just as in a middlegame, is usually superior to a Bishop.

(207)

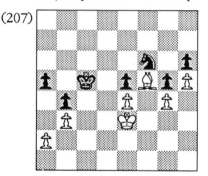

Damjanovic-Fischer, Buenos Aires 1970.
Black to play.

Here we see both Kings waging war against each other and the Black pawns safely placed on dark squares. This position is won for Black because his King is more active than its counterpart and the Knight has much more potential than the Bishop. By this I mean that the Knight can potentially attack virtually any square on the board. White's Bishop can't attack anything and is stuck in a useless light-squared dimension.

To win, Black needs to penetrate with his King. At the

moment though, White's own monarch will keep him out by hanging around e3 and d3. How can Black's King get in? Fischer solves this dilemma by advancing his a-pawn. **1...Kb5 2.Kd3 a4** Now White must choose between two evils: He can play 3.bxa4+ and let the enemy King advance, or he can allow ...a4-a3, when the a2 pawn becomes an indefensible target. **3.bxa4+** Not what he wanted to do, but allowing the pawn to get to a3 also led to a loss: 3.Ke3 a3 4.Kd3 Kc5 5.Ke3 Ne8 6.Kd3 Nd6 7.Bd7 (Black threatened ...Nb5 and ...Nc3) 7...Nc4! 8.Be8 (8.bxc4 b3 queens a pawn) 8...Nb2+ 9.Ke3 (or 9.Kc2 Kd4, etc.) 9...Nd1+ followed by ...Nc3 with a quick win. **3...Kxa4 4.Kc4 Ka3 5.Kc5 Kxa2 6.Kxb4 Kb2** Now Black is winning for two reasons:

1) His King is deep in enemy territory and as a result will be the first to munch White's pawns;

2) When pawns are only on one side of the board, the Knight is superior to the Bishop. This is because the Bishop's long range powers are useless, while the Knight's ability to go to any colored square is of great importance—nothing is safe from the beast!

7.Kc5 Kc3 8.Kd6 Kd4 9.Ke6 Nxe4 10.Kf7 Nf2 11.Kg6 e4 12.Kxh6 White is also hopelessly lost after 12.Bxe4 Kxe4 13.Kxh6 Kf4 followed by ...Nxg4. **12...e3 13.Kg7 e2 14.h6 e1=Q 15.h7 Qe7+ 16.Kg8 Ne4!**, 0-1. White gave up because 17.h8=Q Nf6+ kills the Queen just as it's born, while 17.Bxe4 Kxe4 18.h8=Q Qe8+ 19.Kg7 Qxh8+ 20.Kxh8 Kf4 is also rather one-sided.

Our next example (diagram #208) shows the other side of the coin—an open position leads to a Knight being eaten alive by a frisky Bishop.

(208)

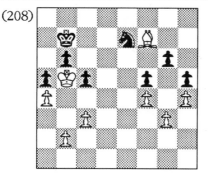

Fischer-Taimanov, Vancouver 1971.
White to move.

What is the difference between this position and the previous one? In general a Bishop is superior to a Knight if there are pawns on both sides of the board, because then its long range powers come into effect. In Damjanovic-Fischer, Black's pawns were safely placed on the opposite color of the Bishop. In the present example, however, Black's kingside pawns are vulnerable because they are stuck on light squares. These weak pawns and the White King's obvious superiority to its counterpart combine to give White a winning position. **1.Bb3 Ka7** Or 1...Nc8 (threatening 2...Nd6 mate!) 2.Bd5+ when both 2...Ka7 3.Kc6 and 2...Kc7 3.Ka6 allow White a further penetration into Black's position. **2.Bd1 Kb7 3.Bf3+** The point of White's earlier play. The King can no longer happily mark time on a7 and b7. **3...Kc7** No better is 3...Ka7 4.c4! Ng8 5.Kc6 Nf6 6.Kd6 Ne4+ 7.Ke5 Nxg3 8.Kf6 and White will scoop up the Black kingside pawns. **4.Ka6** Now White's next step is to put his Bishop back on f7 where it ties the Knight down to the defense of the pawn on g6. **4...Ng8** White gets a winning King and pawn ending after 4...Nc6 5.Bxc6 Kxc6 6.c4 Kc7 7.Ka7 Kc6 8.Kb8. **5.Bd5 Ne7** If 5...Nf6, then 6.Bf7 Ne4 7.Bxg6 Nxg3 8.Kb5 Ne2 9.Bxh5 Nxf4 10.Bf7 wins for White, since the Bishop always beats out a Knight in mutual passed pawn situations. **6.Bc4** White wants Black to move his Knight first, since then Bf7 will be with tempo. **6...Nc6 7.Bf7 Ne7 8.Be8!** *Zugzwang!* Any King move will drop the b6 pawn. Any

Knight move would drop the g6 pawn, and 8...c4 9.Kb5 or 9.Bf7 picks up the c4 pawn. **8...Kd8 9.Bxg6!** White gives up his Bishop for a whole herd of pawns. The Knight's limited mobility generally makes it a poor piece to stop passed pawns. **9...Nxg6 10.Kxb6 Kd7 11.Kxc5 Ne7 12.b4 axb4 13.cxb4 Nc8 14.a5 Nd6 15.b5 Ne4+ 16.Kb6 Kc8** White queens after 16...Nxg3 17.a6. **17.Kc6 Kb8** Or 17...Nxg3 18.a6 Kb8 19.b6 Ne4 20.a7+ Ka8 21.b7+ Kxa7 22.Kc7. **18.b6**, 1-0.

It's clear that most imbalances have the same effect in the endgame as they do in the middlegame. However, some endgame situations *do* change the nature of rules that are taken for granted in the middlegame. Two of these rules are:

1) In the middlegame it is well known that you should keep your King safely hidden behind its pawns. In the endgame the King turns into a fighting piece (the reduced forces make it safe from attack) and must be brought into the center of the board as quickly as possible.

2) In the middlegame you usually want to place your pawns on the *same* color as the enemy Bishop since then it will be blocked and its activity will be curtailed. In the endgame you want to place your pawns on the *opposite* color from the enemy Bishop so that your pawns will be safe from the Bishop's carnivorous advances.

(209)

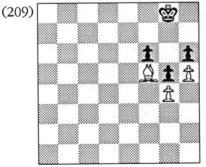

The position in diagram #209 is a simple illustration of this second rule. If this were a middlegame and many more pieces roamed the board, it is not hard to see that Black's King would be extremely uncomfortable (not to mention the Bishop's great activity in this position). For a middlegame, Black would prefer to place his pawns on f7, g6, and h7. Now the Bishop is attacked, no longer has the scope it previously had, and Black's King is infinitely safer.

Aside from considerations like minor piece battles and pawn safety, other imbalances must also be addressed. Something like extra material is self evident, but does a space advantage play a role in the endgame? In the opening it restricts the opponent's options and in the middlegame it takes away his active possibilities. Since space consists of far advanced pawns that map out territory, an endgame situation might easily see these advanced pawns becoming threats to promote, even if they are not passed!

(210)
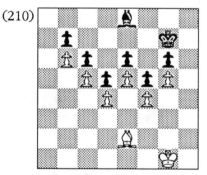
White to play.

White is able to make use of the space advantage and the accompanying fact that his pawns are closer to queening by playing **1.Ba6!** when Black must resign since 1...bxa6 2.b7 allows the pawn to promote.

This tactical idea is quite common. Let's take a look at the position featured in diagram #211 (see next page).

(211)

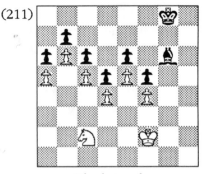

Black to play.

Black loses since he is powerless to prevent Nb4 followed by Nxa6 or Nxc6. For example **1...Be8 2.Nb4 Bd7 3.Nxa6! Bc8 4.Nb4 Kf7 5.a6 bxa6 6.Nxc6** followed by 7.Na5 when Black must give up.

Of course, an advantage in space doesn't only give its owner tactical possibilties—just like a middlegame, you can use it to squeeze the opponent also. Since space is such a useful commodity, it pays to go out of your way to claim it; this means that a plan based on the acquisition of territory is an effective way to play many endings.

(212)

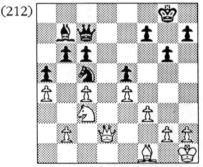

Kuznecov-Silman, Oregon Open 1986.
Black to play.

Black is better due to his superior Bishop (good Bishop versus bad Bishop) and the fact that his Knight can make use of the weakened c5 and d4 squares while its counterpart has nowhere to go at all. What about space? At the moment the territory is basically even. However, Black's superior minor pieces will eventually allow him to annex space on the kingside. His plan is this:

1) Place his minor pieces on their best possible squares.

2) Trade Queens since she has little to do with the interaction of the minors.

3) Tie White down to the defense of the a4 and c4 pawns.

4) Advance pawns on the kingside and grab as much territory there as possible. One of the aims of this is to restrict the White army. The other is to create a possible target on that side as well.

All this takes time, but Black should not be in any hurry since White can only watch as Black improves his position. The feeling of helplessness this gives to the defender leads to depression and eventually to errors. **25...Ne6** Eyeing d4 and f4. **26.Ne2** Defending these squares but also blocking in the Bishop. **26...Qe7 27.Nc1 Kg7 28.Nb3 c5** Ending any White hopes of a c4-c5 advance and nailing down the d4 square for the Black Knight. **29.Nc1 Bc6 30.Qd1 Qd7** The Queens come off so White's minor pieces must take over their Queen's defensive chores. **31.Qxd7 Bxd7 32.b3 Nd4** The White Knight is stuck guarding the sad little pawn on b3. **33.Kg1 f5!** Creating new imbalances. Now White must either view e4 as a point to be defended or he can trade and give Black the possibility of a passed e-pawn via a later ...e5-e4. **34.Bd3 Bc6 35.exf5** With one piece stuck guarding b3 and the other defending e4 White was understandably unhappy. However, a holding pattern by Kf2-e3 was probably better. **35...gxf5 36.Kf2 Kf6 37.Ke3 Kg5 38.Bb1 h5 39.Bd3 h4** Threatening to destroy the base of the f3 pawn with ...h4-h3. White is now severely restricted on the kingside and in the center. **40.h3** Stopping the threat but placing another pawn on a light square. **40...Be8! 41.Be2 Bg6** Showing patience while you build up your position and look for a method of penetration is neccessary when dealing with a spatial edge. So far Black has shown lots of patience, now it's time to find a way to break into the White position. Black's intention is to play ...f4, ...Bb1, and ...e4. **42.Bd1 f4+ 43.Kf2 Bb1!** There are only a few pieces left on the board but White is still being pushed back to the first rank! **44.Ne2 e4!** Threatening to create a passed pawn by ...e4-e3 and more importantly creating a way for Black to enter into White's camp via ...Kf5-e5-d4. **45.fxe4** Naturally 45.Nxd4 e3+ followed by 46...cxd4 with two connected passed pawns is completely hopeless for White. **45...Nxe2 46.Bxe2 Bxe4** It's all over now. Black threatens to win material by ...Bc2xb3, and if White stops this by 47.Bd1 then White's King would also be stuck guarding the g2 pawn. Black would win by marching his King to c3 via ...Kf5-e5-d4-c3. This was all made possible by Black's restriction of the White forces and the placing of White's pawns on vunerable light squares. **47.Bg4 Bc2 48.Kf3?** Ending things right away, but nothing could be done to save the game. **48...Bd1+ 49.Ke4 Bxg4 50.hxg4 Kxg4**, 0-1.

Our final example shows how a little extra space can sometimes work wonders.

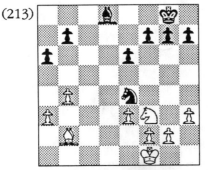

(213)

Mikhalyevsky-Akopov, Rostov 1977.
Black to play.

I can hear the screams now, "This is a dead draw!" Yes, I agree with you—calm down. However, there are two factors that enable White to retain some hope of victory:

1) His King is a little closer to the center than its Black counterpart.

2) Black may not be aware of a little known rule, i.e. *A space advantage can take on epic proportions in a Knight endgame.* The reason for this is that the side with more territory has plenty of room in which to move his Knight to any juicy post that comes to mind. The cramped player though, finds that his Knight is unable to maneuver to its best squares due to lack of leaping space.

1...Bf6? A very natural move that goes right into the Knight endgame that White had been hoping for! Black would have drawn if he had retained the Bishops. One adequate possibility was 1...Nd6 2.Nd2 (keeping the Knight out of c4) 2...f6 blunting White's pieces and preparing to bring the King to the middle. **2.Bxf6 Nxf6?!** 2...gxf6 is stonger since it takes away the e5 square from White horse and keeps his own Knight centralized. **3.Ke2 Kf8** After 3...Ne4 4.Kd3! Nxf2+ 5.Kd4 Nd1 6.e4 White's King would penetrate to the queenside and dine on the pawns there. **4.Kd3 Ke7 5.Kd4** White now has a superior King and some extra territory on the queenside. **5...Nd7 6.Nd2!** Now 6...Kd6 7.Nc4+ Kc6 8.e4 continues White's campaign of space grabbing. **6...Nb6 7.e4 Na4** 7...Kd6 8.e5+ Kc6 9.Ne4 leaves Black facing threats like 10.Nd6 and 10.Ng5. **8.e5** White's advantage in territory is finally clear. He hopes to bring his Knight to d6 when both f7 and b7 are vulnerable. **8...f5** Trading the weakness on f7 for a new one on e6. **9.Nc4 Kd7 10.Nd6 b6 11.f3 Nb2 12.h4!** Tying Black's kingside pawns down and continuing to expand on that side. **12...Na4 13.Nf7 Ke7 14.Ng5 h6 15.Nh3 Kd7 16.Nf4 Ke7 17.Kc4** 17.Nd3!, shutting the Black Knight out of the game, was stronger. **17...Nb2+ 18.Kc3 Nd1+ 19.Kd4 Nb2 20.g4 fxg4 21.fxg4 Nd1 22.g5?** No matter how much territory White owns, if he can't break into the enemy position it won't do him any good. Here White missed his chance to grab the critical c5 square by 22.a4! followed by a5: 22...Nb2 23.a5 b5 24.Kc5 g5 25.hxg5 hxg5 26.Ng6+! Kf7 27.Kb6 Nd3 28.Kxa6 Nxb4+ 29.Kxb5 Nd5 30.a6 Nc7+ 31.Kb6 Nxa6 32.Kxa6 Kxg6 33.Kb6 and White wins. Analysis by Shereshevsky. **22...hxg5 23.hxg5 Nb2** Now a3-a4 has been prevented. **24.g6 Na4 25.Nd3 Kd8 26.Kc4 Kd7??** Black could draw by 26...b5+ 27.Kd4 Kd7 28.Nc5+ Nxc5 29.Kxc5 Kc7. **27.b5 axb5+ 28.Kxb5 Nc3+ 29.Kxb6 Nd5+ 30.Kb7 Ne7 31.a4 Nxg6 32.a5**, 1-0.

This game has always impressed me and acts as proof that the smallest imbalance can lead to real chances for victory if you nurse it and allow it to grow.

OPENING IMBALANCES THAT LAST TO THE ENDGAME

When I was thirteen years old I read that Soviet players would study openings by learning both the typical middlegame and the typical endgame positions that arose from it. At the time, this shocked me. How could a player predict what kind of endgame might arise from any particular opening?

I wasn't able to answer this question until my sixteenth year, when a study of the Exchange Variation of the Ruy Lopez suddenly made things very clear: **1.e4 e5 2.Nf3 Nc6 3.Bb5 a6 4.Bxc6** Giving up the two Bishops to weaken Black's pawn structure. **4...dxc6!** Immediately giving his Bishops open lines, and not fearing 5.Nxe5 because of 5...Qd4. **5.d4 exd4 6.Qxd4 Qxd4 7.Nxd4**

(214)

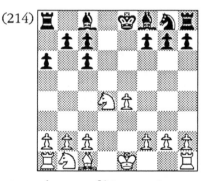

White hopes to make use of his superior pawn structure, which gives him a healthy kingside pawn majority vs. Black's useless queenside clump. Actually, if we were to take all the pieces off the board (leaving on the Kings and pawns), White would win because he can always create a passed pawn on the kingside while Black is unable to do so on the opposite wing.

This means that White should play this opening with the understanding that every exchange leads him closer to the position in diagram #215.

(215)

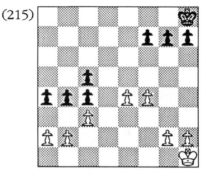

White to play.

If White can reach this position or something close to it, he knows that he will win the game! First on the agenda is to end Black's illusions on the queenside by creating a little V-shaped formation by **1.a3!** Black threatened to steal the game by 1...a3! 2.bxa3, and now either 2...b3 or 2...bxc3 gives Black a passed pawn that will soon promote. After 1.a3, play might continue: **1...Kg8 2.g4** And not 2.axb4?? cxb4 3.cxb4 c3 and Black makes a new Queen. **2...Kf8 3.Kg2 Ke7 4.Kf3 Ke6 5.h4 f6 6.h5 Kd6 7.f5 Ke7** Or 7...h6 (7...Ke5 8.Ke3 takes the opposition and forces Black to back up) 8.Kf4 b3 9.e5+ fxe5+ 10.Ke4 Kd7 11.Kxe5 Ke7 12.f6+! gxf6+ 13.Kf5 Kf7 14.Ke6, etc. **8.Kf4 Kd6 9.g5 fxg5+ 10.Kxg5 Ke5 11.h6** and the game is over.

Fortunately for Black, he is by no means obliged to allow such an endgame to appear. Instead (from diagram #214), he should utilize the advantages of his position by, **7...Bd7** (after 7.Nxd4) **8.Be3 0-0-0 9.Nd2 Ne7 10.0-0-0 Re8 11.Rhe1 Ng6 12.Ne2 Bd6 13.h3 f5 14.exf5 Bxf5** when his Bishops are very active. It's clear that in the Exchange Variation of the Ruy Lopez we get an immediate and intense battle between Black's two

Bishops and White's superior pawn structure where certain endgame situations are already mapped out and assessed as early as the seventh move!

Usually the imbalance we create in the opening does not lead to any specific endgames. However, if you give your newly created imbalance the attention it deserves, it can and often is an important element in the middlegame and a decisive factor if an endgame is reached. The game Villanueva-Silman, Los Angeles 1989, is a fine example of this. **1.e4 c5 2.Nf3 Nc6 3.d4 cxd4 4.Nxd4 Nf6 5.Nc3 d6 6.f4 g6 7.Nf3 Bg7 8.Bd3 0-0 9.0-0 a6 10.Qe1 b5 11.Kh1**

(216)

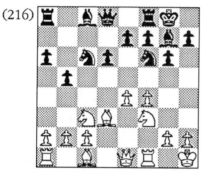

Villanueva-Silman, Los Angeles 1989.
Black to move.

So far White has clearly been preparing for a kingside attack. Though Black will be playing on the queenside, an obvious target is not yet discernable. With this thought in mind, Black decides to go after White's Bishop on d3. The idea is to gain the two Bishops and base his later play on that fact. In other words, Black will try to transform the position into one where Bishops are superior to Knights. Of course, White's kingside attack may crash through first, but that's what chess is about—it's a battle of ideas. **11...Nb4 12.a3 Nxd3 13.cxd3 Rb8** Black is actually a bit concerned with White's potential on the kingside and tries to move as quickly as possible on the opposite wing. If you have a situation where you are playing on opposite sides, it is very important to get your opponent's attention and make him react to your threats. In that way he will never really have time to start implementing his own plans. **14.b4** White did not like Black opening up lines with ...b5-b4, so he stops it once and for all. **14...Bb7 15.Bd2 Qd7** Connecting the Rooks and intending to answer 16.Qh4 with 16...Qg4. Since Black's play will be based on two Bishops, he would be happy to go into an ending—then White's kingside chances would be a thing of the past. **16.Rc1?!** White continues to make natural moves on the queenside, but this is just what Black wants! White must go after the Black King—he has a space advantage there, and his Queen, Bishop, Rook, and Knight all aim at that side of the board. **16...Rbc8 17.Ne2?!** Giving up on his kingside attack for no reason whatsoever! With 17.h3 (to stop ...Qg4) followed by Qh4, f5, Bh6, and Ng5, White could and *should* have started a dangerous attack. Remember: If you don't do what the position needs, bad things will happen to you! The only way you can hope to worry your opponent is by putting pressure on him. White's planless play gave Black great confidence. **17...Rxc1** Black is very happy to trade Rooks. They do little to enhance Black's Bishops but they could very easily help White with his kingside attack. **18.Qxc1** White is playing for trades on the c-file and a subsequent draw. In doing so, he is ignoring all the dynamic potential that his position offered him. **18...Rc8 19.Qb1 Nh5!** Black continues to fight for the freedom of his 'extra' b7 Bishop. White should now play 20.Qb3 with a solid position and just a very slight inferiority. **20.Rc1?** After this, Black takes complete control of the game. **20...f5!** All of a sudden White has nothing on the board to match Black's mighty Bishop on b7. Black's opening strategy of gaining the two Bishops has paid off. **21.Qb3+ Kh8 22.Rxc8+ Qxc8 23.Nc3** Tempting but useless is 23.Ng5 h6 24.Nf7+ Kh7, and White's Knight is trapped on f7. Other moves like 23.exf5 turn the Bihsop on b7 into a fire breathing monster. **23...Nxf4! 24.Ng5 h6 25.Nf7+ Kh7 26.Bxf4 Qxc3 27.Qxc3 Bxc3 28.exf5 g5!** Also very tempting was 28...gxf5 29.Nxh6 Kg6, when Black's two Bishops and central majority should lead to a win. **29.Bc1** To prevent Black from winning the a3 pawn by ...Bb2. **29...Bd5 30.Nd8 Kg7** White is completely lost. The Knight on d8 is dominated by the killer on d5, while the pawn on f5 is about to be eaten by Black's King. Students should take note! On move eleven Black went after the two Bishops and now, nineteen moves later, those same two Bishops are wiping White out. A nice case of an opening idea ultimately winning in the endgame. **31.Kg1 Kf6 32.g4 h5 33.gxh5** Hopeless, but so was 33.h3 hxg4 34.hxg4 Bf3 35.Ne6 Bxg4 36.Nxg5 Bxf5 37.Ne4+ Bxe4 38.dxe4 Ke5 when White can resign. **33...Kxf5** Now White's Knight will never see the light of day. **34.h6 Kg6 35.h7 Bf6 36.Kf2 Kxh7** White should now resign, but he chose to prolong the agony. The remaining moves were: **37.Be3 Kg6 38.Kg3 Kf5 39.h3 Be5+ 40.Kf2 Bb2 41.Kg3 Bxa3 42.h4 gxh4+ 43.Kxh4 Bxb4**, 0-1.

Solve These Problems

(217)

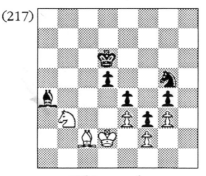

White to play.

Should White play 1.Nd4 and trade the Bishops or should he allow Black to capture on b3 when a Bishop versus Knight battle would ensue?

(218)

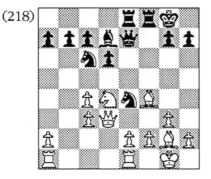

White to play.

After **1.d4 Nf6 2.c4 e5 3.dxe5 Ng4 4.Bf4 Bb4+ 5.Nc3 Bxc3+ 6.bxc3 Nc6 7.Nf3 Qe7 8.Qd5 f6 9.exf6 Nxf6 10.Qd3 d6 11.g3 0-0 12.Bg2 Bg4 13.0-0 Rae8 14.Rfe1 Ne4 15.Nd4 Bd7** we come to the position in diagram #218. White must come up with a clear plan of action. What should he do?

PART FOURTEEN

GLOSSARY

How many people think that *Zugzwang* is a curse, *Hack* is a cough or the act of striking someone, *Fish* is something that swims until you eat it, and *Zwischenzug* is a sound that is made during a sneeze? These unfortunate individuals abound in life and, when they are unlucky enough to visit a chess tournament, they come to realize that a strange language is being spoken that is only understood by creatures that spend their time pushing tiny bits of wood and plastic around a checkered board.

The glossary in this section will finally enable you to translate the terms being directed at you by the big chess guns and the smaller *fish* that surround them.

Active An aggressive move, line of play, or position. When mentioned in lieu of a player's style, it denotes a preference for sharp, tactical, or vibrant types of play.

Advantage Having a superiority in position based on a particular imbalance or series of imbalances. See *imbalance*.

Analysis The calculation of a series of moves in a given position. This can be done in actual tournament conditions (in which you are not allowed to touch the pieces) or in a calmer scenario in which the pieces can be moved about (such analysis is often written down for future study or reference). The purpose of analysis is to discover the best move or plan. There is no limit to its length.

Annotation Written comments (prose or actual moves) about a position or game.

Attack To make a threat or threats against a specific piece or area of the board.

Backward Pawn A pawn which has fallen behind its com-
rades, and thus no longer
can be supported or
guarded by other pawns of
its own persuasion.

In the diagram Black has
backward pawns at d6 and
f7. The pawns on h6 and b7
are not backward because
they can safely advance.

Bind To have a grip on a position which makes useful moves
difficult for the opponent to
find. One often speaks of a
crushing space advantage as
a bind.

The diagram shows an ex-
treme example of a bind; Black
is bound hand and foot and
can undertake nothing positive at all.

Bishop Pair To possess two Bishops vs. the opponent's
Bishop and Knight or two Knights. Two Bishops work
extremely well together and are usually an advantage in
open positions.

Blockade Conceptualized and popularized by Aron Nimzovich
(1886-1935), it refers to the
tying down (immobilization)
of an enemy pawn by plac-
ing a piece (in particular a
Knight) directly in front of it.

In the diagram the Knight
on d6 is blockading the pawn
on d5.

Blunder A horrible mistake that hangs material or makes decisive positional or tactical concessions.

Book Published opening theory. A book player is one who relies on heavy memorization of published analysis rather than on his own creative imagination.

'Taking someone out of book' refers to sidestepping published analysis by playing a new or unorthodox move. This denies him the chance to make use of a good memory and forces him to find good moves on his own.

Break The gaining of space (and thus more freedom of movement) by the advance of a pawn.

In the diagram, White intends to open lines of attack on the queenside by the break c4-c5 (prepared by b2-b4). Black will strive to attack White on the kingside by an ...f7-f5 break.

Breakthrough A means of penetrating the enemy position. This can be done by a pawn break or by a sacrifice involving pieces or pawns.

In the diagram at right, both sides are attacking each other's King. At the moment White is safe, since ...gxf3 can be safely answered by Bxf3. So White uses the time given him to effect a breakthrough on the queenside by **1.bxc5 dxc5 2.Nxc5! bxc5**
If Black does not capture the Knight, White will simply retreat it to d3 and rip Black open by c4-c5. **3.Qb2** and Black will be mated.

Brilliancy A game that contains a very deep strategic concept, a beautiful combination, or an original plan.

Calculation The working out of variations without moving the pieces physically. Though this book has taught you to talk or reason your way through a game, there are many positions that have a purely tactical nature. In such situations the player's ability to calculate variations accurately takes on great importance.

The way to train your combinative (calculative) vision is to study the games of attacking players like Alekhine, Tal, or Kasparov. Follow their opening moves and then cover up the rest of the game score. At this point your should endeavor to figure out all the imbalances, the plans, candidate moves, etc. When this is done, calculate each candidate move as deeply as you can, writing down all this information as you go. All this must be done without moving the pieces around. When you have done all that's possible (take as much time as you need, we are looking for accuracy; speed will follow naturally), look at the move played and make it on your board, and keep repeating the process until the game is complete.

Keep a notebook with all your analysis. At first you may not do well, but with practice and effort you will notice real improvement in every aspect of your game.

Center Usually considered to be the e4, d4, e5, and d5 squares, though the territory within the c4, c5, f4, and f5 parameters can also be thought of as central.

Centralize The central placing of pieces and pawns so they both control the center and extend their influence over other areas of the board. A piece will usually reach maximum maneuverability and power when centrally placed.

Checkmate See *Mate*.

Classical A style of play (sometimes called a school) which is concerned with forming a full pawn center. The strategic concepts that go with it tend to be viewed as ultimate laws and thus are rather dogmatic. A classical opening is an opening based on these views. See *Hypermodern*.

Closed Game A position locked by pawns. Such a position tends to lessen the strength of Bishops and other long range pieces simply because the pawns get in their way. Knights on the other hand, can jump over other pieces and pawns, and thus are very useful in such closed situations. A typical series of opening moves that lead to a closed position is **1.d4 Nf6 2.c4 c5 3.d5 e5 4.Nc3 d6 5.e4**, etc.

Combination A tactical move or series of moves based on the opponent's weakened King, hanging or undefended pieces, or inadequately guarded pieces. Usually involving a sacrifice, it is a calculable series of moves leading to material or positional gains. It is important to note that a combination cannot exist if at least one of the above factors is not present.

Though several players have attempted to create a clear definition throughout the years, the following definition by Silman and Seirawan is the most accurate: *A combination is a sacrifice combined with a forced sequence of moves, which exploits specific peculiarities of the position in the hope of attaining a certain goal.*

Compensation An equivalent advantage in one imbalance that balances the opponent's advantage in another. For example: material vs. development or space vs. superior minor piece or three pawns vs. a Bishop.

Connected Passed Pawns Two or more pawns of the same color on adjacent files. See *Passed Pawn*.

Control To dominate or have the sole use of a file, a square or group of squares, an area of the board, etc. Having the initiative would also put one in 'control.'

Counterplay When the defending side starts his own aggressive action, he is said to have or be initiating counterplay. However, there are varying degrees of counterplay—some equalizing the chances, some not being quite adequate, and some leading to the capture of the initiative and subsequently an advantage.

Cramp A disadvantage in space that leads to a lack of mobility.

Critical Position That point in a position when the evaluation will clearly turn to one side's advantage or stabilize down to equality. In such a position the scales are delicately balanced and the slightest error can lead to a disaster.

Defense A move or plan designed to meet an enemy's attack or threats. It is also used in the names of various openings initiated from the Black side. For example: Petroff Defense, Caro-Kann Defense, etc. These Black systems are called defenses, since White has the first move and thus Black is considered to be defending. The usual flow from Black's point of view would be: Defense leading to equalization, and then the switch over to a counterattack. This is the classical approach. More modern openings are often designed to create immediate imbalances in an effort to seize the initiative as Black. Strange as it may seem, even these counterattacking openings are usually given the title of defenses: Nimzo-Indian Defense, Sicilian Defense, Grunfeld Defense, etc.

Development The process of moving one's pieces from their starting posts to new positions where their activity and mobility are enhanced. It must be remembered that one's pieces should be developed to squares where they work with the rest of the army towards a particular goal. If an individual piece is providing a useful service on its original square, then there may be no reason to move it.

Doubled Pawns Two pawns of the same color lined up on a file as the result of a capture. Such pawns are generally considered to be weak, though quite often their ability to control certain squares makes them very useful.

The diagram shows doubled pawns in a favorable light. The doubled pawn on c3 is guarding the critical d4 square, while

the other pawn on c4 increased White's control of the important d5 square. Also note how doubled pawns often give their owner an extra open file to use. Black's position in the diagram would be considerably improved if he could double his own pawns by placing the d6 pawn on e6.

Dynamic Dynamics symbolize the aggressive potential in any given position or move.

Elo Rating A mathematical system devised by Prof. Arpad Elo to rank chess players. It is used worldwide.

En Passant A French term which literally means 'in passing'. When a pawn advances two squares (something it can only do if it has not yet moved) and passes an enemy pawn on an adjacent file that has advanced to its fifth rank, it may be

captured by that enemy pawn as if the advancing pawn had moved only one square. This optional capture may be made only on the first opportunity, else the right in that instance is permanently lost.

If Black plays 1...c7-c5 White, if he wishes, may capture the pawn as if it had

moved to c6. Thus, 2.dxc6. If after 1...c7-c5 White declines to capture and instead plays 2.c4, then after 2...e7-e5 White could no longer capture the c5 pawn. However, he could capture the e5 pawn by dxe6 if he so desired. In chess notation an En Passant capture is labeled by the letter e.p.

En Prise A French term meaning 'in take.' It describes a piece or pawn that is unprotected and exposed to capture. (Pronounced: on-pree)

Equality A situation in which neither side has an advantage over the opponent.

Exchange To trade pieces of equal worth. See *Point Count*.

Exchange, The A comparison of value between a Rook vs. a Bishop or Knight. Thus, if you have won an enemy Rook for your Bishop or Knight, then you have won the Exchange.

Fianchetto An Italian word meaning 'on the flank.' Though you will hear many different pronunciations, the correct pronunciation is fyan-ket-to. When a Bishop is developed on QN2 or KN2 (b2 or g2 for White and b7 or g7 for Black), it is called a fianchettoed Bishop. This term applies only to Bishops.

FIDE An acronym for *Federation Internationale des Echecs*, the World Chess Federation.

File A column of eight squares. An 'open file' is a file that is not blocked by either side's pawns.

Fish A derogatory term denoting a weak chess player.

Flank The sides of the board—the kingside and queenside. 'Flank openings' are openings that deal with flank development. Typical starts for such systems are 1.c4; 1.Nf3; 1.b3; etc.

Force Material—all pieces and pawns are units of force.

Forced A move or series of moves that must be played if 'disaster' is to be avoided. Two examples: 1) A checked King that has only one legal move to get out of check. That is considered to be a forced move. 2) A Knight (or any other piece) is attacked and has only one safe square to go to. This is also considered to be forced, even though other moves could legally be played.

Gambit A voluntary sacrifice of a pawn or a piece in the opening with the idea of gaining the initiative, a lead in development, or some other compensating factor.

General Principles Basic rules or play designed to serve as guidelines for less advanced players. As one's experience grows, one learns that rules are meant to be broken. For example: The old rule of *always capture with a pawn towards the center* is widely followed, but a good 30% of the time it is correct to capture away from the center. Other rules (such as *avoid doubled pawns, castle as early as possible, develop Knights before Bishops,* etc.) are also just as suspect. The simple fact is that every situation must be looked at with an open mind—dogma is not something to be nurtured.

Ghosts Threats that exist only in your own mind. A fear of your opponent or a lack of confidence will often lead to the appearance of ghosts and the cropping up of blunders in your play.

Grandmaster Conferred by FIDE, it is the highest title (aside from World Champion) that one can achieve. It is awarded to players who meet established performance standards. Other titles (in order of importance) are International Master and FIDE Master. Once earned, these titles cannot be taken away.

Grandmaster Draw When Grandmasters make a quick, uninteresting draw, it is called a Grandmaster Draw. Nowadays a quick draw between any class of players is given the same label.

Hack A derogatory chess term meaning a state of chess ineptitude.

Hanging An unprotected piece or pawn exposed to capture is said to be hanging.

Hanging Pawns Two adjacent friendly pawns on their fourth rank, separated from other friendly pawns, and subject to frontal attack on one or two half-open files. Though often objects of attack, they also possess a certain dynamic potential. Thus the battle rages around the question, 'are

they strong or weak?' The diagram shows a common hanging pawns situation. The hanging pawns on c5 and d5 give Black an edge in space, good control of the central squares, and pressure down the half open b-file. However, they are also exposed to attack.

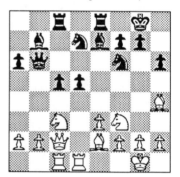

Hog See *Pig*.

Hold A defensive term meaning to 'hang on.' *Such and such a move would have held out longer* means that the move would have offered tougher resistance, but would most likely have ultimately failed. *Such and such a move would hold* means that the mentioned move would have allowed a successful defense.

Hole A square that cannot be defended by pawns. Such a square makes an excellent home for enemy pieces (especially Knights). For example, the opening 1.c4 c5 2.Nc3 Nc6 3.e4 is playable, but leaves a hole on d4 which, after 3...g6 and 4...Bg7, can easily be used by a Black piece.

Hutch A special room set aside for players in a tournament to analyze their games and play skittles. Such a room allows various kinds of activity to go on without disturbing the unfinished games in the tournament. Usually used by the non-masters (called Rabbits), the term hutch becomes easily understandable. See *Rabbit* and *Skittles*.

Hypermodern A school of thought which insists that indirect control of the center is better than direct occupation. In particular Reti and Nimzovich successfully propagated the idea of central control from the flanks. Unfortunately, they took their ideas to extremes—just as the classicists did. Today it is recognized that both schools of thought are correct, and a blending of the two is the only truly balanced method.

Imbalance Any difference between the White and Black positions. Material advantage, superior pawn structure, superior minor piece, space, development, and the initiative are all typical imbalances.

Initiative When your opponent is defending and you are attacking or putting pressure on him, it is said that you have the initiative.

Innovation A new move in an established position or opening.

Intuition Usually a sign of experience, it enables a player to choose a move or plan by feel or common sense as opposed to detailed analysis.

Isolated Pawn A pawn with no friendly pawns on either adjacent file. A common opening that allows an isolated pawn is 1.e4 e6 2.d4 d5 3.Nd2 c5 4.exd5 exd5 5.Ngf3 Nc6 6.Bb5 Bd6 7.dxc5 Bxc5 8.0-0 Nge7 9.Nb3 Bd6 10.Nbd4. The negatives of an isolated pawn are its inability to be guarded by a friendly pawn and the fact that the square directly in front of it usually makes a fine home for an enemy piece, since no pawns can chase it away. On the positive side, it offers plenty of space and the use of two half open files (on either side of it), with the result that one's pieces usually become active.

Kingside The half of the board originally occupied by the King, K-Bishop, K-Knight, and K-Rook. The kingside is on the right of the player with the White pieces and on the left of the player with the Black pieces.

Liquidation A term used to denote a series of exchanges that are initiated to quell an enemy attack or to trade off to a drawn or won endgame.

Luft Literally meaning 'air.' In chess it describes a pawn move in front of one's King that prevents back rank mate possibilities.

Major Pieces Also called heavy pieces. The term applies to Queens and Rooks.

Maneuver A series of quiet moves with the aim of favorably redeploying one's pieces.

Master A player becomes a master when he reaches an Elo rating of 2200, though he will lose this title if his rating drops below that point.

Mate Short for checkmate. It means that you are threatening to capture the enemy King, and nothing your opponent can do will prevent its loss. When this happens, you have won the game.

Material The pieces and pawns, excluding the King. A material advantage is obtained by winning a piece of greater value than the one you gave up. For example, giving up a pawn to win a Rook means that you have an advantage in material.

Mating Attack An attack on the King that is expected to lead to a checkmate.

Middlegame The phase of the game that sits between the opening and the endgame. Grandmaster Tarrasch once said, "Before the endgame, the Gods have placed the middlegame."

Minor Pieces The Bishops and the Knights.

Minority Attack A plan based on the use of two or more pawns (the minority) to act as battering rams against the opponent's three or more pawns (the majority) in order to create a weakness in the opposing camp. Here is the most common opening sequence by which a minority attack is reached: 1.d4 d5 2.c4 e6 3.Nc3 Nf6 4.Bg5 Be7 5.cxd5 exd5 6.Nf3 0-0 7.e3 c6 8.Bd3 Nbd7 9.Qc2 Re8 10.0-0 Nf8 11.Bxf6 Bxf6 12.b4 Be7 13.b5 Bd6 14.bxc6 bxc6. White has carried out his minority attack and has left Black with a weak pawn on c6 and a weak square on c5. After a further Rfc1, Rab1, and Na4, White will have great pressure against Black's queenside. This plan is very important to understand, and situations for its use are constantly arising.

Mobility To have freedom of movement for one's pieces.

Mysterious Rook Move A move with a Rook which seems to have no threat or purpose, but which actually discourages the opponent from a certain type of action (see *Prophylaxis*), or sets up a very deep, well concealed plan.

Occupation Occupation of a file or a rank refers to a Rook or Queen placed in such a way as to exert control over the file or rank. Occupation of a square refers to a piece being safely placed on a square and exerting pressure from it.

Open Often refers to a type of position (see *Open Game*) or file (see *Open File*). This term also refers to a type of tournament in which any class of player can participate. Though a player often ends up with opponents who are much higher (or lower) rated than himself, the prizes are usually structured around classes; with a prize for the top scorers in each different class. The open tournament is extremely popular in the United States and is beginning to be seen more and more in Europe.

Open File A column of eight squares that is free of pawns. It is on open files (and ranks) that Rooks come to their maximum potential.

Open Game A type of position which is characterized by many open lines and few center pawns. A lead in develpment becomes very important in positions of this type.

Opening The beginning phase of a game, which is usually through the first dozen moves but can go much further. It is usually written that the main opening objectives are 1) develop your pieces in a quick and efficient manner; 2) occupy as much of the center as possible; 3) Castle early (King safety). While I can say that these objectives are basically correct, the *real* purpose of the opening is to create an imbalance and develop your pieces in such a way that they all work together in making the imbalance a favorable attribute.

Opposite Color Bishops Usually called Bishops of opposite colors. A situation in which each player has only one Bishop, each being of a different color, and thus the Bishops can never come into contact. This is usually a good attacking imbalance for the middlegame, since one can't defend what the other attacks. However, Bishops of opposite color are known as being rather drawish in endgames, due to the fact that the defender can place his pawns and King on the opposite color of the enemy Bishop, whereupon they are impervious to harm.

From an attacking point of view, a general rule for Bishops of opposite colors is that they are at their best with other pieces to back them up. On their own, they are often impotent.

Opposition An endgame term. The opposition is a means by which one King can dominate another. See Part One, Chapter One, for a detailed explanation.

Outflanking An endgame maneuver with Kings which makes forward progress on the board while: 1) simultaneously preventing your opponent from taking direct opposition; or 2) temporarily giving up the opposition for a higher goal.

Overextended When a player tries to gain some advantages by starting a major advance or offensive, and when this offensive fails, he is often left with various weaknesses and nothing to compensate for them. His position is then said to be overextended.

Overprotection A term coined by Nimzovich. It refers to defending a strong point more times than appears necessary. The idea is that a certain pawn or square may be causing Black (the opponent) considerable problems. By focusing so much energy on it, the Black player would be unwise to break that point because that would unleash the latent energy of the White pieces.

In the diagram, White is overprotecting the e5 pawn. The reason for this is that the e5 pawn spearheads a kingside attack by White. Normally Black might wish to close lines there by ...f7-f5, but now White would answer this and ...f7-f6 with exf6 when all of his pieces have increased their scope and have become extremely active. Thus Black is unable to do anything that would allow White to remove the e5 pawn. As a consequence, his defensive resources are greatly reduced. Also see *Prophylaxis.*

Passed Pawn A pawn that has passed by all enemy pawns capable of capturing it.

In the diagram, White has connected passed pawns on g5 and h6. Black has a passed pawn on a7 and a protected passed pawn on e4.

Passive An inactive move that does nothing to fight for the initiative. A passive position is a position without counterplay or active possibilities.

Patzer A derogatory term that denotes a hopelessly weak player.

Pawn Center Pawns placed in the center. White pawns on f4, e4, and d4, for example, would constitute a large pawn center. A common opening which allows White to build a large center in the hope of attacking it later is **1.e4 d6 2.d4 Nf6 3.Nc3 g6 4.f4**, etc.

Pawn Chain Two or more like-colored pawns linked diagonally. The weakest point of a pawn chain is the base because that is the one pawn in the chain that cannot be defended by another pawn.

Pawn Island A group of connected friendly pawns. In the diagram, Black has three pawn islands to White's two. It is usually considered to be advantageous to have fewer pawn islands than the opponent.

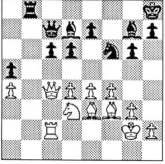

Pawn Skeleton See *Pawn Structure*.

Pawn Structure The positioning of the whole pawn mass. Also referred to as the pawn skeleton. This positioning of the pawns is what usually dictates the types of plans available in a given position due to open files, space, pawn weaknesses, etc.

Pig A slang for Rook. 'Pigs on the seventh' is a common term for Rooks doubled on the seventh rank. Also known as 'Hogs on the seventh.'

Plan A short or long range goal on which a player bases his moves.

Point Count A system of figuring out the worth of the pieces by giving each of them a numerical value. King—priceless; Queen—9 points; Rook—5 points; Bishop—3 points; Knight—3 points; pawn—1 point. The flaw in the system is that it does not take into account other factors (such as position, tactics, etc.) that often drastically change the relative value of an individual piece.

Poisoned Pawn Any pawn that if captured would lead to serious disadvantage is considered to be poisoned.

Positional A move, a maneuver, or a style of play that is based on an exploitation of small advantages.

Post Mortem A Latin term borrowed from medicine which means literally 'after death.' It refers to the sessions which often take place after a tournament game has finished. Both players discuss the game and attempt to find the reason why someone lost—the 'cause of death.' In particular, those with huge or delicate egos love post mortems where they can show that they saw much more than the opponent (who was undoubtedly just lucky to gain the victory). For those of a more open nature, if you had played a stronger opponent than yourself, you can sit back, ask what you did wrong, and hope that the mysteries of the universe will unfold.

Premature A hasty move, maneuver, or plan. To take action without sufficient preparation.

Prepared Variation A deeply researched opening variation which is often strengthened by new moves. It is a common practice to prepare certain lines and new moves for particular opponents, refusing to use it against anyone other than its intended victim.

Problem Child A reference to a shut in Queen's Bishop. For example, the French Defense (1.e4 e6 2.d4 d5) is an attractive opening. Its one flaw is the Queen's Bishop, which has difficulty reaching an active square.

Prophylactic Move See *Prophylaxis.*

Prophylaxis A strategy explored by Nimzovich. Taken from the Greek word prophylaktikos, meaning to guard or prevent beforehand, prophylaxis (or a prophylactic move) stops the opponent from taking action in a certain area for fear of some type of reprisal. Overprotection is a form of prophylaxis.

Promotion Also called 'Queening.' When a pawn reaches the final rank it becomes another piece, usually a Queen. However, the pawn can be promoted to anything other than a pawn or King.

Protected Passed Pawn A passed pawn that is protected by a friendly pawn. See *Passed Pawn.*

Queening See *Promotion.*

Queenside That half of the board made up of the four files originally occupied by the Queen, Q-Bishop, Q-Knight, and Q-Rook. The queenside stands to White's left and Black's right.

Quiet Move A move that is neither a capture, a check, nor a direct attack.

Rabbit A humorous (slightly insulting) term for a non-master.

Rank A row of eight squares. The seventh rank in particular is the subject of much activity, especially when a Rook settles there. Control of the seventh rank is considered to be an important advantage.

Rating See *Elo rating*.

Refutation A move or series of moves that demonstates a flaw in a game, move, variation, analysis, or plan.

Resigns Realizing the hopeless nature of a position and not wanting to insult the intelligence of the opponent, a player can surrender the game (resign) without having to wait for a checkmate.

Risk A double-edged sword. A move, plan, or opening variation that aims for advantage while carrying the danger of a disadvantage.

Romantic The romantic era (Macho era) of chess was a time when sacrifice and attack was considered to be the only manly way to play. If a sacrifice was offered, it was a disgraceful show of cowardice to refuse; thus, many beautiful sacrificial games were recorded simply because proper defensive techniques were not understood. That was in the 1800's. Today, a player who is termed romantic is one who has a proclivity for bold attacks and sacrifices, often throwing caution to the winds.

Sacrifice The voluntary offer of material for the purpose of gaining a more favorable advantage than the material investment. Unlike a combination, a sacrifice is not a cut and dried affair, and there is usually an element of uncertainty associated with it. Though a combination always has one or more sacrifices, a sacrifice need not be associated with a combination.

Semi-Open Game A position with some closed and some open qualities. Typically 1.e4 e6, 1.e4 c6, and 1.e4 d6 lead to semi-open games. See *Open Games* and *Closed Games*.

Sharp A bold, aggressive move or position. A sharp player is one who enjoys dynamic, explosive situations.

Shot A strong move that the opponent did not expect.

Simplify An exchange of pieces to reach a won ending, to neutralize an enemy attack, or simply to clarify a situation.

Skittles Chess played in an offhand manner, often at a chess club or after a tournament game.

Sound An analytically correct move or plan. A safe, solid position.

Space The territory controlled by each player. Thus, whoever controls the most territory has a spatial advantage.

Speculative An unclear or risky move or plan.

Strategy The foundation of a player's moves. The way to achieve a particular plan. See *Plan*.

Style The preference for certain types of positions and moves. It is typical to have one player who enjoys open, tactical positions; while his opponent may cherish semi-closed positions of a positional nature. Thus, the first part of the battle will be to determine who gets the type of position in which he excels.

Support Point A square that acts as a home for a piece (usually a Knight). A square can only be considered a support point if it cannot be attacked by an enemy pawn or if the enemy pawn advance would severely weaken the enemy position.

Swindle A trick from an inferior position.

Symmetry A situation in which both armies are identically placed on their respective sides of the board. For example: 1.c4 c5 2.Nc3 Nc6 3.g3 g6 4.Bg2 Bg7 5.Nf3 Nf6 6.0-0 0-0 7.a3 a6 8.Rb1 Rb8 9.b4 cxb4 10.axb4 b5 11.cxb5 axb5 is a well known symmetrical position that comes from the English Opening.

Tactics Traps, threats, and schemes based on the calculation of variations; at times rather long-winded. A position with many combinative motifs present is considered tactical.

Tempo The unit of time represented by one move. For example: 1.e4 d5 2.exd5 Qxd5 3.Nc3 gains a tempo, as the Queen must move again if it is to avoid being captured.

Territory See _Space_.

Theory Known and practiced opening, middlegame, and endgame variations and positions. Opening theory is also referred to as 'the book.'

Threat A move or plan that, if allowed, would lead to the immediate depreciation of the enemy position.

Time Can be used inseveral contexts. One meaning is the amount of thinking time as measured by special clocks (see Time Control). It is also used in reference to the ability to stop a particular action by the opponent, i.e., 'Black does not have _time_ to coordinate a successful defense against the coming attack.' Thus time also measures development (an advantage in time being a lead in development) and the rate at which an attack is pursued or defended.

Time Control The amount of time given to reach a certain number of moves. In international competition this is usually 40 moves in 2 1/2 hours. If a player uses up his 2 1/2 hour allocation and he has not yet made 40 moves, he will lose the game by foreit no matter what the position on the board is like.

Time Pressure That period of the game when one or both players have used up most of their time and must make many moves with little deliberation. Naturally this should be avoided, since it often leads to mistakes or game losing blunders.

Transitions The changing of one phase of the game into another; the opening into the middlegame and the middlegame into the endgame.

Transposition Reaching an identical position by a different sequence of moves. For example, the Dutch Defense can be reached by 1.d4 e6 2.c4 f5 or by 1.c4 f5 2.d4 e6.

Traps A hidden way to lure an opponent into making an error. A trap should only be laid if it is part of the overall strategic plan. This way, it does not matter if your opponent falls for it or not; you will still be improving your position.

Unclear An uncertain situation. Certain players never use this assessment, insisting that every position is either equal or favorable for someone. It has even been said that 'unclear' is a lazy way to avoid figuring out what's really going on in a position.

Variation A line of play usually referred to about opening lines; but the term also is used in the other phases of the game. Any alternative to the line actually played is termed a variation.

Weakness Any pawn or square that is difficult or impossible to defend.

Wild Extremely unclear. A sharp situation or move with unfathomable complications.

Zugzwang 'Compulsion to move.' A German term referring to a situation in which a player would like to do nothing (pass), since any move will damage his game.

Zwischenzug 'In between move.' A German term for an often unexpected reply thrown into an expected sequence of moves.

PART FIFTEEN

THE SOLUTIONS TO THE PROBLEMS

This section gives the solutions to all the problems throughout this book. I have reproduced the diagram (with its original number) for easy reference and given the question and answer in full. I have also supplied the names of the players—this information was not listed earlier since I didn't want names or dates to influence your decision making processes.

Diagram #19

Question: Black to move. Can he stop the pawn?

Answer: No, he cannot stop the pawn. Even though he seemingly can enter the border by 1...Kg8, 1...Kg7, or 1...Kg6, this proves illusory since White can move his pawn two squares! Thus **1...Kg7 2.a4**, and Black cannot enter the new border. Though the author feels a bit guilty for tricking you in this way, it is better to miss it here rather than in a tournament game!

Diagram #20

Question: Black to move. Can he draw the game?

Answer: Black to move draws but he must be careful after **1...Ke7 2.Kd1!** The direct approach by 2.Kd2 Ke6 (or 2...Kd6) 3.Ke3 Ke5 makes life easy for Black. **2...Ke6** Threatening to make things clear with 3...Ke5 followed by 4...Ke4. **3.Kd2** Setting a trap. Now Black must avoid 3...Kd5?? because White gets the opposition *and* gets his King in front of his pawn after 4.Kd3 Ke5 5.Ke3 (which takes us back to diagram #9). **3...Kd6!** Grabbing the distant opposition. Trying to be fancy by 3...Kf6?? also retains the opposition but allows White's King to surge forward undisturbed by 4.Kd3 Kf5 5.Kd4, etc. **4.Kd3 Kd5** and the draw is finally clear.

Diagram #21

Question: White to move. Can he win?

Answer: White wins by **1.Kd2!** Taking the opposition would only draw: 1.Kc2 Kb7 2.Kb3, and now it's true that White wins after 2...Kc6? 3.Kc4! Kd6 4.Kd4 Kc6 5.Ke5, etc., but Black holds by 2...Kc7! when 3.Kc4 Kc6 4.Kd4 Kd6 gives Black the opposition and a draw, while 3.Kc3 Kd7! 4.Kb3 Kd6 5.Kc4 Kc6 is also nothing for White. **1...Kb7 2.Ke3** Running to the other side of the pawn. Note that from c1 it is only two squares to either c3 or e3. But e3 is much farther away from Black's King, and thus deprives him of drawing chances based on gaining the opposition. **2...Kc6 3.Ke4 Kd6 4.Kd4 Ke6 5.Kc5**, etc.

Diagram #22

(22)

Question: White to move and take the opposition. How?

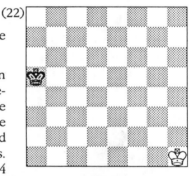

Answer: **1.Kg1!** forms connection points at g1, g5, a5, and a1, and creates all black corner squares. Note that 1.Kh2 would be an error, since the connecting points h2, h5, a5, and a2, do not represent identical colors. After 1.Kh2? Black could play 1...Kb4 and he would then possess the opposition.

Diagram #23

Question: Is it safe for Black to trade Queens in this position?

Answer: Yes, after 1...Qd7+ 2.Qxd7+ (2.Qd6 Rd1+ 3.Rd4 Rxd4+ 4.Kxd4 Qxd6+ 5.exd6 Kd7 is a basic drawn King and pawn endgame) 2...Kxd7 3.Rf7+ Ke8 4.Ke6 (4.e6 Rd1+ leaves White no useful way to get away from the checks) 4...Re1! we have one of the drawing sub-variations of diagram #18 (5.Ra7 Kf8! 6.Ra8+ Kg7 7.Re8 Ra1!, =).

Diagram #27 — Silman-Van Buskirk, Santa Barbara 1989. Black to play.

Question: After **1.d4 e6 2.c4 Nf6 3.Nc3 Bb4 4.Qc2 c5 5.dxc5 0-0 6.a3 Bxc5 7.Nf3 Nc6 8.Bg5 Nd4 9.Nxd4 Bxd4 10.e3 Qa5 11.exd4 Qxg5 12.Qd2 Qxd2+ 13.Kxd2 b6 14.b4 Bb7 15.f3** we reach the position in diagram #27. What are the imbalances and what is White's plan?

Answer: White has a majority of pawns on the queenside, a clear advantage in space in that same area, and his King is well placed in the center. Using his extra territory, White will take his time and restrict the enemy pieces. Once this is done and his Rooks stand on optimal squares, White will advance his queenside pawns and create a passed pawn there. If he can advance this passed pawn he may win; if not the game will most likely end in a draw. The beauty of White's position is that it is devoid of any real weaknesses—Black has no counterplay and no chance to win. The continuation was: **15...Rfc8** Note how White's pawn on f3 blocks the Black Bishop and takes the e4 and g4 squares away from the enemy Knight. **16.Nb5** Eyeing the d6 square. **16...Ne8 17.Bd3 Kf8** The King comes around to defend d6. White welcomes ...a7-a6 since Nc3 would leave b6 weakened and vulnerable to moves like Na4. **18.Rhc1 Ke7 19.c5 d6** On 19...bxc5 White would play 20.dxc5!, retaining a majority of pawns on the queenside. **20.cxb6 axb6 21.Rxc8 Bxc8 22.a4 d5 23.a5** So a passed pawn has been created. The question now is, how far can it advance? **23...h6 24.Kc3 bxa5 25.Rxa5 Rb8** A trade of Rooks would allow White's King to advance to b4. **26.Ra7+ Rb7 27.Kb3** Heading for a4 and a5. Note that White's favorable imbalances were all situated on the queenside and he has been playing on that side of the board for the whole game in an effort to take advantage of them. **27...Rxa7 28.Nxa7 Bb7 29.b5 Nd6 30.Kb4 Kd7 31.Kc5 Ba8 32.b6** The Knight and the passed pawn form a barrier that keep the Black King from approaching the queenside. **32...Nb7+ 33.Kb4 Nd8 34.Bb5+ Ke7** Not falling for 34...Kd6?? 35.Nc8 mate! **35.Nc8+ Kf6 36.Nd6** Fighting for control of the square in front of the passed pawn. **36...e5** Desperately trying to get some counterplay. The passive 36...Ke7 loses to 37.Kc5 Nb7+ 38.Nxb7 Bxb7 39.Bc6. **37.Ne8+** Cashing in. The rest doesn't require any commentary. **37...Ke7 38.Nxg7 exd4 39.Nf5+ Ke6 40.Nxd4+ Kd6 41.Nf5+ Ke5 42.Nxh6 d4 43.Be8 f5 44.Nf7+**

Nxf7 45.Bxf7 Kf4 46.Bc4 Ke3 47.h4, 1-0. I strongly recommend that the reader study this game again after he has finished this book. The sections on pawn majorities, passed pawns, minor pieces, restriction of counterplay, and imbalances that last from the opening to the endgame will enhance his understanding of White's conduct.

Diagram #36 — Kolvick-Silman, World Open 1989. Black to play.

Question: Who stands better and why? Also figure out how Black should best handle the attack on his Knight.

Answer: A highly imbalanced position! Black has a Rook and pawn for two Bishops. This represents approximate material equilibrium but there is always the danger for Black that White's Bishops will become active. At the moment, Black's Knight is attacked and retreats like 1...Ne5 allow 2.Bb2, when White intends to follow up with a3, Ne3, and Nf5. Though this is playable for Black, he would prefer that White not get so much activity.

What are the negatives in White's position? Firstly, his Bishop on c1 is undefended and his Knight on d1 is guarded only once—it's clear that both these pieces are vulnerable. Other unfortunate aspects of the White position are his attacking but off-side Rook on g5 (it can't come back for defense), his hanging pawn on a2, the fact that if Black could somehow take the d1 Knight (via the illegal move ...Qxd1) he would get a big fork on f2, and finally the somewhat insecure position of the White King. This last point has great significance since White's King has only one real defender—the Bishop on g2. With all this in mind, Black realizes that he must react immediately if he is to take advantage of all the White negatives. To this end he decides to eradicate the g2 Bishop, thus leaving the White King in the open. In this way White will be off balance and will not have time to coordinate his forces. **1...Rxe4!** Now the threat is 2...Re1 winning the Queen. **2.Bxe4** Other defenses:

    1)   2.a3 Qe1! with a clear advantage;

    2)   2.Bd2 fails to the simple 2...Qxd2! 3.Bxe4 Qxh2 mate;

    3)   2.Nc3 Qxc3 3.Bxe4 Nf2+! 4.Qxf2 Qxc1+ followed by 5...Qxg5 and Black will easily win the game.

2...Qxe4+ 3.Qg2 No better is 3.Kg1 Qd4+ 4.Kg2 (4.Kh1 Qxd1!)

4...Rxa2+ 5.Bb2 Rxb2+ 6.Nxb2 Ne3+ and White must resign. **3...Qe1+ 4.Qg1 Qxd1!** The beauty of this move is that it also guards the Knight on g4. **5.Qxd1 Nf2+ 6.Kg2 Nxd1 7.a3 f6 8.Rg4 Nc3**, and White resigned in a few more moves.

The lesson to be learned from this example is: If you have various tactical and dynamic factors in your favor, you must use them right away or the opponent will get his pieces to better squares and your plusses will disappear.

Diagram #37 — Amateur-Muller, corr. 1928/29. Black to play.

Question: Black's Bishops look nice, but his center is under a lot of pressure. Who stands better here?

Answer: Both Kings are still in the center, but Black's pieces are much more aggressively posted and he has a lead in development. With a pin on the c3 Knight (which is inadequately protected, since if Black can draw White's Queen away from its defense then the Knight would hang with check and the Rook on a1 would fall next) and pressure on the c4 pawn and the a6-f1 diagonal, Black should look hard for a decisive smash. A move like 1...Rd8 seems threatening, but by playing 2.0-0 White would be able to play on for a long time.

If you suggested 1...0-0, then shame on you! This is much too normal and lazy a move to be correct in a ripe position like this one. Remember, many of your favorite tactical motifs won't wait around for you to use them! If you don't grab the ring right away, it will quickly be out of your reach. By concentrating on the pin and checking possibilities, you should be able to come up with **1...d4!** This wins immediately. If White plays 2.Bxc6+ Kf8 3.Bxa8, Black picks up an extra piece by 3...Bxc3+ and 4...Bxa1. **2.Qxd4 Rd8** So Black has opened up a file for his Rook with tempo. This goes along with the rule of opening up the position if you have a lead in development. White is now lost since there is nowhere he can move his Queen that does not drop the Knight on c3 followed by the Rook on a1. **3.Bxc6+ Kf8 4.Bd5 Rxd5!** White resigns, since 5.Qxd5 loses to 5...Bxc3+ while 5.cxd5 runs into 5...Qxe2 mate!

Diagram #79 — J.Frankle-Silman, San Francisco 1982. Black to play.

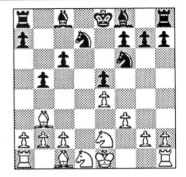

Question: How can Black create a static imbalance that can be nurtured and used throughout the game?

Answer: Black has all the chances because he can gain the two Bishops, which is favorable here since the White Knights have no central support points. **9...Nc5 10.Be3 a5 11.Bxc5** Not a happy decision, but 11.c3 Nxb3 12.axb3 Be6 was very nice for Black. **11...Bxc5** Black's Bishops will torment White for the rest of the game. **12.a4 Ke7 13.Nec3 b4 14.Nb1 Nd7 15.Nd2 Bd4** Offering White the chance to play 16.c3 bxc3 which, however, only succeeds in opening more lines for Black's pieces. **16.Rc1?** Intending 17.c3 bxc3 18.Nxc3 with play against c6, but this turns out to be a serious waste of time. **16...Nc5 17.Ra1** Guarding a4 so the Bishop can move to c4. **17...Nxb3 18.cxb3 Be6 19.Rc1 Rhd8! 20.Nc4** And not 20.Rxc6? Rdc8 21.Rxc8 Rxc8 when Black's Rook decisively penetrates into White's position. **20...Bxc4 21.Rxc4 Rd6 22.Ke2 Rad8 23.Re1 Ba7 24.Rc2 Rd3 25.Nf2 Rxb3 26.Rd1 Bxf2** The rest needs no comment: **27.Rxd8 Kxd8 28.Kxf2 Kc7 29.Ke2 Kb6 30.Rd2 c5 31.Kd1 c4 32.Kc1 Re3 33.Rd7 Re1+ 34.Kd2 Rg1 35.g4 b3 36.Rxf7 Rb1 37.Re7 Rxb2+ 38.Kd1 c3 39.Rxe5 Rb1+ 40.Ke2 c2**, 0-1.

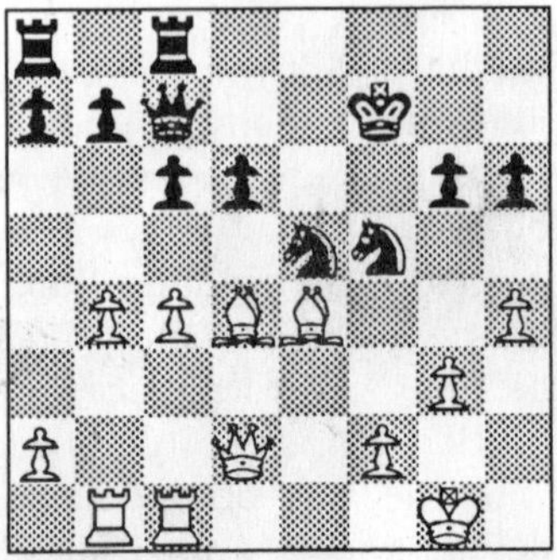

Diagram #80 Capablanca-Milner Barry, Margate 1936. White to play.

Question: What minor pieces rule in this position—the advanced Black Knights or White's two Bishops?

Answer: The Black Knights look strong in the center but they are actually quite insecure. **1.Ba1** One of the best things about a Bishop is its ability to sit at a safe distance from the battle and still exert strong pressure on the position. **1...Rg8** White wins material after 1...h5 2.Bxe5 dxe5 3.Bxf5 gxf5 4.Qg5. **2.h5!** Now the Knight's support points begin to get undermined. **2...Raf8 3.c5!** There goes the second horse. The battle now turns into a rout: **3...d5 4.Bxd5+ cxd5 5.Qxd5+ Kf6 6.f4 Qc6 7.Bxe5+ Ke7 8.Bd6+!**, 1-0.

Diagram #81 — P.Biyiasas-Silman, Berkeley 1983. Black to play.

Question: How can Black play for a superior minor piece?

Answer: White has the two Bishops but they are not particularly active. Of course, Black's Knights are not exactly ripping White apart either. White's a3 pawn is backward but well defended, and if White can play 3.c4 the a3 pawn might eventually become passed. At the moment, White's best piece is the e3 Knight, while Black's Bishop on e6 is his favorite warrior. Black's first move is a logical one; he attempts to trade off his f6 Knight for White's proud horse on e3. **1...Ng4! 2.Nf5?** Strategic suicide. Correct was 2.Nxg4 Bxg4 3.c4 when 3...Qc6 leads to a position with chances for both sides. **2...Nxf5 3.exf5 Bd5 4.Bxd5 Qxd5 5.Qe2 Nf6 6.Bb2 Ne4!** Black hastens to dominate the c4 square, which will lead to a crushing Knight versus bad Bishop situation. Now 7.Rfc1 (intending c4) runs into 7...Nd2! 8.Rd1 Nf3+ 9.Kg2 (9.Kh1 Qc6) 9...Nxh4+ 10.Kh3 Qf3 with an extra pawn. **7.Rfd1 Qc6 8.Rd3 d5 9.Rad1 Qc4 10.Kg2 c6** White is completely lost. **11.g4 Nf6! 12.g5 Qe4+** Ending any hopes White had of a last minute desperation attack on Black's King. **13.Qxe4 Nxe4 14.Bc1 h5 15.Re1 Nd6 16.f6 Nc4 17.fxg7 Kxg7** Black will eventually win White's a3 pawn. The conclusion was **18.Rf3 Re6 19.Re2 e4 20.Rg3 Ra4 21.f3 Kg6 22.fxe4 dxe4 23.Ra2 Rd6 24.Re2 Rd1 25.Be3 Rxa3 26.Bd4 Rd2! 27.Rxd2 Nxd2 28.Kf2 Nf3! 29.Ke3 Kf5 30.Rg2 Ra1 31.Bf6 Re1+ 32.Kf2 Kf4 33.Bd4 e3+ 34.Bxe3 Rxe3 35.g6 fxg6 36.Rxg6 Rxc3 37.Rh6 Rc2+ 38.Kf1 Nxh4 39.Rxh5 Nf5**, 0-1.

Diagram #82 — Silman-Wolski, Los Angeles 1989. White to play.

Question: What is White's correct plan?

Answer: The main imbalance here is Bishop versus Knight. While White's Bishop is active, the Knight still needs to find its proper place. The c5 square has some potential, though the Knight could be chased away at any time by b2-b4. Another possible square is e4 (reached via d7-f6-e4). Though these factors are important, if either side wants winning chances he must be able to create some sort of weakness or achieve a pawn break that leads to penetration into the enemy position. Is there any point in Black's position that is hard for him to defend? The only pawn that might fit this category is the one on a7—the one farthest away from any defenders. To these ends, White comes up with the following plan: He will play b2-b4 (fixing the pawn on a7) and at some time play Qa4 when the pawn on a7 will prove very difficult to defend. Another part of White's plan centers around the break with c4-c5, which opens new lines and can easily create new sets of weaknesses. Since 1.b4 fixes the weak pawn on a7, and b4 also prepares a c5 advance, White's first move becomes obvious. **1.b4 Qf6** Black would have liked to play 1...a5, but this fails to 2.Rd5 when the pawn on a5 will fall. **2.Rfd1** Now the c4-c5 advance (bursting open the d-file) can easily become strong. **2...Nd7 3.Bc6!** Much stronger than 3.Qa4 Ne5 when Black's Knight becomes active. Now Black is tied up. **3...Re7** White threatened to play 4.Qa4 winning the a7 pawn. Now 4.Qa4 is met by 4...Ne5. **4.c5!** Using the power on the d-file to take advantage of the weakness of Black's back rank. Now a new weakness will form on d6. **4...Ne5** And not 4...bxc5 5.bxc5 Nxc5 6.Qxc5! dxc5 7.Rxd8+ and mates. **5.Be4 g6 6.h3** Restricting the Knight and threatening 7.f4 when Black would be forced to shed the d6 pawn by ...Nd7. **6...b5** Hoping to jump to c4, something White has no intention of allowing. **7.cxd6 cxd6 8.Bd5** The position has now clarified. White's Bishop is a fantastic piece, while weaknesses on a7, b5, and d6 also make Black's life difficult. **8...a6 9.Rd4 Ree8 10.Qc7** White finally decides to go directly for material gain. This always must be carefully done, since it is quite typical for your pieces to become temporarily uncoordinated after you rush to the side to gobble something. In this case, White has concluded that Black's counterplay can be beaten back. **10...Rc8 11.Qa7 g5** White would have met 11...Rc2 with 12.Rf4. 11...g5 stops this possibility. **12.Qxa6 Re2 13.R4d2 Rec8 14.Be4! Rc1** Only now did Black notice that he could not play 14...Rxd2 due to 15.Qxc8+. **15.Qxd6** Black's weaknesses have fallen, and the game is now won. **15...Qg7 16.Qd8+!**, 1-0.

Diagram #93 — White to play.

Question: White can gain space on the queenside with 1.b2-b4 or he can gain space on the kingside with 1.f3-f4. Which idea is best?

Answer: There is no question about it, White should play 1.b2-b4 followed by 2.Nb3 and eventually c4-c5. This plan gains lots of queenside space and opens files for the White Rooks, allows both Knights to enter the game, and softens up the g1-a7 diagonal for White's Bishop.

The alternative, 1.f3-f4?, is terrible. This self-destructive move does nothing for White's Knights or Bishop. Instead (after 1...exf4) it actually frees Black's dark-squared Bishop, gives Black's Knight a permanent home on e5, and creates a weak pawn on e4 which rests on an open file.

Be careful that in your desire for space you don't create weaknesses in your own camp and activate the enemy army.

Diagram #94 — Black to move.

Question: Though Black's pawns are pointing towards the kingside (in positions with closed centers you should usually play in the direction your pawns point), he chooses to play on the opposite wing with **1...c5**. Is this wise?

Answer: It is a reasonable choice (and an old favorite of Bobby Fischer's) in this position. White was hoping to get a large space advantage on the queenside with b2-b4 followed by c4-c5 and Nc4. Though Black usually grabs his own territory on the kingside by ...Nd7 followed by ...f7-f5 with a race for dominion in each respective area, he puts this off for a moment (his kingside counterattack will resume on the very next move) in order to make White's queenside expansion more difficult. By stopping c4-c5, Black deprives the White Knight on d2 of the active c4 post and dooms it to spend its life on a less appetizing square.

Black will allow himself the odd defensive move (perhaps ...b7-b6 later) but he must not allow himself to lose sight of his correct strategic plan on the kingside.

Diagram #102 White to Play.

Question: After **1.d4 e6 2.c4 b6 3.e4 Bb7 4.Qc2 Qh4** we reach the position in diagram #102. Is Black a beginner or does he have a method in his madness?

Answer: Black's opening is strange looking but consistent. He allows White to build a nice center and then he starts to attack it and show that it is weak. **4...Qh4** breaks the rule about bringing a Queen out early but it does attack e4 and prevent the e-pawn from being defended by f2-f3. After **5.Nd2 Bb4! 6.Bd3 f5** Black achieves a sharp battle where both e4 and d4 (via Qf6 and/or ...Nc6) can be attacked.

Though theory has finally confirmed that the position in diagram #102 favors White, this assessment only came about after Black scored many nice wins against strong Grandmasters. The point is simple: it's all right to allow your opponent a strong pawn center if you can put pressure on it. If you can't place pressure on the enemy center then you should not have allowed it to be created in the first place.

Diagram #126 — White to play.

Question: Who stands better?

Answer: Black will play ...Ke5 when White's two connected passed pawns are firmly blocked and the e-pawn is in need of constant defense. In the meantime Black can make passed pawns on either wing. The combined weight of Black's superior minor piece (White's Bishop is very bad), superior King position, and more mobile pawns give the second player a winning advantage.

Diagram #127 — Nimzovich-Rosselli, Baden-Baden 1925. White to play.

Question: The position in diagram 127 was reached after **1.Nf3 d5 2.b3 c5 3.e3 Nc6 4.Bb2 Bg4 5.h3 Bxf3 6.Qxf3 e5 7.Bb5 Qd6** White now has the opportunity to give his opponent doubled pawns by 8.Bxc6+. Is this a good idea?

Answer: The doubled pawns could easily help Black in this position. After 8...bxc6 9.e4 Black would avoid ...d5-d4, which would create a weakness on c4. Instead he would leave it on d5 and use his mighty center to squeeze White. Due to this, White first attempts to goad Black into a ...d5-d4 advance before taking on c6. **8.e4 d4 9.Na3** Threatening 10.Nc4 Qc7 11.Bxc6+ **9...f6 10.Nc4 Qd7 11.Qh5+** Creating a weakness on f6. **11...g6 12.Qf3 Qc7** Bad is 12...0-0-0 13.Na5 Nge7 14.Qxf6. **13.Qg4** Stopping Black from castling long and threatening Qe6+. **13...Kf7 14.f4** White plays to rip open the kingside and get to the Black King. **14...h5 15.Qf3 exf4 16.Bxc6 bxc6** If 16...Qxc6 17.Qxf4 gives White a strong attack. However, the doubled pawns that Black accepted are liabilities since the d-pawn has already advanced and created weaknesses. **17.0-0 g5 18.c3! Rd8 19.Rae1 Ne7 20.e5** All of White's pieces join in the attack against Black's vulnerable King. **20...Nf5 21.cxd4 Nxd4 22.Qe4 Be7 23.h4! Qd7 24.exf6 Bxf6 25.hxg5**, 1-0. Black's King gets swamped after 25...Bg7 26.Ne5+ Bxe5 27.Qxe5.

Diagram #128 — Silman-Blankenau, World Open 1989. Black to play.

Question: The position in the diagram was reached after **1.d4 d5 2.c4 dxc4 3.e3 Nf6 4.Bxc4 e6 5.Nf3 c5 6.0-0 a6 7.Qe2 b5 8.Bd3 cxd4 9.exd4 Be7 10.Nc3 Bb7 11.Bg5 0-0 12.Rad1 Nbd7 13.Ne5 h6 14.Bc1 Nb6 15.Qe3 Nbd5 16.Qg3 Nh5 17.Qg4 Nhf6 18.Qh3 Nxc3 19.bxc3 Qd5 20.c4 bxc4 21.Bxc4 Qd6 22.Rd3 Kh7 23.Rg3** It has become obvious that White wishes to smash Black. Is he justified to desire this? Do the positional factors back him up? Black has many defenses; analyze them all and give what you feel is best.

Answer: This game has been a typical *isolated d-pawn* game. White willingly takes on the weakness of the isolated d-pawn in the hopes that the central space advantage he gains from it plus the control of the e5 square will grant him chances for a successful kingside attack. In the diagrammed position, White felt that he was ready to launch a winning assault. Why? White now has a Rook, Queen, two Bishops, and a Knight all aiming at Black's poor monarch! With such a huge amount of force available to White, his attack must succeed! Note that White avoided playing 23.Ba3 since after 23...Qd8 it only amounts to a trade. Why should White wish to trade his attacking Bishop for Black's defensive one on e7? **23...Ne8** Black defends g7 but such passive play does not bode well for his chances. However, it turns out that all the other defenses also fail:

1) 23...Bd5?? Ignores the attack and begs for punishment. 24.Rxg7+! Kxg7 25.Bxh6+ Kg8 26.Qg3+ and mates;

2) 23...Ng8 24.Qg4! Bf6 25.Bd3+ Kh8 26.Nxf7+! Rxf7 27.Qg6 and mates;

3) 23...Ne4 24.Bd3! f5 (or 24...Bf6 25.Ng4! and the threatened explosion on h6 will finish matters shortly) 25.Rxg7+! Kxg7 26.Bxh6+ Kg8 27.Bxe4, and the two threats of 28.Bxb7 and 28.Qg3+ win for White;

4) 23...Qxd4 24.Bd3+! Be4 25.Rxg7+! Kxg7 26.Bxh6+ Kg8 27.Qg3+ Bg6 28.Nxg6 and Black must resign;

5) 23...Be4 is the most important defense. White gets a winning endgame (!) with 24.Rxg7+! Kxg7 25.Bxh6+ Kg8 26.Qg3+ Bg6 27.Nxg6! Qxg3 28.Nxe7+ Kh7 29.fxg3! Kxh6 30.Rxf6+ Kg7 31.Rf1 Rfe8 32.Nc6 Rec8, and now White safely maintains his material advantage with either 33.d5 or 33.Na5.

This last variation is quite instructive since it shows a case of a seemingly crushing attack finishing up as a mundane endgame win. This is actually quite common! A mating attack is not just to achieve checkmate. If you win material or gain some other kind of huge advantage then you must call the attack successful. Don't put blinders on your eyes and only look for one way to win. **24.Bd3+ f5 25.Ng4** Intending 26.Nxh6 or Bxh6. **25...Rf6 26.Ba3** White can no longer mate Black so he settles for a win of material. With that in mind, White starts to exchange pieces. **26...Qd8 27.Bxe7 Qxe7 28.Nxf6+ Nxf6?** Natural but fatal. He had to play 28...Qxf6 if he wanted to continue to resist. **29.Re3!** Here is a very important concept and a big rule that goes with it:

When you win material, it is common for your pieces to be a bit uncoordinated since your plan has presumably come to an end. When this happens, centralize all your pieces as quickly as possible. In this way they will start to work together again.

In the present game White accepts that his attack has come to an end and sees that his Rook on g3 is now out of play. Because of this, White immediately centralizes the Rook and homes in on a new weakness—the pawn on e6. **29...Ne4** Black sees that 29...Qd6 loses to 30.Rxe6! Qxe6 31.Bxf5+, while 29...Bd5 fails to 30.Bxf5+. **30.f3 Ng5 31.Qxf5+**, 1-0.

Diagram #129 — Silman-Blankenau, National Open 1989. White to play.

Question: Explain this position.

Answer: In this isolated d-pawn position Black's b-pawn has advanced to b4; this is in sharp contrast to its usual placement on b6, where it guards the c5 square. In the diagrammed position White can play sharply and try to win the b4 pawn with moves like 1.Qe1 or 1.Rac1 followed by 2.Rc4. This would not be bad (at least you are trying to be forceful), but the outcome would be far from clear. For example, 1.Qe1 Rb8 and the b-pawn is off limits. Instead of going on an adventure, White calmly played to improve the position of his pieces. His first move was **1.Nc1!** Aside from attacking the b4 pawn, the Knight was not very well placed on a2. Realizing that this piece could be put to better use, White redirects it to b3 where it guards the a5 and d4 pawns, and also threatens to jump into c5 if Black is not careful. **1...0-0 2.Nb3** Now that White's main weakness is well defended, he feels free to initiate a multitude of plans. These are: Black's b4 and a6 pawns are in constant need of defenders, the c5 square must be well cared for, and White still has his usual kingside chances! **2...Rac8 3.Ne5** White stands better because while he has many points to attack in the enemy position, Black has almost no counterplay. **3...N5f6 4.Be3 Qa8 5.f3 Nxe5??** A blunder, but Black was getting impatient due to his lack of a clear object of attack. **6.dxe5 Nd7? 7.Bxh7+ Kxh7 8.Rxd7 Rfe8** White has won a pawn, but he must not fall asleep and expect the game to win itself! A new plan is called for that uses the advantages in this particular position. NEVER PLAY WITHOUT A PLAN!! **9.Qf2!** Since Black has the two

Bishops, White prepares to trade one off with Bc5. Once these Bishops go, White's Knight will penetrate on the dark squares and challenge Black's remaining Bishop for superiority. **9...Kg8** White threatened to win immediately with 10.Rxe7 Rxe7 11.Qh4+. **10.Bc5! Bxc5 11.Nxc5 Bd5 12.Na4!** Having found a good square on c5, White quickly vacates it for a better and more permanent home on b6. **12...Qc6 13.Nb6 Rcd8 14.Rxd8 Rxd8 15.Qd4 Qb5 16.h4!** Giving White's King a place to run to on h2 and also preparing to weaken Black's King position with h5 and h6. **16...Rb8 17.h5 Rb7 18.h6!** gxh6 **19.Rc1!** Not allowing Black to dominate the open c-file; White also has a knockout finish in mind. **19...Qxa5 20.Rc8+ Kh7 21.Qg4! Qxb6+ 22.Kh2 h5 23.Qxh5+ Kg7 24.Qh8+**, 1-0.

Diagram #130 — Silman-Magar, World Open 1989. Black to play.

Question: In this position, play continued 1...Ng6 2.Bxg6 fxg6 3.Nf4. Was Black's decision to play 1...Ng6 an intelligent one? Explain the diagrammed position and also the position after 3.Nf4.

Answer: Yet another isolated d-pawn position! In this case Black's Bishops on b7 and d6 are quite active, and the d5 square is well controlled by Black (following the basic rule that you must always control the square directly in front of the isolated pawn to prevent it from moving). As usual, White's main plan is a kingside attack; but he has not played for this in an accurate way, and his only hope now rests in an eventual sacrifice on h6. Realizing this, Black plays **1...Ng6!** and after **2.Bxg6 fxg6** White's attacking chances are completely gone. At this point I can hear a chorus of voices yelling, "But what about the pawn structure?" Yes, Black does have doubled g-pawns and an isolated pawn on e6; but are the weaknesses of these things real or just optical illusions? Let's take a look.

After 2...fxg6 we must compare pawn weaknesses. White still has his isolated pawn on d4. This is no stronger and no weaker than Black's isolated pawn on e6, which has the useful function of controlling the d5 square. This means that these two weaknesses cancel out. So far we have a measure of equilibrium. The Black doubled g-pawns are another matter. Are they weak? Not at all! They make a nice cover for the Black King, hold off White's three kingside pawns, and have the potential for space gaining aggression by a ...g6-g5 advance, restricting the e3 Bishop and the e2 Knight. Indeed, after a ...g6-g5 advance Black's pawns are just as safe as White's, but are actually superior in that they are playing a more active part in the game!

Finally we must realize that to achieve this doubling of Black's pawns, White had to part with his best piece, the Bishop on d3. Due to that, Black now has the two Bishops, an open f-file, and no worries at all concerning his King. It should now be clear that this exchange has led to a Black advantage! The continuation was: **3.Nf4 Qe8 4.Qd3 g5 5.Ng6 Rf7 6.Ne5 Bxe5 7.dxe5 Rd8** Black no longer has the two Bishops, and White's isolated d-pawn has changed into something else. The main imbalance now centers around the Bishops of opposite colors (Black's Bishop is clearly more active than White's) and the potential weakness of the White pawn on e5. **8.Qe2** Bad is 8.Qg6? Nd7, and now both 9.Bd4 Bxg2! 10.Kxg2 Rxf2+ and 9.f4 Nxe5 10.fxe5 Rxf1+ lose for White because his Queen on g6 is unprotected. With 8.Qe2, White hopes to somehow bring a Knight to the lovely d6 square via an eventual Ne4 or Nb5. Naturally, Black will never allow either of these possibilities to come about unless he gets something very big in return. **8...Nd7** The e5 pawn becomes an immediate problem. **9.f4 gxf4 10.Bxf4 Nc5!** All of a sudden White is lost! The threats are 11...Ba6 winning the Exchange and 11...Nd3 forking the Bishop on f4 and the Rook on c1. **11.Qe3 Ba6 12.Rfd1 Nd3 13.Ne4 Nxf4 14.Nd6 Ne2+ 15.Kh2 Rxd6 16.exd6 Nxc1**, and White resigned in a few more moves.

Diagram #140 — Fischer-Gadia, Mar del Plata 1960. White to play.

Question: The position in the diagram came about after **1.e4 c5 2.Nf3 d6 3.d4 cxd4 4.Nxd4 Nf6 5.Nc3 a6 6.Bc4 e6 7.Bb3 b5 8.0-0 Bb7 9.f4 Nc6 10.Nxc6 Bxc6.** Black threatens both 11...Nxe4 and 11...b5-b4. What is White's best move?

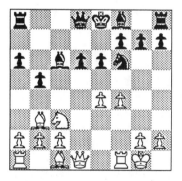

Answer: White has been playing an opening that is designed to grab control of the d5 square. If White takes time to defend against the threats, then he will not achieve his goal. For example, 11.e5? dxe5 12.fxe5 Qxd1 13.Rxd1 Nd7 leaves the e5 pawn in a sad state while White's light-squared Bishop remains lifeless on b3. The only correct way to play this position is: **11.f5!** The whole point of White's opening! Since he is way ahead in development, White does not fear losing a pawn if it means opening up the position. The real goal, though, is to force Black to advance his pawn to e5 when White's light-squared Bishop suddenly becomes very active and the d5 square falls into White's hands. **11...e5** Giving up the d5 square without a fight. 11 ...Qd7 might have been tried, though 12.Qd4! still favors White. Black's most forcing move was 11...b4, since 12.Na4 e5 keeps the White Knight out of d5. However, after 11...b4 White would not comply with Black's wishes. Instead he would sacrifice a piece by 12.fxe6! bxc3 13.exf7+ and gain a very strong attack. **12.Qd3** Simply defending e4 and intending to meet 12...b4 with 13.Nd5. **12...Be7 13.Bg5!** Getting rid of a defender of d5. That square is now a permanent possession of the White forces. **13...Qb6+ 14.Kh1 0-0 15.Bxf6 Bxf6 16.Bd5!** Trading off Black's last guardian of d5. Now White will obtain a crushing Knight versus a bad Bishop. **16...Rac8 17.Bxc6 Rxc6 18.Rad1 Rfc8 19.Nd5 Qd8 20.c3 Be7 21.Ra1! f6 22.a4 Rb8 23.Nxe7+, 1-0.** White picks up the undefended Rook on c6 after **23...Qxe7 24.Qd5+.**

Diagram #141 —White to play.

Question: Should White double Black's pawns with 1.Bxf6, pin the other Knight with 1.Bb5, or calmly develop with 1.Be2?

Answer: When playing the opening you must not just develop your pieces and then ask who is better once you have gotten everything out! The correct way to play an opening is to create an imbalance and then develop around that difference—the idea is to strengthen that difference (be it Bishop vs. Knight, material vs. development or whatever) until it actually starts to favor you.

In the diagrammed position White has clearly been playing to control the e5 square. His f3 Knight, f4 pawn and b2 Bishop all work together towards this goal. Does 6.Be2 help with this plan? No. How about 6.Bxf6? This is even worse since it brings the Black e-pawn (which was doing nothing) to f6 where it keeps all enemy pieces out of e5. Much more logical is 6.Bb5, which intends to snap off one of Black's main defenders of e5. White wanted to develop his King-Bishop, so he finds a square where it aids the other pieces in accompishing the given plan.

Diagram #151 — Silman-Fedorowicz, Lone Pine 1976. White to play.

Question: After **1.e4 c5 2.Nf3 d6 3.d4 cxd4 4.Nxd4 Nf6 5.Nc3 g6 6.Be3 Bg7 7.f3 0-0 8.Qd2 Nc6 9.Bc4 Bd7 10.Bb3 Rc8 11.0-0-0 Ne5 12.Bg5 Nc4 13.Bxc4 Rxc4 14.Nb3 Rxc3 15.bxc3 Be6 16.e5 Ne8 17.Bh6 Bxe5 18.Bxf8 Kxf8 19.Rhe1 Bf6** we reach the position in the diagram. Black has two Bishops, a pawn, and attacking chances against White's King in exchange for two Rooks. How should White handle this situation?

Answer: The beauty of a material advantage is that you can make a sacrifice to quell an enemy initiative or attack and still be equal or even ahead in material. In the present case White gives back one of his Exchanges to get rid of a key Black Bishop and to create a target on e6. This last point is of great importance: Black's position had no weaknesses to begin with. After 20.Rxe6 White is able to create a crack in Black's armor. **20.Rxe6! fxe6 21.Qe3** Attacking both a7 and e6. **21...Qc8** Defending e6 and counterattacking c3. **22.Rd3 Nc7 23.Nd4** Increasing the pressure on e6. **23...a6 24.f4 Kg8 25.Qh3!** All of a sudden White threatens Re3. The e6 pawn is falling unless Black is willing to give up his Bishop and repair White's pawns by 25...Bxd4 26.cxd4. **25...Nd5 26.Qxe6+ Qxe6 27.Nxe6 Nxc3** Black appears to be doing all right, but White is able to show that this is more illusion than reality. **28.Kd2! Nxa2** Black is happy with two pawns for the Exchange, but now White's Rook enters the game and the Black horse is shown to be trapped on the side of the board. **29.Rb3 b5 30.Nc7 b4 31.Nd5! a5 32.Nxf6+ exf6 33.Rd3 Nc3** Tigran Petrosian, who had been watching this game with some interest, thought that Black had to be doing well here and, after the game (when the Fed left in disgust), he honored me by taking the Black side and trying to bash my brains out. After losing with Black repeatedly, the ex-World Champion shook his head in amazement, mumbled some unintelligable comment and walked away. Thirty minutes later Tigran surprised me by dragging me into the analysis room again and trying some new idea for Black (sadly enough, nothing was written down and I remember none of what we looked at). An hour later he agreed with my assessment, patted me on the back, and trudged off into the sunset. I never had the opportunity to talk to him again. **34.Ke3!** The King takes up a dominant position on d4. Note that 34.Rxd6?? lost to 34...Ne4+. **34...d5 35.Kd4 Kf7 36.Re3** Trapping Black's King on the kingside and preparing to stop Black's passed a-pawn. **36...a4 37.Re1 a3 38.Kc5 a2 39.Ra1** White's King and Rook have dominated the poor Black Knight. **39...Ke6 40.Kxb4 Ne2** The poor horse now begins to leap around frantically. **41.g3 Nd4 42.Rxa2 Nf3 43.c3 d4 44.Rf2 Ne1 45.Re2+,** 1-0.

Diagram #152 — Botvinnik-Flohr, 5th Match game 1933. Black to play.

Question: The game has just been adjourned with White sealing 1.b3-b4. Botvinnik thought he had excellent chances to win. Is this true or does Black have resources that his great opponent missed?

Answer: The imbalances in this position are centered around the minor pieces, the Queens and Black's queenside majority of pawns. It appears that everything is against Black: White's Bishop is both good and active while the Black Knight lacks any kind of useful square and seems doomed to passivity; White's Queen is better placed then Black's; the Black queenside majority (which he hoped would be a trump) appears to be nothing more than a weakness needing constant defense. As depressing as it is, this is the way most players would look at the position. Flohr offered up a different point of view, one based on willpower, the desire to turn all imbalances into favorable ones, and an open mind that does not mind the loss of material if positional dreams can be achieved. **1...d5!!** Black realized that his queenside majority was a potential passed pawn. He is quite happy to give up material to make that potential a reality. **2.cxd5 c5 3.bxc5 bxc5 4.Bf1 Nd6** Lo and behold, the whole position has undergone a miraculous change! Now White's Bishop is bad and inactive while the Black Knight has taken up a fine central position. With White's extra pawn solidly blocked, Black is free to start shoving his passer to the ends of the earth. White is the one who is now forced to scramble for the draw. **5.Qa3 Kf7 6.Bd3 c4 7.Bc2 c3** 7...Qb6+ 8.Kf1 Ke7 is stronger but Botvinnik says that White can still draw with 9.Ke2. **8.Qb4 Nc4 9.Qxc3 Qc5+ 10.Kh1 Qxd5+,** 1/2-1/2 by perpetual check.

Diagram #153 — Lyublinsky-Botvinnik, Moscow 1943. Black to play.

Question: Assess this position and figure out what Black should do.

Answer: Black has terrible problems. His queenside pawns are very weak and White will easily win the pawn on c5 by Na4 and Qf2. Though Black has the two Bishops, here this hardly signifies an advantage since they are both very inactive. Since he has no counterplay at all, he does the only thing he can to gain some play. **1...Rd4!** Now the c5 pawn is safe. True, Black is giving up an Exchange; but he will get a solid position, two Bishops, a passed pawn, and an advantage in space in return. This all adds up to factors that he can use in an effort to win. If he had just given up the c-pawn like a lamb, Black would have had no play and would surely have lost. **2.Ne2** The Rook is not going anywhere. **2...Bc8 3.Nxd4?!** Better was 3.Bxd4 cxd4 4.Nc1 followed by blockading the enemy passed pawn by Nd3. **3...cxd4 4.Bf2?** Very poor. White had been expecting an easy victory but 1...Rd4 complicated matters, forcing White to change his mental state and fight for the point. Unable to make the psychological transition, White plays planlessly. Since White's advantage is based on a material advantage of Rook versus Bishop, he *must* open files for his Rooks. Thus 4.Bd2 followed by 5.a3 and 6.b4 was the logical course. **4...c5 5.Rf1 f5** The results of Black's Exchange sacrifice can be seen. Black has a space advantage on the queenside, in the center, and on the kingside. He also has a proud passed pawn and chances for a kingside attack. From rags to riches! It had a price (the Exchange), but all things of quality tend to cost a bit more. **6.Bg3 Bd7 7.Rae1** White would like to play for open lines by 7.f4, but 7...Bc6! 8.exf5 e4 leaves Black with a pair of crushing central pawns. **7...f4 8.Bf2 g5 9.g4 fxg3 e.p. 10.Bxg3** Black would win the Exchange back after 10.hxg3 Bh3. **10...Bh3 11.Rf2 h5 12.Rd2 h4 13.Bf2 Rf8** Poor White has no play at all—a couple of planless moves will do that to you every time. **14.Rd3 Rf4 15.Kh1 Kh7 16.Rg1 Bd8 17.Qe2 Qf7 18.Qd1** Avoiding 18.Be1 g4 19.fxg4 Bxg4! 20.Rxg4 Rxg4 21.Qxg4 Qf1+ 22.Qg1 Qxd3 with a winning ending for Black. **18...Qh5!** Not 18...g4 19.fxg4 Rxf2 20.Rxh3. Now White has no good defense to 19...g4. **19.Be3 Qxf3+ 20.Qxf3 Rxf3 21.Bxg5 Rxd3 22.Bxd8 Re3 23.Bb6 Rxe4 24.Bxc5 Re2** White is hopelessly lost. The finish was: **25.Rd1 Bg4 26.h3 Bxh3 27.b4 Bf5 28.Bd6 d3 29.bxa5 h3**, 0-1. The threat of 30...Be4+ 31.Kg1 h2+ is enough to convince White that further resistance is useless.

Diagram #166 — Sipaila-Silman, Reno 1993. White to play.

Question: Do you think White can get away with 1.Qxd6?

Answer: Black is already way ahead in development. Taking the d6 pawn puts White even further behind and can't be correct, though it must be admitted that White's game is already difficult. In the actual game White was unable to avoid temptation: **1.Qxd6?** If there is a problem with your position (lack of development), never do anything that highlights it! **1...Rad8 2.Qg3** Not falling for 2.c5?? Qa6 3.Qg3 Bxb3 4.axb3 Qxf1+! and mates. **2...a4 3.Bxa4 Bxc4** Black's whole army is beating down on the White position. Thoughts of a pawn deficit should not even enter Black's head—*if your pieces are this active you will always be able to regain a sacrificed pawn or two.* **4.Be3 Qa6 5.Bb3 Bxf1** Black has won the Exchange but White hopes to use his two Bishops to start an attack against the Black King. **6.Rxf1 Nd5** With the gain in material Black rushes his forces back to the center. From a centralized location they will all work together to block the enemy Bishops and stop all White counterplay. **7.Bd4?** Making Black's job easier. 7.Bc1 had to be played but the idea of making a retreating move while material down disturbed White. **7...Bxd4 8.Nxd4 c5! 9.Nf5 c4** With one White Bishop gone and the other inactive, Black is ready to resume an aggressive campaign. **10.Bc2 Qf6** Defends the delicate h8-a1 diagonal and attacks the b2 pawn. **11.Nh6+ Kg7 12.Ng4 Qxb2 13.Ba4 Nc3**, 0-1. The threat of 14...Nxa4 and 14...Ne2+ spells doom for White.

Diagram #167 — Silman-Petranovic, American Open 1989. White to play.

Question: White doesn't fear ...e4 or ...exf4 since both moves allow White's Knight to come to a powerful square on either d4 or f4. On the other hand, White does not wish to play 1.fxe5 since 1...dxe5 leaves the White minor pieces with no advanced posts and gives Black a mobile center. How should White handle this position?

Answer: White has a lead in development but at the moment his Rooks are not playing a part in the game. That's why **1.h3!** was played: White intends to play 2.g2-g4 and rip open all the kingside files. Such an opening up of the kingside will always favor the more developed side—the possible loss of a pawn after g2-g4 doesn't concern White in the least. **1...Nf6 2.g3 Qh5 3.fxe5 dxe5 4.g4 Qh4** Trying to keep the files closed. It's clear that 4...fxg4 5.hxg4 Qxg4 6.Rdg1 would not be healthy for Black. **5.Bxc5** Seeing that Black is not going to allow a crushing attack, White cashes in and grabs some material. **5...dxc5 6.gxf5 Kh8 7.Rdg1 Nh5 8.Rg6 Bxf5 9.Rxh6+ Kg8 10.Rg1** The Rook on h6 is strong but looks very peculiar. **10...Bxc2 11.Kxc2 Rad8 12.Rg5**, 1-0. Black did nothing but react to White's threats after 1.h3; that's what forcefully pursuing the initiative can do.

Diagram #168 — Abramson-Computer, California 1991. Black to play.

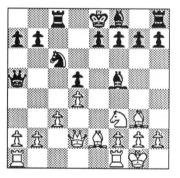

Question: In the diagrammed position Black played for queenside space with 1...b7-b5. Is this a good move?

Answer: **1...b7-b5??** is terrible because Black is starting to attack against a much better developed opponent. This type of thing is always a suicidal undertaking. If someone attacks you from a position of inferiority you must demonstrate a certain type of attitude—you must insist on punishing him for his obvious transgressions! When you have a great lead in development, you must somehow open up lines that allow penetration into the enemy position. Most people think that this means you should attack in the direction of his King. This is completely untrue! If you can open up any front at all your larger army should be able to triumph. Typically, White may try something like the mistaken 2.Rfe1, hoping to get something going down the e-file. Even worse is 2.a3, stopping Black's plan of ...b5-b4. These ideas are much too slow. Remember—you are trying to punish him!

Actually, White has an almost forced win here with **2.b4!** Playing on the side where Black thought he was better! This move is usually rejected by White because it weakens the c4 square and leaves White with a backward c3 pawn. However, Black is in no position to make use of these factors. On the contrary, White has fixed Black's pawn on b5 where it will become a target. He has also gained time by attacking Black's Queen and will follow up with a2-a4, blasting open lines on the queenside. **2...Qb6 3.a4 a6** On 3...bxa4 White will play 4.Rxa4 followed by 5.Rfa1 and 6.b4-b5, when he will win the pawn on a7 and eventually the game. **4.axb5 axb5 5.Qa2!** Notice how Black has not had a moment to breathe since making his fatal mistake of 1...b5? Now White threatens to simply take the d5 pawn with his Queen. **5...e6 6.Qa6!** Gin! Threatening to take Black's Queen, Rook, and b5 pawn. The exchange is forced. **6...Qxa6 7.Rxa6** Black loses the b5 pawn, and with it the game. This was only possible because White reacted with so much energy, not giving his opponent time to regain his balance. Also note that White was not afraid to exchange Queens. He knew that as long as he could fix a weakness and penetrate into Black's position, good things would happen.

Next time you see your opponent get way behind in development, rev up your motor and go get him!

Diagram #169 White to play.

Question: The position in the diagram was reached after the following moves: **1.d4 d5 2.c4 dxc4 3.e3 e5 4.Bxc4 exd4 5.exd4 Nf6 6.Nf3 Bf5 7.0-0.** Black now tried **7...Be4.** What is Black's idea? Is this move any good? What should White do?

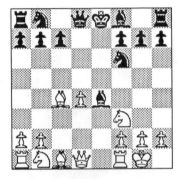

Answer: Black's **7...Be4?** violates some basic rules of the opening. The first violation is that it moves the same piece twice in an open position. This is a very bad thing to do when your opponent already has a lead in development. Another problem is that Black's King is still sitting in the center and the e-file is wide open! When you have an open center you must get the King out of there as fast as possible! Black's idea was to control the d5 square and defend the b7 with his Bishop, but the broken rules give White the chance to play a combination. **8.Bxf7+!** This is made possible because of the open nature of Black's King and the rather loose state of the Bishop on e4. **8...Kxf7 9.Ng5+** Here's that old double attack again! **9...Ke8** Avoiding 9...Kg8 10.Nxe4 Nxe4? 11.Qb3+ and Black will be mated. **10.Nxe4** and Black is completely busted since 10...Nxe4 11.Re1 picks up the poor Knight and leaves White with an extra pawn and a permanent attack.

Diagram #181 Tal-Koblentz, Riga 1957. White to play.

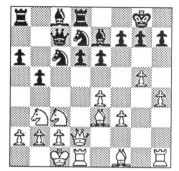

Question: The position in the diagram came about after **1.e4 c5 2.Nf3 Nc6 3.d4 cxd4 4.Nxd4 Nf6 5.Nc3 d6 6.Bg5 e6 7.Qd2 Be7 8.0-0-0 0-0 9.Nb3 Qb6 10.f3 a6 11.g4 Rd8 12.Be3 Qc7 13.h4 b5 14.g5 Nd7.** White is obviously going to attack Black on the kingside while Black will play for a counterattack on the queenside. Should White first prevent ...b5-b4 by a2-a3, or should he immediately continue with his own plans? Also say how White will attack Black's King.

Answer: A move like a2-a3 is terrible since it allows Black to open a file after ...b5-b4. Don't play moves that allow the enemy Rooks to get to you! In the game, Tal played the energetic **15.g6!** White is willing to part with a pawn to open up kingside files for his Rooks. **15...hxg6 16.h5 gxh5 17.Rxh5** Now White has two nice files (the g-file and h-file) for his Rooks. **17...Nf6 18.Rh1 d5!** Following that marvelous rule: *The best reaction to an attack on the wing is a counterattack in the center.* Note that Black also stops White's threatened Qh2. **19.e5!** White reacts in a vigorous manner and prevents Black from opening up the central files. In this way White's Rooks are working and Black's are not. **19...Nxe5** Bad is 19...Qxe5 20.Bf4 Qf5 21.Bd3. **20.Bf4 Bd6 21.Qh2** So White will get into Black's position along the h-file. However, Black is able to run and the battle is far from over. **21...Kf8 22.Qh8+ Ng8 23.Rh7** and White eventually won but Black could have defended much better. I will not mention all the defensive improvements but I will give the rest of the game so that you can enjoy the flashy finish: **23...f5 24.Bh6 Rd7 25.Bxb5!!** White sees that there is no going back so he plays for mate or nothing. He now threatens to chop off the defending d7 Rook. The main point of 25.Bxb5 is to clear the line with tempo so the other Rook has time to get to g1. **25...Rf7** Hanging on. 25...axb5 26.Nxb5 is annoying. **26.Rg1 Ra7 27.Nd4 Ng4! 28.fxg4 Be5** Tal points out that 28...Bf4+ 29.Bxf4 Qxf4+ 30.Kb1 Qxd4 31.Rgh1 threatens 32.Qxg8+ Kxg8 33.Rh8 mate. Now g7 is firmly defended and he has threats of ...Bxd4 and ...gxh6 with a discovered attack on the Queen. **29.Nc6!** Intending to take the offending Bishop on e5 off the board. **29...Bxc3 30.Be3!** Threatening to kill Black with 31.Bc5+. Not as good was 30.bxc3 axb5 31.Nxa7 Qxa7 when Black has a counterattack. **30...d4 31.Rgh1**

Joining in the attack by jumping on the open file. The threat is 32.Qxg8+ Kxg8 33.Rh8 mate. **31...Rd7 32.Bg5! axb5 33.R1h6!** You can't penetrate more on an open file than White has on this one! The threat is 34.Rf6+ gxf6 35.Bh6+. **33...d3 34.bxc3 d2+ 35.Kd1 Qxc6 36.Rf6+ Rf7 37.Qxg7+,** 1-0. Without open files the Rooks could never have played such an amazing part in this game.

Diagram #182 — Silman-MacFarland, Reno 1991. Black to play.

Question: In the actual game Black stopped the threatened Nxc6 by chopping on e5 (1...Bxe5). Was this a good decision?

Answer: Taking the Knight was very poor since White is able to make immediate use of the d-file and the support point on d6: **1...Bxe5 2.dxe5 Nd7 3.Rfd1 Qe7 4.Rd6 Rac8 5.Rad1 Nb8 6.Qg4!** Going after the Black King because White's iron lock on the center allows him to switch to play on the wings. If this were not possible then White would have settled for 6.Qd2 with complete and permanent domination of the d-file. **6...Kh8 7.Bg5 Qc7 8.Be4** Also devastating was 8.Qh4! threatening (aside from 9.Be4) to win the Exchange with 9.Bd8. **8...c5 9.Bxb7** Drawing the Queen away from d8 and preparing the following combination. **9...Qxb7 10.Bf6!,** 1-0. Mate follows 10...gxf6 11.exf6 Rg8 12.Rd8! Rcxd8 13.Rxd8.

Diagram #183 — Silman-B.Satyam, San Jose 1982. White to play.

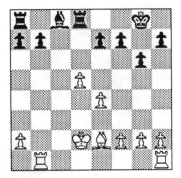

Question: Who stands better and how would the superior side make use of this advantage?

Answer: White has a very large advantage. The main structural imbalance is the mutual pawn majorities. White's central majority gains space, and can transform itself into a passed pawn by a later e5 and d6. Black's majority is stuck at home and thus has very little dynamic potential. Other factors that weigh decisively in White's favor are the superior position of White's King plus the fact that the need to guard b7 prevents Black from completing his development—this will lead to White's Rooks gaining entry into Black's position by the open c-file. **1.Ke3** Getting off the d8 Rook's line. **1...Rb8 2.Rbc1** Now that b7 is guarded, the Rook goes to a more promising square. The other Rook can be used to support d5 by Rhd1. **2...Kf8 3.Rc7 Rd7 4.Rhc1 Rxc7 5.Rxc7 Ke8 6.d6!** Gaining access to the seventh rank. **6...exd6 7.Bb5+!** The immediate 7.Bc4 is not so clear after 7...Bd7. **7...Kf8 8.Bc4 Be6 9.Bxe6 fxe6 10.Rxh7** White has a won game; the immediate threat is 11.Rh8+. **10...Kg8 11.Re7 e5 12.Re6 Kf7 13.Rxd6 Rc8 14.Rd7+ Kf6 15.Rxb7** and with two extra pawns, White eventually won.

Diagram #198 — G.Levenfish-G.Lisitsin, Moscow 1935. White to move.

Question: List the components of White's advantage and figure out how he should proceed.

Answer: White is better for several reasons:

1) He has more space in the center and on the queenside.
2) His Bishop is much more active than Black's Knight.
3) Black's King is somewhat unsafe due to the weakness of the dark-squares (h6 and g7) that was brought about with the loss of his fianchettoed Bishop on g7.

All these plusses won't win the the game automatically though. White must come up with a plan. It turns out that both sides are involved in a dispute over the open c-file. Black hopes to play ...Rxc1 followed by ...Rc8 when the exchanges give him good chances to draw (the side with less space should try to trade the pieces off). Black also threatens 1...Qxa4 and something like 1.b5?? turns the sad Knight on a6 into a powerhouse after 1...Nc5. **1.Rc6!** White makes good use of the support point on c6 and the fact that the Knight on a6 is in an awkward position. Black is now forced to either capture on c6 and give White a crushing passed pawn or to allow White total domination of the c-file. **1...Rxc6** A miserable move but otherwise White will lay an iron bar on the c-file by Qc4 followed by Rc1. Note that 1...Nb8 2.Rxc8+ Qxc8 3.Rc1 also gives White the c-file. **2.dxc6 Qe6** Black would lose a piece after 2...Qxc6 3.b5. **3.Qc3** White now enjoys an enormous advantage in space on the queenside due to his pawn on c6. **3...Nc7 4.Ra1 Rc8** Firmly blocking the passed pawn but leaving his pieces in passive positions. **5.Qd3 d5 6.Rc1 f5** Desperately trying to gain some counterplay. **7.Bf4!** Preparing to break the blockade on c7. **7...dxe4 8.fxe4 Ne8** Both 8...fxe4 and 8...Qxe4 fail to 9.Qd7. **9.exf5 gxf5 10.b5 Kf7 11.Rf1** Aside from the monster on c6, Black also has serious problems with his King. This illustrates a common spatial theme: the side with more territory is able to threaten things on both sides of the board due to his greater flexibility. The lack of maneuvering room makes defense a difficult task for the opponent. **11...Ng7 12.Bd2 Rf8 13.Re1 Qc8 14.Bb4 Re8**, now 15.Qd4 with the threats of Bxe7 and Bc3 would have led to a quick victory. For example: 15.Qd4 Qc7 38.Bc3 Ne6 39.Qd5.

Diagram #199 — Petrosian-Najdorf, Bled 1961. White to play.

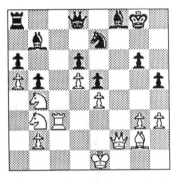

Question: Is White better, and if so, how much? How should White continue here?

Answer: It is clear that White is trying to force a decision on the queenside. Black's only hope is a counter demonstration on the kingside, but it is now too late to accomplish this. Though Black has the two Bishops, we have a closed center which restricts both of the B's. The Knights are superior in this case.

The thing to remember here is that a queenside attack tends to be a longer lasting advantage than a kingside demonstration. This is because a queenside attack goes after weaknesses and squares, and has just as much chance for success in an endgame as in a middlegame. A kingside attack usually has a narrow goal—Mate! This is not an easy thing to force. To make matters worse, if the Queens get exchanged the kingside attack is usually over. In this case, White uses his *endgame odds* advantage and plays **1.Qb6!** Very logical. White penetrates into the heart of Black's position and threatens the Bishop on b7. He also threatens to bring a Rook to c7. Black must trade Queens, but then he is doomed to pure defense since any possible dream of kingside counterplay has ended before it began. **1...Qxb6 2.axb6** Now White has a strong passed pawn on b6, a Knight ready to invade on c6, and another Knight ready to jump into a5. This last point was made possible by the Queen trade, since the advance of the pawn to b6 has cleared the a5 square. **2...Rb8** Black would also lose after 2...a5

3.Rc7. **3.Rc7 Bc8 4.Na5 Rxb6 5.Nbc6 Nxc6 6.Nxc6** Black resigned, since he loses a piece after 6...Bb7 7.Na5 Ba8 8.Rc8 Bb7 9.Rb8.

Diagram #200 — Lilienthal-Botvinnik, Moscow 1935. Black to play.

Question: The position in the diagram was reached after the following opening moves: **1.d4 Nf6 2.c4 e6 3.Nc3 Bb4 4.a3 Bxc3 5.bxc3 c5 6.f3 d5 7.e3 0-0 8.cxd5 Nxd5 9.Bd2 Nc6 10.Bd3** Is Black doing well or will the advantages in White's position lead to difficulties for the second player?

Answer: The imbalances here are quite clear: White has two Bishops and more center pawns. Black has no problem developing his forces and both his Knights are centrally placed. Probably the most important imbalances in this position, though, are Black's lead in development and the fact that White's King is still in the center. If Black plays slowly with ...b6 and ...Bb7, White will catch up in development via Ne2 and 0-0 when the two Bishops may make themselves felt. It is clear that Black must do something quickly if he is to make use of the temporary imbalance of development. What are you to do if your opponent is behind in development and his King is uncastled? The answer is to OPEN THE POSITION! Only in this way can your better developed army force its way into the enemy position.

This may surprise some players, since they feel that they are supposed to keep things as closed as possible if they possess Knights. This is generally true, but clearly wrong and short-sighted in this case. The rule of opening things up for one's better developed pieces takes precedence, since by acting quickly Black keeps White off balance and actually prevents White from using the plusses in his position. **1...cxd4 2.cxd4 e5!** 3.dxe5 The alternatives are also unpalatable: 3.e4 Nf4! 4.Bxf4 exf4 5.d5 Qh4+ 6.Kf1 Ne5, when White no longer has the two Bishops and Black has a great support point on e5. Even worse is 3.Ne2 exd4 4.exd4 Nxd4! 5.Nxd4 Qh4+ 6.g3 Qxd4 and Black has won a pawn. This combination was possible due to White's hanging Knight on d4 and his exposed King on e1. **3...Nxe5 4.Be4 Nc4** Euwe says that 4...Nf6! would have given Black an edge. **5.Qc1 Nxd2 6.Qxd2 Nf6 7.Bd3 Re8 8.Ne2 Qb6** Trying to prevent White from castling. **9.Nd4! Nd5 10.Be4 Nxe3 11.Qxe3 f5 12.0-0 fxe4 13.fxe4 Rd8 14.Nf5 Qxe3+ 15.Nxe3 Be6 16.Rfd1,** and the game was eventually drawn.

It is now clear that Black had at least equality in the starting diagram, and that a lead in development can prove to be quite potent if acted upon energetically.

Diagram #201 — Bronstein-Botvinnik, 1951 World Championship Match, 16th game. White to play.

Question: Is anything wrong with 1.Qd3?

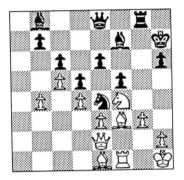

Answer: **1.Qd3?** is bad because it allows Black to create a situation where Black will own a superior minor piece. **1...Bxf4! 2.exf4 Bh5!** Bronstein is faced with a very difficult decision: He can give Black a strong attack after 3.Bxe4 dxe4 4.Qa3 Bf3+ 5.Kg1 Qh5 6.Qe3 Qh3 7.Qf2 h5 and the threat of ...h4 is irresistible, or he can allow Black to take over the only open file after 3.Bg2 Qa8 when Black will effect a penetration into White's position along the a-file. The only other possibility is to allow Black to trade light-squared Bishops and obtain a powerful Knight on e4 versus a very bad Bishop. **3.Qa3** So White takes over the a-file but allows Black to create a dominating minor piece on e4. **3...Bxf3+ 4.Rxf3 Rg7** Hardly necessary, but Black is in no hurry (Black's superior minor piece is a permanent advantage) so he first defends the b7 pawn in case the White Queen later attacks it. Black's plan is to create threats on the kingside which will do two things: 1) Create new weaknesses that can later be attacked. 2) Force White to bring his pieces over to the kingside for defensive purposes which will allow Black to once again dominate the a-file. **5.Kg2 Qd8 6.Kf1 Qf6 7.Rd3 h5 8.h4** Not what he wanted to play but he had to prevent Black from ripping open the Kingside with 8...h5-h4. **8...Rg8 9.Rd1 Qg7 10.Qf3 Kh6 11.Kg2 Ra8** Black now owns the open file, has pressure against the permanent target on g3, and has a vastly superior minor piece.

Diagram #217 — Mephisto (computer)-Silman, American Open 1989. White to play.

Question: Should White play 1.Nd4 and trade the Bishops or should he allow Black to capture on b3 when a Bishop versus Knight battle would ensue?

Answer: White should retain his Knight by 1.Nd4. The computer was programmed to think that Bishops were superior to Knights in an endgame so it happily allowed Black to capture on b3. **1.Ke1??** A terrible mistake. A Knight is usually preferable to a Bishop with pawns on one side of the board because a Knight can attack any pawn and can chase the King from any square. The ability to go to any color is more important than long range powers in such situations. **1...Bxb3 2.Bxb3 Kc5 3.Ba4 Nf7** To answer 4.Bd7 with 4...Ne5. **4.Bb3 Ne5 5.Bc2 Nc4 6.Ba4 d4 7.Bc2 Kd5 8.Bb3 Kc5 9.Bc2 dxe3!** The only way to win. 9...d3 is tempting but does not offer any way to break through. **10.fxe3 Nxe3 11.Bxe4 Kd4 12.Bg6 Nc4 13.Kf2 Nd2 14.Bf5 Ne4+ 15.Bxe4 Kxe4 16.Kf1 Ke3 17.Ke1 f2+ 18.Kf1 Kd3! 19.Kxf2 Kd2 20.Kf1 Ke3**, 0-1.

Diagram #218 — Silman-Getz, World Open 1990. White to play.

Question: After **1.d4 Nf6 2.c4 e5 3.dxe5 Ng4 4.Bf4 Bb4+ 5.Nc3 Bxc3+ 6.bxc3 Nc6 7.Nf3 Qe7 8.Qd5 f6 9.exf6 Nxf6 10.Qd3 d6 11.g3 0-0 12.Bg2 Bg4 13.0-0 Rae8 14.Rfe1 Ne4 15.Nd4 Bd7** we come to the position in diagram #218. White must come up with a clear plan of action. What should he do?

Answer: Black is a pawn down but his active pieces, play against White's weak pawns, and control of c5 give him lots of compensation. White made use of a tactic and played the surprising **16.Bxe4!** Black didn't seriously consider this. Giving up this light-squared Bishop is very risky for White but he accurately judged that Black would have to sacrifice further material to keep his initiative or passively go into a very bad endgame. Since White accepted the pawn in the opening, he is more than happy to take more material—even if Black gets an attack in return. **16...Qxe4 17.Nb5!** The c7 pawn can't be defended without Black fixing White's pawn structure with 17...Qxd3. Refusing to play such a move, Black lashes out against White's King. **17...Rxf4 18.gxf4 Qxf4 19.Nxc7** Wins more material and swings the Knight over to the wonderful d5 square. **19...Re5 20.Nd5 Rg5+ 21.Kh1 Qxf2 22.Qf3 Qh4** The battle that was started in the opening (material versus activity) is still being fought. **23.Rg1** Seeking exchanges. **23...Bg4 24.Qf4 h6 25.Rg3 Ne5 26.Rag1** Black's attack is running out of steam. White's 'take everything' strategy has won out! **26...Qh5 27.Ne3 Bxe2 28.Rxg5 hxg5 29.Rxg5 Qe8 30.Nf5 Qc6+ 31.Rg2** Threatening to win Black's Queen with 32.Ne7+. **31...Qf3 32.Ne7+ Kh8 33.Qh4+ Qh5 34.Qxh5+ Bxh5 35.Rd2 g6** Black saw that 35...Nxc4 is met by 36.Rd4 b5 37.Rh4 g6 38.Nxg6+. **36.Rxd6 Kg7 37.c5 Bg4 38.Kg1 Kf7 39.c6!** Initiating a final series of exchanges that makes the win easy. **39...bxc6 40.Nxc6 Nxc6 41.Rxc6 Bf5 42.Ra6 Ke7 43.Rxa7+ Kd6 44.Ra5**, 1-0.

PART SIXTEEN

RECOMMENDED READING LIST

I love chess books. Any kind of chess book, any age, on any aspect of chess. Unfortunately, many of these books—though interesting from a collector's viewpoint—are completely inadequate for teaching purposes. Others are simply poorly written and are therefore a very poor value for your money. To save the reader from buying useless material, I have put together the following list of books—all of which are the best of their kind available.

Beginner

Play Winning Chess by Yasser Seirawan and Jeremy Silman (Tempus Books of Microsoft Press, Washington, 1990). A fun, easy to read tour of the basic rules and strategies of the game.

Logical Chess, Move By Move by Irving Chernev (Simon and Schuster, New York, 1957). A collection of games which explains each and every move.

Opening

This subject is extremely vague, since no matter how good an opening book may be, it's useless if you don't play the system under discussion.

Your playing strength is also an important consideration. Do you want a detailed treatise on a particular line; or do you want a repertoire book that tells you which openings to play and explains the ideas in detail, but doesn't give all variations (to save space)?

A general book on the openings is useful for non-professionals and professionals alike. *The Encyclopedia Of Openings* (Chess Informant, Belgrade) is the choice of players in the expert class right up to the Grandmaster level. This five volume set covers different openings in each book. One volume devotes itself to 1.e4 e6 plus 1.e4 e5, 1.e4 c5, 1.e4 c6, etc., yet another in the set looks at 1.d4 d5. We could go on and on but I think the point is made. These excellent books go into quite a bit of detail and are superior to the classical *Modern Chess Openings*. MCO (or clones like BCO) is useful for the lower rated player, but here we see a case where its strength is also its weakness: MCO places everything in one volume. This is great for those that wish to take just one book to a tournament, but the lack of space also leads to a lack of thoroughness.

Middlegame

The Art of Attack in Chess by V. Vukovic (Pergamon Press, Oxford, 1965). This classic will make you a master of all forms of attack.

Think Like a Grandmaster by Alexander Kotov (B.T. Batsford Ltd., London, 1978). A complete course on how to calculate. A book that requires a lot of work, but fun to read.

Art of the Middle Game by Paul Keres and Alexander Kotov, translated by H. Golombek (Dover, New York, 1989). A small, inexpensive book that is full of useful insights. Keres' chapter on the art of defending difficult positions is tremendous.

Complete Chess Strategy (1: First Principles of the Middle Game, 2: Principles of Pawn-Play and the Center, and *3: Play on the Wings)* by Ludek Pachman (Doubleday, New York). This series belongs in every chess library.

The Middle Game by M. Euwe and H. Kramer (G. Bell and Sons Ltd., London, 1964). A two volume set (Static Features is the first book. Dynamic and Subjective Features is the second) that has been out of print for awhile and is hard to get. If you see one or both of these books in a used book store, grab them and don't let go!

Pawn Structure Chess by Andrew Soltis (David McKay Company, New York, 1976). Lots of information on an important subject. The other book on this subject is:

Pawn Power in Chess by Hans Kmoch (David McKay Company, New York, 1975. However, Mr. Kmoch goes crazy with all sorts of strange, invented names (Rangers, Fakers, Stops & Telestops, Leucopenia, and dozens more) that do more to confuse than instruct.

Bobby Fischer: A Study of His Approach To Chess by Elie Agur (Cadogan, London, 1992). Explores different middlegame themes by a detailed examination of Fischer's games.

Tactics

Winning Chess Tactics by Yasser Seirawan and Jeremy Silman (Tempus Books of Microsoft Press, Washington, 1992). Detailed explanations of each type of tactical motif. Appropriate for every class of player. This is really the only book you need on the subject, but other excellent choices are:

The *Art of Chess Combination* by Eugène Znosko-Borovsky (Dover, New York, 1959). Is this a good book or am I just prejudiced with happy memories? When I was fourteen years old, I gained 400 points after reading it!

Chess Tactics For Advanced Players by Yuri Averbakh (Sportverlag, Berlin, 1983). Really good, but as the title suggests, advanced.

Endgame

Good books on this subject used to be hard to come by, but now there is an abundance of them!

Essential Chess Endings Explained Move By Move: Volume One, Novice through Intermediate (Revised 2nd edition) by Jeremy Silman (Chess Digest, Dallas, 1988). A great book for beginners through the expert level. Gives only the endings that are useful in everyday play. Every move is explored. **Warning**: This second edition of my work is called Volume One (It's the only volume I intend to do on this subject. I was not aware of this 'Volume One' label until after publication). Chess Digest published a Volume Two, but a glance at the author will show that I had nothing to do with it. I DO NOT recommend this Volume Two by another author!

The Endings in Modern Theory and Practice by P.C. Griffiths (Charles Scribner's Sons, New York, 1976). Covers different endgame groups in a clear, easy to read manner. Useful for Class 'C' to Master.

M.I. Shereshevsky's three books: *Endgame Strategy, Mastering The Endgame, Volume 1: Open Games* and *Mastering The Endgame, Volume 2: Closed Games* (Pergamon, Oxford). Instead of covering different material situations like most endgame books, these books look at different strategic themes in the endgame. Things like Centralization of the King, The Problem of Exchanging, Pawn Majorities, are covered in *Endgame Strategy*. The other two look at typical endgame themes that arise from different openings. For example, Volume Two explores Dark-Square Strategy, Symmetry, etc. This series is expensive but is highly instructive. Useful for Class 'C' to professional.

Now we get into a vast field of advanced books on the endgame:

Basic Chess Endings by Reuben Fine (David McKay Company, New York, 1941). Everything is covered in one thick volume. If you want all endings under one cover, then this is the book to get. However, it makes very dry reading and is more a reference work than a book of instruction.

Yuri Averbakh's endgame series, *Comprehensive Chess Endings: Volume One—Bishop Endings, Knight Endings; Volume Two—Bishop Against Knight Endings, Rook Against Minor Piece Endings*, etc.,—the list goes on and on—(Pergamon, Oxford), is unsurpassed for depth. These books are very advanced and, like BCE, are more reference works than books of instruction.

Endgame Preparation by Jon Speelman (B.T. Batsford, London, 1981) and *Analysing the Endgame* by Jon Speelman (Arco, New York, 1981). Deep discussions of various endgame situations. Very advanced.

Game Collections

One of the best ways to learn about chess is to study the lives and games of the masters. Who you decide to study is a matter of style and taste, but make sure that you look at games with notes that explain what the master was thinking about. Some of the best game collections are:

My Best Games of Chess 1908-1923 and *1924-1937* (two volumes) by Alexander Alekhine (G. Bell & Sons, London, 1927, 1939; or, as one volume, Dover, New York, 1985). Wonderful examples of attack and combinitive insight. Both these books are considered to be classics.

Tigran Petrosian His Life and Games by Vik L.Vasiliev (B.T. Batsford, London, 1974). The reading mixes well with the games to make Petrosian an instant hero. For those who like positional chess.

The Life and Games of Mikhail Tal by Mikhail Tal (R.H.M. Press, London, 1976). Endless stories, games, and analysis by one of the greatest attackers (and most entertaining chess writers) who ever lived.

Grandmaster of Chess: The Complete Games of Paul Keres by Paul Keres (Arco, New York, 1972). Originally a three volume set that has now been abridged into one.

Chess Praxis: The Praxis of My System by Aron Nimzovich (Dover, New York, 1962). A classic that shows how Nimzovich used his positional ideas. Such themes as overprotection, centralization, restriction, etc, are discussed in detail.

Aron Nimzowitsch: A Reappraisel by Raymond Keene (David McKay Company, New York, 1974). This detailed study of Nimzowitsch's games and style is nothing less than brilliant. Fun to read and informative.

Marshall's Best Games Of Chess by Frank J. Marshall (Dover, New York, 1942). This little book is highlighted by a short but interesting bio at the beginning followed by 140 games. Marshall was famous for his swindles and attacks. The games are not subtle, but they are a lot of fun to watch.

One Hundred Selected Games by Mikhail Botvinnik (Dover, New York, 1960). This book covers the years from 1926 to 1946. One strategic masterpiece after another.

My 60 Memorable Games by Bobby Fischer (Faber and Faber, London, 1969). 'Shoot from the hip' annotations from arguably the greatest player of all time.

Other Kinds Of Game Collections

These books are for the serious collector.

A. Alekhine Agony of a Chess Genius by Pablo Morán (McFarland & Co., Jefferson, 1989). A detailed study of Alekhine's life and games after his fall from grace (and love affair with the bottle).

Capablanca: A Compendium of Games, Notes, Articles, Correspondence, Illustrations and Other Rare Archival Materials on the Cuban Chess Genius José Raúl Capablance, 1888-1942 by Edward Winter (McFarland & Co., Jefferson, 1989). Little known information about the great Cuban World Champion. Studies his articles, correspondence, and games.

The Games of Tigran Petrosian: Volume 1: 1942-1965 and *Volume 2: 1966-1983* compiled by Eduard Shekhtman (Pergamon Chess, Oxford, 1991). Covers every game Petrosian played plus notes, stories, etc.

Tal-Botvinnik Match for the World Championship 1960 by Mikhail Tal (R.H.M. Press, London, 1977). Chess reading does not get much better than this!

No Regrets: Fischer-Spassky 1992 by Yasser Seirawan and George Stefanovic (International Chess Enterprises, Seattle, 1992). Covers the Fischer comeback match with Spassky. All the games with detailed notes, plus endless stories, interviews, etc. One of the best match books ever.

New In Chess Yearbook: Periodical Analysis of Current Opening Practice (Interchess BV, Alkmaar). Published four times a year since 1984. A great series that studies the direction of various opening systems by looking at the latest international games.

Chess Informant (Chess Informant, Belgrade). A legendary series that comes out every four months with the best games from that time period. With games listed according to openings, the *Chess Informant* has become a must for all serious players.

Chess Books For The Fanatic Reader

These final recommendations are for people who like to read about the game, its history, and its personalities.

Chess For Fun & Chess For Blood by Edward Lasker (Dover, New York, 1962). Harmless fluff that is lots of fun.

How To Get Better At Chess: Chess Masters on Their Art by Larry Evans, Jeremy Silman, and Betty Roberts (Summit Publishing, Los Angeles, 1991). Fifty of the world's best players give their opinions on questions like, What Books or Players Have Influenced You the Most?, Is Memory Important In Chess?, Is There An Age When Improvement Stops?, etc. The section that deals with anecdotes is tremendous fun.

How To Open A Chess Game by Larry Evans, Svetozar Gligoric, Vlastimil Hort, Paul Keres, Bent Larsen, Tigran Petrosian, and Lajos Portisch (R.H.M. Press, New York, 1974. Stories and opening advice from seven International GMs.